OTHER BOOKS BY ERIC HODGINS

MR. BLANDINGS BUILDS HIS DREAM HOUSE
BLANDINGS' WAY
EPISODE

TROLLEY
TO
THE MOON

AN AUTOBIOGRAPHY BY

ERIC HODGINS

SIMON AND SCHUSTER · NEW YORK

Published by Simon and Schuster
Rockefeller Center, 630 Fifth Avenue
New York, New York 10020

First printing

SBN 671-21440-3
Library of Congress Catalog Card Number: 72-90396
Designed by Eve Metz
Manufactured in the United States of America
by The Maple Press Co., Inc., York, Penna.

S.M.B.
WRITTEN IN DEFIANCE OF
MANY THINGS, BUT IN
PARTICULAR OF
UNITY,
EMPHASIS,
AND COHERENCE

E.H.

CONTENTS

FOREWORD

John Kenneth Galbraith

ERIC HODGINS was a large man, large-framed, with a deep, rumbling voice, an explosive laugh and an exceptionally homely face that resembled, if anything, that of a blotched but very amiable toad. We became friends a few years after this history comes to an end. Friends we remained for the rest of his life. We met more often by accident than by design, wrote each other only at intervals, but our affection and sense of shared identity never diminished. But in my case more than friendship was involved; there was also a large element of worship, for I regarded Eric Hodgins as one of the best writers of his time and certainly the best I was ever likely to know. In the years immediately following World War II, we were both editors (meaning mostly that we were writers) at *Fortune*. In previous years Eric had been an officer of Time Inc., and somehow promotion had brought him into one of the corporate non-jobs in which the enterprise abounded. Then one day he resigned the post and returned to writing. When one of his manuscripts came along, I, with others, put everything else aside to read it. Then we would meet and the comment was always the same: "It's another real Hodgins."

A real Hodgins was marvelously lucid, packed with the most astonishing amount of information, very funny, gorgeously vulgar and invariably at least twice too long. The information was extensively retrieved from Eric's own stock, which was inexhaustible and arranged for total recall. He understood technical processes and more generally how things worked and enjoyed explaining them. More remarkably, he also made the reader want to know. Pompous men and foolish actions were his special joy, but the

1

resulting fun was not so much in the situation as in the writing; Eric's gift, like Evelyn Waugh's, was in finding the precisely outrageous word for whatever he was describing. It was partly because of the vulgarity and length that we preferred the manuscripts to the articles as printed. The late Albert (Bill) Furth, then Executive Editor of *Fortune* and a master of the editorial craft, filtered the bad stuff out. The moral tone of the times and Bill's sense of taste required it.

Eric did not trust his own sense of taste, for he had Bill read his novels too. Our delicacy then was perhaps extreme. In the first of the Blandings books, Blandings gets a bill for extras from his builder, the ineffable John Retch, which Blandings protests. One item is "Extra Screws . . . $3.00." On this Blandings comments, "A very modest sum, but wouldn't it be more customary for you to pay me?" When the book came out, I asked Furth how this had got by. He refused to believe that he had missed such a breach and was horrified. Anyhow, what went was a bitter loss, and so were the pages and pages that had to be cut because there was always too much.

Perhaps more people know of the Hodgins genius than I realize. The two Blandings books—*Mr. Blandings Builds His Dream House* and *Blandings' Way*—were appreciatively read. The first sold well and became a famous movie, and both were major book-club selections. Both novels showed, in addition to all else, a fine ear for the way all kinds of people talk. Hodgins had more than a little of John O'Hara's gift. *Blandings' Way*, in its treatment of Cold War paranoia among the great and the small, was also politically far in advance of its time. No other author viewed the McCarthy landscape with such a devastating eye. Certainly no other book ever showed so well how fear reduced the respectable to driveling idiocy. The book is unstructured and sometimes trivial and has long been out of print. Anyone who happens on a copy should read and treasure it.

Still, too few knew Eric Hodgins, and it was because during his great writing years he was at Time Inc., and the organization always stood between its people and the world. No matter how brilliant the writer, his reputation rarely got beyond the corporate shell. Inside, it was a wonderful story by Hodgins. Outside, it was an interesting story in *Fortune*. This was not a matter of by-lines.

These came into use in the mid-fifties, but made almost no difference; the shadow of the organization was simply too dense.
Archie MacLeish used to take a few months off each summer to
write poetry and assert his own personality. Others left. Eric, who
had come earlier, remained longer.

This book is the story of Eric's early life and his early years at
Time Inc. It is more than the story of a man; it tells also of a time
in our history. And it is, by turns, amusing, evocative and
touching—a wonderful piece of writing. It is the real Hodgins.
Let me here pass it on to the reader and return at the end to tell
something of Eric's later life.

INTRODUCTION

Things I would not tell anyone—I tell the public.
—Montaigne

THE MOST INTERESTING THING about my life, to me, is that it began with the Toonerville Trolley and is ending with footsteps on the moon. So much for more than seventy years of progress in which, thank God, I have played no significant or consistent part whatever. But here I am consoled by the observation of a friend who in his childhood years was feeling some adolescent bitterness at the ordering of things as they were. He had an evil-looking, whiskey-smelling old aunt in whom it was his habit to confide. And following one particularly harrowing occasion, his aunt reared back, swayed slightly and then said, "Frankie-boy, life ain't neat."

Well, it ain't. My life has been a testament to this vast truth. It has been a testament to very little else. Professionally, the profession being journalism, it has been a mild success; emotionally, it has been a disaster almost from beginning to end—a disaster punctuated, as all disasters are, by occasional wild bursts of irrelevancies, sometimes beautiful, sometimes comic.

In my career as a journalist I have met my full share of the pseudo great. I propose to say almost nothing about them. I have, at least beyond the depth of mere interviews, known three men whom I consider truly great: Adlai Stevenson, Henry Robinson Luce and Vannevar Bush. This is a small but bewildering assortment; no one of them would have had anything particularly civil to say to either of the other two. I have seen all three in moments of relaxation—yes, Harry Luce had them—as well as on occasions of greater formality. In dropping these three resounding names on so early a page I must emphasize that I was not the deep confidant or particularly boon companion of any of them. We just happened to get on with each other and that is why I can claim their acquaintances as something more than passing. And with each, I happened to do something—different in each case—that impressed them. The pleasure I got from that was considerable.

Although a journalist from the age of nineteen, I have never been under enemy fire, toppled a corrupt senator, or been the true author of a Plan that falsely and unfairly bears the name of another and less worthy man. So what *have* I done? Well, I *have* been thanked for public service by a President of the United States—Harry Truman—who was simultaneously denouncing me as a traitor to my country because he did not know he was speaking about the same person. That was in the 1950's, and a lot of things led up to it . . . .

* * *

1 · GENESIS, OR, CLOSED ON SUNDAY

MY POLICE RECORD BEGAN when I was three years old. This was odd for, unlike today's three-year-olds, I was in great awe of authority. The scene of the crime was Ocean Grove, New Jersey, which at that time was, and to a large extent still is, a seething hotbed of Methodist Revivalism, overflowing with tabernacles and tent colonies for those seeking redemption. What my parents and I were doing in Ocean Grove in the first place I do not know, for my father was an Episcopalian clergyman and the spirit of the times was not ecumenical. I suppose penury had to do with it, for shabby-genteelism was the background of all my youth. In any event, Ocean Grove, circa 1902, was a unique community and Sunday was not just observed, it was practiced. At 11:59 on Saturday nights the city's wooden gates were closed and locked. Vehicular traffic, more than 99 per cent horse-drawn, came to a complete halt. From then until Monday morning, when the gates were unpadlocked, not a wheel turned; it was a city of the psalm-singing dead. O. Henry once made a simile about something being as "futile as looking up the timetable of Sunday trains stopping at Ocean Grove, N.J." Comparatively few knew what this joke was about, perhaps because it was no joke. The Pennsylvania Railroad, the Central Railroad of New Jersey, the New York & Long Branch Railroad, whose trackage went through Ocean Grove, *outside* the gates, could not be made to suspend Sunday operations, particularly since a large pocket of sin—Asbury Park, with carousels, Arthur Pryor's band, penny arcades and taffy-pulling machines—lay less than a mile to the north, and there was no way of sinning in Asbury Park without going by rail, southward from New York, east- and northward from Philadelphia. But if the archimandrites of Ocean Grove were powerless over these evil forces, they were not wholly without recourse. They could and did pass a city ordinance forbidding any trains to stop at the Ocean Grove railroad station on a Sunday, and even in the days when the railroads were the only means of transport for rich and poor alike, none did.

In the days of which I am speaking, something else was closed on Sundays, too. This was the Atlantic Ocean. (Ocean Grove was not lightly named.) A no-nonsense ordinance forbade any bathing or swimming in that sea on the Sabbath. This prohibition somehow slopped over even into Asbury Park, where fornication was lightly viewed but a dip in the briny was a serious matter if taken on the Day of Rest.

It was on such a day in 1902 that my mother, slightly unconventional for a clergyman's wife, was sitting on the sands and looking at the vacant waves. I, with my pail and shovel, was close by her side. The use of the beach on Sunday was not actually a matter of sumptuary law but was frowned on as being rather coarse, so we were all but alone. In an unaccountable moral lapse my mother removed my shoes and stockings and bade me, if I wished, to go wading. Invitations to pleasure from my mother were not routine, so with a whoop of joy I made for the sea. I was about ankle-deep when I heard the blast of a whistle. Turning, I saw the enormous blue form of a policeman bearing down on me and my mother racing full tilt to intercept him. There was a sort of general collision and a vast hubbub arose. I promptly wet my pants, clinging miserably to my mother's skirts. The law had been broken, and I had broken it. I wasn't actually booked, but my mother had to give her name and address; my name, too, went into the law's notebook. I don't know how my mother talked her way out of our joint act of criminality ("fine or imprisonment or both"); possibly she invoked the Church without explaining that her reference was to the *Episcopal* Church. In any event, after supervising the restoration of my shoes and stockings and satisfying himself that normal order, except for my pants, had been restored, the policeman vanished. Clinging to my mother's hand, and yowling as only a ravished three-year-old can yowl, my wet, sandy crotch a badge of shame for all the world to see, I was led back to The Breeze, a latticework boardinghouse about twenty feet wide, with towers and turrets, which was our vacation abode. My mother's fury, and the bestowals of oh-you-poor-darling on me from *females*, I found unendurable. I took the only way out: I threw up on a rug. If anyone wants to know when senses of sin, guilt and shame were consciously born within me, that was the day. Until then, but seldom thereafter, my life had been one grand, sweet song.

• • •

The front page of *The New York Times* for Thursday, March 2, 1899, makes good reading today. The lead story related that a grand jury had indicted one Robert Burnham Molineux on a charge of feeding poisoned Bromo-Seltzer to a lady friend. Several steamers had been wrecked; one was posted overdue and presumed lost. The Filipino "rebels" were mounting guns, but the U.S. transport *Tacoma* had arrived in Manila Bay "without the loss of a single horse or mule," so obviously escalation was paying off. An approving headline said "WHISKEY TRUST NOW COMPLETE"; the story stressed the length of time it had taken to put the $128 million consolidation together. (Later it took even longer to pry it apart.) A post office had been robbed and a trusted cashier had defaulted. The most important news of that day the *Times* relegated to column five: Rudyard Kipling, who had been desperately ill of pneumonia in New York, at the Hotel Grenoble, his life despaired of, was on the mend and would recover. Medical prose at the turn of the century was much the same as now. Kipling's eminent physicians, after keeping reporters in hours of suspense, had finally officially spoken: "Mr. Kipling is continuing to improve." In its story the *Times* strayed from the straight-and-narrow reporting path by permitting an editorial judgment to creep in: it characterized this bulletin as "succinct." Old F. N. Doubleday of the then Doubleday & McClure Company, Mr. Kipling's American publishers, was quoted as saying, also succinctly, "Thank God!"—as well he might. Eventually Mr. Kipling not only recovered his complete health but the complete virulence with which he attacked, in poetry and prose, all Americans (except presumably his Vermont-born wife) and all things in the America that so idolized him. But it had been a close thing at the Hotel Grenoble.

All of this and more, in a total of fourteen seven-column pages of "All the News That's Fit to Print"—the slogan is older than the century—the *Times* offered for a penny. In fact, the *Times* was quite insistent on its price. The words "ONE CENT - ONE CENT" were carried in 12-point bold caps directly under the title slug. To the right of the dateline below it the ONE CENT theme was repeated, in a lower key and with a modulation: ". . . in Greater New York and Jersey City: *Two Cents Elsewhere.*" Inflation was on its way.

• • •

Of all these events I had no knowledge. Yet on the same date of March 2, 1899, I did figure in the press—not in the *Times*, of course, but some 500 miles away, in the Detroit *Free Press*. I was good for three 6-point lines in which I was not mentioned by name. The item was carried under the "Births—Marriages—Deaths" heading and read "Edith Gertrude Hodgins, wife of the Rev. Frederic B. Hodgins, of a son." This was I, and the archaism "of" delicately implied to informed adults that my mother had been "delivered" of me. My birth in Detroit, Michigan, U.S.A., is a matter involving a moment of explanation and, as my various uncles and aunts viewed it, apology.

My first genealogically discoverable ancestor was one William Hodgins, born in Ireland in 1672. It was not until the 1960's that I discovered to my intense pleasure and pride that my family arose in the same Irish hamlet of Dunganstown, County Wexford, as was also the origin of the Kennedys, later to supply a President and other martyrs to the public service of the United States. I am no enthusiast for genealogy, fortunately, so all I know of my Dublin-based family is that it or portions of it were unaccountably Protestant, and duly came to acquire the label "Anglo-Irish." An aunt used to tell me of a song "Dance with the Hodgins' and to hell with the Pope." That was all she could remember, but that would seem to have been enough. Eventually my ancestors came to belong to the most hated breed of men in Ireland— Agents for the English Absentee Landlords. Blushing over this, let me jump quickly to my paternal grandfather, John George Hodgins, born in Dublin August 12, 1821. By 1833 he had had enough of *something*, for he emigrated to Canada—or rather his whole family did, for if the dates are correct, my grandfather was a boy of twelve when he crossed the Atlantic under sail. The family of James Doyle of Cloyne, County Cork, must also have been seeking pastures greener than Ireland, for in 1849 my grandfather married Frances Rachel Doyle, "eldest dau., Jas. Doyle," and in Toronto, Ontario, she bore him four sons before she died.

My grandfather was the pluperfect picture of the tyrannical Victorian paterfamilias, whiskered and awesome, and the pluperfect figure also of the British Colonial Civil Servant. Canada in my grandfather's day was proud of its Dominion status and proud also of being the largest geographical segment of the British Empire. My grandfather bore all sorts of medals and orders, degrees and fellowships on and about his person, and he bore them as the day and times ordained he should, with a terrible, quietly obtrusive and arrogant pride. As I look back on the old gentleman I realize he must have been quite a person, although all he induced in me as a boy was terror. But then, after all, he died in 1912 at the age of ninety-two, when I was thirteen. As Deputy Commissioner of Education for the Province of Ontario he was the deviser of most of Canada's nineteenth-century educational system. (Then, as now, in British practice, the deputy did the work; his titular superior was ceremonial.) And my grandfather's system, of which I am regrettably quite ignorant, was somehow copied by the Japanese. He was also the author of a multivolume work of suffocating accuracy, *A Documentary History of Canada*.

• • •

But it was in family matters that my grandfather stood, as God intended, absolutely paramount. He chose his sons' careers. The eldest was, naturally, to enter the Army and become at the proper time "My son, the General." He did. The next eldest was to follow the law and become "My son, the Judge." That worked, too. The third son was to apply himself to the technology of the day and become "My son, the Scientist," or at least "the Engineer." That didn't work very well. The youngest son, my father, was to take Holy Orders and become "My son, the Bishop." That didn't work at all. Although my father was the most dutiful of sons he was also the most submissive, and who ever heard of a meek bishop? It must have been a source of galling frustration to my grandfather that although my father dutifully became a Bachelor of Divinity from Wycliffe College after his graduation from the University of Toronto, Class of '88,

11

and was ordained "a priest forever, after the order of Melchizedek," he never rose higher in the ecclesiastical hierarchy than the rectorship of some half-dozen small, pitiful and practically unknown parishes. But so it was to be.

• • •

I said, a few pages back, that my birth in Detroit, U.S.A., was a matter for some apology as aunts and uncles viewed it. My mother was also of Canadian birth (Hamilton, Ontario) and Irish ancestry. There was a distillery somewhere on her maternal side, but much too far back to have been of any practical value. My father and mother were married in 1895 and sometime thereafter, being in Windsor, Ontario, took the unprecedented step of crossing the Detroit River and emigrating to the United States, known in Canada simply and contemptuously as "The States." The reason for the move I do not know but it brought contempt and contumely down on my meek father's head and was widely regarded among his numerous family connections as an act of treason. But by these means and accidents I am a first-generation American. At the age of twenty-one, I had the option of becoming an American citizen (born on U.S. soil) or a subject of King George V (of British parentage). I cast my allegiance with America. Occasionally, *very* occasionally, as in 1968 for example, I have wondered if I made the right decision.

• • •

The Canada I knew as a small boy—and the real reason I knew it at all was because I was constantly being sent off to visit maternal aunts, uncles and cousins during my mother's periodic fits of "nervous prostration"—was a very different kind of Canada from that to which my friend and former colleague John Kenneth Galbraith is also native to. *His* Canada, which he celebrated in one of his lesser books, *The Scotch*, was also Ontario, but *west* of the Welland Canal and my grandfather's clan regarded this whole area, and its people, with deep suspicion. They *were* Scotch (not *Scots*, as Galbraith makes very clear); furthermore they lived west of the Welland Canal, which wasn't done.* Thus on two counts they were the objects of deep distrust

* Of course, Toronto is also west of the Welland Canal, but that didn't count with my grandfather, presumably because it was *north*west.

12

to the emigrated Anglo-Irish who had settled to the east. As for French-speaking Quebec, it was beneath mention, although it was conceded, on my mother's side of the family, that Montreal, with its buggy rides up the switchbacks of Mount Royal, was a city of some glamour.

• • •

My first conscious memory is of music—music on a boat. I know my parents had a summer cottage on the shore of the St. Clair River, the short and narrow waterway that joins picturesque Lake St. Clair with the vastness of Lake Huron.

Excursion steamers used to ply the St. Clair River and the music I heard as a semi-infant came from one of them. When I hear it in memory now it comes back as a mixture of banjo and accordion but whatever it was it was the most exquisite Thing that had ever happened in my life. Moreover, it coincided exactly with my discovery of myself: I remember looking down at my toes and thinking "*I am me!*" My mother sets my age at that moment as eighteen months. Whether she was exact or not, it was a great time to be alive.

• • •

After that, the shadows close in again. I think one of the reasons why was that I was accounted a precocious child. I had acquired somehow some kind of ability to read before I was taught or supposed to, and for years my mother kept a yellowed snapshot of a solemn little boy, his feet encased in high-button shoes, who appeared to be studying an outspread newspaper. The child was I and perhaps I was two-and-a-half or three. That was considered all wrong and accordingly all my books were taken away from me and my contact with literature of any sort was completely severed. Whether there was any cause and effect here I don't know, but I do know, from my mother's incessant remarks to me as I grew older, that I was a sobbing and screaming sort of child, given to incessant and continuing demands, including the demand for reassurance that I was loved, for from the age of less than three onward I seemed to be in doubt on this point. I *do* remember having to learn to read all over again when I was six or so, and remember also, as I was struggling with c-a-t, the feeling, "I knew all this once, and a whole lot more besides."

13

• • •

My father, who must at this time have been in his late thirties, had progressed no farther toward "My son, the Bishop" than to be assistant rector of a church in suburban Detroit. I remember neither him nor my mother as of the time that the revelation "*I am me*" burst over me. My sleeping memory awoke again in a boardinghouse in Philadelphia's Logan Square. (Now Logan Circle: more progress.) I remember a parquet floor and two toys: a mooley cow that gave out with a wonderful bovine moan when her head was twisted and relaxed, and a trolley car. The year must, by dead reckoning, have been 1903. Electrical traction was the wonder of the day, so my toy trolley car was the equivalent of today's spaceship. The trolley's four wheels were attached to a heavy inertia flywheel invisibly set in its belly so that if you repeatedly rubbed the car's wheels across the floor, still holding it in your hand, you stored up quite a bit of energy in the flywheel; then when at last you let the car loose it took off at incredible speed for the ends of the earth—the farthest corner of the room. One day I investigated the anatomy of my trolley car. It was made of the lightest-gauge steel, appropriately painted, and the secret of its construction could not have been more obvious: tiny slugs on the body had been fitted into tiny slots in the undercarriage and had then been bent at right angles to secure the two. It was short work to unbend the slugs and render the trolley car into two pieces. Dismantling wheels and axles was a little harder, but not much. I was well pleased with my work, but by the time my father came home from his office I wanted my trolley car restored. *And he could not do it!* If the music on the boat and the discovery that I was me was my life's first vast ecstasy, here, now, in Logan Square, was my life's first tragic disillusionment: my father was not omnipotent. I was too young for such a revelation and that was why, perhaps, the shadows closed in again and I remember nothing more about Logan Square except, vaguely, falling down a very long flight of stairs.

• • •

The next thing I knew we were living at 59 Fairview Avenue in Lansdowne, a suburb about a twenty-minute train ride from Philadelphia's Broad Street Station.

In 1904 it was possible for a man with wife and child, even one who was still persistently getting nowhere in his profession, to rent a five-room house with ample surrounding greensward within ten miles of Philadelphia's City Hall—and not only that but to keep a servant. I remember two of these: Annie Grady, straight off the boat from Ireland, and Caroline Fauntleroy—Negress, as the word then, without a hint of opprobrium, went. And for some reason I remember their wage scale, which my father was able to meet despite his own lack of prosperity. It was two dollars a month and "found"—i.e., food and lodging also provided. The domestic labor supply was ample, so my mother was constantly firing maids in the hope that the next one would be "better." The firing of Annie Grady occasioned me no sorrow but when Caroline Fauntleroy was fired my world collapsed again, for this old lady had become my dearest friend. I remember still the manner of her going. From an upstairs window I watched despairing as Caroline trudged through the thick dust of Lansdowne Avenue, all her worldly possessions literally done up in a literal red bandanna handkerchief at the end of a literal bamboo pole slung over her shoulder. The helpless sorrow at the loss of my friend bit into me deeply and it was some days before I was civil to my mother again.

But life did have its compensations. At age five I discovered girls and I discovered sex. Unfortunately, these two remained disconnected in my mind and did not fuse until I was almost eight. The wasted years. Across Fairview Avenue there lived a little girl inappropriately named Prudence. Her family must have been filthy rich for they owned a coach and pair. Nevertheless she and I played together and it was slowly borne in on both of us that there was something more fundamentally different between us than just that she wore a little skirt and I wore a sailor suit. Wordlessly we resolved to explore, and crawled under the latticework that formed a sort of kirtle to the bottom of our front porch. There we investigated each other. I don't know how she interpreted what she found out about me, but when I discovered she had no penis and apparently no *anything* (I had done better with my trolley car, years ago), I was simply stumped. The male-female differentiation produced in us nothing but mild bewilderment. Unfortunately for me, Mrs. Fleming, who lived next door, had seen Prudence and me crawl under the latticework and then had seen or inferred what went on thereafter. I had previously loved Mrs. Fleming but now she attacked me with hellfire and damnation. I was terrified, for I had had no consciousness of guilt. She implanted it deeply, and I hope she is frying in hell. Not that she stopped our investigations; Prudence and I merely transferred them to under the couch in my parents' living room. Here there was less space for maneuver and more possibility of other and still more dangerous consequences. But our luck held and we discovered that we both had an anus. We verified this several times and the results were always the same. But we seemed to have reached a dead end and thus our experiments concluded. There was no arousal in any of this—merely the excitement of doing something furtive and getting away with it. Prudence and I reverted to what would have been called "normal" play, having decided that sex had no future.

Not that I didn't, at the same time, suffer the pangs of love. There was a Goddess down the street who wore rimless spectacles and whose hair cascaded down her back. But she must have been all of eleven, and I could not do anything more than cast furtive, fervent, secret glances at her. When she smiled at me she threw me into a state of total, blissful panic.

Let me not give the impression that life for a boy child in 1904 was wholly erotic. True, there was an intense and mysterious excitement in seeing a horse defecate in the street. Since this was always happening, the excitement was fairly continuous. But then there was also my velocipede, which I rode with Jehu's speed and skill. And there were trains. From the very first Lansdowne days I was crazy mad in love with trains and engineers. My father entered with uncharacteristic enthusiasm into a collaboration. On the pipe fence that surrounded our lawn he rigged up a semaphore, string-controlled from his porch seat, so that he could set it at GO, STOP, or PROCEED WITH CAUTION. On my velocipede I would obey these signals with absolute rigor. If the semaphore said STOP, I would wait indefinitely until it changed: compressed-air pump gasping, of course, to keep the brake pipe charged and the blower on to keep the fire bright in the absence of stack blast, for I was the *Broadway Limited*, or whatever else my sign designated. (My father had painted signs indicating what I was, and these I proudly hung on my velocipede's front.) The slow deterioration or outright disappearance of trains is a

16

matter of active sorrow to me still, in my seventy-second year. Waiting in the Lansdowne station I *think* I can actually remember watching the approach of a genuine diamond stacker; if so it was a wood burner and I was seeing a relic of Civil War days. I have never read William Ellery Leonard's *The Locomotive-God*, but I'm under the impression that he and I shared many emotional similarities. However, in Professor Leonard's life there was no Mr. Albert Myers and in mine there was. On that account my life is the richer.

· · ·

Mr. Albert Myers was a motorman for the Philadelphia Rapid Transit Company—the P.R.T., then so called and universally damned. Mr. Myers was day motorman of car No. 1247, a bouncing, swaying four-wheeler that had a very short wheel base and a very short run—two or three miles—between Lansdowne, where tracks' end was only one hundred feet from our house, and the then complicated traction nexus of Darby, where feeder lines from as far away as Chester connected with the big cars that ran through downtown Philadelphia all the way to Front Street and the Delaware River. There ferries carried those inclined to Camden, gateway to the New Jersey shore.

I loved Mr. Myers far more than I loved my parents. The secret of this was, of course, that Mr. Myers treated me with gravity, as an equal and a friend. Since his run was short, #1247 arrived at the Lansdowne railhead every three-quarters of an hour or so. I met its every trip when I was not in kindergarten. And an experienced ear like mine placed against one of the wooden poles that supported the overhead wire could tell by the quality and intensity of its hum how far away #1247 might be when it was still far from sight.

It seemed to be ordained that motormen were short and jolly and conductors tall and dour. That at any rate was so of Mr. Myers and his conductor, whose name I never knew or cared to. When Mr. Myers brought #1247 to its Lansdowne stop, it was the conductor's job to reverse the trolley pole and replace its small contact wheel on the overhead wire. While he was doing this, Mr. Myers would remove his controller handle and reverse lever and, holding them in his gloved hand, make for #1247's other end, now poised for the return flight to Darby. "Better kick the brake shoes," he would say to me, offhand, not a command but a reminder of responsibility. I kicked them with all my force and a small accumulation of dried mud always fell onto the gleaming tracks. This was sublime. I had a useful function in society that was appreciated and acknowledged.

I was "by nature" a tense, whining, screaming, bed-wetting child, but circumstances alter cases. One rainy day as I was racing to meet Mr. Myers and #1247, I tripped and fell full face downward in the thick mud of Fairview Avenue. Ordinarily such a tragedy would have sent me spinning into the horrors, but since Mr. Myers was at stake, I merely picked myself up, greeted him and kicked the brakes, which took a lot of kicking on a day like that. Mission accomplished and #1247 departed, I strolled casually back to the house in a euphoric state of calm, where my astounded mother stripped and bathed me while Caroline Fauntleroy boiled my besmeared clothes. Under the circumstances it had been only the most trifling misadventure.

I suppose there is no consistency in childhood. In mine there was love of Mr. Myers and #1247, of little girls, of trains, of my velocipede and of kindergarten. (I am trying to rank these in order of five-year-old importance.) And there were also my dreams—or more accurately the period of drowsy fantasy in bed that just preceded sleep. The vividness of these fantasies of childhood passes all description. In my happiest I was a motorman, the peer of Mr. Myers. Graduating from this I became a manufacturer of trolley cars. Competitive tests were run and the unanimous verdict was always the same: "Eric's is best." With the plaudits of everyone ringing in my ears, delicious sleep would then come.

• • •

I might say that as a future creator of the best trolley cars I had studied #1247 with some care. Unbeknownst to me, an era of thousands of years was coming to an end—the era of handcraftmanship, whose burial ground might be thought of as that same Detroit where mass production and assembly lines were born slightly after I was. Meanwhile #1247 was two things in one: on one hand she represented the then pinnacle of what, half a century later, came to be called *automation*; on the other, she was handcrafted. True, her motors were noisy and her axles rattled at high speed (i.e., 20 m.p.h.) and her interior was no salon. But her transverse seats were finest shiny rattan and her floor was of ribbed ash. Her enormous swan-curved brake handle—the only means of stopping her—was sculptured out of yellow brass. A lover's eye, like mine, discerned her bell and register cords to be of soft, pliant leather, which ran through fittings of ornamented bronze. Where splices were needed, linked sleeves of copper served. Outside she was thickly enameled in red and cream, with a green "carriage stripe" surrounding her for style. As for her golden numbers, in the shaded gothic then inseparable from anything connected with transportation, they were as genuinely hand-painted as any Rembrandt.

• • •

By starting from Lansdowne in #1247 one could get to Philadelphia for two nickels, one payable at the start of the journey in #1247, the other exacted at the Darby junction. This was quite a consideration for a parson's family, for the Pennsylvania Railroad, which got there in a fraction of the time, charged twenty cents. So whenever it was necessary to use the less expensive route and I was to go along, the start of the journey was pure bliss, for Mr. Myers would station me between his outstretched arms, his left hand on the controller handle, gloved right on the enormous brass brake handle, with instructions to stamp on the floor disc that clanged the warning gong—"to keep the cows off the track"—which was not *entirely* a joke.

It was space flight, that's what. Eternal blessings on Mr. Myers "long in the employ of the P.R.T. who died suddenly at his home in Darby Thursday last." This three-line obit that I came on suddenly in a local newspaper more than ten years after I had last seen him gave me a heavy teen-age pang. A picture of himself, his trolley and his conductor still hangs in my study.

• • •

What I have detailed above represented the brighter side of my childhood. There was also a darker side, which is harder to particularize, except that for times on end I was constantly pervaded by a deep sense of sadness and sorrow. At what? I do not know. I do know that my parents, particularly my mother, were baffled by the child of their union. Equally I could not understand my parents, and in large measure still can't today. I came to realize after a long while that my father had seemed so distant to me in my boyhood because he was a desperately unhappy man, forced into The Cloth by my grandfather, when he wanted to be something else—a journalist, of all things. He made a successful small-parish priest because he was kind, gentle and understanding. His parishioners loved him. I measure my words when I say he was the most Christlike person I ever knew. But there was a trouble. He was a man of no force. At his parochial work he was successful, but he didn't like it and was perpetually trying to escape from it into journalism, at which he was not successful and thus was being perpetually fired. When he was a young man in Canada he *was* successful—prize essayist, Class of '88 at the University of Toronto, and that sort of thing. He had the further distinction of being the first editor ever to publish a work by Stephen Leacock, when both young men were undergraduates. My father and mother and Stephen Leacock were friends and my father was editor of *The Varsity*, to which Leacock first contributed a wonderful little piece called "A Boarding House Geometry." When my father decided to leave Canada, the Governor-General sent an emissary to express the Dominion's regrets, and a Toronto newspaper deplored the loss of "the wittiest after-dinner speaker in Canada." This was never the father I knew. The father I knew lived a miserable, harried life, full of failure and frustration, and although he had many moments of desperate silence, I never heard him complain about his lot, and he never broke down. This is courage of a kind, indeed. But what had happened? I don't know. My best guess, however, is that it had to do with his wife, my mother.

2 · MOTHER LOVE, OR, HELL'S FIRE

MY MOTHER'S FAMILY had its stigma of Victorianism, too. Edith Gertrude Bull was the twelfth of thirteen children—six surviving into adulthood. They were all generally daft, as I viewed them; my mother was the least daft but by far the most discontented and sad. She was an aunt before she was born, since by that time her eldest brother was a married man with children. Because of the size of her family, many of her nieces and nephews were approximately her age. I once asked one of them: "What was my mother like as a girl?" Quick as a flash I got the answer: "Pretty, vivacious and fun-loving—but all that changed *absolutely* when you were born." I have never read any good explanation of this quite familiar postpartum personality change. With my mother, it obviously went to her deepest psychic deeps. While I was still in my cradle she mused aloud, as I suppose every mother does, "I wonder what he'll be when he grows up." She said it to my Uncle Dick, who promptly answered, "That's easy; a low comedian." Even though Uncle Dick was her own brother, my mother scarcely spoke a civil word to him the rest of his life: he had aimed a mortal insult at Her Child.

But there was something even more peculiar in my mother's love for Her Child. Something forced her to emphasize to me, as soon as I was old enough to ask for bedtime stories, that my birth had come close to taking her own life, and wasn't it nice that it hadn't, after all. I was scarcely old enough to understand what birth was, to say nothing of death, so these softly told stories, designed to lull me to sleep, were, in effect, so many fairy tales. But why my mother's insistence on them? Never as a child did I gain the *direct* impression that I was unwanted: quite the reverse, my mother slathered me with love and affection, took the

21

utmost pride in my accomplishments and boasted about me, in my presence, to other adults. This combination of things could have only one outcome: I became a Monster. My mother, seeing that something had to be done, overreacted. From being the loving mother, she suddenly became the punishing mother and whanged me about for doing the same things, I thought, that had previously been praised. I became extremely wary of her, seeing her as inconsistent, unfathomable, unreliable, unpredictable. So, I had a distant father and an enigmatic mother: the perfect psychiatric setup—it would be much later said with authority—for almost anything to happen to the affected child.

My mother today would be called a very sick woman. She became not only an unreliable parent but a nagging wife. When she badgered my father and when he took it lying down I would rush to his defense—thus making everything worse. My father, just then, was enjoying a blessed freedom from parochial work and was, in Philadelphia, an associate editor of *The Booklovers' Magazine* and the Booklovers' Library. These two endeavors were among the many creations of that incredible (for the times) entrepreneur Seymour Eaton, whom H. G. Wells later used as a model in *Tono-Bungay*. Seymour Eaton's rocket went up and up; it seemed that he could market and sell *anything*. I think he must have been a very early first among one-man conglomerates. His adventures led him from groceries to literature. His brands of tea and coffee—the Tabard Inn—enjoyed quite a success for a while in the early century. Then, suddenly, his whole empire collapsed and—bang—my father, now over forty, was out of a job and had to take refuge in becoming assistant rector of Lansdowne's St. John's Church—the first House of Worship I ever remember being in, and in which I remember disgracing myself by suddenly making a loud observation at an unusually solemn moment. Nevertheless I loved St. John's; it had a fine organist and a fine organ. Music, for the second time in my life, intoxicated me as organ and vested choir sang the most stirring Processional in all church music: "Ancient of Days," Hymn No. 311 in the old Hymnal, music by "H. Smart," whoever he was.

> *Ancient of Days, who sittest throned in glory,*
> *To thee all knees are bent, all voices pray;*
> *Thy love has blessed the wide world's wondrous story,*
> *With light and life since Eden's dawning day.*

Not the supplication but the music, not the words but the harmony, stirred me to the depths of my soul. My father was an excellent pianist without being able to read more than a few lines of music; he used to play this for me over and over again and I would swoon with bliss every time. This was the nearest I have in my life ever come to having a Religious Experience, and I was then five.

Of my father's two professions I was from that time forward interested only in the Editorial. I became not only a writer but a manufacturer of books. My books were definitely not as good as my trolley cars, but they were realer. I never did penetrate the mysteries of *quarto* as a child, but *folio* was a cinch for anybody. You just took a couple of sheets of paper, folded them once, put brass staples through the fold and—bang—you had an eight-page book. In this operation, production preceded writing and unfortunately my staying power as an author was not very great; the title page and one page of large downhill-sloping prose were about all I could manage. But I was following in my father's footsteps as best I could.

• • •

One day the horse-drawn hackney bus of the Maplewood School deposited me home as usual. I entered to find all blinds drawn and most windows shuttered. There was a strange smell, later to be identified as the drug valerian, then thought to be the best thing in the pharmacopoeia as a stimulant and antispasmodic. My mother had had the first of her many future nervous prostrations. I, it soon developed, was to be sent away, back to Canada. My father's side of the family wanted nothing of the problem child of the brother who had migrated south out of Canada. My Uncle Will ("My son, the General") had indeed made it as planned: he was Major General William Egerton Hodgins, later to be Adjutant General of the Canadian Expeditionary Force in World War I. My Uncle Frank ("My son, the Judge") had also come through: he was the Honorable Mr. Justice Hodgins of the Ontario Supreme Court. No hope there. My mother's side of the family proved much more hospitable and I was shipped off to the Toronto suburb of Mimico, where my Aunt Lil and her husband were the owners of an Enchanted Garden called Erindale. It seemed as big as the whole Province to me, but I suppose it might have been several acres or even

more. And it did front, for a hundred feet or so, on the sandy
shore of pristine Lake Ontario. It was a heaven of houses, bun-
galows, fences, pathways, pony carts, gardens, flowers—*and a
boathouse and a windmill.* I promptly forgot about my mother;
I was in heaven. I was to visit Mimico and Erindale many times
in my childhood and boyhood—sometimes because of my
mother's illnesses, sometimes on vacation with my father and
mother—and it was always the same—Enchantment. Here I always became not a problem child but a model child. Racing about
the twisted paths I was the locomotive, the train and the passengers all in one—either of the *Royal Blue,* the *Black Diamond*
or the *Broadway Limited.* On a less intellectual, more sensual
level there were red, black and yellow raspberries to be picked
from the warm redolent vines that clung to the rough stone walls.
It was almost enough to make me stop missing Mr. Myers.

Another reason why I was a model child in Erindale was that
I was in mortal fear, and quite rightly, of Aunt Lil's husband,
Thomas Jermyn. Since my Aunt Lil was the second of my grandmother's brood of thirteen, she and her husband were so much
older than my parents that *their* children, my three cousins
Evylyn, Eileen and Percival—God help him, but mercifully he
was called "Pete"—were mid-age between my parents and myself. Uncle Tom was bearded and terrible. When the eight or
more of us sat down to dinner, there was the usual chatter. Uncle
Tom would let this go on for a moment, then slam the butt of
his knife on the polished table and bellow "Com-*pose!*" We composed, all right. Uncle Tom's wife and children were as terrified
of him as I was, I am sure. This was his intent. This was the
way things were. This was God's Plan. To have questioned any
of Uncle Tom's unilateral decisions would have been somehow
worse than questioning Christianity. At any rate, the lightning
bolt would have struck faster.

Uncle Tom's cowed son, Pete, was in my eyes, and the eyes
of others too, a kind of genius. On the one hand, he was a ne'er-
do-well. On the other hand, he could do everything. He owned
a sailboat, a boom-and-gaff-rigged sloop, a most ordinary vessel,
and inevitably came in first in every Saturday race of the Mimico
Yacht Club. Eventually the other skippers tired of this monotony
and banded together to ask Pete, most politely, if he would be
willing to race one Saturday in a boat not his own, but in the

24

slowest, dumpiest craft, by common consent, in the whole regatta. He promptly consented and crossed the finish line first in her, too—with a wider gap than usual between him and his followers. *That*, I think, was showing off.

That was not all he could do. He was gently gruff with me but I always watched him with wide-eyed admiration, and he did not seem to mind the devouring intensity I bent on him. With my own eyes, over one long summer, I watched his every motion as he built a sleek motorboat out of raw lumber until it emerged, varnished and sanded to a fare-ye-well, a craft whose every subtle curve faired perfectly into every other. Did he build the engine from rough castings? Did he sculpture his own propeller? In my estimation he could have.

Eventually Pete married, judiciously after his father's death. His choice fell on a luscious girl "of Italian extraction" who cuckolded him in what must have been record time for those or any other days. Eventually there was a divorce. I never heard of Cousin Percival again. He was never good on land.

• • •

Yet all in all I preferred my mother's side of the family; it certainly produced much more interesting aunts and uncles than my father's side, which was totally stuffy and stupefyingly null. But in addition to the maternal aunt I have specified, I knew three of my maternal uncles. Anyone named Harcourt Bull, wherever in the world found, is a relative of mine, but the original (so far as I know) Harcourt Bull was my Uncle Hadge, a lawyer who was full of fun, if you can believe me. My Uncle Dick I seldom saw, because of his sister's enmity, but according to Uncle Hadge my Uncle Dick, in his boyhood, had a unique gift, much envied and admired: the ability to vomit by volition. On some distant boyhood day my uncles Hadge and Dick had committed some violation of the penal code, or at any rate were being chased by the town constable. The chase led in and out of an orchard with the constable gaining. It led eventually to a ladder propped against the side of a house. My uncles started climbing. So did the constable. Things were approaching a cul-de-sac when Uncle Hadge turned to his younger brother just below him and commanded, "Throw up, Dick!" The chase ended.

I loved Uncle Hadge for sharing that story with me, all the

more so because it so obviously offended my mother. As for Uncle Dick, not present to verify or amplify, my admiration was boundless. Did he, now adult, whiskered and a father, still possess this gift? I could not ask.

Uncle Ned was a different sort of character but he had his virtues too. He was a magician who could take ten-cent pieces out of anybody's ear or cut a cork into quarters before your very eyes and then, by covering the dismembered cork for an instant with a handkerchief, render it whole again. He was a marvel, but he was an optometrist who died young, a grievous loss.

• • •

Every time in my life that I was sent to Mimico or Toronto I would leave a wraith and come back chubby. My mother always remarked on this, but no hint of cause and effect ever seemed to cross her mind. It was very simple. My various aunts and cousins treated me kindly but firmly. The rules of the establishment were precisely and clearly announced. Violations would not be tolerated. Period. Except for what was forbidden or *de rigueur*, I was a free man, encouraged to have fun, with or without their help, as I pleased. There is—or there was—an answer to "please don't eat the daisies." Children are demons with very clear and subtle minds, and the excuse "You never told me not to" is a fabrication made instantly, *ad hoc*, falsely, faultlessly and with a reaction time too swift for an adult. My cousin George Kelley, married to my lovely cousin Evylyn, at the time childless, was supposed to be a cold fish and "not understand children." So there was much morbid speculation when I was sent to board with them. This proved groundless. Cousin George, having tucked me offhandedly into bed, turned at the door and said in a calm, quiet voice of unassailable authority, "There is to be no noise or disturbance coming from this room until eight o'clock tomorrow morning. Any questions?" There were no questions, not even about the extra drink of water, and there was no noise. Not ever. And no bed-wetting.

In due course I returned home, chubby again, turned my own home into chaos and grew wraithlike again on demands for three and four extra drinks of water per evening. They did not quench my thirst, which was not for water at all but for disruption. I had learned how to cause it, and what I knew about disruption, which was a lot, I used to the hilt. No wonder I was a sad and sorrowful little boy. In Canada, as by Mr. Myers, I was treated as a *person;* at home I was a piece of property.

• • •

When I was five my mother became pregnant again. If I had known it I would have been puzzled and surprised for reasons that will appear later. But all I knew was that once again the blinds were lowered and the smell of valerian filled 59 Fairview Avenue. The time was late 1904, and after Christmas had passed I began to look eagerly forward to another date—St. Valentine's Day, which would mean, O thrill of thrills, that my breakfast place would be piled high with a large assortment of envelopes all addressed to Master Eric Francis Hodgins. In those days mail dispatch was swift, sure, copious, dependable and regular. St. Valentine's Day, 1905, was bitter cold, with freezing rain, but despite that the trudging postman at 2 P.M. delivered another big batch of envelopes on the front porch. In going to collect them my mother slipped on the icy boards in a severe fall. Soon there began still another episode of drawn blinds and the smell of valerian, and in due course I was shipped off to Canada again. This, by now, was just fine with me; I preferred almost any household to my own. After a long while, there arrived for me a letter in my father's exquisitely scholarly handwriting explaining that it had been planned I should have a baby brother but that God had kept him in heaven because he had not been strong enough for this earth. This seemed to make the best of sense to me, although perhaps not in the way my gentle father had intended, and I was a bit puzzled by the long faces of my cousins. Not until several years later when I had accidentally come upon the facts of life did I learn that my mother had been delivered at full term of a stillborn child. Thereafter she would more than occasionally speculate gently to me whether there was perhaps any connection between her fall, in her loving eagerness to get my valentines, and her subsequent obstetrical tragedy. She didn't *know,* of course, but she rather thought . . . .

I was not unduly affected by the soft implication that I might be a murderer because a much heavier blow had fallen. I was to be parted from Mr. Myers. Something had gone pop in my father's affairs again and we were leaving Lansdowne for Morton,

27

Pennsylvania—a little suburb on the same P.B.&W. commuter line of the Pennsylvania, but four stations farther out. For the first time my father, who was now forty-five, was a full-fledged Rector—of a tiny, ugly little House of Worship known as the P.E. Church of the Atonement. The move was a wrench for everyone, and why it was made I don't know. Lansdowne was quiet, well barbered and serenely middle-class, but Morton was a tough little town. If Lansdowne had a slum I had never seen it. But my father's new church and its rectory were right on the fringe of the slum—the white slum. The Negro slum was, literally, on the other side of the railroad tracks. Morton teemed with colored people, and none of the whites even pretended to like it—not even my saintly father. The Negro population was 98 per cent servile—"which is what they ought to be"—and 99 per cent suppressed, although as everywhere, there was the occasional "uppity nigger." After all, in 1906 the country was still full of people who had lived and fought through the Civil War—and then had forgotten why they had done it. The Memorial Day parades of the G.A.R. were of course beginning to thin but the continuing prevalence of Civil War songs was amazing. When orchestras played "Dixie," the audience would drown the first five bars in its applause, which meant, I came to learn, "All is forgiven."

• • •

In many ways it was good to have been born in the last year of the nineteenth century. For one thing the village blacksmith *did* stand under the spreading chestnut tree and the ring of his hammer on his anvil was a deeply romantic sound. As for the chestnut trees, their blight had begun to strike, but its terrible extent, which would eventually destroy every such tree in America, was still anything but evident. I doubt I ever appreciated the beauty of these trees, or of their sawed wood, until later life, but in 1907 I did indeed appreciate the joys of going chestnutting: picking up the big prickly burrs that littered the ground about, prying them open, with some pain, and extracting the gorgeous shiny nut inside. My generation must have been one of the last to do that, and as for the clang of the blacksmith's hammer on his anvil, the glow of his hand-bellowsed forge, and the splendid stink of the smoldering horses' hooves as the glowing iron shoes were fitted—all these were already beginning to lessen a little as my boyhood progressed. The smith, a mighty profane man was he, and his language to a restive horse—"Whoa up there or I'll ram this file up your ass"—was most impressive as children coming home from school looked in at the open door. And none more impressed than I, the preacher's son.

As the blacksmith and the chestnut trees began their slow decline, the horseless carriage shed that label and became frankly the automobile, variously shortened to "the car" or "the auto," and it caused horses to rear and shy. No wonder. There were precious few of them, and one of the most conspicuous, to be remembered with greatest affection, was the one-lung Cadillac. Having a two-cycle engine with but one cylinder, it depended on the heaviest automotive flywheel in history to keep it under steerageway between explosions in the cylinder. These were real explosions—tooth- and window-rattling detonations. No wonder they frightened horses; they frightened humans, too, except small boys. It was a tossup which was the most exciting: a runaway horse or the occasional passage of an auto down Franklin Avenue. The standard juvenile witticism of the day was yelling at the goggled auto driver: "Hey, mister, your wheels are going around," and I remember my father's gentle rebuke from the rectory porch: "Son, that is not a very polite thing to say."

• • •

At that time I had not passed beyond the juvenile-intoxication stage with life and nature. One of my last visitations by this emotion, comparable to the *"I am me"* revelation or the discovery of music, was standing knee-deep in a field of daisies, buttercups and black-eyed Susans and being quite overwhelmed by the beauty of life. It was one of the last pure things of the time, although a little later I was made gloriously drunk by A Smell. To this day I cannot identify that Smell, which I have smelled only three or four times since childhood. On no evidence I have come to think of it as Eucalyptus, but I have no way of verifying it. All I know for sure is that it was as beautiful as sex—and noninvolving.

Being eight, the velocipede of my youth had given way to a bicycle, with New Departure coaster brake and acetylene lamp for nightwork. I still remained a railroad, however, and here acknowledge my deep debt to the Mead Cycle Company, manufacturer of the Ranger Superb. (They published a catalog that afforded me reading and rereading for several years.) It is impossible to convey how rural the United States still was. We were now twelve miles from Philadelphia but vacant land, not even tilled, abounded, and if you had the courage you could pedal to, and maybe through, the Secane Woods—a forest primeval. If you had the courage to go through the woods you came out at the Secane station of the P.R.R. Then you had to pedal back. Those woods were dark and the trees were a virgin stand. No boy would venture into them alone, but there was courage in groups. We would try to make our way through the trail without snapping a twig underfoot, like Natty Bumppo, but it didn't work.

• • •

I have described Morton as a tough little town, and it certainly was. It was also primitive. The sidewalks were mostly wooden planks, like those of Dodge City in *Gunsmoke*. The streets were dirt, of course, and in dry weather they made dust, as fine and dense as cement, which fell backward in little fountains from the iron tires of the wagons. Street lighting was far in the future and except on moonlight nights the dark was ferocious. For the benefit of those who today deplore "crime in the streets" it can be noted that prudent gentlemen at night carried sword canes as a matter of course. There was no law about carrying concealed weapons, and a sword cane, after all, was a practical necessity. The distant barking of a dog or the ringing of the fire bell—an old steel locomotive tire in which the blacksmith had cut a slot so it would vibrate when struck with a sledge—these were also fearsome things in the dark.

In the rectory at night, bells were not always distant. There were occasions—not many but some—when our front doorbell would ring at, say, three in the morning, followed by a pounding on the door. This, I learned detachedly, was because somebody was dying and my father was wanted at the bedside. It was seldom the doom of the elderly that brought forth these nighttime calls. The man at the door was more likely to be an anguished young husband or an anguished father whose wife or daughter was dying in labor, less likely from the childbirth itself than from an overdose of chloroform administered by the lone local doctor. By the time my father was home I was of course deep in sleep again, and would be told in the morning, solemnly, that young Mrs. Cooke was dead. This passed my understanding. Later, much later, it was not to.

But even in those days faint new things were stirring in realms connected—faintly—with medicine. The Emmanuel Movement had begun. It delighted my Aunt Nance to call it "The Enameling Movement" but it took its name from the Emmanuel Church in Boston, where the eminent Reverend Dr. Elwood Worcester was Rector. Eventually, *Religion and Medicine* by the Drs. Worcester, Samuel McComb and Isador Coriat (this last being an actual M.D. psychiatrist) came out and provided the lay American world with one of the first primitive expositions of psychodynamics it had ever heard of.

My father was fascinated; my mother (who needed all the psychic help she could get from anywhere) was contemptuous. Her sufferings were "real" and here was a suggestion that they were "imaginary." It's a bit discouraging that this lay confusion on a fundamental of psychiatry still persists today. But my father got the message and strove to put it into practice. Practical, practicing psychiatrists simply did not exist except to deal with the "insane." So my father picked up the Emmanuel Movement and tried to run with it. There is no evidence he ever got very far, but his rectory office was open to parishioners or any others with one kind or another of the psychic heaves. Then, as now, the commonest trouble lay with alcohol; then, as now, nothing much could be done about it unless the problem could be turned into a do-it-yourself project, which it never was until the eventual growth of A.A., of which I was one day in my forty-fifth year to acquire some direct knowledge. Eventually the Emmanuel Movement was to peter out, but not without leaving some interesting traces behind.

• • •

If I am later to give—as I am—some evidences of childhood depravity, social justice to the young dictates that I should also record some normalities of the times. There was no problem of playground space—it was all about us. We played kid football ("Tackle 'im low!" was the war cry) and kid baseball. I preferred the latter, of which the practical variety was "worky-up," in which players on each side set rotations of position every inning. (There was no outfield, and no need for one.) Three men on a side—pitcher, catcher, first baseman—would do, although four were better. That covered second. The baseball problem was economic. There were five-cent balls and ten-centers and balls that cost a quarter of a dollar. The five-centers were no good; merely cotton waste stuffed into leather and even an infield hit would knock them lopsided. The ten-centers were our staple, although when we were in funds, presumably by stealing from our parents, we were able to buy the twenty-five-cent ball, which usually lasted until it got lost. When we learned, from the Spalding and A. J. Reach catalogs, that a real professional-league ball cost $1.25, we yearned to fondle such a precious object, but we never did. They were not on sale locally. No effective demand.

• • •

A few depraved adults smoked cigarettes in those days, and we followed them avidly. Folklore described smokes as "coffin nails" fifty years before the American Cancer Society caught on; habitual users were "cigarette fiends"—i.e., tremulous and emaciated chain smokers. We never happened to see one. Although we experimented—very mildly—with cubebs, coffee grounds and corn silk, these were not worth the hand-rolled effort, and for boys of eight real tobacco was distasteful. The reason for our interest in Sweet Caporals and Piedmonts (five cents for twenty) lay in the colored cards of baseball players each pack contained. There was the 150 series, of low value. The 350 series had a much more active market. Eventually there was issued the 450 series—better than tax-free municipal bonds any day. Mordecai "Three Finger" Brown, renowned pitcher, whose missing digit was regarded as an asset. Larry Lajoie (*La-zu-ay*). Rube Waddell. Christy Mathewson. Walter Johnson. The immortal Chicago Cubs infield, "Tinker [ss] to Evers [2b] to Chance [1b]." Topsy Hartzell. Tyrus Raymond Cobb. These were the heroes of the day, and their bright-colored images were the currency of boyhood. The Great American Pastime was close to its zenith. Football was college only, basketball had been invented but that was about all, and hockey was unorganized. Baseball was *the* thing. When my father, much later, took me to see my first professional game in Shibe Park, it was to see a game destined to be unique in baseball history and unquestionably destined to remain so forever . . . .

The game was between Connie Mack's then invincible Philadelphia Athletics (also the *Athaletics* and the *Alfaletics*) and the Detroit Tigers. In the journalism of the day it was the page-one lead story even in *The New York Times*, and the *losing* pitcher, later to be the Reverend Aloysius Stanislaus Travers, S.J., went the whole route for Detroit, giving up twenty-five hits on which Connie Mack's men scored twenty-four runs. He lost the game, all right, but he saved baseball's honor and I saw him do it. I had no business being there.

It all began, as so many things used to, when Tyrus Raymond Cobb, one of baseball's greatest and unquestionably dirtiest players, had climbed into the stands and assaulted a fan who had been riding him.* (This had been in New York some days earlier.) Ban Johnson, president of the American League, slapped an indefinite suspension on Cobb. The Detroit players then announced that if the suspension wasn't immediately lifted they would not take the field against Connie Mack's men in Shibe Park, next on their schedule. To this threat Ban Johnson replied that in that case he would lift the Detroit franchise, and how would anybody like *that?*

With this, even Connie Mack set out to help his rival manager Hughie ("Ee-YAH!") Jennings. Young Steve Travers was assistant baseball manager for a local Catholic college, but was not a player. For the lure of twenty-five dollars he agreed to pitch. His stuff consisted of a curve and what was later described as a "no-smoke" ball. Enough other bodies were rounded up at ten dollars each to make a team. What I cannot explain after almost sixty years is why Connie Mack used the cream of his own pitching staff (Pennock and Coombs) against these particu-

---

* Sports page prose has gone pallid with the years. This is the lead paragraph in which *The New York Times*, with no by-line, described what happened. "Everything was very pleasant at the Detroit-Yankee game on the Hilltop yesterday until Ty Cobb johnnykilbaned a spectator right on the place where he talks, started the claret, and stopped the flow of profane and vulgar words. Cobb led with a left jab and countered with a right kick to Mr. Spectator's left Welsbach, which made his peeper look as if someone had drawn a curtain over it. Silk O'Loughlin, without a license from the boxing commission, refereed the go. He gave the decision to Cobb and then put him out of the ring. The spectator went to a lawyer's office to make out his will."

lar rivals, and how *they* managed to score two runs, for somehow they did. But it was a day to remember.*

Even I realized that earthly existence could not continue to provide a continuous life like this.

•   •   •

More prosaically, there was Turner's Pond. It served for hockey in the winter and for bent-pin-and-worm fishing with bamboo poles in summer. Occasionally somebody might hook a catfish but very seldom. Turner's Pond was a mud-banked pool covered at the edges and patched in the center with rich green slime. An occasional adventurer would try to swim in it, but I was much too fastidious—and besides, I could not swim. But kids and water have always had a natural affinity, and in the warm summers, tracing the rocky and refuse-filled creeks was real exploration, and fascinating less for geology, of which we knew nothing, as for the discovery of dead dogs, bedsprings and sodden upholstery. Anyone who thinks stream pollution to be a wholly modern thing has another think coming, although rocks and ferns also then abounded.

•   •   •

The isolation of my parents' life impressed even me. There were not many Episcopalians in Morton but I think my mother's flustered incompetence as a hostess had something to do with it, too. Although my father made his conscientious parochial calls, it was gradually borne in on me that he only faintly believed in what he was doing, and my mother believed not at all. Unto the third generation we had all been trapped into religion by my grandfather, and although I did not see it that way then, I jolly well knew that *something* was amiss.

My parents seemed to have only three friends, plus their wives—the Senior Warden of the Vestry, the Junior Warden, and the Superintendent of the Sunday School. But in these friends, I too was lucky. The Senior Warden, Mr. Sanford, who also sang bass in the choir, worked in some department of the Baldwin Locomotive Works, then located on Spring Garden Street, spang in the middle of downtown Philadelphia. He had

* For helping me remember what I saw I am much indebted to Mr. William Marshall, head of *The New York Times* Indexing Department.

innumerable pictures of historic locomotives over which he would let me pore. His wife, like all wives of the times except my mother, baked her own bread, thus also gaining a passport to my youthful heart. As for the Junior Warden and his wife, they were even more fascinating. He was Dr. Arthur Parker Hitchins, a bacteriologist and then head of the H. K. Mulford Laboratories in nearby Glenolden, who was destined to play a large role in my older life. He introduced me to the microscope, which was, I think, the first scientific instrument I had ever seen. His wife was a young blond goddess of twenty-six recently out of Bryn Mawr and, I am quite sure, the first woman of college cultivation I had ever encountered. I looked upon her with love and awe. As for the Sunday School Superintendent, his case was simpler: he was a jovial wisecracker (term then unknown) with whose daughter, Josephine Smith, I was deeply smitten. Even more important, the Smiths owned a music box—a large, ornate mahogany music box and, like our bathtub, an item I should think would be worth thousands to a museum. It played from a variety of slow-circulating steel discs studded with little teeth that, as they passed under a bar fixing down-hanging metal reeds, produced arpeggios and other forms of twangs. The phonograph and the player piano were both struggling to find markets but had not yet succeeded. The music box still remained the last word, although its days were numbered.

• • •

There is a further mystery about my father and mother. Although my father was a university graduate and my mother had the kind of education thought fitting for a young lady in the 1890's and had spent a year in Paris to acquire the sort of European buffing then thought necessary to culture, I remained in complete ignorance that I lived a mile and a half from an even then well thought of seat of learning, Swarthmore College—at the next stop west of Morton on the P.R.R. Although my father was musically literate and a good amateur pianist, I never heard a symphony orchestra until I was a college student going under my own steam. I was never taken to an art museum or gallery. My reading was never guided. Where in hell *were* my parents?

3 · "ERIC, OR,
LITTLE BY LITTLE"

My mother hated Morton and the role of Rector's wife, which she performed inexpertly. My father's salary was $700 a year, with the rectory thrown in. J. P. Morgan the Elder was Trustee of a Fund for Undercompensated Clergymen and from that source my father drew another $300 a year. A blacksmith made more, but my father had to be a Gentleman, and when not in his canonicals, he wore a frock coat green with age. There was then, however, the boon of the "clerical discount"; railroads and department stores gave the proper card-carrying clergy a discount of 10 per cent. Physicians usually charged the clergy and their families nothing at all.

My mother hated not only Morton, but Philadelphia and Pennsylvania. She never got over a wonderment about the United States based on the bewildering fact that in this new land "people didn't know their place." She had affection only for New York—which she regarded as a wonder city, which actually it then was. The broad, unpolluted Hudson sparkled, the swift innumerable ferryboats crisscrossed it like water beetles, the sun shone on the gleaming buildings, and a British novelist—I forget who—described, among New York's enchantments, "the champagne air," by which he actually meant the atmospheric air.

I first crossed the Hudson because my mother's sister Aunt Nance lived there with her Colonel Blimp husband in an apartment house (Philadelphia had at the time no such thing) at 103rd Street and Amsterdam Avenue. For safety, I had rather be in Vietnam than near that neighborhood now, but half a century ago it was solid middle-class white, full of twelve-story apartment houses *with elevators and uniformed attendants.*

Golly. Only an occasional corner saloon gave evidence of the brutish side of man's nature.

I seem to have stayed with my Aunt Nance a good many times when my harassed mother needed a rest. (Aunt Nance's three children were adults.) And I developed a great fondness for her. The vestments of her day made her look like one of the Whoops Sisters with whom the young Peter Arno broke into *The New Yorker* twenty years later. But she was large and jolly and—admirable trait—rather fond of alcohol.

• • •

One morning in 1907 I was watching from our sixth-floor window while a colored man industriously hosed clean the sidewalk in front of the corner saloon opposite. (I was a great watcher of people at work: two men with muck rakes cleaning a clogged sewer would give me a morning's fascination.) My aunt paused to see what was claiming my attention. She made the remark to me that it looked as if a giant had piddled on the sidewalk. This suddenly excited me and I felt my penis harden. I was far from unconscious that I had one and had long ago ceased to puzzle why little Prudence hadn't. But mine, up to now, had been a source only of pain because some contemporaneous Dr. Spock had diagnosed "adhesions" between prepuce and glans and had given instructions on how to "break them up." Most male children are born with "adhesions" to which the medical profession, now grown wiser, pays little attention. Not so in my day. My mother was instructed how to go about breaking the physical bond between the mucous-membrane glans and its protecting sheath. This involved soap, very hot water, gauze and a steel instrument with a small spoonlike head. I screamed at the pain and indignity of what was being done to me (in the name of love, naturally) but my mother was nothing if not conscientious and I can remember four or five screaming sessions. Subsequently, I came, for a while, to regard my penis not as a liability exactly, but at best a convenience for emptying my bladder. But this morning everything was different. I was having, without knowing what it was, an eight-year-old erection. I was about waist-high to the window sill so I swept my body decorously across it. The result was a feeling of intense pleasure where I had previously felt only pain or nothing. I repeated the maneuver. The pleasure compounded. In a moment or so I had lost all volition and was automatically striving for I knew not what, but only that I had to have it or die. And in a moment I had it, and my whole being was flooded with ecstasy. I had achieved an eight-year-old orgasm. I had discovered masturbation.

• • •

Well! This changed the whole color and complexion of life, which was turning out to be quite worth living after all. But if I had such a bliss-producing mechanism, all self-contained, why had no one told me about it? Here must be a conspiracy of silence. Very well: I would meet secrecy with secrecy. When I went to bed that night I would test the efficacy of the bottom bed sheet against a small but erect penis and see if the divine experiment could be repeated. I did, and it was. Then and there I formed a resolve: I would masturbate (of course I didn't learn the word until much later) on every occasion of which I could take advantage. But since secrecy seemed to be the convention, I would observe the convention.

I have heard it remarked in medical circles that male children who learn to masturbate and achieve orgasm before the age of potency are giving evidence of a high degree of neurotic disturbance. You can't disprove it by me. What I have not heard remarked is that boys before potency can masturbate as girls and some women can, that is, as often—per day—as they wanted to. Just a little rest was necessary before the whole process of excitation, pleasure and climax could be achieved again. Only after potency has its beginnings, I was later to learn, did ejaculation and detumescence bring an end to things, perhaps for a day. At a desk beside me at the Rutledge Institute, my new seat of learning (in the fourth grade), there sat a girl, Dorothy by name, who was constantly doing something to herself as her wriggles and facial expressions almost continuously made clear. She aroused in me disapproval, bewilderment and envy. The disapproval was because I had formed the moral opinion, with nobody's help, that autoeroticism ought to be a private secret affair. The bewilderment was because Dorothy provided strong circumstantial evidence that girls must possess some sort of equipment that I had missed in my Lansdowne investigations of little Prudence. And the envy sprang from the fact that *if* (it was an unresolved and tantalizing question) little girls were also equipped to experience genital bliss they could gratify themselves in semi-public, with practically no one the wiser, whereas little boys could not. These practices and observations went on during spelling, reading and arithmetic, in a mixed roomful of perhaps twenty boys and girls, with a pleasant woman teacher, Miss Lemmo, presiding and giving her attentions successively to the third, fourth and fifth grades, who sat in separate ranks before her in the same room. A constant hubbub went on among the little boys, but of the five little girls, all was demureness except for one lovely incorrigible, Helene. She was not a mischief-maker—she simply flashed a brilliant defiance at any order she was given of which she did not approve. I envied her her staunchness, and still do.

I had reached now the age, however, when I was *against* girls. They were too mamby-pamby and sticky-sweet, and a little boy could see through the blatant hypocrisy of little girls dealing with adults as through the clearest crystal. There was just nothing to them. Moreover, I had a private resentment. When our monthly reports were issued, four of the five little girls—the exception was always Helene—inevitably headed the list. I came fifth. The issue was "deportment," which was given a numerical grade that affected the averages and always pulled mine down. It was outrageous. I can never remember seriously misbehaving in school. I was just a victim of sexual discrimination. It was unjust, unfair and lousy, although anyone who would then have dared to use that last word would have been thrashed. Its only use then was literal and an unutterable vulgarism.

• • •

In 1907, boys traveled in gangs—not gangs in the modern sense, but in the sense of *packs*. I was a member of a pack, but a rather straggling rear-rank member. (There was no warfare between packs; they were mere subdivided social groups, not subdivided by any interests or prejudices but by random fission. Colored boys and white intermingled in these packs because although adults had prejudices, and "separate but equal" schoolhouses were the law of the land blandly accepted by both races, children could see no difference.) No difference except in sex—a colored *girl* could not have roved with a boy pack, but then she would never have dreamed of trying, nor would her white sister. Girls had their own organizations, beneath contempt, all of them, with activities of jacks, rope skipping, etc. I suppose every boy had a *secret* love for a little girl, but it was a tortureproof secrecy. Mine was, anyway.

My low status with my pack was the result of my bearing of three hideous crosses. In the first place I was a minister's son and my nickname hence was "Preacher." Second, my Christian name was Eric, and although this has since grown to be a fashionable and even a romantic male tag, in 1907 it was just as bad as Marmaduke, Percival or Montmorency. Added to the horror of all this, there was a book called *Eric, or Little by Little* by Frederic W. Farrar, Dean of Canterbury. This "Tale of Roslyn School" was mercifully unknown to my kid contemporaries, but all too well known to my parents' friends, who threw it up at me constantly. A copy of this fictionalized morality tale was in my father's study. I read it many times—reading for the sake of loathing, which I seem so often to have done. The fictional Eric was fair and beautiful, brilliant and gifted, and in fact had everything, having been born into the Upper Upper Class. Roslyn School was obviously on a par with Eton and Harrow. Eric makes a brilliant beginning, the darling of all. Somehow he oh-so-gradually falls in with evil companions, is falsely accused of cheating, and things start, little by little, going to hell. A terrible climax is reached when Eric shows up for chapel "in an intoxicated condition." He runs away from school, ships aboard a lugger, breaks his leg and is remanded home, where eventually, shriven and gentle, he dies a beautiful death, at about age seventeen, amongst the beautiful gardens and lawns of nineteenth-century England. I still have a copy of this really horrible book because to this day when an adult friend finds one in a secondhand bookstore for twenty-five cents he cannot resist the "joke" of sending me a copy.

The copy I now have is an American edition, obviously pirated, for it carries no copyright line. But it *does* say "Twenty-Fifth Edition," and the date on the title page is MDCCCXCI, which by my translation is 1891. I cannot establish when the sainted Dean wrote his goddamn book, but it must have been no later than the 1880's, and anything past that mid-century cannot be ruled out. I go into this personal trauma because it only occurred to me recently and suddenly that schoolboy drinking must have been a recognized thing almost one hundred years ago. And Dean Farrar was not talking about small beer—it was brandy he had in his book. Who says youth has changed? *I* did, a few pages back—but now I think myself wrong.

• • •

I hated my name and tried signing myself "E. Frank Hodgins," but it couldn't be made to stick. About this time I learned from my parents that when I was a baby I looked more Irish than Tim Costello ever had, and my aunts and uncles had spontaneously taken to calling me "Dinty." Dinty Hodgins—there would have been a name to conjure with. But my fool mother had passionately stamped it out and there I was, irremediably stuck with a sissy handle. My third cross was that I was myopic and had to wear glasses, with the result that when I was not called "Preacher" I was called "Four-Eyes." From these built-in humiliations there seemed—there was—no escape. Under these conditions I thought myself lucky to be allowed to run with a pack at all, and I vowed to myself a vow: that no matter how badly I might be hurt at any of the disorganized kid sports of football, baseball, shinny, prisoner's baste (that was what I thought it was called), I would never, never cry. And only once do I remember so much pain that I was forced to break the vow. Nevertheless, in choosing up sides for football or baseball I was always the last to be chosen, and thus my inferiority was constantly thrust before me. So it was not surprising that I developed another secret vice. This was reading.

The first book I remember reading cover to cover was Horatio Alger, Jr.'s *Strong and Steady*. I loathed it. I read it again and again, for the sake of loathing it more deeply. At age eight I knew that it had no more relation to real life than a blob of clay—less, in fact. Was this the world of books? It seemed so. More Horatio Alger. Oliver Optic. G. A. Henty. I read them because I wanted to read for reading's sake, and it was something to do on a rainy day. But Literature was certainly a fraud. With *The Wolf Hunters* and *The Gold Hunters* by James Oliver Curwood things brightened a little. Here was *some* relation to reality, I thought, possibly because I had never hunted wolves, prospected for gold and was unacquainted with the Ojibways or any other

Indian tribe. All boys were warned against "dime novels"; these cost a nickel but a deeper mystery was why they were on the Index: they all packed a morality wallop that would have nauseated an Amish.

And then an incredible thing happened. I came across a copy of *The Adventures of Tom Sawyer* by Mark Twain, a name unknown to me. (He was still alive, with his white mane, white evening clothes, and a fully recognized genius. Perhaps it was just as well I did not know this: it might have made me suspicious of him.) He burst into my mind like a rocket. Here was a man who used words with grace and power, whose characters were real, and who could tell a rattling yarn.

But wonderful as these things were, there was a more wonderful thing still. Tom had been unfairly treated by Aunt Polly, he thought. Put to bed, he brooded and brooded on his sorrows. They were insurmountable, so *"He turned his face to the wall and died."* Here was an adult, a writer, who actually knew what it was like to be a boy. *I* had turned my face to the wall and died a thousand times in my eight years, and here was someone who understood and wrote about it. The effect was overwhelming.

I sought out all the Mark Twain I could find. *Tom Sawyer, Detective* didn't quite measure up, but then there was *Huckleberry Finn* and, above all, *Life on the Mississippi.* I think I must have spent a year reading and rereading those books. Why had my parents not put me wise? I didn't know, and still don't. In fact I can remember only one literary experience with my parents. By the light of a green-shaded lamp my father read aloud to my mother and me Dickens' *Our Mutual Friend.* It took a long time, and it passed largely over my head, but the words were pleasant to hear in my father's grave voice.

• • •

Before I revert to more lurid things, there is a word to say about that green lamp. The rectory, a pleasant house, must have been relatively new for it was equipped for "the electric light." But every fixture was also a gas fixture because "the electric light," later shortened to "electricity," was unreliable, even then. Moreover, since there was no such thing in the world as an electric "appliance," the only use for electricity in the home was lighting. Thus, the first generating stations did not begin to spin a wheel until dusk. It was great fun on a winter's afternoon turning on the clumsy switches at about three thirty and waiting for the lamps to begin to glow. They were bulbous, fragile things, with a point where the glass had been drawn and sealed together. They enclosed a single strand of looped filament and most of them bore the mark SHELBY-32 CANDLEPOWER. They burned out incessantly. When the generators started up, the filament would begin to glow cherry-red, then eventually yellow. This was 32 candlepower.

I have said that we lived on the edge of a slum, and we certainly did. The rectory, church, lawn and a shed where high-flying parishioners could stable their horses during morning prayer stood at the corner of Franklin Avenue and Yeadon Road. The rows of run-down shacks and houses that stretched northward on Franklin Avenue were lighted by neither gas nor electricity but by coal oil, which is to say by lanterns. The house opposite was perpetually dark and was haunted—everyone knew that. The rectory, come to think of it now, must have been a very advanced bit of house technology. It had plumbing. It had an inside bathroom. This was an enormous room that could, and sometimes did, hold three people with space to spare. Its linoleum floor was a bit wrinkled from water splashings. The washstand was the big feature. It was a porcelain bowl topped by a huge marble slab. (Some things came cheap in 1907.) The water closet, to give it the accepted name of its age, was less technically advanced. Its two essential features, receptacle and water tank, were separated but connected by six feet of vertical lead pipe, subtly bent where required, for plumbing was really plumbing in those days. Flushing was an experience over which one paused an involuntary moment before grasping the wooden chain handle because the release of waters was so ominous and prolonged that even a small boy knew that he was involved in an irrevocable act. Both tank and receptacle were encased (the distinction between encasement and concealment was blurry in 1907) in strips of glued mahogany. A similar veneer encased the bathtub, which was made not of porcelain or anything enameled but of a buckled and crinkly metal, tin-coated, which groaned and snapped as you shifted your weight.

It was the day of the Saturday Night Bath, for those who bathed at all. (Mary Baker Eddy, for one, was against it, except among consenting adults.) Those now accustomed to sneer at the Saturday Night Bath are forgetting the hot-water problem. Our hot water was produced by a gas heater semi-integral with the gas stove in the kitchen. (The kitchen also had a coal stove, generally preferred because it was more reliable and "easier" to use.) Preparations for the Saturday Night Bath were usually begun before lunch and consisted in turning the gas flames up to their highest within the cylindrical iron cover that encased coiled copper tubes. Why the water heated in those tubes among these fierce blue flames for half a day yielded such a niggardly supply of hot water in the bathroom above is a thermodynamic problem I have yet to figure out. But the despairing cry "The hot water's getting cold again" was constantly being heard. Why did *every* member of the family have to take to the bath only on Saturday night? Simply, it was the custom of the country.

Let me return momentarily to the kitchen. It, too, was a vast space. Equipment: gas stove, etc., coal stove, sink, and icebox. Ah, the oak-covered icebox, with the huge drip pan underneath that rewarded forgetfulness by overflowing so subtly that only a slow stream oozing across the floor gave an eventual reminder. By then, the drip pan was so brimming that it could not be moved without a gunnel going under, and an emergency call for mops.

But the fascination of the icebox lay in the iceman. His wagon called twice a week. The impoverished ordered "a five-cent piece," cheerfully chopped and carried by tongs to the back porch. We were sufficiently above the poverty line to give the order for "fifty pounds." I think this must have cost fifteen cents. It fascinated me to see the iceman use his ax: very gently chopping at the surface until the whole 200-pound cake split like a cleft diamond. He then weighed our chunk on his spring scales (he was never more than half a pound off) and toted it into the top of our icebox, where it settled down with a delightful crackling.

Come to think of it, *everything* was delivered in 1907. The huckster's wagon called twice a week; the fruits and vegetables, really garden fresh, were bought from him. The huge yellow-colored horse-drawn vans of the big Philadelphia department stores, twelve miles away, clinked and rattled through the dust of the roads. My mother was stopped from shopping at one particular Philadelphia grocery store because its delivery wagon said

ACKER, MERRILL & CONDIT—FANCY GROCERIES, WINES, LIQUORS
AND CIGARS and such a wagon could not be seen stopping at a
rectory. But every local store also had its horse-drawn delivery
system. Even on a $1,000-per-year stipend one need not ever carry
bundles. Traveling tinkers and peddlers were not confined to the
nineteenth century—they carried well over into this one. But
to a child, of course, the most fascinating vehicle on the road
was the hokey-pokey wagon—a pushcart with a set of jingling
bells that could be heard for half a mile in the noiseless air,
and from which came forth penny ice-cream cones, penny ice-
cream sandwiches made on the spot with a mold and, for the
wealthy, a nickel cone. I had only one of these in my entire
boyhood; the occasion must have been a really heady celebration.

•   •   •

One reason, I think, for the vastness of the kitchen in what
was emphatically not a farmhouse was that it doubled as the
laundry; space had to be provided for the maneuverings of
movable galvanized-iron tubs and boilers, for scrubbing boards
and ironing boards. I have a recollection of a colored laundress
who came once a week for this operation. My mother certainly
didn't conduct it for by now she had elected semi-invalid status;
also the days of the Annie Gradys and Caroline Fauntleroys were
over, perhaps because the wage scale had advanced to three dollars a month and we were no longer able to afford profligate
spending; in whatever event, we had no servant.

I know the year we moved to Morton; it was 1906 because
it was there, in our dining room, that my father read out the
news of the San Francisco earthquake from the front page of
the Philadelphia *North American*. It was my last good year;
1907, the year of the Rich Man's Panic, was also the year that
saw me blasted by a succession of shattering personal events.

It had begun auspiciously enough. I had a set of electric trains
in the attic, together with a stationary steam engine that belt-
drove a toy tool shop. Dry batteries existed for the trains but were
much inferior to wet batteries, self-constructed out of a set of
quart jars into which one poured a mixture of sulfuric acid and
potassium chromate. One then lowered boughten zinc electrodes
into this mixture, wired the appropriate circuits and—zip went

the trains. I also had a magic lantern, with half a bed sheet for a screen, and a jigsaw, as well as a small cylindrical press that printed from rubber type you set yourself. It was not enough. I was one of those infuriating children who wandered about the house on rainy days whimpering that they "had nothing to do." Of course there was always masturbation, but this was now strictly a nighttime affair.

•   •   •

My complaint of "having nothing to do" when actually surrounded by copious resources did not make me at all a unique child, I realize from conversation with even today's parents. In one sense, I was right, in 1907. No movies, no automobiles (practically speaking), no radio, no TV. It was an age compounded of illustrated lectures, music boxes, pyrography, player pianos (for the very well-to-do). The phonograph existed but not the disc—not commercially at least; the morning-glory horns amplified what the stylus picked out from the wax-cylinder idea of Thomas Alva Edison.

The only wonder is that books and magazines were not more at a premium than they were, in a child's world. *The Youth's Companion* (of which, twenty years later, I was to be the last editor) had an enormous circulation among readers who turned its moralistic pages every Thursday evening by the light of candles and lanterns. The *YC* was undisputed as having the largest magazine circulation in the eighties and nineties—far outrunning *The Saturday Evening Post.* My parents would not, for some reason, bring me up on it. I was a *St. Nicholas* child, and this, too, was somehow demeaning: I had no taste for Frances Hodgson Burnett's Rackety-Packety House and not *too* much for Ralph Henry Barbour's *The New Boy at Hilltop,* although this latter was obviously of a higher order of literature. (These were the current offerings in the December 1906 *St. Nicholas;* the respective authors' more famous works, *Little Lord Fauntleroy* and *The Substitute Quarterback,* had preceded them.)

•   •   •

Out of an odd miscellany I did discover that despite my woeful athletic ability I did have what J. B. Conant was, years later, to call "a marketable skill"—I could read aloud! And I had an audience! A set of parents up Franklin Avenue, named Brown, had three sons, the eldest, my eight-year-old contemporary. And it developed that the three Brown kids liked reading—or more exactly, liked to be read aloud to, themselves being not very adept with the Roman alphabet but avid to hear a good yarn. None of us had ever been to a theater, which was a morally doubtful institution in the first place, didn't flourish in Philadelphia, and was beyond economic reach in any event. So on rainy afternoons I held readings—my audience being the three Brown brothers plus an occasional transient. We read kid stuff exclusively, for that was all that was available to us. The miserable little town of Morton had no library, and the books on my father's shelves were mostly theological works, I then thought (I was wrong), and the "Sunday School Library" of the Church of the Atonement contained exactly what you would have expected. But whatever we read, I was the E. H. Southern of Morton, Pennsylvania, and I reveled in it.

• • •

The adult moral code of the 1900's was extremely confusing to the young, just as it is today. Although the delivery wagon of Acker, Merrill & Condit—Fancy Groceries, Wines, Liquors and Cigars could not stop at the rectory door, things were not so simple as all that. The King's Daughters always gave my father a new Bible at Christmas; the Senior Warden always gave him a quart of Scotch; my father, in whom the last spark of humor had yet to be entirely quenched, delighted in placing these gifts conspicuously side by side. Such was my father's consumption of whiskey that last Christmas's bottle was *almost* gone when next Christmas's bottle arrived. My own career as an alcoholic, like my police record at Ocean Grove, began in my very early years—about five, I think, in Erindale, when my cousin Pete's Italian wife fed me most of a box of chocolate-covered brandied cherries and was enchanted when I got high as a kite. A mixture of chocolate and alcohol is not to be recommended under any circumstances, so presently I got violently, desperately ill from the excess of both, and when the truth came out, Pete's wife was placed deep in the doghouse. This experience must have acted as what I was years later to learn of as the "avulsion treatment" for alcoholics, for I never had a drop of hard liquor to drink

47

until I was twenty-four and the U.S.A. was deep in the coma
of Prohibition. The consequences of *that* are another story
altogether.

The boys of the era knew there were "fallen women." We
also knew that big cities like Philadelphia had "red-light dis-
tricts." We had no definite idea what the terms meant but we
could and did conjecture, and when, in later years, we learned
All, it turned out that we had hit the problem, if that was what
it was, right on the button. Long before then, however, I was
in for my series of shocks that eventually led me to an eight-year-
old version of a "nervous breakdown."

• • •

In the first place, at last but inevitably, my mother caught
me masturbating. Perhaps her shock was genuine, perhaps not.
In whichever event, she gave me the full hellfire-and-damnation
treatment. She pronounced for me the awful four-syllable word
that described what I had been practicing with such innocent
delight. (Innocent? Then why had I been secret?) And she told
me that this indulgence led directly to insanity and early death.
In this she was not making things up out of her own moralistic
head: the weightiest medical opinions of the day, expressed in
print, completely backed her up. The session with her was awful
and aroused in me two tremendous emotions. On the one hand
I was in abject terror. On the other, I was filled with the earnest,
high-minded resolve never to get caught again. I never was. Insanity and early death were not altogether pleasant prospects,
but *some* games were worth the candle.

• • •

A further shock lay in wait for me. One day while I was busy
still regrouping my psychic forces, I wandered toward the hedge
that marked the rear boundary of the rectory's pleasant lawn.
I often walked through that hedge but today I stumbled over
something. It was a boy's prone body, the body of the boy next
door, and it was a very active body. It lay on the willing body
of a little girl who happened to be one of the boy's younger sisters,
and the two were having what I later, much later, learned to
call sexual intercourse. I watched in fascination. Now it was
proved beyond a shadow of a doubt that although little girls

48

did not have penises, they did have *something* corresponding and complementary . . . . Eventually the boy, Donald Greene, having completed his act, stood up and, with a wave of his hand, offered his sister, who must have been about age seven, to me. (Donald and I were friends, after all.) At this I turned and fled in terror. Why terror, I wonder? The reason for the differentiation of the sexes had been made clear to me with a thunderclap suddenness and with equal suddenness it had been made evident that the Pleasure Principle here must be the same as that involved in autoeroticism. Still, why the terror? And also why, of all things, did I flee straight to the arms of my mother—who only weeks before had coupled in my mind the idea of sex with the ideas of insanity and early death? I don't know, but this is what I did, and poured out to her the gasping story of what I had just witnessed.

She was, naturally, very grave. I did not know that I had witnessed incest, and my mother did not dwell on this aspect of things at all. In this I think she was, for once, wise, for I'm sure the introduction of still another phenomenon-*cum*-taboo would have capsized me altogether. She obviously didn't know, herself, how to deal with the situation, and the most I can remember, in the midst of her grimness at everything, was her sorrowful lament, "Now little Agnes has lost her virginity." Here was yet another new concept to handle. Over long, thoughtful, solitary periods, I did reasonably well with it.

To the parents of today's youth concerned and confused by the actions of their children, I ought to be able to offer a mite of consolation. Here, in only partial concealment, within the grounds of a church, in daylight, incestuous cohabitation was taking place—not between adolescents, but between children. And it was in the suburbs. And it was more than fifty years ago. And there was a lot of it. Boys were forever cross-comparing the merits—I almost wrote *virtues*—and the satisfaction ratings of various little girls. Some of this could obviously be set down to braggadocio, but although these not-yet-potent boys may have had their share of swaggering fakes, they knew what they were talking about—and they talked about it constantly, although not one was more than ten. They were rural slum children, it is true—tough, but *not* parentally neglected or abandoned, *not* poor to the line of destitution, and only semiliterate. And there was no question of race: no wops, kikes, spiggoties, Polacks, micks or niggers. (The latter word was in perfectly good repute then, and when my mother said, as she so often did, "Housework is nigger work," it was in no way a strange expression to fall from the lips of a lady.) Underneath their grime, these kids were as white, Anglo-Saxon and Protestant as any Methodist bishop. I, the innocent among them, learned the value of the knowing smirk. It was my only defense.

I can think of only two things that are problems today but unknown in 1907. Juvenile drinking was one. Even the most depraved Keeper of the Old-Fashioned Saloon would not sell a drink to a minor, for this really went against the grain of the times (when more alcohol was consumed per capita than today) and the risk wasn't worth the price. If a minor tried to enter a saloon he was merely—but immediately—kicked out. That ended that. As for narcotics, a schoolboy coming on the word—which wouldn't have been likely—would have had to look it up in a dictionary. But sex, except for innocents like me, why any fool . . . .

•   •   •

There were other parallels between 1907 and the 1970's. There was the identical grumbling among the nonpoor that the poor were poor "because they wouldn't work." Anything like the state welfare systems that grew up beginning with the F.E.R.A. (Federal Emergency Relief Act) of the first New Deal would have been regarded as way to the left of Emma Goldman, Alexander Berkman, the I.W.W.'s Big Bill Haywood, the MacNamara Brothers, or other anarchists of the times. Charity was purely a private affair. Moreover, there were the same complaints as now, that the male head of the family—the *white* family, this time, if you please—was a drone, a drunk, or both. (The status of the Negro was so low he wasn't even counted in.) Male indolence among the poor was even enshrined in song:

> *Everybody works but father,*
> *And he sits around all day . . . .*

This song was much sung in my youth. And there *seemed* to be something in it. The white slum in Morton was full of males who sat on their porches, stockinged feet on railing, hour by waking hour, while their wives took in washing or otherwise held together what is today called The Family Unit. A much later-day contemporary friend of mine who had been brought up on the Pacific Coast had noticed the same thing in his California boyhood and had a theory about it. The theory was that these drone males had been young wage earners when the long and devastating depression of 1893 had knocked them out of the job market with such force and ferocity that they were first stunned and then made permanently hopeless and spiritless as the depression dragged on and on. There does seem to be some kinship between this idea and today's sociological view of why today's male Negro family "head" so often deserts, gives up and cops out, socially castrated.

In 1907, children lied to their parents, just as children do today. My generation of youth looked at its adults and its lips curled in scorn, just as today. We saw through adult hypocrisy with the same crystal clarity as today—but there *was* a difference. We did not lash out at anyone. Part of *our* hypocrisy was that we kept secret our knowledge of theirs. Along with earning our contempt, they had also engendered our fear. The generation gap (unknown phrase) was as wide in 1907 as in 1970. In the years between, only the *tactics* of struggle between youth and adult authority have changed.

● ● ●

I had scarcely had my baptism of sex before the day of confirmation arrived with its final revelation. The same Donald Greene who had offered me the use of his sister had somehow got hold of a medical handbook for laymen. In it was a vivid color plate showing a woman's body in cutaway sections. The innermost section showed a large sac in which there lay, unquestionably, a baby, with captioning that said "Natural position at time of birth." Donald's attitude was "There! See what I told you?" But it was also obvious that despite his sophisticated working knowledge of sex, he himself had been somewhat enlightened by this explicit illustration.

Once again I rushed to my mother. I forget what cock-and-bull story I had previously been told about the origin of species, except that it was something better than cabbage leaves or "The Doctor." Now, I demanded of my mother, was the illustration I had seen true or fake? If fake, to what end; and if true, *why had I not been told?* I think my insistence here was less a demand that I be told the truth for truth's sake than it was a furious and humiliated reaction to being one-upped by the likes of Donald Greene. Yes, my mother answered sadly, it was true. She described pregnancy and delivery, but she stopped well short of answering the question I dared not ask: How did the baby get there in the first place?

Donald Greene and the pack and I discussed this matter at great length. We were richly endowed with the spirit of scientific inquiry, and although our laboratory equipment was defective, we still, by sheer induction, reached an incontestable conclusion. There was some direct causal relationship between fucking and babies. But just what? We were scientists, groping at the edges of a mystery without being able to get anywhere near its center. Eventually, an older boy, a real senior citizen of fifteen, bursting with masculine pride over his ability "to make the stuff come," supplied the missing link in our chain, and when my mother at last brought herself to the point of Revelation, it was anti-climax. Jimmy Reed had long before told all.

But a puzzle still remained. Why the reticence? Why the adult evasion and holding back? Why the lies? Everybody did what I had seen Donald Greene and his sister doing. Nobody—at least nobody in Philadelphia in 1907, it seems—had ever heard of Sigmund Freud, although there were nasty doctors in Switzerland; Paul DuBois, for example, had written a book called *The Psychic Treatment of Nervous Disorders*, which I was some time later to come on in my father's library—not exclusively theological after all! Years later, Freudian psychoanalysts used to be very rigid on the doctrine of the Primal Scene—the supposedly inevitable moment when the child first *sees* (not infers, *sees*) his parents in the act of intercourse. I don't know the status of the doctrine today, but if I ever witnessed the Primal Scene myself, I have repressed it out of all consciousness. So an incongruity remained; I simply could not imagine my father and mother doing what I had seen Donald Greene and his sister doing.

Later, when I was all of eight, another revealed truth burst on me. It was a little like the *"I am me"* discovery of self at eighteen months, but not nearly so pleasant. It was that I owed my existence to the fact that my father had lain on my mother and impregnated her. This fact was not repellent but it would simply not digest. I was given a book, *What a Young Boy Ought to Know* by the Reverend Sylvanus Stall, D.D., in which the reverend doctor beat about the bush so furiously as to raise impenetrable clouds of dust to obscure the total landscape of the sex complex. It's a good thing I was given this work *after* Jimmy Reed's explanation of potency; if I had been given it before, I think it would have beclouded even Jimmy's vivid style.

• • •

Most of the new revelations were not only pleasant, they were also wildly exciting. But they had come too fast one upon the other and I was overwhelmed. I remember terrible nightmares, continuous bed-wetting, screams, scenes and tantrums. I was standing upon the verge of my eight-year-old nervous breakdown. When it came, the precipitating factor was not sexual—it was Long Division. There was an evening of homework that had its climax in a terrible, horrible outburst of convulsive, hysterical tears because I couldn't do it. And shortly after that my mother met me with the news that I was to be taken out of school for a year, and wasn't that lovely? My father would tutor me at home.

4 · PHILADELPHIA, OR, "CORRUPT AND CONTENTED"

BY KNOWLEDGE my father was not badly equipped for his task; by technique and method, very badly. I cannot remember a single thing his grave and conscientious instruction taught me. As a student, I was better versed in current events, as I picked them up from the Philadelphia *North American*, which under the editorship of E. A. Van Valkenberg was a crusading newspaper by the standards of the day—i.e., it was a violent partisan of Theodore Roosevelt's. I remember Taft's 1908 victory over Bryan and exclaiming at the smallness of the vote. My father explained to me that this was the *electoral* vote. Anyway, William Jennings Bryan had been defeated and the Republic was again safe.

My father's lifelong yen for journalism had somehow led him into a mild association with the *North American*. He used to submit small versifications for the editorial page—and in 1908 he hit a bull's-eye. For Memorial Day—then more frequently called Decoration Day—he had submitted a longish poem. He was knocked flat with pleasure and pride when the newspaper printed it—not only on page one but all over page one, with ornate art-department borders, taking up all news space on page one except for columns one and seven. I remember how the first verse went:

> *Don't talk to me of San Juan hill*
> *Or that scrap in Manila Bay,*
> *For I was one of the boys in Blue*
> *That fought with the boys in Grey.*

The thing to be said for that flight into poesy, of which there were seven stanzas more, was that it reflected the spirit and taste of the times. Despite the passage of forty-odd years, the Civil War was, journalistically speaking, only day-before-yesterday;

the acceleration of history had yet to begin. As a nine-year-old I had my ghastly troubles, there was misery within a stone's throw of anywhere, vice and grand larceny were rampant, medicine was still in its horse-and-buggy days. Trains with wooden cars collided fatally, ships sank regularly, and Fourth of July first-degree burns were a major medical problem. But for the world of Adult Institutions these were halcyon days, or so it seemed when one was nine.

The United States celebrated Independence Day with a racket that proclaimed us still a pioneer nation. "Isolationism" was an unknown word because everyone was an isolationist and thank God for that. When, about this time, my father became a naturalized American citizen, he had to swear generally to renounce all foreign kings and potentates and in particular King George V of Great Britain and Ireland. My father confessed that that last phrase gave him a twinge. It gave my mother a worse one. She was of course automatically Americanized at the same time, yet even in her last years she kept up her comments on the strange ways of the Nation to the south of Canada where she had lived ever since 1895. There was nothing chauvinistic here; it was merely that Things were not done Properly. Practically no one knew the proper way to leave calling cards, for example: a married lady calling upon another married lady would leave three cards, one of her own, two of her husband's, signifying that wife was calling upon wife, but that husband (who might not have come calling at all) was calling on husband *and* wife. And cards were never handed to anyone but a servant. I received a furious dressing down from my mother once because I intercepted the three cards the calling lady had sought to place on the hall table, as was proper under the circumstances since we had no servant . . . . Have I not mentioned that we lived on the edge of a slum? It made no difference.

• • •

I think my father's minor involvement must have been responsible for my meeting my first journalistic celebrity. He was my father's friend Leigh Mitchell Hodges, who for year upon year in Philadelphia wrote a daily column called "The Optimist." He was a lecturer too, and several times my father invited him to entertain the Church of the Atonement Men's Club in Morton,

55

which my father had manfully organized. I cannot remember the quality of the Hodges prose; I can only now reflect on the instant, the automatic fate today of a newspaper column called "The Optimist." But I was in awe of someone who could write so that somebody else would print it. (My father and grandfather didn't seem to count, being relatives, or something.) My father took me to Philadelphia and the *North American* offices several times, where I met such heroes as Walter Bradford, the *North American*'s one and only strip cartoonist, creator of John Dubbalong and Enoch Pickleweight, to whom a son was duly born, named Dill. It was fine 1908 humor. I remember the shock my mother handed me when she revealed that Walter Bradford had a vice. He drank. That was why his cartoons were occasionally missing! The *North American* had a really great page-one political cartoonist—Herbert Johnson, later to be stolen by *The Saturday Evening Post*, whose mammoth offices were then cattycorner to Independence Hall. Johnson was thus given a mass audience but was also thereby largely robbed of his pen's virility. It was from such offices that George Horace Lorimer unerringly guided the *S.E.P.* by the lights of the day and Edward W. Bok, the sultan of the *Ladies' Home Journal*, had conducted his famously successful campaign against the all-but extinction of the egret, to supply the plumage for ladies' hats. Such things were beyond me, but it didn't matter, for back at the *North American* I had actually shaken hands with Jimmy Isaminger, the sports editor and columnist on whose every word I hung, and that was enough to last half a year.

Did I say a few pages back that these were halcyon days? Perhaps I was not altogether right, for they were also the days of the muckraker (coinage of Theodore Roosevelt)—the days of Lincoln Steffens' *The Shame of the Cities*, which fastened on Philadelphia in perpetuity the masterly phrase "Corrupt and Contented," of Ida Tarbell's *The History of the Standard Oil Company*, of Tom Lawson's *Frenzied Finance* in magazines like *McClure's, Ainslee's* and *Everybody's*. I don't know why or when these bursts of journalistic vitality died out, but I do know, in my own private calendar, when they were modestly reborn—in 1923 with the first issue of *Time*. Meanwhile, back in 1908 *et seq.*, I was joyously content to be reading in *The Saturday Evening Post* the Lawrenceville stories of Owen Johnson, the outpour-

56

ings of Irvin S. Cobb and the Get-Rich-Quick Wallingford stories of a now neglected American comic genius, George Randolph Chester. The political punditry of Samuel G. Blythe and Samuel Crother was beyond me, with good reason I now hope, but in retrospect it does seem that the granite-faced George Horace knew precisely what he was doing. From Sam Blythe I do remember several articles called "Cutting It Out" on the subject of booze and its renunciation. Apparently alcoholism was the occupational scourge of journalism then, just as it is today. Sam Blythe seemed to have conquered it.

• • •

In 1909 I was again considered fit for school and was sent back to the little Rutledge Institute—still standing and unchanged when I visited it fifty years later. I was again placed in the fourth grade, just where I had been before, and for which I was at last considered psychologically ready. I can remember absolutely nothing that I learned there, academically at least. The school day began with the whole school—it must have had between forty and fifty students—marching to the top-floor assembly hall to the music of a piano. Then we all listened to one or another of the Psalms as read by Miss Stellwagon, the principal. Deathly silence reigned during this, not out of respect for the Deity, with Whom we were supposed to be in close contact, but because even the toughest of the kids were scared stiff of Miss Stellwagon. I wonder why. There was nothing fearsome about her; she was just a trim, crisp old maid, but somehow she had The Eye. When a messenger arrived in class saying "Miss Stellwagon wants to see———," it could be Wilfred, Helene, DeMarr or some other chronic hell-raiser, the whole class would fall silent as the delinquent was led away. Five minutes later he would be back, his demeanor hangdog, his cheeks tear-streaked. I never found out what she did to these toughs that reduced them to such quivering blubber. I was "sent" to Miss Stellwagon's headquarters only once, for after all, I was "Preacher." She did not threaten me with decapitation or anything else; she merely fixed me with The Eye and said, her voice muted: "You, of all boys, being sent to me—*and I'm not coming back next year!*" The inference was ghastly clear: one thoughtless deed of mine had ruined her life. Like all before me I returned tear-stained and in a state of shock. Many times since then I have pondered the deep mystique of Authority and on what it was based. It was not on fear of force: force had gone completely out of usage. Yet Authority remained. Awe remained. The use of The Eye, the twitch of a brow, the crease of a forehead, all produced Awe, *provided* the Authority was Awesome. That's as far as I was able to get then—and I am not much further along now.

• • •

The year 1909 turned out pretty badly. The Payne-Aldrich Tariff Bill had been passed (without my knowledge). My reading consisted of a mixed bag of mail-order catalogs, *The Scottish Chiefs* by Jane Porter—which was regarded as "too advanced" for me, and still is—and *Pinky Perkins, Just a Boy* by a retired naval officer writing in *St. Nicholas*, who should, in my ten-year-old opinion, have been ashamed of himself. There was also O. Henry, whose star had been brilliantly ascending with *The Four Million*, *The Trimmed Lamp* and *Heart of the West*. But he, too, Drank. Moreover, there was a rumor, not then authenticated, that he had once been in jail. It seemed to me then that everybody who wrote or otherwise created had something wrong with him. It still seems so. Mark Twain was to die the following year; not until his obituaries flooded the front pages did I have the faintest notion that my favorite author was the world-acknowledged towering genius of contemporary American literature. Talk about the relevancy of school to life! In school we memorized the poems of Alice and Phoebe Cary, James Whitcomb Riley, John Greenleaf Whittier, with heavy doses of *Hiawatha*. We did not know why we were doing it, and I think it remains a good question today.

• • •

In 1909 my mother underwent a serious operation at the hands of William Wayne Babcock, whose fame was very and justly great, but who later mutilated me. For a while it was thought she would not live. Death to a ten-year-old has no meaning, so I was merely puzzled by the tension in my father and his friends, and felt no other emotion. But she recovered and continued leading a miserable, nagging life until a stroke ended it with merciful suddenness when she was seventy-eight.

There was no question that my father's family looked down on my mother's. My father's family was distinguished; my mother's was not. But although I preferred my father to my mother (and she knew it), I continued strongly to prefer my mother's side of the family to my father's. Even when we visited my Uncle Will ("My son, the General") and his daughter Betty in a shacklike summer cabin in the then-wild Gatineau River country I was conscious of a certain stuffiness pervading, despite the beautiful roaring river and the logs that came tumbling over the great falls from operations upstream. I suppose the whole place is now a paper mill, but then it was virgin wild, and trying to ride the logs would have been like surfing if surfing had been invented. But obviously my father did not feel at home with his more distinguished brothers, and the veriest child can tell where there's stiffness in the air.

By contrast, in my harsh young judgment my mother's family were all fools, but fun. For my maternal grandmother (who, like my father's father, lived to be ninety-two), however, I had a deep and reverent affection. She played games with me, from backgammon to tiddlywinks. Her maiden name had not been Anne Evylyn Donnelly for nothing, and she had wild and tempestuous stories to tell of her youth and girlhood in Dublin. The youngsters of my day had a fascination for the past, the long-ago; it was *much* better than fiction, and I wonder what has happened since. My grandmother had been widowed when she was sixty-five and always thereafter wore a widow's cap, white and tailless for informal indoor wear, with tails if there was to be an Occasion. But the shortest venture out of doors absolutely decreed a change to black, and there was no such thing as tailless black. When once I saw my grandmother in her room before she had put on her cap, it was as if I had seen her nude. When I walked beside her in the street I felt pride in her cap and the rustling of her heavy black silk dress. And she radiated toward me a feeling of love that neither of my parents seemed capable of. Her defect, as I saw it, was piety. Now that I know a little more about the Irish temperament than I did then, I better understand its wild and apparently causeless swings between abandon and holiness. Whenever my grandmother would come down from Canada to visit the Morton rectory, my father would every morning hold post-breakfast kneeling prayers in deference to my grandmother's conception of what was fitting. I knew the whole thing was a fake put on for my grandmother's benefit. But it was not against her that my scorn was directed; it was against the howling hypocrisy of my parents. Much later on I came to learn that my mother hated *her* mother, despite all outward sweetness. More hypocrisy, for which children have a keen sense.

• • •

Our whole family of three narrowly escaped tragedy or extinction shortly after my mother was brought home from the Samaritan hospital in Philadelphia, but was still bedridden and helpless. One morning I suddenly became conscious of a vast scurrying up and down stairs. I looked into my father's study where, poor man, he used to compose his sermons. It was a mass of flame, and the scurrying I had heard was my desperate father racing up and down stairs to get some source and container of water. The study couch was on fire. My father had lighted his pipe from a kitchen match (safety matches were rare those days), and when its head had ignited but broken off, my father, with the kind of dunderheadedness that frequently overcame him, had merely put another match to his pipe. Meanwhile the broken, flaring head had fallen under the couch and ignited the excelsior stuffing. By the time I saw it, it was incandescent and the heat was cracking picture glass all over the study. Panic-stricken as I was, I seized a half-filled kettle and dumped its contents on the inferno. The result was just a little steam, mingling with the smoke and flames. I have made some unflattering remarks about my father, but on this day, when his carelessness had started a disaster, he displayed a courage and resourcefulness that must have been in him all the time, but eternally squashed. He laughingly pooh-poohed the whole thing to me and told me to go and keep my bedridden mother company. By that time, the study was an inferno, a job for a professional fire department. But Morton had no fire department at all. There was the bucket brigade, in which a group of sweating men ranged along both sides of a strange, long iron-tired vehicle would hand-drag it whither it had been summoned. The vehicle carried a long ladder on its top; its sides were festooned with buckets, one to a man. Three miles an hour must have been as fast as the men could haul it by its straps—one to a bucket. No help possible there. What my father did was open the one study window and in some unfathomable fashion manage to shove the whole flaming couch out of the window to the ground two stories below, thus sustaining third-degree burns of his face and hands. He didn't even collapse from the burns or shock. A skeptical insurance claim adjuster equipped with steel measuring tape later declared there was no way in which Samson himself could have forced the dimensions of that couch through the dimensions of that window frame. Yet there was the charred evidence.

So now both my parents were in bed, my father's face covered with a mask of ointment-saturated flannel, with slits only for the eyes and nostrils. He was not exactly disfigured by the burns afterward, but the contours of his face were never exactly the same again. With both my parents in bed I must have been hard for *somebody* to handle but someone—I suppose a vestryman's wife—took charge of me for some days. When, thirty years later I found myself on a psychoanalyst's couch, describing this scene as the terror among the many terrors of my life, he said, "Oh, I think those are just screen memories, designed to block off what you really don't want to remember." How the hell did *he* know?

• • •

But 1909 was not wholly terror and tragedy. Not long after the January fire, the snow had begun in the gloaming and busily all the night and two days and nights thereafter had made everything into a series of beautiful, white, undulating lumps. It was heaven to be snowbound, and when, after days, horse-drawn wooden snow plows, weighted with rocks, cleared some paths, the banks they piled up were twice as tall as I. Buggies disappeared and sleighs with lap robes took their places. Occasionally a kindly adult would let you hitch your Flexible Flyer sled to his sleigh's rear and give you a dizzying ride of, at a guess, ten miles per hour. This was Living.

But unbeknownst to me a grand decision had been taken. We were to leave Morton and go to live in the heart of Philadelphia. And my father was to give up his parochial duties and actually cast his lot with journalism, for better or worse. It turned out, actually, to be worse but we did not know that then and all three of us felt jubilant at the prospect before us.

5 · THE USES OF AWE, OR, THE BOY SOPRANO

IN PHILADELPHIA TODAY the district known as Society Hill is one of that city's triumphs of urban restoration. It stretches east and west from the Delaware River to 8th Street and north and south from Lombard to Walnut, and it includes 712 Spruce Street. Now Spruce Street, even in 1911, had its points. The Pennsylvania Hospital fronted on Spruce at 8th Street. Above 11th Street, Spruce became quite handsome, and from 12th Street to Broad it was the Doctors' Row of the day: fine brick buildings with marble steps that were scrubbed to alabaster whiteness every day by the industrious underprivileged. But below 7th, Spruce Street degenerated fast. So once again we were living on the fringes of a slum—this time an urban one. Number 712, close to the corner of 7th Street, called itself The Spruce. It was two houses thrown into one, camouflaged by a double-width glass canopy to disguise what it *really* was: a boardinghouse for the shabby-genteel. We certainly qualified. My father had been hired as religious editor of the *Evening Telegraph* and occasionally doubled as an editorial writer. His salary in 1911 was twenty-five dollars a week; the cost of one large room to house all three of us at The Spruce plus three meals a day was twenty-one dollars a week. The margin of four dollars was a little thin even in the days when, at my age, you could sit all afternoon in a movie house for five cents. The nickelodeon had been perfectly named.

• • •

In those days Philadelphia had three evening newspapers (as well as four or five morning) and *"Bulletin—Telegraph—Times"* was the evening newsboys' cry. They had the ranking exactly right. The *Bulletin* was excruciatingly dull, and since that was exactly what Philadelphia wanted, it overflowed with prosperity. The *Times* was a Munsey newspaper and thus eventually doomed to extinction. The *Telegraph* was in the middle, losing money, but putting up a good fight. The present "In Philadelphia nearly everybody reads the *Bulletin*" was already on its way to being true.

I seem to have been less interested in my father's job than in the mechanical side of journalism. Mr. Price, the *Telegraph*'s managing editor, wore a cutaway coat to work: the uniform of authority or of a highly placed man in any profession. This combination of cutaway coats and roll-top desks was unexciting, so I gave my total love and admiration to two wholly noneditorial characters: Jim Newman and Fred Kelsey. Jim Newman was in the advertising art department, and from him I learned what a silver print was: a pale-blue flimsy photocopy of something or other. It was Mr. Newman's job to trace the faint outlines of the silver print in India ink. This done, the silver print was gently lowered into an enamel dish of "acid," whereupon the last traces of blue disappeared and lo—we were left with a damp copy of an India ink "original." It was miraculous. The original then went to the engraving and stereotyping departments, on its way to the rumbling presses in the basement of 704 Chestnut Street. For almost the first time in my life I had learned something—not by being "taught" but through my own observation.

Mr. Kelsey was even more fascinating. He belonged to that now vanished breed of man, the wire-service telegrapher. Before him slanted a rickety typewriter. To his left, encased in a three-sided mahogany box, was the brass sounder, whose dots and dashes he instantly translated into letters and words. An empty tin of Prince Albert or Velvet pipe tobacco was always clipped to the sounder box, to add resonance. And what has been said about the press telegraphers of the day I can testify to out of my own knowledge. While Mr. Kelsey was listening to his sounder and pounding his typewriter he was simultaneously capable, without any effort at all, of conducting a running conversation with me on any subject under the sun. Only casually, once in a while, did he open his key to tap out a terse query to "the other end." Where was the other end? I never knew. I did pick up a little Morse code by my association with Mr. Kelsey, but never enough to serve much useful purpose. Despite all the incredible gadgetry of today's "communications"—a word then as unfamiliar in working circles as "media"—it still seems to me a shame that the skills of the Mr. Kelseys of the century's preteens should have vanished off the earth.

I was disloyal to the *Telegraph* in a minor way. The basement presses of the *Times*, close to Independence Hall on Chestnut Street, were visible behind big plate-glass windows, and I would watch them endlessly as the web roared through the spinning cylinders first, then to be shaped into a V on its way to the folders. The Hoe Perfecting Press—what a name that was! The editorial departments were pretty dull by comparison to these marvels, I thought, and in this I had made a judgment wiser than my years.

• • •

In one respect it was an advantage to be a preacher's son in Philadelphia. I didn't have to go to one of the even-then frightening public schools to which the family four-dollar margin would otherwise have condemned me. At the corner of Locust and Juniper streets in 1911 stood a large, lovely brownstone building, gabled and ivy-covered. It was the Protestant Episcopal Academy, and because I was my Rector father's son I could be admitted there, tuition-free, so long as I maintained a satisfactory scholarship record.

Insofar as any twelve-year-old can be said to love school, I loved the Episcopal Academy. Somewhere along the line it dropped the *Protestant* from its name, but it still exists, in most distinguished form. The lovely brownstone building in the heart of Philadelphia was long ago torn down to make way for a third-rate hotel; faced with this urban renewal the Academy moved to spacious grounds in the Main Line suburb of Overbrook, where it continues to carry on.

Things were done with style at P.E.A., then its acronym and rallying cry. On the first floor were the Benson Vestibule, the Benson Library, the Benson Chapel (I never did know who Benson was), and the headmaster's office. Below were locker rooms, giving onto the yard where shinny and touch football were played; above were two tiers of classrooms, the whole topped by a gymnasium. When the school day began, everybody rushed to the Benson Chapel pell-mell, but an instant hush fell when

Old Nifty entered, robed. Old Nifty was the headmaster, with a glistening bald pate and splendid white Taft mustache. He was the gentlest and kindest of men but, like Miss Stellwagon before him, he, too, had The Eye. At his approach the unruliest bunch of twelve-year-olds would freeze into postures that were parodies of innocence, but if there was a culprit to be found, Old Nifty found him. We never knew how, but fifty years of dealing with boys must have had something to do with it. Old Nifty, whose real name was William Henry Klapp, had been a student at P.E.A. in his own boyhood, had left it only for his years at Harvard and at medical school, and then returned to teach. "In practically a lifetime spent here—" was usually the introduction to the sentence saying that what had happened yesterday was the most outrageous thing during that period.

• • •

The Benson Chapel over which Old Nifty presided at morning service was a magnificently handsome room. Old Nifty stood before a lectern on a large raised platform or else sat in one of two great carved oak chairs at the back, the other chair being reserved for a bishop or someone else almost as eminent with a special message for a special occasion. There were two hymns, and a fine two-manual organ was accompanied by a twelve-voice boy-soprano choir. I got to be a boy soprano in my Third-Form year, and it was simply great because the choir stayed behind for twenty minutes of practice for next morning's hymns, and this got us out of almost half of the first-period class.

Old Nifty would read a lesson from the King James Version, make whatever the day's announcements might be, and retire to his throne. In two oaken pews flanking him sat the Masters, ranked by seniority. We underformers sat in ordinary cushioned pews facing one another across the center aisle, but the giants of the Sixth Form sat, each one, in carved oaken stalls that formed a semicircle at the chapel's rear. When the last hymn had been sung and the benediction pronounced, Old Nifty would bow dismissal first to the Masters on one side, then to the other. After these solemn processions had filed out there would be a significant pause, and then Old Nifty would call "Sixth Form" and these men of the world would soberly depart. So it went, all the way down to the Second Form, lowest in the Middle School. In all parades and processions, boys were never ranked by short, medium or tall, but solely by scholastic rank, which altered slightly from term to term. There was no palling around between Masters and boys. You were called by your last name and nothing else. I think it was a good system.

• • •

My first days at P.E.A. put me through a lot. One of the first things I learned was that, preacher's son and all, I was a little mucker. The Academy's other boys came in general from Main Line families; they had not had a shabby-genteel upbringing on the fringe of a slum. What I had to learn, even faster than the Latin declensions, was proper manners. I knew no mode of address to any other boy except "Say, kid—" but I learned swiftly. I also learned about doffing my cap should I pass a Master on the street. He would incline his head in recognition. This was S.O.P. I think I really learned the value of manners in a single flash one day. I was walking down Broad Street when I spied three Masters coming abreast in a group. I doffed my cap. But since I was in the company of a lady—my mother—ironbound etiquette required the Masters, all three of them, not only to uncover but to bow, not only to my mother but to her "escort"—me. This was heady stuff: manners had *use*.

• • •

So far I seem to have given the impression that P.E.A. was entirely peopled by perfect little gentlemen. Nothing could be farther from the truth. The same irrepressible mischief, the same unending warfare between The Boy and The Enemy that Owen Johnson so beautifully depicted in his Lawrenceville stories, pervaded all of P.E.A. But there was something decorously left out of the Lawrenceville stories and this was Sex.

When I entered P.E.A., girls vanished completely from my life. "And good riddance" was my feeling at the time—an emotion that I have also occasionally felt in maturer years. But the disappearance of girls did not mean the disappearance of Sex—indeed it heightened it. An inexperienced young Master who

66

taught geography expressed himself once as delighted that the volumes of the *National Geographic* in the Benson Library were so obviously well thumbed. They were indeed, but we were not studying the continents—we were looking for tits. They were Balinese or other brown tits, but they were tits, they were female, and there were no other things to look at and be so excited by. They promised something unknown but ecstatic for the future, when you were to be more than twelve.

6·THE HEALING ART, OR, ONAN TRIUMPHANT

So MUCH HAS BEEN WRITTEN in the last decades about homosexuality among all ages, all kinds and all sexes that I feel well justified in putting my own oar in here. At P.E.A. in the subteens of the century I saw almost nothing of it, and heard very little. An older boy once asked me if I knew what a "fairy" was—then the exclusive and universal term—and when he saw through the fake of my knowing smirk, he was obviously pleased, although he did not enlighten me. As to my own direct experience with homosexuality, it was with Venus.

Venus was not a schoolmate; he was the headmaster's office boy. Large liquid eyes, full red lips and a girlish voice—at about age sixteen, I should judge—amply accounted for his nickname. One afternoon, going down to the locker room to stow a sweat shirt, I suddenly came upon Venus. He was leaning against a wall, his fly was open and he was masturbating. This came as a shock to me but not to him. Without a trace of embarrassment he invited me to his side and put my hand on his penis. It was very hard and erect and—to my twelve-year-old eyes—*huge*. He instructed me what to do and I needed the instruction, for his mode was different from mine. But as he approached his climax he took matters into his own hand and as I witnessed his orgasm and ejaculation the emotion that filled me was less excitement than bewilderment. My illicit reading had of course by this time made me aware of the consequences of male climax, but reading about it and actually seeing it were two completely different things. Venus and I had two more locker-room encounters, in which I fondled him and he fondled me. The results, from my point of view, were deplorable failures. I envied Venus his size and powers. I told him so and received from him the comforting assurances that, for my age, I was doing all right. Venus was a chronic masturbator and, it soon turned out, the whole school knew it. He thought he had discovered a dark slat-walled storeroom under the stair well where he could lie down and practice to his heart's content, unobserved. But he was not unobserved. One day when Venus entered Pinky Anderson's class with a note, when Pinky was momentarily out of the room, the thorough little gentleman who was also the Number One scholar of the Form called out in a loud voice at his retreating figure, "Hey, Venus, you'd better quit jerkin' off under those stairs." Even the class was jolted by this sudden public unveiling of what everyone knew but somehow no one discussed, and Pinky a moment later returned to an unusually silent and thoughtful class, which was not thinking, as it was supposed to be, about nominative clauses.

Long before that time I had fallen out of Venus' favor, which he had then bestowed on a still younger boy. I didn't care because although I had heard of group masturbation I had never seen it, and to me secrecy and solitude were the essence of the whole business, and sexual sharing with a girl was an apparently unattainable ambition. I knew no girls. Besides, even if I had . . . mystery, mystery. Meanwhile I was stuck. The Lord's Vengeance, even when added to my mother's dire warnings now three years gone by, was still insufficient.

We were all sex-ridden, and since it was unthinkable to discuss the subject with an adult, we discussed it, endlessly, among ourselves. I kept out of these discussions, in effect taking the Fifth against the possibility of self-incrimination. But I remember the locker-room conversation between two boys as to how "They" could tell if you "Did It." It seemed that if the skin of your cock was wrinkled when it was flaccid, "They" (presumably the medical profession) know you "Did It." I examined myself with some care. I was wrinkled, all right.

My preoccupation with my penis was certainly excessive, so much so in my mother's eyes that once she sewed up my trouser pockets. I screamed so loudly with twelve-year-old indignation and outrage at this invasion of privacy that she quickly unsewed them again, for another plan was forming in her mind.

Despite my comparative happiness at P.E.A. I was still a sickly and miserable child, given to tantrums, incessant colds and bedwetting. Something drastic had to be done—and was. First, my nasal turbinates were "burned out"—which meant cauterization with a cherry-red-hot electrode. Cocaine dulled the pain but was powerless against two other sensations—the heat of the electrode and the inhaled smell of your own searing flesh. This operation changed nothing in the slightest, so six months later it was performed again, and again without results. So a further plan was formed. My mother confided to me, if that is the verb, that I was to be taken to the Garretson Hospital where I was to be circumcised and at the same time have my tonsils and adenoids removed by the same redoubtable surgeon, William Wayne Babcock, who had operated on her. The tonsil-and-adenoid job by itself would have been enough to throw me into fits, but it faded into nothing when I thought of surgery attacking the only part of my body I really cared for. My mother modestly and judiciously explained to me that *everything* was not going to be cut off. But my foreskin was an integral and highly valued part of me, and I did not wish to be parted from it. But tears, fits, entreaties, and everything else I could muster were not enough to prevail, and in due course I was railroaded. I can remember only one act of gentle understanding as I lay in twelve-year-old terror on the operating table. A young intern, a Dr. Oliensis, who I hope is still alive and flourishing, said, as he placed the gauze mask over my nose and mouth and prepared the ether drip, "Now, sonny, when you smell something, blow it away just as hard as you can. That's fine! Do it again." A few such deep inhalations and I was gone. Of my coming out again I don't feel like saying very much to this day. I looked surreptitiously at my bloodied penis, its glans, still mucous membrane, but now bare, with horror. Not nominated in the bond, Dr. Babcock had passed a steel probe into my bladder seeking, I think, he knew not what, so that for some postoperative days the acts of swallowing or urinating were tortures no one had led me to expect.

When, about thirty years later I lay on the couch of a psychoanalyst whose services I by then had considerable need of and recounted this tale to him, he showed the first and only outburst of emotion I have ever experienced among his impassive breed. "That was damned rough treatment to hand an adolescent," said Dr. Prescott Giniger. He reflected on his remark for a moment. Then he added, "Goddamn rough treatment." Then his mood altered again: "Nowadays, an Irish Circumcision is favored in many quarters." I told him I didn't know what that meant. "Let him wear it away," said Dr. G., who thereupon resumed his impassivity.

•　•　•

So, after more than a quarter century had gone by, I had expert testimony to back up my feelings of 1911. I had been outraged. I had been irremediably mutilated. From that moment on I actively hated my mother as a cruel and stupid woman determined to wreak whatever in her invincible way she wanted to have wrought. I did not include my father in these damnations since, typically, he didn't seem to have been around and could not have prevailed against my mother if he had been.

As the physical pains began to disappear and I was left (only!) with the psychic trauma of my mutilation, an awful question suddenly presented itself: Would I still be able to practice self-abuse? If not, I would take the only remaining course open and commit suicide, or something. No sooner was I home again than I used my first moment of privacy for the crucial, the final test that would determine if life was still worth living. Well it was. Things weren't *exactly* the same, but there was nothing to warrant complaint. Thereafter one of my attitudes toward my mother, and to some degree to the whole stupid and venomous world of adults, was "There! You see I have outwitted you after all!"

7 · OLD GOBBO, OR,
THE SECRET OF FAILURE

I HAVE DWELT a good deal on sex in what has preceded because, after all, it was the great overriding Topic of Interest among boys of eleven, many other than myself. But there were others— many others. Before I plunge into them I want to stay a moment more with the Episcopal Academy. Even as I look back through more than sixty years since my class ('17) graduated, it still impresses me with what a genuinely fine school it was, even then.

The emphasis on Forms and Masters, not on "grades" and "teachers," suggested that, like the fashionable boarding schools of the day, it modeled itself on the English public schools. But from what I have read of Englishmen's reminiscences of *their* schools, the American imitation surpassed the British model. The teachers knew how to teach. There was no "fagging," nor corporal punishment of any kind, no favoritism I could ever discover. And believe me, I looked for it. My hated spectacles and my shabby clothes set me somewhat apart from the other boys, but my stigma as "Preacher" disappeared. After all, this was a church school. Although I was never popular I was not shunned, and for this I was deeply grateful. For intramural-sports purposes all classes were divided into Auroras and Vespers. (I was an Aurora, but contributed nothing of value in anything.) Rivalry was intense between the two; any Aurora would come charging to the defense of another, set upon by Vespers. School discipline was so good that we scarcely were conscious it existed. The Senior Masters—"Pinky" Anderson (English), "Old Jeff" (Jefferson Shiel, Mathematics), "Pop" Williams (History), Mr. Doolittle (Latin)—all had The Eye and could quell anything with their brows. Only Charles Sawyer Shinn (English and Math) used the raised voice: *"Go back through that door and enter this room correctly!"* or *"Get out of this classroom for the rest of the hour!"* This was a terrible banishment. What was the criminal to do from then until the gongs sounded at the next hour? Suppose he met another Master in the hallway! How could he explain that Mr. Shinn had kicked him out of class?

Of course, there were a few exceptions. M'seer Maubert (French) had his difficulties with discipline, perhaps because he also had his difficulties with the deeper subtleties of the English language and could be confused. But the inexplicable failure was Mr. Watson (Physics and Chemistry), promptly christened Old Gobbo. (We were Shakespearean scholars.) Despite the looks and build of a varsity fullback and the fact that he had apparatus to perform "experiments" that should have fascinated us, Old Gobbo was powerless over his classes. The little angels of Pinky Anderson's brow-controlled room became rampaging demons in Old Gobbo's. Spitballs crisscrossed the room and landed with gorgeous *splats* on the blackboards. Stink bombs (hydrogen sulfide encased in fragile glass balls that shattered when unobtrusively dropped) went off, and the room would have to be cleared out and aired. Torpedoes and itch powder, readily obtainable at a nearby "novelties" store, found ready uses. Old Gobbo lasted through one harrowing (for him) academic year and was then fired—literally harried out of the school by a group of Perfect Little Gentlemen, average age fourteen. What was the secret of his failure? In addition to his build and the advantages of the subjects he was supposed to teach, he had bushy brows, a deep voice and a manner of seeming authority, yet he could not prevail, and it was not that "he didn't know his stuff," a deficiency any ten-year-old would be quick to detect. So what was his lack?

Of course we were all essential rebels, but we were not nearly so open rebels as Owen Johnson's Lawrenceville boys. Our best ploy was the Derailment—the throwing of the Master off his subject. Despite his long experience, Mr. Doolittle was the most easily derailable. Any boy who could establish some sort of bridge, no matter how flimsy, between *"Ubi eo ventum est"* and the issues of women's suffrage, or the then tentatively proposed income tax, received the grateful glances of the rest of the class for this meant that the rest of the hour's Latin recitation was probably over. Mr. Doolittle regarded both issues as the products of degenerate socialistic minds, and just a few quiet respectful questions could keep him going through the rest of the hour—not that we knew anything or cared a fig about these remote affairs.

Pinky Anderson could occasionally be derailed; Jefferson Shiel and Pop Williams never. There was *a* way of derailing Charles Sawyer Shinn in Math, but of its nature it could be used only rarely. The ploy was to ask, in a knowledge-pleading voice, "Sir, what is the *real* use of studying plane geometry?" Now this, in reality, is a complex question to answer to the satisfaction of a twelve-year-old, and as I have said, Mr. Shinn was by nature a combative personality. Thus a sufficient series of pleading, knowledge-thirsty questions made a pretty safe guarantee that we would never reach Euclid's Proposition VI that day. Thus, in the language of today, we had every Master taped. Did they know it? Of course they had us taped too, and our basic weakness was that of this we were insufficiently aware.

• • •

At Episcopal (another short form for the Academy) I even discovered, spasmodically at least, the joys of learning. When Mr. Doolittle once warned me that I was on the verge of flunking Latin and had jolly well better do something to avoid this disgrace, I took to getting up at five of a spring morning and swotting away at Greenough and Kittredge until I had really learned what I was supposed to know. And it was *fun*—this was the great discovery. Youth is a series of spasms, and this Latin spasm, like most spasms, did not last indefinitely. I never led my class in anything. Even roll calls were taken not alphabetically but by scholastic rank. Two really brilliant boys, neither of them grinds, fought it out perpetually for first and second places, alternating constantly. There was a steady, consistent third placer. Memory tells me I usually came in fourth or fifth, which meant, I think, that I must have been in the top third of the class, but by a whisker. This must have been due to my efforts in Pinky Anderson's English class. There we were required to write weekly themes. Mine caught Pinky's ear, and he gave me warm encouragement and wide latitude. I even wrote a theme in which I parodied the theme styles of a few of my classmates. This was pretty close to the line of downright impropriety, and when Pinky said that when the headmaster arrived in person,

74

as he always did to take the roll, he would call on me to reread the theme in his presence, I was terrified. Would I be expelled, disgraced, refused admission to the French Foreign Legion, which would be my only remaining recourse? I could tell nothing from Pinky's bland face. When Old Nifty arrived with his roll book, Pinky called me to the platform, where I shakingly reread my five-minute essay. Now for the blow. But Old Nifty smiled a pleasant smile and said, "Good. In fact, rather good," and inclined his head to indicate that I could take my seat while he finished checking the roll. Suddenly I ascended into heaven and sat on the right hand of God the Father Almighty. The jeers and gibes of my classmates, when the hour ended, affected me not the slightest; I had suddenly come to favorable public notice—I, of all people. After a while that towering school figure, the seventeen-year-old editor in chief of *The Scholium*, the student monthly magazine, asked me to contribute a piece. I did. It was a flop. I received my life's first rejection slip, which took me down quite a few pegs. But I had nevertheless discovered something: in writing I could be facile and I could be versatile, and I made the most, for a long time, of these twin gifts. Not until middle age did I come to realize that these "gifts" were the very hallmark of the quite successful Second-Rater—the light in which I view my adult career as I prepare to meet my Maker and, if possible, ask Him a question or two.

• • •

So, from then on I was happy at P.E.A. Despite my glasses, my shabby clothes and my total athletic uselessness, I was elected to The Secret Seven, a Third-Form group. Unfortunately I attended only one meeting because a week later Old Nifty abolished The Secret Seven and I never even learned what our Secret was.

But there were other compensations. I have said that P.E.A. did things with style, and style rose to no higher peak than at the services that marked the beginning of the Christmas and Easter holidays. All parents were invited and all parents came. The Benson Chapel was jammed. Old Nifty wore his Harvard academic robes with appropriate doctor's hood; the faculty wore cutaways with carnations in buttonholes. All boys wore blue serge and their parents lived up to them. A bishop, dean or some other ecclesiastic sat on the throne chair next to Old Nifty and would later make a brief speech to which he had given not even a moment's nonconventional thought, and to which there was no response. A First and Second Lesson was read, and the soprano boys' choir sang hymns and carols—in Latin, thank you. After these warming-up exercises, Old Nifty took charge at the lectern.

"I shall now read out, not without pride, the names of those boys who have distinguished themselves academically during the term just closed. There are three groups: those Commended with Highest Honor, those Commended with Honor, and those Commended. As I call each name the boy will rise and remain standing until the last name has been called. Parents will appreciate that every boy commended is deserving of high praise and has added to the honor of the School. I shall now call out the names."

And he did. No boy knew beforehand whether he had made this list; so although there were some sure-thing shots, the tension was electric. I never made it higher than just plain Commended, but even so one felt pride in the act of standing. But even as I stood up a shadow would fall on my pride. I was conspicuous. I was conspicuous because I was the only boy in the school who wore an Eton collar. I wore it because my mother forced me to and would buy me nothing else. Regardless of how violently I fought her, I could not break the soft, whining, tyrannical hold she had on me. It took the First World War to do that.

8 · NINETEEN TWELVE, OR, THE REPUBLIC ENDANGERED

WHILE THINGS WERE going well at school, they were going terribly at home. It was the era of the boardinghouse, one of the least regrettable of our present-day urban cultural losses. The meals at The Spruce were so vile, the gassy turnips and sulfurous butter so intolerable, that a contract was renegotiated whereby we kept our room there but went elsewhere—to another boardinghouse—for dinners. The dining room had one long and narrow table, seating maybe forty, and our meal tickets were punched as we went in. The clientele was shoe clerks, shopgirls and retired railroad brakemen. This was our economic level. My mother resented mingling with these social types, and her own Anglo-American manner did not go down well with them. And it was, one way or another, my father's fault, of course. Why could he not develop any respectable earning power?

The star boarders were a Mr. and Mrs. Carroll. He clung to a worn cutaway and she—well, my mother told me, in a secret and portentous whisper—*Mrs. Carroll shaved and penciled her eyebrows*, the next-to-last word in depravity. (Younger readers should know that although Fallen Women used rouge and perhaps even lipstick in 1911, the makeup equipment of a Lady consisted of a bulky box of *poudre de riz* and a powder puff the size of a baseball and that was that. Used sparingly and for special occasions only, otherwise people might gain the impression that one was "fast.")

• • •

Off the dining room of our new eating house there was a parlor with an upright piano. The music of the times had gone far beyond Tosti's "Good-bye," "Just a Little Rocking Chair and You,"

"In the Shade of the Old Apple Tree," "Pony Boy" and similarly affecting ballads and had entered the decadent era of "Alexander's Ragtime Band," "That Mysterious Rag" ("sneaky, freaky ever melodious rag"). Even such songs as "Come, Josephine, in My Flying Machine" and "He'd Have to Get Under—Get Out and Get Under—to Fix Up His Auto-mobile," which were filthy enough, were falling under the sinister shadow of ragtime. Some shipping clerk or shoe salesman was always pounding them out on the mistuned parlor piano. All this provoked my father to the only open display of temper and irritation I had ever seen. Whether his objections were moral or because he was a good pianist, I never knew. As for my mother, she grew daily more petulant, irritable and bitter with her lot in life, given to violent outbursts of temper at my father as well as me. I had a theory about my parents even then, and beyond verification. It was that my mother had been in love with Stephen Leacock, who in the language of the day had "thrown her over," whereupon she had married my father on the rebound. However that may have been, my father remained forever a deeply loving husband, although how he managed it at times passed my understanding and still does.

• • •

I think it must have been the sinking of the *Titanic* in April 1912 that first aroused my interest in news qua news. In 1908, when the S.S. *Florida* had sunk the S.S. *Republic*, I was too young to comprehend what wireless operator Jack Binns had been able to do with the aid of Signor Marconi's wireless, but the *Titanic's* incomprehensible tragedy brought me to full alert. At the time, of course, I knew nothing of the timeless feat of Carr Vattel Van Anda, the *Times*'s managing editor, in organizing his whole staff to cover the story before there was firm verification that the ship had gone down. (First rumors merely referred to the iceberg collision and "damage.") Many details, but not enough for me, filtered through to the Philadelphia papers, and when, some three years hence, my family and I moved to New York, I used to spend day after day in the New York Public Library's newspaper room reading and rereading from the back files every smallest detail of the tragedy that began when lookout Frederick Fleet in the crow's-nest sounded three bells to the bridge—warning of an object dead ahead—and was made inevitable when First Officer William Murdoch, on watch, made his fatal decision to try to sheer off, thus letting the iceberg rip his ship's hull for half its length instead of hitting head on and sustaining a hideously crumpled bow with which the vessel *might* have remained afloat, at least for longer. All of this I read and reread, column after endless column; this, and also the most chilling, thrilling, hair-raising publication of its kind I had or have ever come upon. It was a large volume, *The Report of His Majesty's Wreck Commission*, Lord Mersey, Chairman, issued, I think, after an investigation of a year or more. It delved into every minutest technical detail of the tragedy. The deliberately unemphatic low key of the prose makes Walter Lord's highly successful book, *A Night to Remember*, read, by comparison, like *Rebecca of Sunnybrook Farm*.

•   •   •

Returning to other aspects of 1912, my father's rather weary job on the *Telegraph* held one great advantage for me: a season pass to Shibe Park (now Connie Mack Stadium). Cornelius McGillicuddy's Athaletics were then at the height of their powers—World Champions in 1910, 1911 and 1913. They were American League Champions also in 1914, but of the ensuing tragedy of that year, more later.

These were the days of pitcher Eddie Plank, Herb Pennock, Jack Coombs, and Chief Bender, half Indian, and of Ira Thomas and Jack Lapp, catchers. They were the days also of the "$100,000 infield"—a colossal sum—with Stuffy McInnis at first base, Eddie Collins (a college graduate, it was rumored) at second, Jack Barry at short and "Home Run" Baker at third. Home Run Baker got his name because he could be counted on to produce from eight to thirteen (his top) four-baggers *every season*. Eddie Murphy covered right field, Amos Strunk was in center and Rube Oldring was in left. A relief pitcher as contrasted with a starter was then unknown. To get knocked out of the box was one thing, but to get relieved in mid-game because you were tiring would have been nothing but disgraceful. You went the full nine innings if your stuff was working at all, and Eddie Plank once pitched both games of a double-header, winning each time.

79

• • •

It seems to me I must have used my father's season pass every summer day. Baseball was really The National Pastime then. The afternoon papers stopped their presses frequently to replate with the current local scores. And for the final innings there was The Fudge. The Fudge was a metallic plate screwed into the impression cylinders. You *hung* the plates, by the way. On The Fudge there were raised squares of soft metal. Left untouched, they printed merely as black squares. But as the final innings' scores were telegraphed down from Shibe Park (about three miles distant, but the telephone was, then as now, not a reliable instrument), they were sped to the basement. The presses were stopped, and a man with hammer and steel punch would whang the appropriate numeral into the proper lead square. Then the presses were started again and The Fudge would print the new number as white on black. Mind you, this was all Page-One Stuff, even in April and May.

My first journalistic thrill was to be allowed to sit beside William G. Weart, sports editor of the *Telegraph* and the author of the column "Weart's Warblings," in the press box. Weart would dictate slowly to the telegrapher by his side: "Midkiff picked out a slow one and put it over Collins' head into short center for the first hit of the game." The telegrapher's key clinked out the dots and dashes, and someone in the city room three miles away (Mr. Kelsey, maybe, perhaps the while simultaneously talking about the soon forthcoming 1912 Presidential election) translated it back into prose on his spavined typewriter. Mr. Weart fascinated me because he could see plays and possibilities far more acutely than I could, for all my twelve-year-old reaction time.

• • •

My father must have had a raise from twenty-five dollars a week because early in 1912 we moved into infinitely better quarters than The Spruce. It was still a boardinghouse—Miss Cashew's—but in a downright respectable neighborhood, close by Episcopal (1221 Walnut Street), with a good dining room and a high clientele. Here I first met three fascinating people: Mr. and Mrs. John C. Trautwine, Jr., and their son, known as

Third. The Trautwine family was then so famous in engineering circles as to influence the rest of my life and this influence was so all-pervasive that I defer its telling until later in favor of the feverish excitement of the 1912 political campaign, and most particularly the night of Tuesday, November fifth.

• • •

Boies Penrose was Senior Senator from Pennsylvania and Leader of the "regular" Republican Party in the days when the candidate was chosen in a smoke-filled room. So defective was my political education that I did not then know that Boies Penrose had once been a member of an ancient class at my own school. Penrose was a Political Boss, Old School, and his reputation was none too savory. Also, horrors, He Drank to Excess, according to persistent rumor. (His personal formula for Southern Comfort, apparently one of his favorite tipples, compounded of bourbon whiskey, brown sugar, two combs of honey and many other things, to be buried in stone crocks for two years of aging, sounds emetic to me now, but when I first saw it published it sounded like nectar.) Anyway, there he was entrenched impregnably in his Senate seat and as Party Boss. (The popular election of Senators was yet to come—and, as memory now recalls, was still another socialist evil that could derail Mr. Doolittle.) Scott Nearing was at that time a firebrand professor of economics at the University of Pennsylvania's Wharton School of Finance who actually advocated the creation of the Federal Reserve System of banks; an obvious heresy, unfortunately unusable to derail Mr. Doolittle because none of us knew how to ask a question about it. But Scott Nearing was obviously of the then extreme left and had a habit of speaking out vigorously on all topics. (His son, whom by coincidence I years later hired at Time Inc., went by the name of John Scott). But the sentence that got the heave-ho for Scott Nearing from the U. of P. was memorable indeed: "I would rather see a son of mine in hell than educated at the institution that gave Boies Penrose his start in life."

Boies Penrose was in complete control of the Republican Convention that renominated incumbent William Howard Taft for the Presidency. Well before that time Theodore Roosevelt had broken with Taft, once his protégé, and had also had heavy afterthoughts about his earlier "No Third Term" vows. (Since he had succeeded the assassinated William McKinley in 1901 he had had only one *elected* term, that of 1904–08.) When Teddy could not get his delegates seated in Chicago, he bolted the convention and his idolater, the *North American*, bannered "PROGRESSIVE PARTY IS BORN!" There followed the Bull Moose movement and the attempt on Roosevelt's life in Milwaukee, where the assassin's bullet was stopped just short of the victim's heart by the thickness of the speech manuscript still folded in his breast pocket. The first stirrings of interest in the Life Political could be felt in my thirteen-year-old bosom.

Election night, 1912, made the bosom thump. My father took me down, through torchlights and red fire, to the jammed offices of the *Telegraph*. On the second floor a magic lantern had been rigged, its carbon-arc light focused on a double-bed sheet strung aloft on Chestnut Street at 7th. Wild, dense crowds blocked all of Chestnut Street as far as the eye could see. The city room was in a frenzy of activity because the advance of technology meant that as A.P. returns poured in by telegraph to Mr. Kelsey and his associates, artists stood by to paint the figures on glass slides that were then rushed to the magic lantern, which, with uncertain focus, occasional right-for-left or top-for-bottom reversals, displayed them to the cheering or groaning crowds below. So *this* was journalism! I had never conceived of anything so exciting, but not unnaturally I didn't make much connection between it and the art of writing.

• • •

When it finally appeared that Woodrow Wilson, a Democrat, a scholar, a school teacher, a college professor, a college president, and to cap it all the first minority President of the twentieth century, was indeed slated to move into the White House on March 4, 1913, Republican Philadelphia was glum. The bitterest pill to swallow was that the split Republican Party had helped to put an avowed, confessing low-tariff man into the office that the journalese of the day referred to as the nation's Chief Magistrate. What would happen now, above all with William Jennings Bryan Secretary of State? Nobody knew, but forebodings were deep. As things were to turn out, nobody knew less than Woodrow Wilson.

9 · MR. TRAUTWINE, or, THE AIMS OF EDUCATION

The year wore into 1913, and the Trautwine family began to loom large in my now-beginning adolescent life. Mr. Trautwine "Junior" was then a man in his early sixties, but so illustrious had his father's name been in the 1870's and 1880's that his son remained Mr. Junior to the end of his days. He wore gold-rimmed bifocal spectacles, a kindly expression, and a beard. Beards were no longer tumbling Victorian waterfalls, of course; they were referred to in journalese as "hirsute adornments," an indication that they were on their way out altogether; those that remained, like Mr. Trautwine's or Pop Williams' at Episcopal, were trimmed every week and barbered to a sharp, stylish point.

Mr. Trautwine, half a generation older than my own father, treated me exactly as a son hopes, for some reason almost always in vain, that his real father would treat him: *as an equal*, but of course an equal still needing some widening of Horizon. This he undertook. Why did the shabby, hopeless little boy I was capture this kindly man's interest? To this day I don't know, but perhaps it was partly because his own son, Mr. Third, a man in his thirties at the time, treated him with such hostility, which *must* have been of long standing. Father and son were editors and proprietors of *The Civil Engineer's Pocket Book*, of which Grandfather Trautwine had published the original edition in 1872. It was the unquestioned progenitor of all the hundreds of engineering handbooks that were to follow, and was still famous in its own right half a century later. Grandfather Trautwine must have been quite a gent. He lost his right arm in a field accident but this seemed to have occasioned no more than a long pause in his career: with steel-weighted T squares, steel-weighted triangles, steel-weighted "French curves," reversed

83

ruling pens and other devices of his own invention, he retaught himself his trade and became what surely must still be a world rarity—a one-armed, left-handed engineering draftsman.

As I write this today I have before me a copy of the "20th Edition, 3rd Issue, 150th Thousand" of this famous work, now vanished, in which I was later to play some part, and my eye falls on a page familiar to me for almost sixty years. It is headed "PREFACE to the First Edition, 1872," and I can almost write down its first paragraph without looking at it:

> Should experts in engineering complain that they do not find anything of interest in this volume, the writer would merely remind them that it was not his intention that they should. This book has been prepared for *young* members of the profession; and one of its leading objects has been to elucidate, in plain English, a few important elementary principles which the savants have developed in such a haze of mystery as to render the pursuit hopeless to any but a confirmed mathematician.

The last sentence of this four-page introduction reflects the certitude of the nineteenth century, now gone: "There is no table of errata because no errors are known to exist except two or three of a single letter in spelling; and which will probably escape notice."

• • •

Well, I think perhaps another reason for Mr. Trautwine's interest in me lay in some innate desire to help, instruct and encourage the young (as his father had done) if the young showed any signs of response, which I did. He spoke German to me, by way of seeing how much of the language I was acquiring from Mr. Peck, Master of German at Episcopal. It wasn't very much. But it was exciting to realize that you could *converse* in German, instead of reciting *"Du bist wie eine Blume,"* so my German picked up. There was no hint of the pedagogical in his manner toward me, nor of *stooping* to explain anything, yet he explained a lot, by simple exposure and the unspoken assumption that I would be interested. He took me to his office, where he, his son Third and a staff of eight or ten were working on still another revision and expansion of his father's classic book. Had I ever heard of a logarithm? No. Well, if I would reach up to the second shelf and hand down that four-inch-thick book by Herr Dr. C. Bruns, he would show me vast tables of *seven-place* logarithms. "Seven place?" "Yes; carried all the way out to seven decimal places"; that was the sort of thing the Germans were particularly good at. A logarithm's virtue, or one of them at least, was that if an engineer wanted to multiply two huge numbers that might take him a couple of days and still have a mistake in it, he looked up the two numbers in Dr. Bruns's book, wrote down their logarithms, merely added them and then worked backward with Dr. Bruns to find the number corresponding to the addition; that number would, hey presto, turn out to be the *product* of multiplier and multiplicand. Vast timesaver; particularly now that adding machines existed, which after a while could be run by electricity. It was too bad there weren't better devices on the market for mechanical computation, but there weren't—not through lack of effort, however. There had been an Englishman, Charles Babbage, back in the early 1800's, who had wrestled with the problem but his inspiration was way ahead of the technology (there was a nice word: *technology*) of his times. And even before Babbage there was Blaise Pascal (he was French, of course), who had had a great headful of ideas that had also proved too grandiose for his day. But logarithms remained great things. There were two parts to them: the *characteristic* (left of the decimal point) and the *mantissa*. But we could go into that later, if we liked. Meanwhile, this slide rule (point) has its numbers arranged in a logarithmic scale and an arithmetic one, so when you pulled its slide in and out and centered the glass with the hairline where you wanted it, you were using logarithms to multiply, divide or do other even fancier things. "This particular slide rule is made by Keuffel and Esser, but a lot of people call them 'Teufel und Fresser.'" I got it, and was proud! Mr. Trautwine had done something Mr. Austin, Master of Algebra, had never succeeded in: he had captured 100 per cent of my attention, and he had done it not by instructing me, but by his manner of casually discussing shared interests.

• • •

Only once in a rare while did Mr. Trautwine turn quizmaster:
"Why does a mirror reverse right for left instead of top for bottom?"

"Why do we speak of *heat* in such a different way from how we speak of *cold?*"

Very difficult questions.

"You're familiar with pi, of course." Oh, yes, I assured him, brightly, we had "had" that in geometry and algebra. I even reeled off its value: 3.1416. "Well not *exactly*," said Mr. Trautwine. "In engineering we usually use 3.14159, but that's not exact either."

No such heresy had ever been heard in Mr. Austin's class at Episcopal. "As a matter of fact," said Mr. Trautwine, "John Napier, the same man who invented logarithms, once carried the value of pi out to several thousand decimal places in hopes he would come on a repeating decimal."

I was silent in the face of this startling news.

"Why do you suppose he was so blooming anxious to find a repeating decimal?"

I hadn't the faintest idea.

"Well, for example, 0.3333 is a repeating decimal, isn't it? What's its value?"

"One-third," I said, wondering what the game was.

"No matter how many threes there are after the decimal point the value stands exactly at one-third?"

"Yes."

"*Now* can you make a guess at why Napier was so keen to find a repeating decimal in pi, other than the fact he was a Scot?"

I still hadn't the faintest idea.

"The answer is right in your hands," said Mr. Trautwine. "If Napier had ever hit on a repeating decimal he would have established an *exact* value for pi, wouldn't he?"

Of course!

"But he never hit one, no matter how complicated," said Mr. Trautwine, in mock sadness for these vast and frustrated labors in the sixteenth century. "So only God knows the *exact* value of pi."

Wow. Now I knew something no other Third Former at Episcopal knew. It was Knowledge—not everyday *useful* knowledge, but Knowledge. I felt a fourteen-year-old's scorn for Mr. Austin, who had given us pi equals 3.1416 as a Verity. *Perhaps Mr. Austin didn't know any better himself!* Delicious, wonderful, iconoclastic thought!

• • •

Every schoolboy knew about "wireless" if for no other reason than the *Titanic* disaster, but the time was still well in the future before kids would acquire cat's whisker and galena detector sets. Radium had been discovered, but we didn't know that; we had not yet "taken" chemistry.

"This radiation business," said Mr. Trautwine. "To tell you the truth, I don't understand very much about it myself. We might go to the Franklin Institute for one of those Sunday-night lectures the next time Professor Goodspeed [Professor of Physics, University of Pennsylvania] is giving one." It was a magnificently casual throwaway suggestion.

The Franklin Institute of those times was far from the magnificent creation of today. In 1913 it was housed in an unimposing gray stone building on North 7th Street—a sleazy neighborhood to begin with. The second and third floors were given over to a sharply raked amphitheater for lectures. Professor Goodspeed was not the only lecturer I heard there, but he was a standout, with an easy manner, touches of appropriate, mild scientific humor and a gift for clear exposition. Best of all, his lecture platform was filled with glassware with which he would demonstrate his points. I well remember one of his opening paragraphs on Radiation, and although I obviously can't quote him verbatim after almost sixty years, it went something like this:

"One day in 1895 one of my senior students rushed into my office to say that some German with a difficult name had discovered a Ray that would penetrate solid objects. I expressed polite interest and began thinking how I could politely get him out of my office in the shortest possible time, for I was very busy."

Professor Goodspeed may have been telling a good story at his own expense, but that did not matter. These were "popular" lectures and this was how Professor Goodspeed introduced Wilhelm Roentgen and his discovery, with the confessedly bewildering name of X ray that he gave it, awaiting a better one that has never in three-quarters of a century appeared.

The wonders of the pre-Roentgen age had been the Geissler Tubes and their slightly more sophisticated successor, the Crookes Tubes. The Geissler Tubes were interesting and apparently useless curiosities. You exhausted a glass tube to as high a vacuum

87

as you could in the nineteenth century, introduced some inert gas into it, sealed the tube, attached platinum electrodes to the ends, connected them to a source of high-frequency current and lo—the tubes glowed in the dark, with many colors, depending on the rare gas used. The trick was to make these tubes into fantastic examples of the glass blower's art, full of angles, whorls and wriggles, and introduce fluorescent artifacts in the shape of butterflies, for example, thus showing that the mysterious glow would move as freely as the tube listeth, and make the butterfly fluoresce at the same time. Marvelous. The sixtyish Mr. Trautwine sat in full attention beside his fourteen-year-old, goggle-eyed companion, never once committing the sin of "explaining" anything. The unspoken presumption was that I could take things in as well as he could. *We were equals!* No senior can confer a greater sense of self-worth than this—and damn it, a father can't do it because he remembers when he had to change your diapers.

Professor Goodspeed had other wonders to perform. From the Crookes Tubes he went on to what must have been the newest thing in the world—an elemental cathode tube. With all lights turned out and current applied to the tube, a stream of electrons (what were *they?*) was made visible inside the tube. But the grand climax was still to come. Professor Goodspeed held an ordinary horseshoe magnet in his hand and slowly lowered it over the neck of the tube. As he did so, the electron stream was slowly deflected upward; as he slowly withdrew the magnet, the stream sank again. When the lights were turned on again the audience burst into wild applause, and no one clapped harder than Mr. Trautwine or I. I was sitting on the extreme outward edge of all Physical Knowledge, and that was quite a place for a four-teen-year-old to be, not *better* than Shibe Park, of course, but different, quite different.

10 · EIGHT CENTS AN HOUR, OR, GIRLS

MR. TRAUTWINE was a Socialist. ("Heavens!" said my mother.) This meant, in those far-off days, that he was an *almost* contented American citizen who regularly voted for Eugene V. Debs for President, an incessant writer of Letters to the Editor, a "sympathizer" with the cause of labor.

As the name suggests, the Trautwine family was German, and one branch of it stuck to the spelling "Trautwein." Without really knowing anything about it I suspect that some revolutionary great-grandfather must have fled Germany for the United States. In any event the spirit of freedom, of nonconformity, was still deeply at work in the bosom of the now elderly Mr. Trautwine, who had become my hero. He, like his father before him, had been born in Philadelphia and I can remember his strong disapprobation for the Germany of Bismarck, which he first visited as a young man on his *Wanderjahre*; it had outraged him when his hotel asked him, most politely, of course, to visit the nearest police station and register there, as all foreigners were supposed to do even in those days before passports. He did, of course, and the interrogation was most polite, but it *was* interrogation. Had he ever been "detained?" Detained? There was some momentary translation trouble here; then at length it appeared that the ultrapolite sergeant of the Polizei was using a euphemism, and "Have you ever been detained?" really meant "Have you ever been arrested?" No. But this kind of thing rankled in the Trautwine breast eternally. He loved the free air of America, except that he wanted it to be freer still. But above all he was a Utopian, a strong believer in the Perfectibility of Man and other such ideas as have now gone down the drain of History. He was also a strong believer in the ideas of Henry

George, the man who had not only advocated but invented that heretical idea the single tax, the confiscation of rents. Mr. Trautwine gave me a copy of *Progress and Poverty*, which I read with avidity but no comprehension at all. "What started me thinking," said Mr. Trautwine, "was a book called *Looking Backward* by Edward Bellamy." He gave me a copy of that, too, and I have never gotten over it.

• • •

My fascinating mentor kept on taking me to the Sunday Franklin Institute lectures, to hear, for example, Ralph Modjeski, an eminent bridge designer (and son of Madame Modjeska, the Polish actress), lecture on the then famous and horrible Quebec Bridge Disaster, and Charles Proteus Steinmetz, then the stogie-chomping hunchback "genius" of the General Electric Company, talk about Alternating Current. (A.C. *vs.* D.C. was one of the burning issues of the engineering day, in which Thomas Alva Edison, of all people, eventually turned out to be on the wrong side.) And there were lots more.

Moreover, he was going a week from Monday afternoon to inspect a North Philadelphia high-pressure fire department pumping station. Would I like to go along? And there was a new filtration bed near Torresdale. Had I ever seen one? Would I like to? Would I like to go with him to a convention of the American Society for Testing Materials, in Atlantic City, where he was down for some short remarks? Would I just.

"My father had quite a reputation as a civil engineer, entirely apart from starting the book," said Mr. Trautwine on the train ride down, "and somebody asked him the inevitable question about the secret of his success. My father said, 'It's quite simple. You build a reservoir, and it leaks; you build a filter bed, and it won't pass the water. So I build filter beds and call them reservoirs.' "

• • •

But the apex of everything came when Mr. Trautwine offered me a job as an after-school-hours office boy and errand boy. "I have to clear it with Third, of course, because he's the head of the office now." I had met Mr. John C. Trautwine, III, only once or twice. He was a pale young man, with an ascetic face and jet-black hair overhanging one brow, and so shy that I

90

suffered with him. He played the violin quite creditably, and his doting mother was always inviting people into their small suite at Miss Cashew's at which he was forced to give a recital. On the basis of this tiny acquaintance, Third gave approval to his father's plan, and I became part-time office boy for the Traut-wine Company, Publishers of *The Civil Engineer's Pocket Book*, 257 South 4th Street. My pay was eight cents an hour, and if I was able to put in enough time, Saturdays included, I might earn as much as $1.40 a week. Wow. Tootsie Rolls, chewing gum, nickelodeons, an occasional ten-cent seat at DuMont's Minstrels, all these were within my power now, and perhaps the world was not such a terrible place after all.

• • •

The portentous year 1914 opened quietly, as I remember. The first and second Balkan wars had occurred without my knowl-edge, and, I suspect, without the knowledge of most of my elders either. It was to be a portentous year for me, too, and not because of anything that was going to happen in Europe, so far, so very far, away. When the Austrian Archduke and his wife were as-sassinated in a country then called Serbia, this was news dis-tinctly subordinate to how Connie Mack's Athaletics had per-formed on that same June 28. My father seemed to be doing well on the *Telegraph*, although just what the job of religious editor was I didn't know and didn't care. I was too much inter-ested in myself to give much of a hang about my parents.

A year or so before, a single pubic hair had curled its way into existence, and now an imminent forest was creating a thin fuzz on my lower belly. Better than that, I had some evidence of prepotency. The orgasm of prepubescent masturbation amounted to something like a highly exalted sneeze, but now the orgasm was accompanied by a feeling of slight, fascinating, mysterious internal flow. Nothing *appeared*, but the feeling of flow gave rise to the fervent hope that my balls were on the verge of being useful as well as ornamental. And they were un-mistakably growing heavier; the scrotal sac was growing longer in response.

• • •

The year 1914 was portentous in even a finer way than that. Some happy destiny had led us for a month's vacation to Point

Pleasant, New Jersey, then a paradise. The Curtis House and Cottages were just that—an old farmhouse, with a parlor, containing an insane upright piano, and a huge dining-room-pantry-kitchen complex. The upstairs had been chopped into about eight double rooms, with, at the end of a long corridor, one bathroom dragged only partially out of the nineteenth century. This room was strictly for bathing (infrequent) and defecating; after all, every room was equipped in the most modern way with pitcher, washbasin and slop jar.

The grounds were enchanting, for six or seven one-family cottages made an L around the farmhouse, and two patches of lawn with bald spots on them and a net between proclaimed them tennis courts. Across the road there was an occasionally tended six-hole golf course.

The location of all this was perfect—a fact attested to when, a decade ago, I tried to seek it out and discovered every vestige gone and the acreage surrounded by a high ornate brick wall, now obviously enclosing a wealthy man's estate. And why not? The ocean was only ten minutes distant (by Model T Ford), and the southern bank of the Manasquan River, just before it gave in to the sea, was a five-minute ramble through woods to "the dock." So there was sea bathing, yachting and canoeing on the Manasquan, a noble stream, bicycling on the red-dirt Jersey roads, ramblings through the woods and all that one could ask for, plus a sudden, heaven-sent miracle—Girls!

Girls hit me with such a bang at age fifteen that I still grow a little breathless over it more than half a century later. There I was, one June day after lunch, sitting in a wooden porch swing attached by creaky iron links to the rafters and listening to the vivacious chatter of Miss Constance Curtis, fair and comely, with her hair already "put up"; a year older than I but not using this lamentable disparity to make me feel inferior. Suddenly a scepter touched her and transformed her from Girl into Goddess, she all unknowing. My reaction was instantaneous. I left the swing, dashed upstairs and began scrubbing my face and hands. I must have emptied three basins of filthy water into the slop jar before I was satisfied. Then I began to turn things upside down hunting for a brush and comb. Something had to be done about my tangled and matted hair, and I had to get back to Constance as fast as possible. My mother was in our room at the time, and her instinct must have told her that my hetero-sexual life had begun five minutes ago. She laughed, and it was a loving laugh but, damn it, it was also compassionate. She tried to hug me, but I wanted none of this: I wanted to be back with Constance, and in a flash I was.

Nothing had changed. She was still in the swing and she was still a Goddess. Things were plain to me now; girls existed to bring, by nothing more than their existence, joy and meaning into the lives of boys. That girls might entertain similar feelings toward boys did not then occur to me; this was to be Lesson B, and not to be very well learned when its time was to come. Meanwhile, O the tragedy of the wasted years! I had it bad.

• • •

Constance, to make matters better—or worse—had a younger sister, Hester, just my age, with chestnut hair that hung down her back almost to her waist. The Curtis girls, with an elder brother (another ne'er-do-well) and their parents, lived in sum-mer in the biggest of the cottages, directly across the quadrangle from the farmhouse. Their father, a dignified old gentleman with a limp, was a country lawyer who daily rode to his one-room office on a bicycle path through the woods. (The woods were everywhere; we had not yet begun destroying America.) Momma was frankly, openly, dotty; mostly sitting in silence, with occa-sional bursts of laughter, meaningless conversation or sudden abuse; I suppose a modern diagnosis would be schizophrenia. A Catholic priest had thought his ministrations might do good. Mrs. Curtis was converted but not otherwise changed, and brought her two young daughters devoutly into the bosom of the Church with her. Of the two, Constance was somewhat the prettier, slightly more brainy and definitely the more partial to me. So of course I fell madly in love with Hester, but without ceasing to love Constance either.

• • •

The world was thereafter, for quite a while, a different place. Not only did the Cosmic Plan stand revealed, the Earth had shifted its axis and the Universe had expanded. (In this discovery I thus anticipated Sir James Jeans, Sir Arthur Eddington and

93

numerous other deep thinkers, whose works I was to come on later.)

Here, writing as an old man, I am forced into the use of an old-fashioned dirty word. The word is "purity." Although I was "in love" with Constance and Hester, and they with me, I dared to think, I never made the slightest attempt to embrace them, to hold hands with them, to put my arm around either girl's waist. As for trying to kiss either one of them, this would have been to defile the Goddess-Girl. Of course I had the wildest night-time sexual fantasies about them, Hester particularly. But this was adolescent love, pure, if not simple. And it went on for three more summers. There were plenty of other boys and girls about, and we all played tennis, swam and sailed together. We even went, in a fleet, on canoe trips together, up the Manasquan above "the Island," where it all of a sudden narrowed to a twisting rocky, rushing stream, crisscrossed with fallen tree trunks and other portage hazards. The objective was to get as far as the "deserted village" of Allaire, the only remains of which, in 1914, was the wreck of an old water wheel. There and back was an all-day excursion, strenuous and exciting. All this part of New Jersey in those days was primitive, the nearest incursion of anything smacking of Commerce being the New Jersey truck farms. The ocean beach had a half-mile boardwalk and a few shacks of bathhouses. My last summer at Point Pleasant with the Curtis girls was 1917, and I wish, for romance's sake, I had never gone back. When I did (long after), en route elsewhere, the tiny village of Brielle had flourished into a yacht-club establishment, Point Pleasant Beach was a minor-league Coney Island, steel bridges spanned the river in place of the old wooden draws—in short, my youth had been destroyed. I resented these evidences more than the slow degeneration of my own physical body.

• • •

In the midst of the rest of youth surrounding us, the two Curtis girls and I formed an unshakable trio. In the summertimes we were constantly and joyously happy; in the wintertimes we wrote one another long letters. I formed the conviction, not to desert me until I was in college, that when I grew up Hester and I would marry and, because she was a devout Catholic, would have nine children. I didn't want, even at age fifteen, to be the father of nine children. Neither of the Curtis girls was of the flirtatious or boy-teasing type. This was fortunate, for if they had been I think I would have gone crazy. In the secret honoring of my love for Hester I once abstained from masturbation for ten days before I caved in. But outwardly we three remained simple, tennis-playing, sailing, bathing and canoeing playmates of innocence undefiled. It was simple acute shyness and a deep conviction of my physical unattractiveness that held *me* back. Another factor in our strange stability was that, I think it must be confessed, we were three bright kids, and enjoyed being bright together.

• • •

War had been declared in Europe, of course, and Sir Edward Grey had made his famous, ominous and all-too-true statement about the lamps of Europe. President Wilson had issued his famous plea to Americans "to be neutral in thought as well as deed," and nothing was easier for a sex-obsessed adolescent.

But in 1914, it seemed, it was pretty easy for everyone. The Curtis House clientele was *not* the boardinghouse clientele that my mother so despised and my father and I suffered in silence. My father's salary must have risen to some such scale as forty dollars a week; otherwise how could we be in the company of such important people as a real live editor, Karl Edwin Harriman (of *Red Book*), and his family, or T. S. Sullivant, whose animal drawings in the old *Life* were famous, or Guy Pène du Bois and his family? Sullivant, an endlessly industrious pen-and-ink illustrator, was a formidable Irishman, with a hair-trigger temper, who used to, occasionally, in the dining room, hurl his laden plate face downward on the floor in protest at the meals, which were vile; an interesting scene never failed to develop thereafter. Guy Pène du Bois was of a much more equable temperament. I did not know of his eminence, which was then perhaps only growing, and was thus unawed when he would take me on for tennis. (I could give him a fairly good game.) A Houghton, of Houghton, Mifflin, no less, joined his family in one of the cottages every weekend. This was pretty high company, after all; my parents and I were still shabby-genteel, but we had somehow moved up a notch and—very important—the penury of a clergyman's family was here understood and allowed for.

And none of these imposing adults seemed at all concerned about the war, except a Mr. Oliver, a banker, who was in a state of agitation because the New York Stock Exchange had been closed.

• • •

A small chip fell off my Innocence, thank God, as the fate-laden summer wore to a close. A new girl, Virgilia, and her parents arrived for a fortnight's stay. She was dark and picturesque and wore picture hats. The other girls did not like her, which should have told me something, but didn't. Unlike the "wholesome" out-of-doorsy girls, apparently unconcerned about sex, Virgilia had one predominate interest, and it was boys. Whether because I was the nearest available boy, or whether I somehow attracted her, I could not tell—except that I could not credit the latter. Yet there we were, in late evening, blessedly alone, in that wooden porch swing with the creaky iron links. I ached to as much as hold her hand, but I was too cowardly. In a moment I was given a lesson that, alas, I did not really learn till later: when a boy is too shy to give a girl attention, and the girl would like it, she waits a decorous period and then *she* makes the advance—protected in her own self-esteem (I am surmising, of course) by her "instinct to mother" the forlorn or helpless.

In any event, my head was shortly in Virgilia's lap, and her hand was gently stroking my cheek. A ton of paralyzing ice fell off me, and in a moment we were out of the swing and into a hammock where at last we embraced; I kissed her, first on the cheek, then, when she was far from objecting, on the mouth.

I thought my heart would burst. But there was another factor, also, to contend with. I had an erection. How horrible, I thought, if Virgilia would become aware, for our bodies were close. I was still too dense to realize that *if* Virgilia had perceived anything the probabilities were high that she would have been gratified by this proof of her feminine power of arousal. The question of what to do next was all too easily solved; a step was heard on the porch floor. We sprang out of the hammock, pulled ourselves together and decorously bade good night to Mr. Raber, the manager, who was making his final rounds.

Virgilia and her family were due to leave next morning. With a new-found courage I planned to take her for a farewell stroll through the woods to the river, "Kiss her parting lips as her waist I gathered slow," and then . . . .

So in the morning I did indeed take Virgilia for a stroll, but when it came time to make George Meredith's lovely image real, I could not convince myself that last night had ever happened and it was obvious that Virgilia was not going to take the first step the second time. So we said halting, clumsy, awkward goodbys and parted—not quite forever.

Alone, despite cursing myself for lily-livered cowardice, my heart remained slightly above the water line. After all, at age fifteen, I had for the first time in my life kissed a living, breathing girl, and she had kissed back. I did not know how long it would be before I kissed another.

11 · THE HORRORS OF WAR, OR, THE SALE OF EDDIE COLLINS

BACK IN PHILADELPHIA, the autumn began inauspiciously. The newspapers were giving some attention to the war, and apparently the headlines were proclaiming that Von Kluck's drive on Paris was failing under Allied counterattacks. But the general tone of America toward this European holocaust was best expressed, I think, by a paragraph from the *Telegraph*'s daily, anonymous humorist: "If the Allies keep on checking Von Kluck, he'll begin to look like an actor's trunk."

All in all, a much more serious situation was brewing at Shibe Park. Connie Mack's Athaletics had won the American League championship again, but earlier, in Boston, a nasty situation had arisen. The National League's Boston Braves, in last place in mid-July, had undergone a spurt, unknown in baseball until the Mets of 1969, that had carried them to the top of the pile by September's end and won the National League pennant. This was all very well, but when the Braves' braggart manager, George Stallings, announced to the whole United States that his bedraggled ex-last-placers would win the World Series from the A's in four straight games, Philadelphia denounced the upstart in much the same language that Theodore Roosevelt had been using in stating his opinions of President Woodrow Wilson. And quite rightly. Yet that is exactly what the upstart's team did, in October 1914, in the eleventh World Series ever to be played.

Philadelphia went numb with shock. It was nice that Paris had been saved from the Germans—but *this!* The tragedy was over, yet a sense of foreboding still hung over the city. And with cause. On one grim Philadelphia afternoon the newspapers were bannering the incredible news: "CONNIE MACK SELLS EDDIE COLLINS."

98

It was the beginning of the end. Connie Mack was breaking up his $100,000 infield. In fact, he was breaking up the entire championship ball club that had so suddenly and inexplicably disgraced him and Philadelphia, and was to begin anew. A thing like that, one never gets over. I haven't.

• • •

About this time, the Philadelphia *Telegraph* fired my father. I knew something was amiss in the household that day, but not what, until my mother said gravely that evening, "Daddy has lost his position." I was full of anxious questions. Would we have to leave Miss Cashew's? Yes. Would I have to leave Episcopal? Probably. What would we do? Well . . . .

As it turned out we did have to leave Miss Cashew's and landed up in a rooming house in North Philadelphia, which was a slum even in those days. And I did have to leave Episcopal, although not right away. My two most terrible fears, so terrible I could not voice them, were that my links to the Trautwines and to Point Pleasant would be broken. As things were to turn out, they were not. My father was able to find a reasonable succession of temporary jobs while hunting for a permanent one. But our Philadelphia days were numbered.

My father's inability to hold a steady job, other than a parochial one, might suggest that he was lazy or stupid or had a personality no one could get on with or even that he took an occasional nip from the bottle. But none of these things was true. He was hard-working, conscientious, affable and of steady habit. He was even learned, not that that counted for much. But he was a door mat on which anyone could wipe his shoes. So everyone did. While loving him I also vowed that I would not be like him. It took some doing, for like him I could never achieve a sustained faith in myself, despite some tenaciously held opinions on this or that. "I love you," a sweet young lady once said to me, "but you're a son of a bitch." So to *some* extent, I had succeeded.

• • •

Eventually, my father got a job as news editor of *The Church-man*, which meant, to my mother's delight, our removal to New York. I can remember our arrival in Jersey City, on January 15, 1915, with our belongings packed in four bulging straw suit-

99

cases, and our passage under the Hudson in "The Tubes," which smelled then as they still do, and our winding up at Miss Proudfoot's Boarding House—which sounds like something invented by David Graham Phillips but unfortunately was real. It ran between West 57th and 58th streets, hard by Columbus Circle. My parents had a basement room on 57th Street; my cubbyhole was on the top floor of the 58th Street side. Here began two ghastly years. Once again my status as a clergyman's son made me eligible for entrance into Trinity School, Class of 1917. Trinity is an old, fine, distinguished school and I have nothing to say against it except that I hated it. At P.E.A. my grades were good if not spectacular; at Trinity, they fell with a crash, and for many reasons. The least of these was that I entered in midterm; thus, everybody knew everybody else, and I was the sole stranger. The greatest of these was Mr. Victor M. Fitch-Bonsall, Master of English. He is long ago dead and to my intense regret, not at my hands. Doubtless it is unhealthy as well as un-Christian to hold a murderous wish in your heart, more than half a century later, toward someone the Lord has many years ago already seen fit to summon, but I do, I do, I do.

At Episcopal, in Philadelphia, dear old Pinky Anderson, as I have said, offered me latitude and encouragement in the childish themes I wrote for him. Quite beyond recapture lie my preteen thoughts about what I would someday "do" when I grew up, but I must have had them and they must have somehow involved writing, for it was in composition that I felt most natively at home. So I started out, with my only reference point Pinky Anderson, to compose the required weekly themes in the same spirit for Trinity's Mr. Bonsall. (It was the American custom in dealing with hyphenate names to use only the latter half, to my mother's violent disapproval.) I don't remember what my subject was, but I treated it with the kind of levity that had pleased Pinky. And there will always be graven on my memory the sudden, thunderous devastating demolition Mr. Bonsall accorded me. He was really angered. "You're new here," he said. "You'd better learn *right now* we don't write themes in that fashion in this class. I want no more of that sort of thing again, ever! Grade, Zero. Next boy."

Here was a kind of public rebuke and humiliation I had never suffered before. I was not the bright kid Pinky Anderson and

100

Mr. Trautwine, in their several ways, had thought me. Once again I was a bumpkin and a boob, a mockery of a human being. A more thorough and complete devastation and destruction of a student by a "teacher" could not be imagined.

This catastrophe roughly coincided with my sixteenth birthday. In all New York, where I had now lived for less than two months, I had not one friend. Confiding in my parents was not to be dreamed of; it was something to recoil from. I was hopelessly and permanently cut off from all human society, the outcast of outcasts. My father, anxious and insecure in his new job, was too abstracted to give me anything more than the most casual notice; my mother was herself so sunk in self-pity and hypochondrial ill-health as seldom to emerge except into occasional fits of fury at something or other. "I have nourished a viper in my bosom" she burst out at me in Sarah Bernhardt style over something or other. This was just what I needed.

• • •

My Trinity grades went down and down in all subjects. I was sunk in an adolescent lethargy from which I could find no escape. It was mildly encouraging to see in the hallways of Trinity a familiar face, that of André Mesnard, whom I had known at Episcopal, but since he was a Vesper and I was an Aurora we scarcely knew each other. The teachers at Trinity—always with the exception of Mr. Bonsall, in my own mind—were kind and good and of a competence quite equal to those at Episcopal. It made no difference. Day after day, following a miserable morning and lunch (the school day ended at 1:30 P.M.), I would walk home, swearing by every oath I knew that *this* afternoon would be different and that I would really study next day's lessons, hard.

And in the solitude of my fourth-floor room at Miss Proudfoot's I would begin earnestly enough. But nothing is quite as infirm as adolescent resolve, and I was mired hub-deep in caramels and self-abuse and there was no truck or tugboat to pull me out. Parents *are* useless or worse during the ages of fifteen and sixteen. I terribly needed a Mr. Myers or a Mr. Trautwine, but I had lost them both. As for falling back on my own resources, this was, in a simile Stephen Leacock was yet to compose, "like falling back on a cucumber frame." As for my apparently unconquerable

101

vice, I was two-drops potent now, which made things both better and worse, for following the climax there would be a few moments of blessed peace and tranquillity, but as they faded I would be overcome by guilt and shame. Doubtless I was headed for the insanity my mother had some years earlier predicted for me, but I had the minor satisfaction of knowing her wrong about "early death." At age sixteen it was already too late for that.

12 · SCIENCE AND THE ARTS, OR, "MYSTERY AND CLEVERNESS"

THERE MUST HAVE BEEN something more to my life than that; in fact there was. Without adult help or guidance I discovered the New York Public Library (but not the Metropolitan Museum of Art; as for art galleries, they were obviously not for the likes of me). Among the open shelves of the vast and then uncrowded twin reading rooms I read an undifferentiated collection of masterpieces, miscellany and junk. But at least the junk was not such junk as *Silas Marner* or *The Mill on the Floss*, which we were fed in school. (My hatred for Mr. Bonsall ebbed a fraction when he said he thought *Silas Marner* was the worst book he had ever read, but that he was helpless; it was in the curriculum.) What was *not* in the curriculum was any author later than Robert Louis Stevenson; *Dr. Jekyll and Mr. Hyde* had apparently closed out English literature for good. Yet these were the very days when Shaw, Wells, Arnold Bennett, Kipling, Maugham and Conrad were not only alive but at the height of their powers. Nope, "never heard of 'em"—in school, that is. An even greater hush surrounded the Greats of earlier centuries, unless of course they were Sir Walter Scott or someone equally likely to bore the living ass off a twentieth-century reader of *any* age. The only "assigned" book I can remember reading with high interest and pleasure was Thackeray's *Vanity Fair*; Mr. Bonsall had forgotten to tell us it was a Masterpiece. (His definition of a masterpiece, by the way, being "a work combining Mystery and Cleverness.")

Thus in the New York Public Library I had to pick my own way, not knowing the difference between Tolstoy and Gene Stratton Porter. It didn't take too long to catch on, but a little help would have gone a long way. One day I came on two books side

103

by side, neither of them great, but each so fascinating to me that I must have reread them a dozen times, as young people are likely to when something really hits them. They were *On the Art of Writing* by Sir Arthur Quiller-Couch and *A Study of Versification* by Brander Matthews. The former in particular so fascinated me that for years thereafter I tracked down everything he had ever written or was in future to write or compile, including the *Oxford Book of English Verse* and the *Oxford Book of English Prose*. Thus, suddenly, in the midst of despair the Universe expanded again as, in the autumn of 1916, a miracle hit me.

• • •

About a year after Mr. Bonsall crushed me to death, I transferred out of the "classical" course into the "scientific" one. This brought me into sudden and wonderful contact with Mr. Sydney Ailmer-Small, Master of Physics and Chemistry. Mr. Small was the most wonderful teacher I had ever encountered: patient, humorous, human, and brimming over with the imparting gift. His manner was easier and more informal than any other Master, whether Trinity or Episcopal, and he called the boys by their nicknames. (Mine at the time was "Hodgie.") Nevertheless, the strictest order prevailed in his classes; he did not decree it, as Mr. Bonsall, or demand it, like "The Harp" (Julius Adenaw, Master of French), he merely expected it, and it was given. You could ask him anything, and he had a good, perhaps even a discursive answer, but he could not be derailed; in fact, nobody tried it. He was too obviously interested in what he was doing: *teaching*. And he had the born teacher's knack of finding something immediately at hand—a piece of chalk, length of string—to illustrate what he was talking about. I never knew whether *he* knew I was a wounded bird, but it didn't matter.

The miracle was not just that my marks shot upward in Mr. Small's classes; they rose markedly in all of them—even Mr. Bonsall's—and ambition was reborn in me. The two top sharks of the senior class scientific section were going to go to M.I.T.— could *I* aspire to this then toughest of all universities? I consulted Mr. Small, who pursed his lips, cocked his head to one side, thought a moment and then said, "If you work very hard to make up for lost time—yes!"

104

• • •

Holy Mother of God! Mr. Small actually thought I might be able to make it. Mr. Small went on talking about boys and colleges, and here a reminder is due that no so-called educational explosion had taken place in 1916; anybody could go anywhere he liked provided only that he could pass the tests of the College Entrance Examination Board, which were tough, but not unscalable, mountain peaks. "Now you take a boy like Black," said Mr. Small; "he's a nice kid, and his marks are fair, but he just shouldn't go to college at all. When he graduates from here, which he will without much trouble, he should just go out and find himself a job; he simply isn't college material."

That kind of talk today would be regarded as heretical, anti-democratic, discriminatory, anti-civil-rights and Racist, but Mr. Small held, in 1916, the view, now in 1970 held defamatory, that higher education should be for people who showed promise of being able to profit from it. And Mr. Small thought I was material for M.I.T.! Mr. Bonsall had effectively indicated that the doors of the life literary were closed to me, but now another, quite different door, while not exactly open, was at least ajar.

The result was that last year's human wreck, interested in nothing save self-pity, was transformed into a student who could not be torn from his books. I forswore everything except getting ready for the next day, week, month, whatever the challenge.

In the second half of the year, Mr. Small singled out the class's top shark and me. "How would you two like to stay after school on Friday afternoons and do some extra experiments in the chem lab?" Would we just. Imagine being *privileged* to stay after school!

"Here are two chunks of something. Use your blowpipes with the Bunsen burner and tell me what element or elements you think you can identify. Here's another chunk. Is the material organic or inorganic?" Lester Stanley Champion and I, in our laboratory aprons, those Friday afternoons, would not have traded places with Count Rumford.

• • •

In the Trinity Class of 1917, there was a chubby adolescent who stood out from his fellows mainly because, alone among us, he wore a derby hat. Alone among us, also, he was to achieve international fame, for it happened his name was Humphrey Bogart. But in the spring of 1917 his name was mud. This was no fault of his own; he had come down with scarlet fever and we were all quarantined at just the time we should have been sweating it out for our College Boards. And the Class of 1917 was thrown into further confusion for President Wilson's 1915 post-*Lusitania* speech, "There is such a thing as a man being too proud to fight," had by April 1917 been transmuted into the American mission to make the world "safe for democracy," and the United States was in the war. Some of the seniors wanted to enlist—an inclination the faculty did its best to discourage.

I presented no problem. The Army and Navy were pretty choosy about whom they wanted in their ranks, those days. The concept of "warm bodies" belongs to World War II; in World War I they would have nothing to do with you if you wore glasses; you would be "helpless in the field."

But as to my going to M.I.T., a problem presented itself: there was no money. Although I had graduated third in my class, just behind the two sharks who *did* go to M.I.T., I had most inconveniently flunked one College Board exam—in freehand drawing—and was thus one credit short of M.I.T.'s requirement. Mr. Small again provided wise counsel: go to Cornell for a year, make a good freshman record and then transfer. But there was no money for that, either.

This idea of Mr. Small's was a master stroke for it gave me an idea. John C. Trautwine, III, was a Cornell alumnus; maybe he would give a Cornell aspirant a job for a year to earn some money. I wrote him. It turned out that he would. So I would leave New York, leave my parents, and go back to Philadelphia. An independent life was about to begin. It had been a long time in coming.

13 · WEST ACROSS THE SCHUYLKILL, OR, THE SILVER CORD BROKEN

TODAY, AS AN OLD MAN, I confess to being deeply hurt by the indifference and neglect I so often encounter at the hands of my own children. Yet as I set down these recollections I am bound in honesty to record the joy, the absolute *joy*, with which I cut loose from my own parents when I was eighteen. Of course, there were a few differences. When I cut loose from my parents this included cutting loose financially as well as in other ways. Thus I was shortly to experience not only the joy of personal independence but also the joy, as it then was, of being self-supporting.

In the realest of real senses, it was a forced decision. Between 1911 and 1917 my father's earning power had risen from twenty-five dollars a week on the Philadelphia *Telegraph* to forty-five dollars a week as news editor of *The Churchman* in New York. But just as I was graduating from Trinity my father got fired from this job, too. The editor in chief of *The Churchman* in those days was the Reverend Charles K. Gilbert, later to become the Right Reverend Charles K. Gilbert, Bishop of New York, and his way of letting my father know he was fired was to write a news item announcing that a young clergyman from the Middle West, the Reverend Guy Emery Shipler, would shortly take over the post of news editor; my father learned of his fate only when he read it in galley proof. If this proves, as I think it does rather conclusively, that one quality not necessary to becoming a bishop is moral courage or direct dealing, I think it also sadly proved my father's almost total lack of talent for journalism. The Reverend Mr. Shipler, who succeeded my father in 1917, went onward and upward in *The Churchman*, eventually not only becoming the editor in chief but transforming it from a pallid and spineless jellyfish of invertebrate Christianity to a courageous and crusading magazine that not only reported religious news but *made* it by espousing views and causes that were in the very forefront of the social thought of the day. All hail Dr. Shipler. His reign was long and brilliantly successful: he knew what his convictions were and he had the courage of them. And my unfortunate father had, of these attributes, neither.

• • •

So it was from a passive father and a raging and desperate mother that I was taking my leave. I remember telling my father of my decision that I was going to study to be an engineer. He considered the news gravely for a moment and then said, "Oh. I had always rather hoped that you would want to go into journalism." And I remember also, and vividly still, that this was the only moment of true rage I ever felt against my father. I suppressed it because, damn it, with all his faults and failings, I loved him and did not want to hurt him. But within me there raged the sentiment, "Then, goddamn it, why didn't you ever *say* anything?" For he never, never had. Throughout all my years so far, I had looked toward my father for cues and guidance and received none; from my mother I got a huge surfeit that I had not asked for, placed no value on and did not want. This was the home, these were the parents, I was leaving. I wish, even now, that I could pump up a little sentiment about it, but there is none to pump.

• • •

Geographically I wasn't going very far, or to a strange place. Nor was I to be friendless, for in addition to the Trautwines, father and son, there were Dr. and Mrs. Hitchins. Four more devoted elder friends a young man never had—*effectively* devoted. They must, I think, have sensed the size of the emotional deficit that existed between my parents and myself and deliberately set out to fill it. All through my youth, as I look back on it now, I was being helped and encouraged by elders to whom I was in no way related, who had no motives for their kindness except the kindness itself. I *think* I must have been a bright boy, and when I italicize that word it is not out of a modesty that would be ridiculous with boyhood now more than half a century gone by, but out of a bewilderment equally long. I was never brilliant scholastically; I was bookish but not bookwormish. I had neither good looks nor easy manners. I *did* have the typical Irish trick of being able to catch on fast, use terminology correctly when I didn't *really* understand it, and a memory well above average. And—I blush to confess it to any modern youth—I was *interested*. So far as I can remember I was interested in everything, which is just the wrong thing to be now—and does of course have the obverse that there's nothing very deep about you—but it was quite the right thing to be when the country was, like myself, still in its teens, when all knowledge was accessible and the perfectibility of man was beyond question. So at a guess, it was qualities like these that caused older people to befriend me.

• • •

Well, whatever my qualities were, I took them to West Philadelphia. The Market Street subway had to turn into "the elevated" to cross the even-then stinking Schuylkill River and remained so all the way to its then terminus at 69th Street. I found a boardinghouse at 56th and Walnut streets, or more accurately I found a storybook Irish family named Kelly that had a house that had "a room" that Mrs. Kelly would rent to an applicant who could pass her exacting standards. Himself was a teetotaling, God-fearing nonunion carpenter who even then must have made much more money than my father, for Mrs. Kelly's food was ample and luscious and Mr. Kelly's house smelled of lovingly oiled woods and the freshest of fresh laundry. Mrs. Kelly was always in her kitchen, and Himself, by the time I usually got home, was already sawing and planing away in the cellar for a cabinet "to go, you know, in that place in the hall"—for when I called Himself merely a carpenter I did him an injury: he was a *ship's* carpenter. For my comfortable room I paid $3.50 a week—"Unless you think that would be asking too much," Mrs. Kelly had said. (Mrs. Kelly had taken an immediate shine to me for a shocking reason I'll reveal in a moment.) At $3.50 a week, which I did not think too much, meals were obviously *non compris*, but if the weather was cold when I was going out in the morning, "It wouldn't do to let you go out without a cup of coffee," and this often expanded into a pair of fried eggs, bacon, biscuits, and a glass of milk. Similarly on a cold evening I might be thought to need a cup of hot chocolate "and a piece of pie that'll just go to waste if you don't eat it." No money arrangements for this canteen were ever discussed. I was away from home and Mrs. Kelly was mothering me, along with her six- and four-year-old colleen daughters; to have suggested pay would have been a monstrous breach of manners. Memory's gauzy film has probably softened a few edges here, but I wonder what the neighborhood of 56th and Walnut is like now. A festering slum, a ghetto, a trysting spot for junkies? When I lived there (through the coldest winter and the hottest summer in Philadelphia history), it was a frontier, an outpost. Philadelphians who lived east of the Schuylkill made topical jokes about the "Middle West." But the supposed boon of the subway-L really rapid transit was new, so there were still almost as many vacant lots as there were houses. Trees abounded; street traffic was a major domestic focus of war activity because of the shipbuilding at Hog Island; you were perhaps more likely to hear the clop-clop of horseshoes than the rattle of the Tin Lizzie.

Philadelphia had its Negro problem in 1917 and whites were pretty sore about it, except that I'm sure they didn't use the word "problem," and they didn't know whom they were sore at. The growing Negro slum was then tightly confined to South Philadelphia; if you were white you didn't feel quite comfortable south of Lombard Street, day or night. But it was hard to say whether this was because you feared bodily harm (probably not) or hostile looks (probably) or because you couldn't bear to see what you were looking at (most probable). That *North* Philadelphia would one day be an unparalleled Negro slum was unthinkable. North Philadelphia was deeply depressing in 1917, but it was entirely white depressing. It stretched as far as the eye could see, and each side of every street was lined with machine-made little double houses, every one complete with gabled roof, front porch and a semipermeable septum of lath and plaster dividing family from family. But neat repair was what made the whole complex livable. Now that is gone and the result is The Jungle—*perhaps* not the worst but almost certainly the most extensive Negro slum in any American city. In the days of my father's tenure on the Philadelphia *Telegraph* a bouncy little streetcar used to take me through this endless neighborhood to reach Shibe Park, where Cornelius McGillicuddy's Athaletics used to play their flawless baseball. But, my heart having been broken by their rout of 1914, already described, I never went there again.

Besides, I was too busy at my job with the Trautwines. Mrs. Kelly's solicitude for me became more and more evident as the autumn deepened and the weather grew sharp. She did not know anything about how I earned the money out of which I gave her her $3.50 a week. For an Irish lady she was very quiet and self-restrained, but one evening in the warm kitchen she overcame these qualities enough to ask me. I told her I was working to earn money to go to college. She thought that was wonderful. And what did I want to be when I got out?

"An engineer," I told her.

"Oh." There was such manifest disappointment in her voice that I couldn't leave the conversation there, so I began to describe, in what must have been condescending teen-age terms, the social value of the engineer, as it had been revealed to me.

"It's not that I don't think highly of the profession," said Mrs. Kelly.

"Maybe you don't think I'd make a good one?"

"Oh, I'd never say that," said Mrs. Kelly. "But here I've been thinking of you in another profession altogether. And Himself agrees with me. We've talked about it and we think you'd be perfect for it."

This was fascinating. I'd had no idea I'd been the subject of family concern for my future.

"And what do you and Mr. Kelly think I should be?" I asked. It was not an idle question, for at eighteen, despite the Trautwines, I was just as hazy about my life's future as anyone else.

Mrs. Kelly drew a breath and a seraphic smile suffused her.

"A *priest*, Mr. Hodgins! Oh, you'd make a wonderful priest!"

14 · THIRD, OR, RUINED BY DRY CELLS

THE OFFICES of the Trautwine Company were at 257 South 4th Street, a slightly seedy neighborhood in extreme downtown Philadelphia, with priceless architectural and other relics of colonial days neglected, run-down, and scattered all about. The Trautwines, father and son, were supremely suspicious not just of the capitalist system but of the most ordinary business enterprise. The original Trautwine's famous civil engineering *Pocket Book* had gone through nineteen editions in thirty-five years, had sold 150,000 copies, and was now being shamelessly imitated in the then burgeoning fields of mechanical and electrical engineering. These were the days when it was still possible to cram the essentials of these engineering arts into handbooks, which were, however, getting to be three inches thick in $3'' \times 7''$ format, printed mostly in 6-point type. In short, "Trautwine," as it was inevitably known, had been a gold mine for the better part of these fifty years and during most of this time had been published in America by the illustrious firm of John Wiley & Sons and in England by Chapman & Hall. But the Wiley firm did next to nothing "useful" in Mr. Trautwine, Jr.'s socialist view of things, collected most of the swag, and paid the Trautwine author-editors a mere "royalty" on sales. So around 1912 the Trautwines took their book away from Wiley and became their own publishers, taking on all the jobs of contracting for paper, printing, binding and distribution, in addition to all the writing and editorial necessities. And for a while, dear old Mr. Trautwine, Jr., the Fabian Socialist turned entrepreneur, made a pretty good go of things. There were just two little troubles: the large sums of money to be saved by junking the "parasitical" publishers turned out not to be quite so large as theoretical calculations had foreshadowed;

and the jobs of manufacturing and distribution took up so much time that the business of editing fell farther and farther behind schedule. Sales began to languish a little in consequence; the book was slowly getting out of date. The little company didn't have the credit resources of John Wiley & Sons either.

• • •

And there was another problem, a problem independent of time, place, occupation or any other external variable. This was the eternal problem of father-and-son. I think I have sufficiently described the kindly and bearded John C. Trautwine, Jr., utterly benevolent and fearsomely Radical. To describe his son and only child, John C. Trautwine, III, is extremely difficult, for he was a genius.

Third, as he was universally known, had graduated from Cornell as a civil engineer in 1900, which means he must have been about twenty years older than I. Where his father was open and amiable, Third was darkly brooding, shy and suspicious. There existed in him that strange affinity so often encountered, the affinity between engineering and music: he played the violin and viola with much more than amateur skill. And he was a mine of ideas, all of which he had too soon. Since Third's father was not only receptive to all these ideas but had placed his son in command of the little company, it was a complete mystery why Third hated him, but hate him he did. Since I liked them both, and they were both more than kind to me, I often felt sadly torn, for I early learned that the way to create high vexation in Third was to say something kind about his father. A real revved-up dynamically oriented psychoanalyst could have no end of fun with all this, for in addition Third's mother was a truly beautiful old lady: soft gray hair framing an ethereal face, calm, reposeful and as quiet as her lovely voice. Third hated her, too. He was much in love with his first cousin, whom Mrs. Trautwine in her turn detested. "She's everything he loathes in everybody else," she said to me one day, not dispassionately. And indeed that was how she seemed to me, too. Through whatever resolution of forces, Third never married, and Mary MacManus died an old maid. "Cousins shouldn't marry."

It was Third who introduced me to a literary curiosity: Arnold Bennett's *How to Live on Twenty-Four Hours a Day*. The reason it was a curiosity was that Arnold Bennett had written it: it reads (although the prose is lots better) like a collaboration between Dale Carnegie and Elbert Hubbard. And I well remember its opening lines: "There are some men who are much more capable of loving a machine than of loving a woman. They are among the happiest men in the world."

The author's next sentence was an instant disclaimer that this was intended to be a nasty remark about womankind; it was merely that there were certain *lasting* satisfactions in tinkering with a machine that tinkering with a woman would not provide. And I think it was by no accident that this book so enthralled Third, who was not a particularly bookish man. For Third *was* in love with machines—deeply, passionately. Eventually they ruined him, just as women or drink ruin other kinds of men.

For a first example: Third, the violinist, could not play the piano. But he owned a 1907 player piano and was mightily (and quite correctly) dissatisfied with the pumper's inability to control its dynamics, except in the crudest way. So he invented, and eventually got a patent on, the Trautwine Shader. The Trautwine Shader permitted the piano pumper individual control of the force with which any one of the eighty-eight hammers would strike any one of the eighty-eight strings: *forte, mezzo forte, piano*. This involved, however, the ability to manipulate eighty-eight tiny three-position valve handles, affixed just in front of the keyboard. To learn to play the Trautwine Shader conscientiously thus required a higher order of practice and discipline than determining to be a concert pianist in the first place, so the invention never found a ready market. But I used to marvel at the prototype machine, abandoned in a dusty back room—a tangle of brittle-dry rubber tubings of very small bore, and dust-plugged auxiliary brass tracker bars, and other paraphernalia of a dream from which the dreamer has been awakened by an unfortunate sound in the night.

Again: Third was rightfully dissatisfied with the copying processes available to the engineer in the early days of the century. The blueprint existed, of course, but not yet the photostat. Third got himself deeply involved in the LeClercq Black Line Process, and in so doing hovered for a while on the ragged edge of Discovery. The Black Line Process gave highly defined reproductions of the India-ink work of engineering draftsmen, and with a few

114

different twists and turns of luck, and better timing—plus enough money—might just conceivably have turned into a progenitor of Xerox, as the Haloid Process did half a century later. But it didn't. The point is that Third was angry—that's the right word—about the deficiencies of blueprints and carbon paper well before World War I and tried to do something about it. And if he was not the inventor of the now-universal vertical filing system for offices, will the real innovator please stand up?

•　•　•

There were no electric clocks in the teens of the century. Third thought there ought to be. This was a tough one, for alternating current was not universal; there was no such thing as a small, reliable, self-starting synchronous motor. Even if there had been, the voltages and frequencies that emanated from powerhouses were far from constant. There were, however, large wall clocks whose minute hands could be notched up every sixty seconds by an electrical pulse delivered to a solenoid. Third bought half a dozen and put one in every room in the offices, so wired that the first clock would activate the second, and so around home, on the falling-domino principle. It would be about ten seconds before the last clock would respond to the initial impulse from the first. But where was the initial impulse to come from? That was easy: from a combination of an eight-day grandfather's clock of chronometer accuracy and about a dozen Eveready dry cells, which in those days were each about as big as two stacked Campbell's soup cans. Third hitched a make-break electrical contact to grandfather's second-hand wheel so that every time the second hand reached thirty the contact would close and one tick later open again. The cycle commenced.

But how did it end? It ended with the "chek clok." (Third was an ardent believer in Simplified Spelling, and the 20th Edition was so spelled.) This, like grandfather, was a spring-driven chronometer and it, too, was electrically wired—wired so that if the impulse from the last solenoid clock reached it more than fifteen seconds late an electrical contact would be broken and red warning arms would rise diagonally across the face of every clock in the system. One of my jobs was to supervise, maintain and repair this system, for which there was absolutely no need, and I loved it.

115

• • •

How much was I paid? I can't *exactly* remember, for I was paid by the fractions of an hour. On every employee's desk was a register: a mahogany box with two rows of six buttons labeled "Editorial," "System," "Manufacturing," "Distribution," "Nonproductive," etc. Whenever you were at work one of those buttons had to be pushed in. These boxes were connected into the electric clock system and inside every box was that individual's "rate wheel." Every individual was known by a symbol, not by name. I was H9 because I was the ninth person whose name began with H to be employed by the Trautwine Company. Other fellow workers were B8, S4, M1 and W4. Mr. Trautwine, Jr., was of course T2 and Third was T3. (Third solved the problem of his mother; although not an employee she was T2.5.)

When I, as H9, punched in, the rate wheel in my register began slow revolutions. When one of its sparse spiked lugs engaged a contact *and* grandfather actuated the clock system, a counter in my register would notch up. I had thereby earned one cent. A whole bank of interconnected counters in Third's office could tell him at a glance who was (supposedly) working and at what. And every evening he would add, in varicolored inks, to the running graph of the month: so many pennies had been spent on Editorial, System, Manufacturing, etc. The main thing the graphs showed was the heavily disproportionate time spent by everyone except T2 on System, for System was forever breaking down, or T3 was further elaborating it. The day of reliable low-voltage electrical equipment simply hadn't arrived but Third was trying to force it. A bank of miniature traffic lights stood outside his office door; white meant enter, and when you did, a door trip changed the white to green, meaning to the next person, you may come in if you like but someone has got there before you, so think it over. And red meant what red always means. When you left, another door trip changed green or red back to white—except that Third had a controller handle on his desk by which he could override the door-trip mechanisms, and pilot lights to remind him of what he was doing. His rationale for all of this was that he had an extremely poor memory and needed these artificial aids to his fallibility. Actually, of course, his memory was highly tenacious. He was the arch type

116

of Arnold Bennett's machine lover, and since at the time so was I, I could not possibly have fallen into a happier milieu. But I was lucky in other ways as well. T2 gave me informal lessons in German, in the Morse code, and on the wheezy little parlor organ in his study, and this was fine. But finer still was the way in which I got my very first introduction to the processes of writing, editing, proofreading and an assortment of the printing arts.

15 · A DOSE OF CLAP, OR, WHERE IS MY WANDERING BOY?

I SAID A few pages back—and then sidetracked myself—that I didn't remember how much I got paid by the Trautwines. But dead reckoning will do it. I *do* remember that T2 as senior member of the firm got paid two cents a minute. (*Two cents a minute;* how wonderful to be in such economic command!) At an eight-hour day and a six-day week that came to $57.60 per week. And I remember something else: every Saturday morning one of my chores was to take a company check for seventy dollars, signed by T2, to the Provident Bank and Trust Company, 4th and Chestnut, and come back with the cash, which took care of the whole weekly payroll except for T2 and T3. My recollection is that sometimes I got almost as much as seventeen dollars out of this. Since I worked a ten-hour day and usually a seven-day week (not because I was exploited, but because I was fascinated) that seventeen dollars was for a little less than a seventy-hour week, and this must have meant I got paid one cent every other minute. A young man could save at a rate like that. Board, $3.50. Seven breakfasts per week (Automat—glass of milk and two dough-nuts), total: 70¢; seven lunches (Automat—ham sandwich, hot chocolate, piece of pie), total: $1.05; seven dinners (Y.M.C.A. cafeteria—*carte du jour*), total: $2.00; transportation and miscellaneous, total: 90¢. That came to less than half of my salary; even with slippage I could buy a ten-dollar Postal Savings Certificate almost every week. By putting in a twelve-hour day now and then I could save close to five hundred dollars in a year. And darned if I didn't! The movies were no temptation; the theater was beyond me; I had no girl. So to complete the budget I have given above I should have added: Recreation, two cents per day.

That was the cost of a towel at the Y.M.C.A.—15th and Arch streets.

• • •

Dr. Arthur Parker Hitchins, once my father's Junior Warden at the Morton church and head of the H. K. Mulford Laboratories in Glenolden, was now Lieutenant Colonel Hitchins (M.C.), U.S.A., based in Philadelphia. He was one more of the elder persons I've spoken of who was determined to make life easier and pleasanter for me. So was his still-beautiful wife. Dr. Hitchins was determined to introduce me to athletics. Despite his busy schedule, he said, "We're going to join the Y and play some handball." And we did. I had never played handball before, and what was more I had the shy, uncertain and guilt-ridden boy's fear of a locker room: a place where you stripped, ran around nude in and out of showers and were thrown into intimate contact with members of your own sex in some way that I found disturbing. I think Dr. Hitchins knew all that when he made his suggestion.

The Y, in the First World War, was a haven for young doughboys and gobs of our volunteer Army and Navy. Once again, the *innocence* of America half a century ago comes back to me vividly. A much heavier odor of sanctity clung to the Y in those days than does now, I imagine, and the staff was on the pious alert for transgressions. "Cigarettes are forbidden, Brother," said a red-haired Christlike young man behind the desk to a gob who had absent-mindedly lighted up a fag (the word was innocent of any other meaning in those days). The lobby of the Central Y in Philadelphia was quite large; every evening a professor from the University of Pennsylvania would lecture on English Literature to a crowd of eager young servicemen, undisturbed by the bustlings of lobby traffic in and out. I wish I could remember his name, for he was a gifted teacher and richly deserved the rapt attention he got. The movies you could see free in the basement were no worse than those you could see for twenty-five cents at a theater. (The day of the movie palace was just dawning; in New York the Rialto was the nearest thing to swank; the Rivoli and the Capitol were yet unbuilt; Philadelphia lagged far behind.)

And the Y had a library, too. It was a pretty dull library,

119

but it was a library, and a place of quiet. I remember that it was there that I first read Dr. Hugh Cabot's *What Men Live By*, which made a vast impression on my eighteen-year-old mind. There was no such thing as an Identity Crisis in those days, but the young men even then yearned for guidance, and most people or things or books failed them. Youth, by which I mean, at least momentarily, the eighteen-year-olds, was, I suspect, divided into the 3 per cent/97 per cent split that continues to characterize them—the 3 percent who knew exactly what they wanted to do or be and had known it all their conscious lives, and the 97 per cent who hadn't the vaguest idea—all the young Mr. Micawbers of the world. I had once belonged to the 3 per cent, so I had thought, only to be jarred out of it by the precious Mr. Bonsall of Trinity School. And I was unconsciously trying my hardest to get back into the 3 per cent even in the library of the Philadelphia Y.M.C.A.

A wise old Catholic Rector, Father Bunn of Georgetown University, said to me once, years later in life, "Adolescents aren't very much interested in *subjects*, you know, but they're intensely interested in the personality of the teacher, and if *he* interests them, his subject will interest them."

So, at the Y, I read, I listened to the U. of P. professor, I saw movies, but principally I paid the two cents a day for the big clean towel that was my passport to the gym, the handball and volleyball courts. And to my intense surprise and gratification I discovered that I liked athletic enterprise after all, and that I had some qualifications for it.

● ● ●

One summer evening as I was leaving the Y, I encountered a youth of my own age dressed in a sailor's uniform, U.S.N., standing disconsolately on the front steps. We greeted each other with a shock of surprise, for he was Lester Stanley Champion, one of the two sharks of Trinity who had been bound for M.I.T. I felt a moment of hot shame that he should be in uniform while I was not, but this passed somewhat because Stan was so utterly cast down. "My ship's been here for a week," he said, "and may be here for another week. How do you ever *meet* anybody? I tried to pick up a girl on Filbert Street last night, and she said, 'What the hell do you want; a fuck?' I didn't want a fuck; I just wanted somebody to talk to." We had been in the war for four months or so, and the need to make some sort of provision for hundreds of thousands of homesick youths suddenly cast adrift from home had scarcely occurred to anybody except the Y, and its appeal was to lonely God-fearing Youth, not to lonely tough Youth, which can also exist.

• • •

Colonel Hitchins soon got an assignment that sent him traveling away from Philadelphia a good deal. As a bacteriologist he was enchanted with his assignment: chief traveling inspector of venereal-disease-control operations as far west as Oklahoma. I missed him sadly when he was gone, but whenever he came home he had some fine tales to tell—all the more so to me because venereal disease was in 1917 not only not a subject for conversation, it was not a subject for newspaper stories either. Our Boys were Pure.

"Positively the worst dose of clap I ever saw in my life, I saw at a cantonment in Oklahoma," said Colonel Hitchins. "He was a corporal, and it was a beaut. So I put on what I thought was my best military manner and said, 'All right, soldier, why did you violate regulations and not use your prophylaxis kit immediately after exposure?' And the corporal looked very uncomfortable for a minute or so and then he said, 'Because, sir, Colonel, sir, no gentleman would use one of those things in front of a lady.' " Colonel Hitchins, who had been a military man for only about ninety days at the time, had a hard struggle with himself not to break up but succeeded in preserving aplomb. It made me feel splendidly worldly to be the honored recipient of such stories and I always welcomed Dr. Hitchins' return from a long trip for two reasons, of which that was one. The other was that he would be out of practice at handball and I could beat him.

• • •

Dr. Hitchins and my friend and boss Third never met. They would not have gotten along, I felt. But it was strange they didn't meet because Third, too, was a patron, occasionally, of the Y—but for totally different reasons. Third played the viola in the Y orchestra, a very uncertain musical group that did have the distinction of being conducted by a member of the Philadelphia Orchestra. When Third and I were not busy at the office we might be spending a Saturday or Sunday afternoon at his apartment, he with his violin, I at the piano. Now I cannot play the piano. But there was no need. Third, having long ago given up on the Trautwine Shader, had now an ordinary player piano that he had tricked out with a lot of homemade and improvised improvements. Many of them antedated the actual marketing of the Duo-Art and Ampico instruments, which were the ultimates in sophistication of mechanical musical reproduction until the combination of radio and electrical, as opposed to the merely acoustical, recording of music on discs slowly drove them to the wall. Third had accumulated a great collection of rolls to which he had added his own tempo and dynamic markings, and there was never a more passionate player-piano player than myself. The number of times we played Beethoven's Violin Concerto in D or Wieniawski's "Serenade" was uncountable. But we played some non-war-horses, too. Third was abnormally fond of the music of Edward MacDowell, so out of favor then that pieces like his "Keltic Sonata" or "Schattentanz" or "Sonata Tragica" or "Sonata Eroica" were scarcely to be heard. But we played them and played them until strings or roll all but wore out. At last, I was having my part as a "creative" musician.

• • •

Third's operating principle seemed to be that if you couldn't bring a machine to the aid of a man in doing a piece of work, there must be something wrong with the nature of the work. He belonged to the Computer Age and didn't know it. As I am able to look back over a half century to his brilliant, unhappy and essentially unsuccessful life, it seems to me as if he had groped toward dozens of things that were to elude his hands because, so to speak, the stepladder he was using to try to grasp stars was too short and too rickety to give him the aid or comfort he needed. He was, for example, constantly trying to devise a whole range of gadgets that today are called servomechanisms, but he was trying to do it before what Vannevar Bush later called "the age of reliable complexity" had arrived, when low-voltage electrical equipment was no more reliable than a child's set of toy trains of the period.

But his spirit for innovation was unquenchable. His first job after graduating from Cornell, I remember his telling me, came to him from the efforts of a Mr. Smith, who called him up to say, "Trautwine, I've got something for you. Just call Mr. Jones and tell him that you're the young engineer I told him about. It's a job surveying a mine in Scranton."

"But Mr. Smith, I've never done any mine surveying," Third protested.

"Well, don't tell him that; don't tell him that," said Mr. Smith. "Just go and say I sent you—and then do the job."

So Third did—and not only got to be an accomplished mine surveyor but invented a large handful of special devices to make the task easier, including a gas-inflated balloon (known in the office as Phat Phinney) that would hold the stadia rod against the mine ceiling, where no human hand could go.

He brought the same spirit to his father's office. For example, one of my first jobs was to be "copyholder" while T2 had spread out before him the first galley proofs for the 300-odd new pages on railroads that would distinguish the 20th Edition from the 19th. The job of the copyholder is to read aloud to the proofreader what the printer should have set. In an engineering work, crammed with necessary boldface and italic as well as roman, and with complex formulas full of tiny superior and inferior numbers, the task of identifying all these by voice would have been formidable, and Third would have none of it. Consequently, as copyholder I had in front of me a box with six push buttons. These were variously connected to a high-pitched buzzer, a low-pitched buzzer, a doorbell, a chime and red, white and green lights. In general, the sounds were for punctuation or mathematical symbols; the lights were to indicate numerators, denominators or other equational apparatus. It was vast fun; furthermore, it invested me with a sense of importance, and that was no unimportant thing. And furthermore still, I was no longer a mere spectator at the art of printing; I was a participant in it. For it was my job to cart the proofread galley strips back to the composing room and help interpret the markings to its superintendent and often to the Linotype operators themselves, for this was the most difficult kind of technical composition; most mistakes were *not* self-evident and most of the equations required the most exact horizontal alignment of three successive Linotype slugs. In fact, there were plenty of experts in composition who were willing to stake their reputations that such a job *had* to be set on Monotype and couldn't possibly be accomplished on Linotype in those days. But Third was unshakable that it could; not only was it cheaper (in first cost it was; I'm not so sure after all the bills for corrections were in), it was less susceptible to errors accidentally introduced between last proofreading and foundry. Proper handling, however, did require another Trautwine special invention—the Juggle Spotter.

The biggest hazard in handling Linotype metal is transposed slugs; in an ordinary book such an inadvertence is an embarrassment and defacement; but when this happens in a book loaded with equations, utter hash and nonsense is the most probable result. The Juggle Spotter was merely another box—bigger than the copyholder's marvel—with a ground-glass top and inside it as bright a Mazda bulb as the times afforded. You took two galley strips, one the revise, the other the corrected, and you brushed the revise with a light oil that rendered the paper translucent. Then you aligned them over the ground glass and any slug displacement showed up instantly. I was placed in charge of the Juggle Spotter; lo and behold, juggles showed up with a fair enough frequency to invest this job, too, with high importance. Then there was the matter of proofreading wax engravings for engineering diagrams. In the nature of things this had to be a one-person operation and I was that person. I was learning and growing at a terrific rate, and I was very happy.

● ● ●

Suddenly, the little company was hit by a tornado. Most orders for the book (still 19th Edition) came for single copies, one or two dozen a day. Now and again a big wholesaler would order fifty or a hundred copies. That was all. But one morning there arrived from the U.S. Army Engineers, Procurement Division, in an innocent-looking franked envelope, an order for 1,275 copies!

Panic resulted. There were only about 500 copies in stock. Of course the printer had sheets, but the job was to unstore them, ship them to a bindery, buy Fabrikoid for covers, and do half a dozen other things without keeping the Army waiting too long. Since the book was printed on India paper, so called, and from forms that made sixty-four pages to a sheet, the folding and collating were dainty jobs—and all of this fell to my lot to arrange. Somehow it got done, I forget just how, but I know I learned something about a bookbindery in the process.

After a while things quieted down again, and I went back, happily, to the proofreading machine and the Juggle Spotter. We were now into the winter of 1917–18. In the front windows of every newspaper office huge machines had been installed. They worked on the same principle as Wall Street "broad tape" tickers: an inked wheel with raised letters on its rim notched its way across a sheet of paper, held taut between take-up and supply reels six feet apart, printing out in type an inch high wire-service bulletins for the silent, gaping street crowds. And at least twice a day a man armed with thumbtacks and a roll of red tape would step into the window to alter one detail or another of the front lines between Allied and German troops on a large-scale map of France. On the giant teleprinter, Eugene Debs was clamped into jail for violation of the newly passed Sedition Act; on the map of France as seen on Chestnut Street, British troops under General Byng made a sudden breakthrough at Cambrai; so it went, one day better, one day worse. We were hearing a lot about Herbert Hoover in those days; President Wilson had appointed him U.S. Food Administrator and after a while the city's billboards in addition to proclaiming "Uncle Sam Wants YOU!" emblazoned "Food Will Win the War." We began having "meatless Mondays" and other days on which the whole country was to do, successively, without wheat or pork or—and it was a bitterly cold winter—coal for heat. In a very mild way America slowly began to experience an occasional rigor of war. But what brought the war home hardest to Philadelphia was Hog Island, where a massive shipbuilding program was so bogged down that inbound freight trains on the Pennsylvania Railroad, unable to unload, began building up a solid mass of cars halfway back to Pittsburgh. William Gibbs McAdoo, as director-general of railroads, bounced Samuel Rea as chief of operations of the Pennsy—not because of this but because Mr. Rea wouldn't take orders from anything called "the government," war or no war.

The one man totally unaffected by any aspect of the war was T2—John C. Trautwine, Jr. Being a Socialist, he was also a pacifist, and a perfect one. The war was "an outbreak of international anarchy"—I remember his words well—and a rational human being would not cooperate in any way with a world gone mad. If a band were to strike up "My country, 'tis of thee . . ." he might as likely join in with *"Heil Dir in Siegerkranz,"* for this hymn tune was international in having words appropriate to American, English or German sentiments, and only through internationalism could the world be saved.

And, thank you, T2 would buy no Liberty bonds. Not a dollar's worth; not a nickel's worth. In a mad, irrational world, brother was slaughtering brother; this insane horror would enjoy no subsidy from him. Since T2's name was prominent in Philadelphia's civic and professional affairs, he was much waited on to change his mind, and the local Drive Committee used to send "loyal" German-Americans, some of them with almost musical-comedy accents, to plead with him. In return, he was calm, courteous, quiet—and totally immovable. I began to fear for the sweet old gentleman, with his German name, his German ancestry, his love of things German in the worlds of art and music—fearful that some overheated 100 per cent patriot would someday turn him in for his stubborn refusal to conform to any American wartime pattern, and that someday a U.S. Marshal would arrive to lead him away. If this ever happened I felt sure Mr. Trautwine would just quietly go, and from his prison cell write innumerable Letters to the Editor, not of protest at injustice but just quietly objecting to the absurd logic of putting him away. But the time happily never came. I think it must have been the old gentleman's complete dispassion that saved him from harassment.

• • •

As the long winter slowly gave way, the office was thrown into another uproar. This time the order for *The Civil Engineer's Pocket Book* that came from the U.S. Army was for 2,275 copies. They didn't exist, nor did the sheets for them. There had to be a printing order for enough sheets to make, eventually, 5,000 copies.

By now, T2's attitude toward the war was putting him in an odd position. He proclaimed that if he were the head of the firm he would refuse to fill the order—but since he had long ago abdicated this position to Third, it was Third's decision to make—but in whatever event, he, T2, would take no part in helping. Since Third was totally immersed in editing copy for the 20th Edition and didn't like dealing with crass commercial people like printers, he simply turned the whole job over to me.

And in so doing he simply turned me loose in a whole field of clover. Now I was no longer a visitor in a pressroom; I had a right and duty to be there. A double row of huge flat-bed Miehle presses stretched endlessly before me. Some of the electrotypes for the older sections of the book were pretty worn and battered and I—I!—had been given discretion when to make the old plate do or when to order a new plate made from the actual ancient pages of type, some set in Monotype, but some in actual hand composition (in 6-point!), all stored in the vaults of William F. Fell & Sons, Printers. This inevitably introduced me to the process of make-ready, of which I had never before heard. With a thirty-two-page form locked up I would watch the pressman pull a trial sheet and take it to the pressroom superintendent, who would study it for minutes before he began marking it for places too light or too black. What the pressman then did with a razor-sharp knife, cutout tissue shapes, and a magical glue that he placed on the back of his left hand, in the depression between thumb and forefinger, well, this was really being let in on the ground floor, an authorized witnessing of a Rite.

I shall have to leave it to some future reader of this manuscript to explain why I was born into the world loving music and printing before I knew what they were. I have already recorded my intoxication, at age eighteen months, with the first musical sounds I ever heard, and how this intoxication coincided with my *"I am me"* self-discovery. I am not sure I have said anything corresponding about the making of books, except to record that I was busy at it as a four-year-old. From my earliest memories, right down to the present day, composing rooms and pressrooms are the most exciting places in the world to be. Wherein does this excitement reside? I don't know. All I know is that it has nothing to do with the nobilities of A Free Press—although I am for that, too—or any grandeurs about A Better World Resulting from a Wider Diffusion of Knowledge—about which I am extremely skeptical. Or any high-flown trash like it. I have already recorded that in youth I was bookish but not bookwormish. And my love of printing never led me into being a bibliophile, for example, any more than my love of music led me into being an instrumentalist. I *suppose* that my inability to be a scholar

127

in any field is due not only to a lack but also to an excess. The lack is the lack of sufficient depth of mind. The excess shows up in a high impatience: when I think I'm on the trail of something I tend to go wild with excitement and jump to the nearest plausible-looking conclusion that can just as often turn out to be wrong as right.

• • •

Well, the signatures got printed, I found out what type lice were, the sheets got folded, collated, bound and cased in—and the Army got its "Trautwines." Early in this year, 1918, an unbreakable bond had been forged between me and the printing press—not an ideological bond at all, just a practical case of what would now be called shacking up. I thought—and had good reason to think—that I was shacked up with engineering, and was to live the next four years of my life under this misapprehension. But it was not all wasted. Just most of it.

Meanwhile, I would willingly have stayed with the fascinating Trautwines in their fascinating office at the fascinating venture, but for two facts. First, a new college year was approaching and I had the money for it. Second, it appeared that the United States Army now wanted me, glasses and all. Congress had widened the age brackets for the Selective Service Act—alias the Draft— from ages twenty-one to thirty-one to ages eighteen to forty-five.

16 · FAR BELOW CAYUGA'S WATERS, OR, THE DEATH OF HEROISM

SOMEPLACE THE NAME of the real father of the S.A.T.C.—the Student Army Training Corps—must be known, but I don't know where to look. It *sounded* like a great idea: with the extension of the draft to age eighteen, a college-bound youth would be inducted into the Army and then permitted to go to the college of his choice. Boys already in college would stay where they were but don uniforms. Every college campus in the United States would be thus militarized; dormitories, fraternity houses and all other suitable structures would become barracks or mess halls, and a twelve-hour day would be split into two six-hour halves— academic work in the morning; close-order drill in the afternoon. "We must not grind up the seed-corn of the future," Abbott Lawrence Lowell had said, perhaps to give this new idea an academic push. But it all turned out to be a disaster, just the same.

When, one night, with my draft card in my pocket and my heart in my mouth, I boarded the special Ithaca cars of the then-immaculate Delaware, Lackawanna & Western ("Mile for mile the most highly developed railroad in America") Railroad's New York–to–Buffalo crack train, I knew I was really on my own at last. I was not only going to college; I was simultaneously going into the Army. It was one thing to have been in Philadelphia, the city of my boyhood, and among friends, but now I didn't know what I was going up against. It was, later, small consolation that the U.S. Army didn't know, either.

My first memories are consequently confused. The beautiful Cornell campus was full of disoriented professors, brand-new shavetails who were to be our company commanders, and a vast confused jumble of the civilian and the military, going in opposite directions. It all looked as if a battle of no small proportions had just been lost—by whom, it could not be determined. But after a while, long lines of student-inductees began converging on a huge armory where the Cornell-S.A.T.C. Commander had set up shop by installing the quartermaster corps, the medical examination post and several other essentials. All I remember was walking around, aimless and nude, among several thousand other naked young men, all of us carrying our induction papers in our hands. Slowly, we began to file past a line of doctors. One did nothing but look down throats. Another examined eyes. A third gave searching looks at genitals, fingered pairs of balls at a rate of about a pair a second, also directing the uncircumcised to "skin it, for Christ's sake," which would make the line move a little slower for a moment or two. Cases of hydrocele, if sufficiently gross, were shunted aside. Except for my eyes (I had 20/200 vision in O.S. and not much better in O.D.) I did all right until I reached the heart man with his stethoscope. He moved it from place to familiar place on my chest, and had just released me to his next colleague, after having written "O.K." in the right space, when he suddenly called, "Hey—come back here." He put his stethoscope back on my chest and listened for a long minute in obvious disbelief. Then he said, not to me but to the surrounding air, "Well, I'll be damned." Then, repeating that he would be damned, he scratched out his O.K. and in its place wrote "Systolic blow in aortic area." I had no idea then what this meant, but at last, when I came to the final, the evaluation, desk, presided over by a chicken colonel, he looked the whole sheet over, gave me a piercing glance, and wrote my summing up: "Class C; fit for limited service only; eyes and heart."

That was that. In a misery of fear I now stood before the quartermaster's counter where supply sergeants were doling out uniforms, shoes, hats and other gear without reference to the size or shape of the recipient. I was assigned to Company A, which was bivouacked at what had been, in civilian times, the Cosmopolitan Club, on the "wrong" side of Cascadilla Creek and hence off campus.

We were, all of us, a pretty ratty-looking bunch, and I don't mean just A Company; I mean the whole encampment. Even after, by swap and barter, we had managed to attire ourselves better, even after the principles and practices of close-order parade-ground maneuvers had been thoroughly drilled into us, even after hours and hours of marching and countermarching and singing the songs of World War I as we did, our self-esteem was pretty low. Or am I thinking only of myself? I don't believe so; one afternoon as we were marching, company front, across the beautiful Cornell Quadrangle, we bore down on a crosswalk where two little girls were walking unaware. The elder spied us first and called a warning to her little junior: "Jeannie, Jeannie, look out for the *soldiers!*" And I remember the snigger of self-contempt and hatred that rose, in defiance of all military etiquette, from our own ranks. Soldiers, forsooth!

As for me, I was back among the lowest of the low. I can remember no benefits derived from being in Class C and fit for limited service only. I was excused from no drill; on the contrary, I drew an abnormal number of K.P. assignments as a dishwasher, and miscellaneous jobs as a headquarters orderly. Of the academic side of my S.A.T.C. life I can remember no slightest wisp except, uniquely, a course labeled "War Aims," on which I kept an incredibly full notebook. I credit this industry to the genius, as a lecturer, of that justly famous professor of political science Samuel Peter Orth. (Of Austria-Hungary, the Orth description was "that syphilitic empire, dropping to pieces of its own rottenness"—rather hard to forget.) The rest of Cornell, as a university, might as well not have existed during the S.A.T.C. days so far as I was concerned. I think the University felt the same way about it.

• • •

There came one evening what was universally called "Smut One"—the introductory lecture given all troops on venereal disease. At the Cornell S.A.T.C. the chief medical officer was a Colonel Harris, a surprisingly genial and informal man, who could not, I think, have been Regular Army. Maybe he was a professor in uniform. In any event he knew how to present facts and organize material for large crowds. Whatever the total muster strength of the Cornell S.A.T.C., it was all present and accounted for on the night of Smut One—obligatory. In due course the houselights dimmed for the presentation of lantern slides. That this was in the days before Kodachrome mattered not a whit: the hand-coloring equaled or perhaps outdid it in the close-up display of the male and female genitalia, starting

131

with normality and progressing relentlessly by soft and regular degrees to the ultimate horrors of suppurating and ulcerative decays and dissolutions.

Long before such a point was reached, I heard a soft thump. Then I heard another. Not until I had heard two more did it dawn on me what was going on: these were the Tough Guys passing out, having previously lain with prostitutes. Medical corpsmen pulled them out; they revived, vowing eternal chastity thereafter, just in time to see full-length portraits of untreated tertiary syphilitics with no noses. It was a great night for male virgins.

• • •

The Medical Corps was soon to have its hands fuller than anyone on earth had dreamed of. Unwittingly, it had provided itself with a dress rehearsal for disaster, first class, when the inevitable time arrived for typhoid-paratyphoid inoculations. We were to get the so-called lipovaccine, in which the transporting vehicle for the bacilli was not water but oil; the theory of the French bacteriologist whose child this was being that with oil as the "disperse phase" of the colloidal vaccine, the absorption rate into the body tissues would be only one-third as fast as with water; consequently the three hitherto customary spaced shots could be condensed into one. This called for needles and syringes of close to veterinary size, and once again some potential military heroes passed out as they saw the gigantic thrust, just inboard of the right shoulder blade, with which the man just in front of them got stuck.

Our only instructions were to go immediately back to barracks after the shot and remain indoors the rest of the day; there would be no drill. But a lot of us, including me, never got as far back as barracks. I walked, feeling perfectly normal, as far as Cascadilla Gorge; suddenly on the bridge the whole world turned upside down and stayed that way for some time before it began spinning. I do not know how I was gotten to the hospital, but I do remember realizing, after a while, that I had lots and lots of company—about half the encampment. But we were all right again in three or four days.

By a strange coincidence, it fell to my friend Colonel Hitchins, back in Philadelphia, to be one of the demonstrators of what was wrong with the lipovaccine. It was simple enough; when the oily suspension hit the watery serums of the body, the emulsion simply broke, and the absorption rate then became exactly the same as with the older vaccine. So all the Army proved, at our expense, was that you could give three times as heavy a dose of typhoid-paratyphoid vaccine as anyone had dared give before and still not kill the subjects. Science had taken another forward step.

• • •

It was not until mid-October that the 1918 influenza epidemic hit Ithaca, but it struck with the same savage and stunning force there as everywhere else. There were a few differences, however. Ithaca was not a large city. It was not near any large city. Ezra Cornell had planted his college there for the very reason of the beauty, tranquillity and isolation of this site far above Cayuga's Waters. I don't know that the death roll was any higher here than anywhere else. I don't know, either, how that fraction of the Army and its doctors coped with this incredible act of Fate. Company commanders died. The toughest top sergeants died. Between 10 and 20 per cent of the entire Cornell-S.A.T.C. was stricken, and all of a sudden, with "the enemy" still thousands of miles away, we were in the midst of battle-casualty conditions.

Also suddenly, therefore, my status as "Class C; fit for limited service only" took on a significance I had not thought for it, for there was a great need for orderlies—i.e., message runners and chore doers. I got assigned to Cascadilla Hall, a huge ark of a building that was converted into an emergency hospital. There was no one—absolutely no one—who could not give me an order; in consequence, everybody did: officers, medical corpsmen, civilian doctors, nurses, convalescent patients—from one end of the spectrum to the other. It was a poignant job, too; I had never seen death before, and now I was seeing it all about me. It was hard to be sure toward whom my feeling of helpless compassion was the more directed: the deathly ill patients or the desperately overworked staff, themselves all but helpless, who had the responsibility of trying to keep everything from sinking with all hands on board.

One cold night I was on duty outside the makeshift hospital's main entrance, before which, in as near military manner as possi-

133

ble, two sentries paced. A man and a woman approached one, who came to Order Arms as he listened to them, and then bawled "Orderly!" at me. "This here is the father and mother of Private Smith," said the sentry. "They got a telegram to come, and they want a pass to get in." It was my job to convey this message where it should go. Inside, at a desk shoved into a corner, a civilian doctor was answering everybody's questions about everything, his own face ashen gray. I conveyed my message. The doctor rummaged in a shoe box filled with $3'' \times 5''$ cards until he found the one he needed. Then he scribbled on a pad in front of him, tore off the leaf and handed it to me. "Pass, admitting one," he said.

I was green enough to say "Just one, sir?" He started to give me a hard look, and then all the energy drained out of him. "That's right," he said in an almost inaudible monotone, "just one."

When I had to confront Private Smith's parents with a pass good only for one, I had a terrible sense of having failed them. And the discussion, in which the mother wanted the father to use the pass and vice versa, was too painful to listen to. I didn't. How many times that same scene was played out, with how many different casts of characters, God alone knows . . . . In the intervening fifty years the amount of heartbreak in the world has increased so many more millionfold, one memory of one heartbreak seems scarcely worth recording. Perhaps it isn't.

But because this is a personal history, perhaps it is worth recording that Private Hodgins, Class C, fit for limited service only, and in his still earlier years an almost constant sufferer from upper-respiratory infections, went through the Great Influenza Epidemic of 1918 under conditions of maximum exposure and never even sneezed.

• • •

Often today I wonder, and at the very same time that I may be cursing modern Youth, what in hell was biting Youth when I was young. For in 1917–18 male Youth wanted to go marching forth to war. Our secret dream, which even the scruffiest among us clung to, was of being picked for Officer Training School, then to be shipped to France to be slaughtered—although of course that was not the way to put it. The way to put it was that dreams

134

of military glory filled the heads of all of us, with of course hordes of beautiful girls swooning over us. The impulse was to Heroism: the inconveniences of Heroism, ranging from ghastly death to having half your face blown off or half your intestines blown out, were suppressed to the vanishing point. There were, of course, draft dodgers, like the notorious Grover Cleveland Bergdoll, and a few small groups of genuine conscientious objectors, who enjoyed scant public sympathy or support. The impulse to Heroism was in the young; it was their parents who had the long second thoughts. What fools we were!

Just what fools may be judged by our reaction to the arrival of November 11, 1918. The Armistice produced hysterical—but not universal—joy. For example, there was little joy in Ithaca, or at least among the S.A.T.C. Our fantasy of Heroism, which was the thing sustaining us, now without foundation, collapsed. The job ahead for the military was now only demobilization.

Because of the decimation of A Company by the flu (this slang shortening was barely in use in 1918), I had been moved from rear rank to front rank in my squad; that is, I had become an Acting Lance Corporal. But promptly when the front-rank man was duty-fit again, I returned to the rear rank. That happened on November 12. So of my military service to my country during what was known for a scant score of years as the Great War, I can only say, with Kipling's Mullvaney, "I *was* a corporal, but I was re-joosed."

• • •

When I got back to Ithaca after demobilization and a Christmas vacation spent partially with Third in Philadelphia (he was avid for news of how Cornell had changed in the eighteen years since his own graduation) and partially with my parents, I was still in Army uniform. So were, at a guess, about 10 per cent of the freshmen. This was not because of any lingering of material spirit—that had suffered a painful death—but I couldn't afford a suit of civilian clothes. When I finally was able to, I had, of course, to wear the "Frosh cap"; any freshman caught by an upperclassman wearing any other headgear was subject to severe physical manhandling, for with the end of the S.A.T.C., the spirit of Siwash had returned to American colleges.

But at least my physical surroundings had taken a tremendous

135

turn for the better. Gone was my incarceration in the "barracks" of the Cosmopolitan Club; I now had a room, a luxurious room, in North Baker Hall, one of a set of beautiful dormitories built just before the outbreak of war. I knew no fraternity would ask me to join, and none did. From January until June I lived a life of unrelieved loneliness, but one thing sustained me. I was out to compile the best academic record I could so that I might be able to transfer successfully to M.I.T. for my sophomore year. I was dead set on chemical engineering as a career and Cornell offered no such course. Consequently I was in Cornell's Sibley College ("of Engineering and the Mechanic Arts"). The freshman curriculum was innocent of anything much later to be called The Humanities. So we were given instruction in forge and foundry work; differential and integral calculus; physics; chemistry, including qualitative analysis; and—oh, yes—military science and tactics, where some of the same officers who had treated us like the scum we were in S.A.T.C. days now would begin instruction by saying, "The subject for today, *gentlemen*, is . . ."

But that was all. No English, except that Martin Wright Sampson, imported from Oxford or Cambridge to be Goldwin Smith Professor of English Literature, gave, out of the goodness of his heart, the so-called Sibley Readings, whereby late every Friday afternoon he would read aloud, very rapidly and never stumbling, and with beautiful intonation, some significant fragment or two from the masterpieces, major or minor, of the past. (We were still interested in the past in 1919.) Attendance was voluntary, and you received no credit from the Registrar's Office, but the large room was always crowded.

• • •

Not until much later years did I learn that Cornell, in those days, anyway, took conscious institutional pride in the quality of its teaching, particularly to freshmen. But I was certainly conscious that I was being splendidly taught, whether by accident or design never occurred to me. In analytical geometry and elementary calculus I drew a section presided over by Professor Wallie Abraham Hurwitz, black-bearded and rabbinical, but a teacher who, although he must have been barely out of his twenties, knew how to bring the total resources of his personality to the job at hand. His resources were considerable; he was humorous, vivid and learned—not just in mathematics: how the Greeks constructed the Parthenon, how a certain song went in Gilbert and Sullivan's *The Gondoliers*, by what means of intersecting hyperbolas the Allies had located the Germans' Big Bertha; whatever it was that came into Professor Hurwitz's mind at the moment, he could use then and there as a "teaching aid," a phrase blessedly unknown in an age more ignorant than this one. And, of course, he was interested in what he was doing; more than that, he was interested in his class and treated its members as if they were his equals, which they were not. Once, in the course of developing a set of equations, he fell into a quagmire. He instantly acknowledged it.

"I'm stuck," he said. He spent several moments trying to get unstuck. "Any member of the class have any helpful suggestions?" There was a long silence while our supposedly all-knowing professor stared in bewilderment at his blackboard. Finally a tentative voice spoke up from the rear. "How about figuring the slope of the curve at the Origin?" And that turned out to be the missing clue. After five more minutes of blackboard writing, the now unstuck Professor Hurwitz turned back to the class and said, "Who was the brilliant man who made the suggestion about the slope at the Origin? Mr. Rieber! Well, Mr. Rieber, many thanks for getting me out of that hole." And there was not one of us who did not wish that he had been Mr. Rieber. But compliments were not Professor Hurwitz's sole stock by any means. He allowed full play to his wide range of emotions; if he felt scorn he was likely to break his piece of chalk into fragments and hurl them at the blackboard—or the dolt—in disgust.

I suppose he's dead, now; either dead or ages since emeritus or retired. They must all be dead, those men in full vigor before the twenties had even begun. I wonder if a generation grew up behind them as dedicated to teaching as Professor Browne in freshman chemistry or Professor Gibbs in physics. The two men were as different as any two could be: Professor Browne, lively, dancing and hyperfull of beans; Professor Gibbs, dry, pawky, and as eternally composed as his wispy hair. Yet each was equally successful in bringing *his* individuality to bear on the baffling process and problem of memorable teaching.

Years later, forty or so, I had an assignment from the Ford Foundation to interview a certain number of university professors who had made a widely acknowledged name for themselves as instructors of youth and to ask them if they had developed any set of Principles. Not much came of it, but I vividly remember talking to an old chemistry professor at Haverford on the eve of his retirement. "Obviously," he said, "after teaching freshman chemistry for forty years I don't need to spend much time in formal preparation for a lecture. But I do insist on one thing. For the full hour before the lecture, I insist on absolute solitude. And how do I use this solitude? I just look out of my window, and I *meditate*."

17 · THE OLD FALL RIVER LINE, OR, PILGRIM'S PROGRESS

GOING TO BOSTON was once a great experience—the trip, I mean. At least half a dozen steamship lines operated between New York and Boston, but proudest and most prosperous was the old Fall River Line, which of itself operated four massive side-wheelers— the *Commonwealth*, the *Priscilla*, the *Plymouth* and the *Providence*. The *Commonwealth* was the flagship of the line, and when I stepped aboard her at her near-the-Battery pier on a blazing July day, 1919, I was glad my parents were with me, for I doubt I would have had the courage to face her magnificence by myself. The Dining Salon ran the whole beam of the ship on the uppermost deck, and as the *Commonwealth* trundled from her Hudson River pier, around Manhattan's lower tip and so into the East River, through Hell Gate, and into Long Island Sound, you got, as you dined, a panorama of New York that was unforgettable—if you were twenty. The stewards—no landlubber's term like "waiters" could conceivably do—were all Negro, all more than six feet tall, all darkly handsome, all immaculate in white uniforms, and all combined deep dignity with deep deference. Or so it goddamn well seemed at the time. The food, needless to say, was ambrosial.

I can't remember now why my parents were with me, for the purpose of my trip was to visit M.I.T., my Cornell freshman grades clutched in my hand, to ask about my chances for admittance as a sophomore in September. The Fall River Line ran to Fall River and no farther because there it connected with the Old Colony Railroad, which, like the Fall River Line, was a subsidiary of the once proud New Haven. It took three trainloads of rattling, swaying wooden cars to transport the *Commonwealth*'s complement to Boston and way stations, and the instant

139

you debarked in Fall River you knew you were in New England; speech, railroad stations bearing names like Segreganset, customs, usage, clothes, appearance—all were different, and radically different, from the part of the country you had left just twelve hours before. It was marvelous. Travel did *not* mean a string of Howard Johnsons and Holiday Inns.

Arrived in South Station, then happy to be the largest handler of commuter traffic in the country, it was enchanting to see that the Boston police (alone, it must have been, in the entire country) still wore helmets the shape of a London bobby's; that Summer Street became Winter Street on crossing Washington; that Milk Street ran close by Water Street.

But the trip, having been arranged by my father, had the usual and characteristic flaws. He had no idea where our hotel was. Like an immigrant family, each of us carrying a straw suitcase, we set out to find it, my father remembering only that it had advertised itself as "on Beacon Hill, in the shadow of the State House." The ad was quite truthful, and after an endless trudge we found it. What the ad had naturally not mentioned was that "in the shadow of the State House" was a semislum street, and the hotel a semislum hotel.

There we were again!

• • •

I took leave of my parents as soon as I could and trudged across Longfellow Bridge to Cambridge. There I turned left and began the long walk on Memorial Drive and the rim of the Charles River Basin until I finally arrived opposite the Dome and Colonnade that stood between the two outflung arms and pylons that enclosed the massive Great Court. I must have stood in awe for ten minutes, seeing with my own eyes the words incised in foot after foot of Indiana limestone: MASSACHVSETTS INSTITVTE OF TECHNOLOGY, and thinking to myself, "I am here, I am here." It is one of the ironies of their craft, which architects insist on creating for themselves, that this head-on view of the Institute's noble façade is a view that the Institute's class-going students very rarely see, and I myself have been able to pause and study its classic grandeur perhaps only a dozen times since that first far-off day. But despite everything that was to happen to me in the close vicinity of this site, much of it extremely disillusioning, my feeling of reverence remains. Here was the almost over-powering embodiment of a Great Idea that had yet to go so fatally wrong.

Meanwhile, on this broiling summer day, my mundane job was to sound out the possibilities of my own entrance to this enchanted palace, "the most difficult seat of learning to get into and to get out of in the United States." On this score I received cautious encouragement, but nothing could be guaranteed; I would simply have to go the rounds of professors when the fall term opened and explore my luck. I went back to Boston and my parents, mission more or less accomplished, and feeling quite sure that if M.I.T. would only let me in all of life's future problems would be thereby solved. As my parents and I lugged our straw suitcases back to South Station for the return to New York, I caught what was to be my last glance, forever, of any Boston policeman whose distinction was that he wore a helmet like an English bobby's.

• • •

Nineteen-nineteen, particularly when viewed in the perspective of half a century gone by, was quite a year: locally, nationally, internationally. The Treaty of Versailles was signed. President Wilson, in his efforts on behalf of the League of Nations, begged the Senate of the United States not to "break the heart of the world" by rejecting the Covenant; Henry Cabot Lodge, senior senator from Massachusetts, led those senators who succeeded in breaking it. And while President Wilson was desperately traveling the country over in the League of Nations fight that was to end in the breakdown of his health and the wreckage of all his plans and hopes, his Attorney General, A. Mitchell Palmer, was engaging, unimpeded, in a "Red hunt" that was not to be equaled in mindless ferocity until the era of Senator Joe McCarthy. The Communist Labor Party was founded upon the symbol of the hammer and sickle and the slogan "Workers of the World Unite." The American Legion was also formed. Whenever the Supreme Court decided anything, it was likely to be by a 5-to-4 decision. The 18th Amendment to the Constitution was ratified, whereupon the Volstead Act was passed and Prohibition became the law of the land. These were *not* halcyon days.

141

• • •

Particularly were they not in Boston. The Boston I reached in September was an armed city, with the National Guard patrolling the streets. The reason why, of course, was the Boston Police Strike. So long had been the record of corruption of Boston municipal government that the city's Commissioner of Police had been made an appointee of the Governor of Massachusetts, not the Mayor of Boston; thus Governor Calvin Coolidge was much more directly involved in the strike than he would otherwise have been. If memory serves, the District Attorney of Middlesex County was himself in jail and the citizenry was in the mood for some righteous talk. Cal supplied it. "To restore the public safety to the hands of men who have sought to destroy it, would be to flout the laws the people have made," he said in turning his back on suggested amnesty for any striking cop. "There is no right to strike against the public safety, by anybody, anywhere, any time," he also pronounced, and these two statements, plus a perverse Fate, were later to produce more out of less than the wildest skeptic would have thought possible. But Boston in September was a tense city, with the Guard not only patrolling the streets, but painfully learning how to direct traffic. Commissioner Curtis had vowed that not a single member of the old force would ever be reinstated, and none ever was. So the Guard was in for a long term of duty while a brand-new force, over many months, was recruited and trained.

• • •

The academic year 1919–20 was to be both momentous and tragic for M.I.T., but this fact was deeply hidden from me as I trudged its halls, visiting professor after professor as a transfer student trying to get enough credits "signed off" to permit my entrance as a sophomore. It was a long and discouraging process, during which I more than once considered giving up and going back to Cornell. But at last it was accomplished, and somehow, mysteriously, I got a scholarship grant that paid half my tuition. This was a great break, for in those days M.I.T.'s tuition was $350 a year, this huge sum being due, the catalog explained, to the high costs of a scientific education that had to be supported by expensive laboratory equipment. Fortunately, also, my father now had a job with the Interchurch World Movement that paid him the highest salary he ever achieved—sixty dollars a week—so he was able to send me an occasional check large enough so that I did not have to wait on table for supplemental income—which my mother would have considered a social disgrace. I did manage to pick up some spare change by tutoring backward kids in high-school algebra. I pretended I was Professor Hurwitz of Cornell, which made the job lots of fun.

Somehow I had come on a classified ad that said a single room was available in the home of an Episcopalian clergyman in West Roxbury, so thither I went, and fell into great good luck. The clergyman happened to be the Reverend Howard S. Wilkinson, who in later years moved to Washington as Rector of the church where Franklin Roosevelt went for his Sunday worship. Mr. Wilkinson, in addition to being Rector to his little church in West Roxbury, was a member of the National Guard, so I never knew when I was going to encounter him in his canonicals or in military uniform. There was nothing contrived about this latter, for Mr. Wilkinson could ride a motorcycle, and his night beat—the strike was well into its second month now, and the Guard knew what it was doing—was South Boston, no garden spot in the best of times. The Reverend Mr. Wilkinson made a jaunty outrider and relished his job. "But I don't mind telling you," he said to me soon after we got to know each other, "that all the first week I was so scared I had to go out back and throw up before I took off." So it was with the Reverend Mr. Wilkinson, his wife, and a mischievous daughter of nine that I made my home during my first year at my new Alma Mater. It was a fairly long commute from West Roxbury, a pleasant, leafy suburb on the New Haven line that ran between Dedham and Boston, and once in South Station I had to take "the L," which ran underground except where it crossed the River Charles, to either Kendall or Central squares, then walk about half a mile to the Institute itself. Elapsed time: About three-quarters of an hour each way.

• • •

Without knowing it, I had become a member of the largest class ('22) in the Institute's history. Without knowing it, I had also elected one of the Institute's most sought-after courses: Chem-

143

ical Engineering. The end of World War I had resulted in an enormous vogue for technical and engineering education; the Institute's registration peaked like the early days of a fever chart. Fortunately, the physical plant, having been brand-new only four years earlier, was large and lavishly designed; it could bear the new and unexpected load with ease. Not so the instructing staff; department heads were out whacking the bushes for new instructors in freshman and sophomore subjects. And there was an almost instantaneous need for—nobody but a college president could guess—more money. An endowment drive was thus under way, with a goal, almost fantastic in its magnitude, of several million dollars.

This year 1919, which saw me enter as a new student, also saw two comparatively inconspicuous additions to the faculty. Both were geniuses, not yet in flower. By the luck of the draw I was assigned to the calculus section taught by the then more inconspicuous of the two: a brand-new instructor in mathematics whose name was Norbert Wiener, and who was not, repeat, not, a very good teacher of sophomores. He had entered Tufts at the age of eleven and taken a Harvard Ph.D. before he was nineteen. But this made him a strictly local New England genius; west of Providence, nobody had then heard of this odd young man, somewhat obese, with bulging eyes and a waddling walk, and quite unsure of himself. ("Are my explanations *clear?*" he once asked me after a classroom session. I lied and said Yes, silently blessing the teaching genius of Wallie Abraham Hurwitz, who had imparted to me enough momentum to cope with some of Wiener's higher obscurities.)

The other 1919 newcomer was also from Tufts: a salt-drenched Yankee from Cape Cod, both of whose grandfathers had not been sea captains for nothing. This was Vannevar Bush, who had just joined the faculty as an associate professor of electric power transmission. Years later it was to turn out that Van Bush and I were to become friends and collaborators, but as of 1919 we were total strangers. Aside from the admitted pleasure òf name dropping, I do have another reason for coupling these two men together, and in the frame of 1919. Both Bush and Wiener started their permanent careers then. Neither knew the other well; in fact I have always suspected that a certain mutual denigration existed between them. Yet both, working in their separate ways, were

144

at the top of the genealogical tree from which is descended, for better, for worse, the twentieth-century computer age in which now we live. And it all *started* to begin in the portentous year when the Versailles Treaty was signed, sowing the seeds for World War II, when Wilson was stricken and the senior senator from Massachusetts killed American participation in the League of Nations, when the Boston Police Strike made Calvin Coolidge a household name, when the American Legion was founded, when the American Communist Party was also founded and when John Reed wrote *Ten Days That Shook the World*.

And something else had its faint, far-off beginnings. I spoke a few pages back about M.I.T.'s endowment drive. As an ingenious gimmick to establish new money sources for the Institute, someone had thought up a something to which was given the name of the Division of Industrial Cooperation and Research. The idea was that through this division the Institute would consult with the industries coming to it and would, for a fee, make available its most appropriate physical facilities and faculty brains.

At this proposal, a good deal of hell broke loose. The arguments *for* were, in addition to revenue, that the Institute would gain by being brought closer to Industry's problems, to the benefit of professor and student alike; that Industry in its turn would learn that there were ways of getting benefits from the Institute other than by raiding its faculty and luring its most gifted men away for good—in those days a real and vexing problem. The arguments *against* were that this sort of contact with Industry would be a soiling and corrupting experience for a university and that, once sanctioned, there could be no telling where it would all end. Education was Education and Business was Business, and no matter how "practical" the ends the education might eventually serve, there had to be a Zone of No Contact. It was hard to define but less important to define than to acknowledge.

The first nonclassroom event I got up my nerve to go to was what was then called a "smoker." Of it I remember mostly wandering aimlessly about in one of Walker Memorial's halls. I seemed to be the only person there who didn't know anybody else, but then there came up to me a thin pipe-smoking young man who might have been either a junior faculty member or a graduate student. "What do *you* think of this idea of 'selling Tech'?"

145

I didn't know. But it was clear what *he* thought. It was also clear what half the roomful thought: they thought it was an idea reared by the devil himself.

That did not prevent the very successful establishment of the Division of Industrial Cooperation (the "and Research" was later dropped), which still functions after a fashion. After a fashion only because the contentious idea of 1919 was so completely over-ridden by subsequent events that in the vast complex of Education-Industry-Government it became hard or impossible to tell where one left off and the others began: the Zone of No Contact was superseded by a three-way overlap. And of course, if the brilliant Vannevar Bush, as the head of the F.D.R.-created Office of Scientific Research and Development during World War II, had not enlisted or conscripted university scientists and labora-tories in the development of modern war weaponry, we might not have won that mortal combat.

But it so happens that I am setting these words down exactly a half century after the establishment of that once contentious little Office of Industrial Cooperation and Research. And as I write, the current news is that right at M.I.T. a group of faculty and graduate students has struck against further government-sponsored hardware research and that the strike idea is spreading from campus to campus. The M.I.T. statement said:

> We feel that it is no longer possible to remain uninvolved. We therefore call on scientists and engineers throughout the coun-try to unite for concerted action and leadership . . . . To devise means for turning research applications away from the present overemphasis on military technology toward the solution of press-ing environmental and social problems.
>
> To convey to our students that they will devote themselves to bringing the benefits of science and technology to mankind . . . .

It would seem that a gigantic wheel is about to turn full circle.

And it would seem that I have strayed very far from my sopho-more year.

• • •

My abiding recollection of my first M.I.T. year is of unremit-ting toil. "The Institute is a place for men to work, not for boys to play," President Francis Amasa Walker had thundered during his nineteenth-century tenure, and the student body took a sort of pride in this pronouncement. *"We are happy! Tech is hell!"* was not the student cheer for nothing. The Institute's grading system consisted then of only three marks at term's end: C meant passed with credit, P was for passed and F meant failure. It was not the inhuman place then popularly pictured. But the teaching system was geared to the pace of the above-average student; others had to gallop or limp to keep up, according to their aptitudes. It was generally recognized in those days that the Department of Electrical Engineering made the heaviest demands on student capacities and that Chemical Engineering stood next. The Chemical Engineering students liked to boast (and the boast was not empty): "We get more chemistry than the chemists and more thermodynamics than the mechanical engineers." But this was not for a sophomore to know. Not until his junior year did the student come into real contact with his professional department or even take any courses in which the word "engineering" was descriptively used. The sophomore was still having pounded into his head the necessary groundwork in mathematics, in physics, in analytical chemistry. And in English and history, too.

• • •

The English Department of M.I.T. was a miracle. I call it that because I don't understand how, in those days, it was possible to attract and hold, on the faculty of an engineering school, so many men of scholarship or intellectual brilliance, or both; where the student body, no matter how bright, was not much concerned with "literary values" or the niceties of composition; and where a small but distinctly measurable fraction of the engineering faculty itself thought that all time taken away from its specialty was wasted, and no waste more conspicuous than studying *words*, for heaven's sake, when formulas were what made the world go round. (It must be remembered that this Philistine's view of things was probably quite an accurate reflection of the general state of affairs in the U.S.A., post-World War I.)

The intellectual star of M.I.T.'s English faculty in those days was Associate Professor Frank Aydelotte, later to become president of Swarthmore and later still to be president of the Association of American Rhodes Scholars. It was he who devised the mandatory English and history course for second-year students,

147

and a beauty it was, both for what it offered to the student and because it was also a gun-spiker for the enemies of Culture hidden here and there in the more hard-bitten core of the faculty. It was, quite simply, a course designed to show the impact of science and technology on nineteenth-century literature, with pure belles-lettres out of bounds but otherwise nothing barred, prose and poetry intermingled, running up, down and crosswise from J. S. Mill to Carlyle, from Swinburne to Matthew Arnold. Such a course will sound very simple today, particularly at M.I.T., which now has a full-fledged School of Humanities that stands on an equal footing with the schools of Science and of Engineering, but with the 1920's yet to begin it was vastly stimulating medicine. Belles-lettres were ruled out of bounds, but so were scientific apologetics, and there was more of Ruskin than there was of Huxley. In short we were brought face to face with the protests, despairs, frustrations, angers and panics that afflicted the thinking mind as it saw the Age of Faith collapse, to be succeeded by the Age of Who Knows What? Confronted with the evidence that the generation of our grandfathers and great-grandfathers had gone through hang-ups (I am borrowing this convenient phrase from the generation that invented it under the misapprehension that it was theirs who had the first) worse than our own, we lost, to our great advantage, some of that feeling of never-before uniqueness that afflicts all youth.

• • •

The 1920's began without any announcement, anywhere, that the most fabled decade in American social history had officially opened. But for M.I.T., January 1920 was planned as a month of special, deliberate excitement. Richard Cockburn Maclaurin, the Institute's president, a man who had taken the most coveted prizes at Cambridge in both mathematics and law, was reaching a summit of his brilliant career. Dr. Maclaurin had attracted to the cause of M.I.T. a mighty benefactor who over seven years had insisted on anonymity and was known to M.I.T. and the world only as "The Mysterious Mr. Smith." He had given the Institute quite some few millions of dollars, and now, this January, with a gift of $4 million to crown the endowment drive, his identity would at last be revealed at a triumphal dinner of all M.I.T., over which Dr. Maclaurin would preside. But three

148

days before the dinner Dr. Maclaurin fell ill. The dinner could not be postponed, and the evening, somewhat muted by his absence, went off as scheduled, with The Mysterious Mr Smith unveiled as George Eastman, whose benefactions to M.I.T. totaled, ultimately, more than $20 million and who was stepping out from anonymity now not because he wanted to but because the only way he could make this gift was by signing stock transfers of Eastman Kodak common.

So there was dancing in the street, and all manner of celebration, but it stopped abruptly, for two days later, surrounded by the cream of New England medical practitioners, Dr. Maclaurin died of pneumonia.

• • •

I had never seen Dr. Maclaurin in life, but now I saw him in death, as one of a long winding line that filed past his casket, lying in state, housed by the walls of travertine and glass that gave onto the Great Court. He had presided over this; in the twelve years of his presidency he had created a new meaning and a new dignity for technical education and brought into being a new concept for what, in 1909, he had inherited as "Boston Tech." The Institute did not pause long before resuming its immediate work, but perforce it had to pause for ten years of interregnum before it found again the proper succession. It was a bleak decade for the Institute, and it was during this decade that I knew it best.

• • •

The Greek-letter fraternity system flourished at the Institute. I was never asked to join it. Worse than that: one of my Trinity schoolmates who had gone on to the Institute issued me the conventional invitation, "Come on over to the House for lunch and meet some of the boys." I did, and the matter ended there. Anyone who thinks that this silent, passive, completely polite rejection doesn't hurt has another think coming. The fraternity system is now on the wane, and when I say I'm glad, I am gleefully, vengefully glad. Yes, thank you, it is a step toward a Greater and More Meaningful Democracy, but balls to that: this has nothing to do with my glee, the roots of which are entirely personal and vindictive.

As a matter of fact, I was a Brown Bagger. How odd that the possession and use of a minor piece of luggage could make a razor-sharp class and caste distinction—yet it did. The Brown Bag was eminently sensible. It was a leather book bag, a sort of miniature valise, big enough for loose-leaf notebooks as well as texts. In theory everybody should have had one. But the possession of one dropped you instantly five notches in the undergraduate social scale—a fact I didn't know when I bought mine, else I would not have. But carry a Brown Bag *once* and you are a Brown Bagger the rest of your life. Thus, when I got rid of mine, it was too late.

• • •

It came down to this: no fraternity man, doubtless from indoctrination, ever carried a Brown Bag. But the converse was not true: the noncarrying of a Brown Bag did not reliably indicate a fraternity man. Despite all these intricacies, the hard fact remained: the Brown Bagger was a second-class citizen. And these second-class citizens had no ability and apparently not much wish to form a cohesive society of their own.

My first friendship with a fellow Brown Bagger came in the Quantitative Analysis Lab, because our lab benches faced each other. He was one Lewis Tabor, with whom I retained a constant friendship to, through and after graduation. By the oddest of coincidences, the first job he was offered was as teacher of chemistry and physics at—guess where? At my former school, the beloved Episcopal Academy, outside Philadelphia, where he grew old in its service.

• • •

When I think of that Quant Lab, I *really* get some idea of how old I am. Wash bottles that we made ourselves, given only a flask, a rubber stopper pierced with two holes, lengths of glass tubing and heavy cording for wraparound heat insulation. Lessons in simple glass blowing. Inserting a glass bead in three inches of rubber tubing too small for it; later when you attached this rig to the bottom tip of your burette and pinched it, you let a single drop of the burette's liquid fall into the beaker beneath. You were titrating something against something else, with

150

phenolphtalein as the indicator. (Hydrogen-ion concentration was a brand-new concept.)

And the analytical balances, kept in their separate room, each one in its glass-fronted mahogany case. You worked to four decimal places with these beauties, whose counterweighted window was always down for draft protection in the final stages as you remote-controlled the rod-and-hook by which you inched the tiny platinum rider along the calibrated right side of the balance beam until at last the swaying needle came to rest neither a hairline to the right nor to the left of the zero mark on the scale. It might take half an hour to weigh 3.1427 grams of something and hope your arithmetic was right. This beautiful apparatus and the rest of the stuff we worked with were mere superficial refinements of laboratory equipment of the nineteenth century. Indeed, it comes over me, as I think of it now, that in the 1920's we were taught seventeenth-century mathematics, eighteenth-century mechanics, and that most of the *ideas* of the nineteenth century were presented by—of all things—the English Department.

•   •   •

It was a strange, isolated, solitary and girl-less existence I led, commuting between West Roxbury and Cambridge every day. I still faithfully corresponded with the Curtis girls, Constance and Hester, from the now rapidly receding happy days of Point Pleasant. Constance presented no emotional problems to me, but Hester did. Although we had never so much as kissed and had never exchanged even verbal endearments, I was somehow internally convinced, and had been for some long time, that Hester and I were destined to be married. I had no basis for such an idea—and the idea, instead of being wholly comforting, was also disturbing. For Hester was a Catholic and a devout one. Thus, in all the fantasies I had about her, and they were many, there ran the recurring theme, "So we'll have to have nine children, and I don't want nine children." I had held this fantasy long and persistently, and along with my innocent love for Hester I was using up a lot of psychic energy combating the Fate that was going to condemn me to fathering nine brats.

And then the strangest of strange things happened. One wintry 1920 morning as I was going through the motions of bathing

151

in my third-floor quarters at the Wilkinsons', I suddenly said to myself, and almost out loud because of the force with which the thought hit me, "Well, now, who's ever said you've got to marry Hester? Certainly not Hester! Maybe she wouldn't have you if you asked her. But in any event you don't *have* to marry her, and you don't *have* to father nine children."

Whereupon a great sense of happiness and relief came over me. I cared for Hester no less, but our engagement, so to speak, was then and there broken. Years later I told a psychologist this tale of the strange relief from a bondage that had never existed, and asked him if he could account for the instantaneousness with which the imaginary chains had fallen away. And with the usual conciseness of his kind, he answered, "I don't know."

It was a relief not to have to support those nine children any more, but now I *really* had no girl.

18 · TUBBY ROGERS, or,
THE ANARCHIST AND THE ALCHEMIST

EVERYTHING HAPPENED TO ME in my junior year at M.I.T., and everything else happened when I was a senior.

I had spent the summer of 1920 in New York with my parents, in an effort to get up enough courage to apply for a summer job. A friend of my father's had given me a letter of introduction to the secretary of the General Chemical Company. Its offices were deep in Manhattan's financial district. Every day I would take the subway from 145th Street and Broadway down to Wall Street, and then, afternoon after afternoon, I would pace up and down in front of the company's Broad Street headquarters, trying to get my nerve up to go up to the offices and present my letter. And day after day my nerve would fail me. It was a colossal struggle but I always lost. But then one day at last I won, and thereby got my first lesson in how effectively impeccable manners could be used to fend off the unwanted. My letter of introduction was from a weighty citizen, so it brought its high-executive recipient into the reception room to see me within three minutes. He greeted me with delightful courtesy and explained that he was in a board meeting but that he would speak to the company's general manager about me immediately afterward; he felt sure this gentleman would be able to see me if I would present myself again tomorrow. He deeply regretted that the board meeting interfered with a lengthier conversation now.

Well! There had been nothing to be afraid of after all. Next day, my silly cowardice put behind me, I presented myself as requested, and the general manager kept me waiting no more than a few minutes. He, too, was the soul of courtesy, asked me five minutes' worth of questions, assured me that it had been a pleasure to meet a young man interested in serving the chemical industry, said he would canvass the situation and that I would hear from him promptly. Thank you, sir, thank you very much. Not at all; it had been a pleasure to meet a young friend of Mr. Blank's. He would communicate.

He did, all right, and his promise of promptness was so honorably kept that the very next day (the mails were prompt in 1920) I was excited and gratified to get an impressively long envelope, impressively engraved with the name and address of the General Chemical Company. The heavy, crackly bond sheet inside was signed by the general manager in person. It was with regret, he informed me, that his canvass had not revealed any situation in which my services could be utilized, but he was nonetheless mine most sincerely.

Thus ended my search for employment that summer. But I did derive a lesson from the experience, to prove useful in later years: when you want to get rid of somebody, do it with the utmost punctilio, and promptly; it is more completely defeating than any other way. The courtesy shown by these two important men toward a pimply, cadaverous and bespectacled youth who had intruded on them with a letter they could not ignore had been flawless. I had utterly nothing to complain about, and the door had been shut in my face all the more effectively on that very account. Secretly, I was relieved. If the general manager's letter had instead told me to report to the assistant superintendent of the Punxsutawney plant the following Monday, I would have turned chicken all over again.

•   •   •

So the summer was over. In the manner of youth I had vaporized it. When my junior year began I deserted West Roxbury and the kindly Wilkinsons and went to room with five other nonfraternity men in a pleasant firetrap on Massachusetts Avenue, in Cambridge, only about twenty minutes' walk from the Institute. There were six of us: three would-be chemical engineers, an electrochemist and two electrical engineers. They were all good students, and one of the electrical engineers was a gifted pianist and amateur artist adept enough at drawing pretty girls to be a regular contributor to the *VooDoo*, the undergraduate funny magazine. It was thoroughly good for me to be

154

thrown in with congenial contemporaries, yet nothing could banish some residual and unaccountable *Weltschmerz:* I remember one sunny autumn morning walking down Massachusetts Avenue toward the Institute when all of a sudden there went through my mind the thought: "Life is not going to hold very much for you; why don't you have done with everything and kill yourself now?" It was a question that would recur from time to time.

But it didn't recur that year. All juniors were required to take one of a long list of so-called General Studies courses; that is, something that had nothing to do with their major field. I applied for something or other to do with astronomy, but the section was already full. All right: I ran down the list again and encountered "Contemporary English and Continental Dramatists, Asst. Prof. Rogers, M., W., F., 3–4 P.M." It fitted into my schedule, and the section had one place left. I registered and thereby with one casual choice changed the course of my life back into that same creek bed out of which the precious Mr. Bonsall of Trinity School had sluiced it five years before.

"Asst. Prof. Rogers" was Robert Emmons Rogers, A.B., A.M. At Harvard his nickname had been "Bobolink" and he had been a portly and literary young man, editor of the Harvard *Advocate.* At M.I.T. his nickname was "Tubby," and since he was scarcely over five feet tall and seldom succeeded in weighing under 200 pounds, the name was apt, literal and inevitable on the tongues of students and colleagues alike. After a while it dawned on me that I had had the incredible luck of falling under the influence of a genial anarchist. Of all the shapers of my early life, he was the major one—and our coming together had been an accident.

Tubby was a brilliant lecturer. He also required weekly themes, themes of criticism and comment on the plays in Thomas Dickinson's *Chief Contemporary Dramatists.* For my first effort I picked William Butler Yeats's *The Hour-Glass* ("A Morality") and subjected it to my heaviest twenty-year-old scorn. The class was sufficiently small so that the conscientious Tubby would be able to hand the themes back, with his written comments, a week after they had been turned in. When I got my first one back Tubby had written, "A little overexcited, perhaps, but I like your style—it has *drive.*"

That was all I needed: I was back in the days of Pinky Anderson, except now this was college, and my mentor was a *professor* and not just a schoolteacher. Successively, as week followed week, I took out after Arthur Wing Pinero, Henry Arthur Jones, Lady Gregory, Dion Boucicault. It was gorgeous fun. Tubby gave me my head completely. Thereafter, for the rest of my Institute career, I took every course that Tubby gave. Slowly the teacher-student relationship was supplanted by friendship, eventually deep and abiding friendship with Tubby, his wife and little-girl daughter. I had found, for good and all, it seemed, where I belonger. There is much, much more to be said about Tubby, and later on I'll say it.

• • •

About the rest of my education, I was becoming increasingly doubtful. (So were portions of the faculty.) Juniors were given a stiff course in organic chemistry, and this I loved, and still do. The sight of a benzene ring in a structural formula to this day arouses in me a deep nostalgia. The professor who gave this course was the venerable Forris Jewett Moore, whose feats as a lecturer were extraordinary. In *The Light That Failed*, Rudyard Kipling refers to M'sue Kami as "a leaden painter but a golden teacher," and so it was with F. Jewett Moore as a chemist. Indeed, I think he made very little pretense of being an experimental chemist, to say nothing of an innovative one. But as a teacher of chemistry he was gold, pure gold. In this particular course he lectured three times a week for a full year, with never a note in front of him, covering the blackboard with successive waves of the most complex symbols and equations, never pausing in his calm, lucid explanation of why the Friedel-Crafts (or the Grignard?) reaction worked because, you see, a molecule of water splits off here. (Large looping ring on blackboard envelops two atoms of hydrogen and one of oxygen between the reacting substances.) Only once in that entire year did he falter. He suddenly stopped writing an equation—"Ah . . . the reaction escapes me. My apologies." It was actually reassuring to know he was fallible.

In the Organic Chemistry Laboratory I was by no means as good a student as I was in the lecture hall. One day I was doing something and all I can remember is that it was not what I was supposed to be doing. I had added reagent A to reagent B and a drop, let us say, of dilute sulfuric acid. After a moment of bubbling, the solution in the test tube turned such an exquisite liquid emerald-green that I hurried to the professor in charge of the lab to ask him what it could be. He asked me what I had done; when I told him he said in a musing way, "I think you have produced some potassium manganate. This is hard to do, for it is very unstable, so if I'm right it will oxidize in a minute or two into potassium permanganate. Let us watch it and see." We did, and within the minute the emerald color began changing, first at the top of the tube. Then, moving slowly downward, the purple of stable potassium permanganate supplanted the enchanting green of unstable potassium manganate. "Yes," said Professor Davis, "that was it. I don't know just how you did it."

I thanked him and turned to go. "Wait a minute," he said. "I think I ought to tell you the impression you make on me."

Professor Davis was a shy man with a slight hesitancy in his speech. I waited.

"The impression you make on me," he said slowly, "is that you have the soul of an alchemist."

He had hit it painfully on the button.

• • •

Alchemists have no business studying chemical engineering. I was able to enjoy Professor Davis' quiet remark, but it did not escape me that this gentle professor was in his unique way issuing certainly not anything as definite as a rebuke, but certainly a warning. This was reinforced in spades by my first encounter with a course called "Industrial Chemistry," designed to lay the groundwork for the summit course of the senior year, "Chemical Engineering I." I can remember a quiz question that asked to know the optimum capacity and diameter of a tank designed for the evaporation of one hundred gallons of water per hour from a 10 per cent solution of Glauber's salt at a temperature of X degrees F. I cannot remember my answer, except that it was wrong, but I vividly remember my emotional reaction, which was, "Jesus Christ, is *this* what I have committed my life to?" After a long internal agony, I went to see Tubby. After all, I was in my junior year, and I was on a path that was turning out to be a vast mistake. English, mathematics and organic chemistry (in lecture form) had turned out to be joys. So had some miscellaneous short courses like "Precision of Measurements." I cannot account for the intellectual satisfaction this one gave me, but for some reason it was terrific. Perhaps, again, it was because of a brilliant teacher, Professor "Ma" Goodwin. But otherwise things were in bad shape.

Tubby's advice was crisp and succinct. "Keep on," he said. "You can't drop out or turn back now. Do just enough work not to flunk anything, but give your engineering studies as much constructive neglect as is safe, and concentrate the rest of you on your reading and writing."

And that is what I did, thenceforth.

•   •   •

In Harvard's Widener Library the Farnsworth Room used to be immediately to your right after you had climbed that preposterous set of steps leading up to the main portico. Its door bore a fearsome legend: THIS ROOM FOR CULTURAL AND RECREATIONAL READING ONLY. (Maybe some of today's campus revolt isn't so bad after all.) It was in the Farnsworth Room, at Harvard's expense, that I got a good part of what education I possess. Number 907 Massachusetts Avenue, where I lived, was actually closer to Harvard Square than to the Institute; so on Saturdays and Sundays particularly, when I should have been concentrating on the puzzling and unwelcome problems of physical and industrial chemistry, I was instead in the Farnsworth Room. I think its hours were 10 to 10. If so, so were mine. And over the weekends the only place to get a decent student meal in Cambridge was in a cafeteria on Dunster Street, a five-minute walk away. So, over the weekends I used to put in hours of reading, the like of which I would have rebelled against violently had they been required. I cannot remember everything I read there. I do remember that in addition to contemporary works there were endless bound volumes of the literature of the eighteenth and nineteenth centuries. Don't forget how young the twentieth century was; in library terms it was scarcely back from the bookbinders. I do remember one jewel beyond price: a set of bound volumes of *Punch* going back to Vol. I, No. 1, in the mid nineteenth century. With these I curled up for endless weeks. There was no better way of learning about the changing social and political history of England than through these pages, and this I did, not knowing that I was doing it. "Learning put lightly, like powder in jam." Indeed, the reading of the bound volumes of other English periodicals was a great experience; the Farnsworth Room had them all. To come on Chesterton and Belloc and Shaw and Beerbohm not as Names but as sweaty working journalists was a considerable experience. Here also was where you could read all of Shaw's plays, particularly those that are never produced, like *John Bull's Other Island* or *Widowers' Houses*, or come on such total surprises (to me) as George Meredith's *An Essay on Comedy and the Uses of the Comic Spirit* or "Love in the Valley" and H. G. Wells's *Boon*; *The Mind of the Race* and *The Wild Asses of the Devil*. This was the place to discover *The Perfect Wagnerite* or the innumerable short stories of Saki or *Zuleika Dobson*. There were also things I read (as in my boyhood) loathing them, like Thomas Hardy's novels, or loving them, like Thomas Hardy's poetry.

•   •   •

Through my assiduous reading of F.P.A.'s "The Conning Tower," first in the New York *Tribune* and then in the New York *World*, I had gone quite bughouse over the French Fixed Forms: the Ballade, the Rondeau, the Rondel. Another rhyming idol of mine was W. S. Gilbert. I started imitating the Fixed Forms and Gilbert, using contemporaneous M.I.T. matters for the incongruity of the subject matter with its form, and, my spine straightened by Tubby, I sent these off to the *VooDoo*, which, being hard pressed to fill its columns, printed everything I submitted. In the language of the day all such printed matter was known as "drool," and pretty accurately. But it was a lot more fun composing verse than it was studying applied mechanics, another course that mounted the evidence growing in my mind that I was not cut out to be what I was trying to be.

"Applied Mechanics" is a very misleading title for a course. It sounds like the study of mechanisms—which was also a course, but a completely different one. Applied Mechanics was designed to teach you to apply the math you had previously learned to actual engineering problems; the calculation of Moments of Inertia, for example. I was very, very bad at it. And I had had the ill luck to be assigned to the section taught by Slave-Driver Smith. Even the best students conceded that Slave-Driver Smith deserved his title. He was a dry, bald Yankee, a martinet who piled on the work load and was a ruthless marker-down of even the most strenuous student efforts. Almost all of us in his section were chemical engineers, so we had plenty of group opportunity to discuss him. And discuss him we did. Our favorite fantasy was the fantasy of castrating him; the satisfaction came in our long, elaborate discussions of method, which could occupy us for hours at a time. But one day a dissident voice spoke up, saying, "I am not in favor of castrating Slave-Driver Smith." All heads turned toward the speaker. "No," said Pete Franklin, "wrong principle: completely wrong. We will leave his balls intact; we will feed him a diet rich in aphrodisiacs, and we will amputate his cock at its root so that he will live all the rest of his life under the tortures of Desire from which he will be unable in any way to rid himself, forever and ever, Amen." This new idea won instant acceptance and a subcommittee was appointed to discuss ways and means. A minor disagreement arose as to whether a rusty hatchet should be used or conditions of strict surgical asepsis should prevail. An undergraduate biologist swung the votes for strict asepsis. He did not want Slave-Driver Smith to die of an infection; this would be self-defeating. What we wished for him in his altered state was the ripest of ripe old ages.

Meanwhile, in Slave-Driver Smith's class, full decorum was always preserved, there was no complaint, and full outward respect was rendered by student to professor. I really think it was more fun like that: hates lovingly cherished and sublimated into fantasies that were rich in their own rewards. Slave-Driver Smith drove on, wholly unconscious that in the students who sat rank upon rank before him all minds were dwelling with delight on the thought of cutting his intromittent organ off at the very root.

The day of the Confrontation has taken a lot of imaginative joy out of collegiate life.

• • •

So I ended my junior year at M.I.T. in a state of high but not wholly disagreeable confusion. I had the soul of an alchemist, which was not a good foundation for a career as a chemical engineer. Yet I was three-quarters through with my undergraduate career and not in any danger of flunking out. In Tubby Rogers I had found a hero-teacher, and in writing things for him or for the *VooDoo* I had rediscovered an activity to which I could give my unlimited spontaneous enthusiasm. The thing to do, apparently, was to follow Tubby's advice and consciously persist in taking the wrong path until I would duly come to the end of it. Then we would see what we would see.

160

19·LEWIS AND LITTLE, or, A CONTRAST IN DOCTORS

Like Harvard's, like Princeton's, like even the University of Pennsylvania's, the undergraduates of the Institute had their Dramatic Society. Like the Hasty Pudding, the Triangle, or the Mask and Wig clubs, this baldly called *Tech Show* was *not* organized for the improvement of the Drama as an art form, and even less to be "experimental theater." Its purpose was simply to put on a student musical comedy that should be strictly an undergraduate affair, with libretto, lyrics, music and acting carried out by them alone—the only three professionals being the coach (i.e., the director), the ballet mistress, and the orchestrator of the music, who, when performance time finally came, would be found directing the student pit orchestra. The Institute had pitifully few coeds in my day, but if there had been 300 they would all have been debarred from any connection with *Tech Show*, for part of the elaborate charade was the obligation that the Ladies of the Ensemble, as well as the Gentlemen, had to be males.

Perhaps I was inspired by the play-reading binge I had been on since I took Tubby's course in nineteenth-century drama. I was definitely not encouraged by Tubby, or by anybody else, but the determination rose in me that summer between my junior and senior years to write a libretto for the 1922 *Tech Show* and submit it when the fall term began. So all summer long I slaved at dramatic construction, which turned out not to be so easy as it had seemed to a casual critic. I have only the faintest remembrance now what it was all about, but I was much impressed in those days by the so-called Well-Made Play, so I am sure I tried to follow the principles of Sardou. And it won the competition. I was in seventh heaven and, being hopelessly stage-struck from my earliest days, I attended all the auditions for parts, all conferences on words and music, all cast and orchestra rehearsals, from beginning to end. Since it took from early October to get things into shape for performances the following April, I was obviously committing another large block of my time to non-chemical-engineering affairs. More than that: The editor in chief of the *VooDoo* got put on probation, which meant he had to resign his job; I was next in line, so I got it. The curious result of all this was that I suddenly emerged from total obscurity into being a campus figure—not a towering figure like the editor of *The Tech* (student newspaper) or the class president, yet still a sort of figure. But this had a curious effect on me; once rejected, always rejected. So I pushed away most new friendships now possible and stayed pretty strictly with the small circle of friends already made.

• • •

But along with my new distractions there came also the unsettling experience of becoming once again interested in engineering. Just when I thought I had myself figured out at last, a new gauze of uncertainty enveloped my mind. For this, a genius of an engineer, a brilliant teacher and a unique personality, all wrapped up together in one man, was responsible. The man was Warren Kendall Lewis, Ph.D., Senior Professor of Chemical Engineering and Head of the Department. He was known invariably to colleagues and contemporaries and students as "Doc"—a nickname that *I* always slightly resented as being unworthy of his stature as thinker and teacher.

One remarkable thing about Doc Lewis, the first that would occur to any observer, was that despite a lifetime spent in his profession there was nothing about his appearance or manner that suggested any of the stereotypes of the teacher. He was not the absent-minded professor that Norbert Wiener was later to typify so perfectly. Nor was he the urbane charmer, the classroom entertainer, the ruminative pipe-puffer, nor the master of the flashing retort that would have made him a campus Character. He was of average height and weight, neither the stooped scholar nor the ramrod martinet. His clothes inclined to be a bit rumpled and baggy but with no hint of academic eccentricity in the bagginess. He wore the same necktie three months at a time, and his glittering gold-framed spectacles sat only slightly askew on a somewhat lumpy nose. His face usually bore the slight suggestion, only slight, of a frown. When he entered a classroom he neither strolled nor stalked; he just walked in. Nevertheless, when he did, an instantaneous hush fell, for there was not one undergraduate who was not terrified of Doc. I have spent some years trying to account for this, and the best thing that I can come up with was that Doc always looked as if he were going to explode, and a shard from him was going to rip through your intestines any minute. Yet I knew him, as it was to turn out, not only as an undergraduate but for twenty-five years thereafter—and he never did explode. Nor did he ever cease looking as if he were going to.

Doc Lewis lectured to a large class thrice weekly on the principles of chemical engineering, and what even the poorest student in the class felt was the tremendous force of his desire to transfer what he knew from his head to yours. It was this force, I am sure, that caused him to speak in italics: "Now the *result* of this finding was to bring to *everybody's* attention the *importance* of the *parameter.*" This was one of only two peculiarities in his classroom style. The other was pausing after a long sentence, taking a deep breath, and then blowing his cheeks out to their full elastic limit before exhaling and going on—perhaps a sort of *visible* meditation before plunging further.

Listening to Doc and learning something from his lectures was only one of the excitements of the chemical engineering of the day. Another considerable one was that there was no textbook—none had yet been written. So we worked from syllabi—badly mimeographed sheets of paper that were a mixture of text, tentative statements of principles, theories and problems, which might, or might not, have solutions. We were, in effect, guinea pigs; after undergoing countless revisions, our mimeographed study sheets would eventually become the preliminary manuscript for the eventual textbook, not published until some years after the Class of 1922 had graduated, *Principles of Chemical Engineering* by Walker, Lewis and McAdams.

It isn't much to say that these three men, particularly the first two, aided by the distinguished chemist-alumnus Arthur Dehon Little, *invented* chemical engineering and brought forth, out of such empirical and messy nineteenth-century arts as leather tanning, glue boiling and papermaking, an engineering discipline susceptible to mathematical and other scientific manipulation. Dr. Little had been visited by inspiration a few years earlier and had proposed the concept of "unit operations"—heat transfer, filtration, distillation, evaporation, etc.—which not only brought order out of chaos to the chemical industry but made the engineering of chemistry a logically *teachable* entity. And Doc Lewis was the teacher of teachers.

When his course began in the fall of 1921 I was aghast to discover that by the luck of the draw I had been assigned to Doc's own recitation section. Being an indifferent student, I was deathly afraid of him; being near him always, in those early days, made me feel as if I were standing in wet shoes close to a 100,000-volt transformer, which was not only humming but crackling. As a matter of fact, Doc *did* crackle, almost constantly, but no lethal bolt from him ever struck down a student. He was much too wise—and humane—a teacher to humiliate a pupil, but I was too green to know this. So I was scared. Like Miss Stellwagon, he had The Eye.

The climax of my scaredness came early in the first term of Doc's recitation section. For the preceding week we had had a mimeographed sheet of problems to mull over; today was the day we were supposed to have constructive ideas about them.

Doc sent his crackling glance around the room. "Let's take up Number Four first, just to get out of a rut," he said. Problem No. 4 had to do with a blast furnace. From the data given it was not functioning properly. So the problem posed was: What steps would you take to restore the furnace to normal operation?

"Russell," said Doc, "let's have some suggestions from you." Robert Price Russell, in later years to be president of the Standard Oil Development Company, the research arm of the Standard Oil Company (New Jersey), frankly admitted that he had no suggestions that morning.

"Greenewalt," said Doc, addressing Crawford Hallock Greenewalt, in whose horoscope it was written that he would at suitably later times become president and then board chairman of E. I. du Pont de Nemours & Co., "maybe you have an idea how to tackle it." But Greenewalt confessed that he had tried several approaches, none of which had proved fruitful.

Now this was very bad. In fact, it was horrible. It was horrible because out of all the problems on the sheet the only one I thought I perceived how to tackle was No. 4—but if two of the best students in the class were stuck, then obviously my naïve approach must be wrong. I stooped and untied my left shoelace so that I could then slowly retie it; I wished to be invisible; I wished Doc to think me seriously if not totally indisposed. When I looked up, he was staring straight at me, and the morning sun glittered dangerously on his spectacles.

"Well, Hodgins," he said, "we seem to have a hard time getting started this morning. How are we going to get off dead center? What's the first thing you'd do?"

I was trapped. Either I would have to say I didn't know or I would have to give my home-brewed foolish answer. "You can't make things any worse," said Doc encouragingly. "Was there a big dance last night or something?"

"Well, sir," I said, my voice coming from far, far away, "the first thing I think I'd do would be to run a carbon balance on the furnace."

"A carbon balance!" said Doc, not only in italics but boldface.

Now, Doc would explode at last. At last the long-caged lightning would strike.

"A—carbon—balance," Doc repeated, gathering up his powers. "Well, I don't know about the rest of you, but that's how *I'd* start."

I think I must have fainted, or something. Anyway, I remember no more about the rest of that hour except its ending. I never knew Greenewalt well in undergraduate days, but Bob Russell and I were good friends from being deskmates in a class on chemical German several years before. So I was pleased when he waited for me in the corridor. His message was quite brief. "You son of a bitch," he said. This was the high point of my career as a chemical engineer. It was close to the end of it, too.

• • •

Tech Show got produced in April 1922, and quite successfully. Although I can't recall the slightest wisp about my libretto, I can still hear the music of the student composers; an electrical engineer and a chemist provided most of it, and it was good enough to be reorchestrated and played by the Boston Pops Orchestra that summer. But the student pit orchestra of the actual

165

showtime was pretty good, too. These were days of high formality; tuxedos were not high-toned enough for the orchestra; white tie and tails were *de rigueur*.

With the show out of the way, and May being the month when the heads of all student activities gave way to their successors of the class behind them, little was left in prospect except the coming final examinations. What was I going to do after graduation? I had only one notion. It swiftly came to nothing. Arthur Dehon Little, M.I.T. Class of '85, was very much alive in 1922 and active head of the firm he had founded. Unknown to him, I had put him on a very high pedestal indeed. He was handsome and distinguished; he was an illustrious chemist; he had codified chemical engineering; he was an after-dinner speaker of grace and wit and, withal, so highly literate that he was a contributor to the *Atlantic Monthly*, no less. So I very much wanted to work for Dr. Little, but "as a report writer or something" was as close as I could come to imagining my utility to his even then large and prosperous consulting firm, fronting splendidly on Memorial Drive, scarcely a mile from the Institute. I told Tubby of my ambitions and Tubby promptly supplied me with a letter of introduction.

That had put me in fine fettle. Dr. Little and Tubby knew each other more than casually for Dr. Little was president of the Alumni Association that year and Tubby had been for five years editor of *The Technology Review*, a quarterly published by the Alumni Association, and the only nonalumnus ever to hold that post.

So when I was granted the appointment to present Tubby's praiseful letter, I looked forward to a cordial time. And that's not what I encountered at all.

The handsome Dr. Little, seated behind his handsome desk in his handsome office, whose windows gave on the placid beauty of the Charles River Basin, politely read Tubby's letter. Then, gracefully opening a silver cigarette box, he gracefully lighted an elegant cigarette and raised his eyebrows into an inquiring arc: "Whatever you have to say, pray begin." I stammered my ill-thought-out piece. Dr. Little emitted a meditative puff of smoke. No, he said distinctly, he did not think that quite fitted in. Did I have any further ideas? I did not, of course. Well, said Dr. Little, rising from behind his desk, he was very glad to have met me, and if anything occurred to him . . . . It was all over in six minutes. My hero had not cottoned to me at all; in fact, I had been given the Push-off Polite about as quickly as possible. It was actually more disconcerting than discouraging. No finger of help had been raised; no hopeful or helpful sentiment had been expressed. I had come warmly recommended; my necktie was straight; I was especially washed. I must have done something very wrong, or else the business of finding a job had a lot to it that I didn't know about. Ivory hunters from the large corporations of the day were already thronging the Institute corridors, but they were hunting for high-markers, and I had long ago ceased to be one; besides, I didn't want to go to China for Standard Oil even if they'd have me. So once again I lapsed into vagueness. In spite of that I had a job before I had my diploma.

• • •

The graduation ceremonies of the Class of 1922 were unlike anything ever before or since in Institute history. For one thing we were the biggest class until then to be graduated; the Institute had no auditorium or hall of any kind to house us, our proud parents, sisters, cousins and aunts, and others entitled to attend. For another, in a curious burst of formality, completely countercurrent to the age of the flapper, the hip flask of warm bathtub gin, and the New Necking, which had just opened, the Class of 1922 had voted for an academic procession with caps and gowns, hitherto eschewed in Institute tradition. And for still another there was no president to preside or to hand out the degrees of Bachelor of Science. As things turned out, no degrees whatever were handed out that graduation day. An Act of God intervened.

After a lot of conferring between faculty committees and student government it was decided that the graduation exercises would be held in the Great Court; the vast expanse was open to the Charles River Basin but was enclosed on its other three sides by the Colonnade, capped by the Great Dome, and the pyloned embracing arms on either side. Today, the Great Court is a thing of beauty, landscaped with noble trees, shrubs and carefully tended flowerbeds, but in 1922 it was a void floored by coarse pebbles as the top dressing of the made land—for where the Institute now stands were once the clam-rich tidal flats of the River Charles. So on this sea of pebbles it was decided that the Class of 1922 would be officially launched into the world. Duly, the Department of Buildings and Power contracted for a

167

huge circus tent to be erected in case of rain; within it was built an appropriate platform and were placed several thousand of what are appropriately known as undertaker chairs. This huge expanse of canvas was put up by experienced circus riggers under the eternally watchful eye of Major Smith, the Institute's Superintendent of Buildings and Power.

• • •

Graduation day dawned gray and breezy, but without rain. As the day wore along—ceremonies were to start at 2 P.M.—the wind freshened and the sky was full of scudding clouds. The academic procession from Walker Memorial to the Great Court was distinctly a flappy affair, for the wind was now playfully gusty. But only a few caps got blown off, and soon everybody was within the shelter and safety of the vast three-ring tent.

The most memorable speech of the day—because the worst— was delivered by Colonel John Buffalo Christian, Head of the Department of Military Science and Tactics. Why he was on the program at all, I don't know, but it was he who lost the battle that was soon to ensue. During several preceding speeches, mercifully short, the wind had steadily risen in force, and the canvas, which had up to then been merely flapping rather heavily, began making much more resentful sounds.

Colonel Christian, who manifestly had been supposed to speak five minutes and then sit the hell down, launched instead into an interminable flux, rich in allusions to a happy boyhood. All the while he spoke, the wind rose. The canvas roof was now beginning to belly upward and then slap down with a thunderous *whumpf*. The forest of the tent's internal bracing poles, of four-inch diameter, began first to sway and then to groan. Colonel Christian, obviously inured to battle conditions, plowed indomitably on.

By now his audience was distinctly restive. It was clear we were in the midst of a line squall; Colonel Christian's words were now all but inaudible in the midst of the thunderous *whumpfs*; all his audience's eyes were not on him but on the wildly billowing tent roof and the dancing support poles.

After two externities, Colonel Christian sat down, well pleased. Elihu Thomson, that distinguished scientist who had been called on more than once to be the Institute's figurehead president during one or another unhappy interregnum, then rose, but before he could utter two sentences there was a rifle-sharp crack. There were some screams and the audience sprang from its undertaker chairs. One internal bracing pole had snapped in two, on a long diagonal fracture line. The bottom half crashed across the chairs; the top half, still attached to the roof, began a wild series of lashing swings. That was the limit of endurance for Major Smith. Cutting in on Acting President Thomson he bawled "All Out!" at the top of his lungs. It was a happy thing that the tent had no skirt; it could be vacated from any of the 360 degrees of the compass, and it was. But 2,000 compacted people make a slow-moving mass, so it was obvious that the next command would be "All hands to the guy ropes" in the hope of keeping the tent from complete collapse while there were still people inside. A continuing series of rifle-shot sounds indicated that one by one the internal supporting poles were giving way.

About twenty people per rope—students, faculty, anybody—dug their heels in and strained to hold on. It was a losing fight; the tent would be satisfied with nothing but complete collapse—fortunately with nothing under it now but those undertaker chairs. As I clung to my particular guy rope I had a momentary flash into what Major Smith must be thinking about Colonel John Buffalo Christian—for the Boston newspapers next day would inevitably have a lot of fun with M.I.T., whose graduates could tame the Yellow River in China or build the longest bridges and the highest dams in the world, but who could not peg down a tent so it wouldn't flop over in a breeze.

Eventually my guy rope went with the rest. Slowly and with dignity it pulled its four-foot peg from the ground and went where the wind listed. I was conscious of being dragged, nose and belly down, through several feet of the Great Court's rolling pebbles. When I sought to sit up I realized I was entangled with someone. When we disengaged I found myself gazing into the face of Assistant Professor of Mathematics Norbert Wiener. He returned my gaze.

"Haven't I seen you before, somewhere?" he asked me.

"Yes, sir," I said. "I was in your sophomore calculus section once."

"Ah," said Professor Wiener, "so that was it. Well, nice to have seen you again."

And in that fashion, more or less, I was graduated from the Massachusetts Institute of Technology.

20 · RUINED BY LOVE, OR,
ALCOHOL DISCOVERED

BEFORE ALL THIS had happened, some little time before, in fact
I had begun having some truck with the Assistant Dean of Stu·
dents, Harold Edward Lobdell. It was not about disciplinary mat
ters or scholastic, either. I was a little puzzled to know what
it *was* about.

Lobdell, Class of '17, was three years older than I, and brand
new in his job. So was the Dean, Professor Talbot, Head of the
Chemistry Department. He had not wanted to be Dean very
much, but Mrs. Talbot wanted to be Mrs. Dean with a passion
So it came about that Professor Talbot became Dean Talbot. Dear
Talbot was not a very outgoing personality so he swiftly cas·
about him for an assistant who could compensate for his deficien·
cies. And in Lobdell he found his ideal man.

Lobby knew everybody in the Institute, high and low. He was
artful, shrewd, deft, with an easy manner, a genius for academic
political infighting, and a streak of sadism in him a mile wide
But he had one virtue that overrode almost all his vices: where
the good of the Institute was concerned, his was the sword that
knew no brother.

His infallible instinct to find the center of action and make
straight for it was not only valuable to him but valuable to the
Institute he served so wholeheartedly.

In 1922 Lobby sniffed out a growing dissatisfaction within
the Alumni Association. The presidency of the Association was
almost wholly honorary and its term ran for only one year, so
the fact that Dr. Little, the illustrious chemist, was about to be
succeeded by Harry Johann Carlson, an illustrious Boston archi
tect, meant next to nothing; the work-horse officer of the Alumn
Association was always the secretary-treasurer. And he, one

Arthur Hopkins, was quite dissatisfied with the way the Association's affairs were going. In particular, he was dissatisfied with the Association's official organ, *The Technology Review*, a dun-colored quarterly that Tubby Rogers edited with his left hand—an arrangement that had begun as a wartime emergency measure and then outlasted the war. Tubby didn't particularly relish the job and was the first to agree that an alumni magazine should be edited by an alumnus, but nobody had come along to supplant him, and since he was paid an extra $500 a year—quite a supplement to an assistant professor's salary then—he felt no pressure to give it up.

All this Lobby knew. And none of this did I, until several years later. But Lobby's earlier and seemingly aimless conversations with me were actually sizings up, and once he felt satisfied with me, he went to Tubby, having somehow found out the affectionate bond between us, saying that Arthur Hopkins, in the name of the Alumni Association, wanted him, Lobby, to take over the management of the *Review*, which had previously never had any—all true enough—and would he, Tubby, relinquish his editorship and its annual $500 if I were hired as managing editor? Tubby promptly said he would, whereupon Lobby ceased being vague with me and unfolded such portions of his plan as he thought it appropriate I should know. There was nothing shady or dishonest about this; it was just very adroit manipulation. Lobby would be editor, he told me, and take the $500 a year that had been Tubby's. I would be managing editor at $1,500 a year. And that wasn't all, said Lobby. He had wangled out of Arthur Hopkins an agreement that if the new *Review* (it would henceforth be a monthly) should show any profit at the end of the year, it would be divided—70 per cent to me, 30 per cent to him. True, the *Review*, which was just my age, having been founded in 1899, had never once shown anything but a deficit, but the arrangement was nice in principle.

• • •

Professionally, all this left me in seventh heaven. I not only had a magazine to edit but to create, for it was agreed that the *Review* should be completely redesigned—frequency, size, format, policy, the works. And it was all mine to do, under Lobby's genial and easygoing supervision. The Alumni Office was right across the hall from the Office of the President, and Lobby, who knew how to get anybody to do anything, got Major Smith, of Buildings and Power, to carve out a separate cubicle for me, my name on the door and everything.

From June all through the summer, I worked top speed and top power at everything. Lobby was much more interested in the *Review* than in the Dean's office (which was as good as closed during the summer anyway), so, with him, I flung myself into the job of remaking the *Review*, working day and night, seven days a week—and as in the old Trautwine days not because I was being exploited but because I loved it so. I don't know where I found the nerve to fire the old printer and sign a contract with a new one or how to specify and order a year's supply of paper, but I did. We had until October 25 to put out our first issue. I had guidance from Lobby, but for staff I had one girl who for the five years had minded all the office routine between Tubby's quarterly visits, and being at least double my age was not disposed to take any orders from the likes of me. With Lobby's backing I fired her, with ardor, and in her place was lucky enough—or unlucky enough, in view of some subsequent events—to find a crack secretary and stenographer named Rose Emma Lawson, red-haired, pert and extremely attractive. For that first issue I wrote most of the copy myself, in between chasing ads and writing circulation letters. But we had a break of luck, although it involved still more writing, this time at real breakneck speed: the Institute Corporation had elected a new president—Samuel Wesley Stratton, who had founded the National Bureau of Standards—and we were able to break the story in our first issue. Things turned out to be a great success. The *Review* for the year 1922–23 made a profit for the first time in its history, and my 70 per cent of it had the effect of almost trebling my salary. Everything was going absolutely swimmingly for me, except in the Girl Department. Things were terrible there, all the more so because girls have never, never, *never* been more beautifully attractive, more exquisitely girlish than they were when the flapper era was just beginning and all the world was young.

• • •

The offices of *The Technology Review* could hardly have been more perfectly placed. As I have said, the Office of the President was directly opposite, but that scarcely counted. Adjoining or facing on the opposite side were such organizations as the Alumni Office, the Division of Industrial Cooperation and Research, the Publications Office, the Placement Bureau and the News Service. It was headquarters row, and it swarmed with interesting people on interesting errands, interesting visitors asking interesting favors.

As head of the Placement Bureau, the ubiquitous Lobby had recently managed to install his highly competent friend and near classmate Kenneth Reid. Ken, like Lobby, was a graduate of the Institute's Department of Architecture. After the war he had stayed in Paris for a while and then rather mysteriously vanished into India, to get mixed up in the jute trade on behalf of the Bemis Bro. Bag Company. He remained an excellent draftsman, but did not feel any urge—then—to practice his profession. Instead, here he was, a big, handsome, super-six-footer, sporting a waxed mustache that would have been a status symbol if the term had been invented, the Institute's new Placement Officer.

Ken was more Lobby's age than mine, but we became the best of friends and I looked up to him very much—because he was a trained architect, because he had been in Paris and could speak knowingly of the Dôme and Les Deux Magots. He knew and introduced me to that splendid Renaissance Man Samuel Chamberlain, etcher, lithographer, painter, photographer, author and gourmet cook. Ken also introduced me to another architectural friend, Leon Keach, not as multifaceted as Sam, although he, too, had lived in Paris and was now back in Boston, wearing a purple beret and yellow smock and being a draftsman in the architectural offices of Guy Lowell. Ken and I for a while got our lives all mixed up together and I suffered a great deal of pain on his account, though God knows not through his fault. But putting that memory momentarily aside, let me dwell on how, through Ken and Leon, I had the first alcoholic drink of my life.

• • •

Prohibition was in its infancy; the Supreme Court had yet to rule that the *possession* of beverage alcohol was not a crime, only the sale of it. Well, Leon Keach, being very advanced, had a bootlegger, a very furtive and nervous Mr. Cohen, who sold nothing ready-to-drink: his specialty was square cans, with screw caps, that looked as if they were for kerosene, but which contained instead one gallon, more or less, of Belgian alcohol. Mr. Cohen mysteriously did not cater to the bathtub-gin set. The gallon of alcohol cost five dollars, but along with it Mr. Cohen would supply three tiny vials of flavoring: Curaçao, Cointreau or Benedictine. For a slight premium, Grand Marnier, Crème Yvette or Crème de Cacao were also available. Leon favored Curaçao and Benedictine. He was a meticulous worker. He would dissolve just so much sugar in just so much Poland Spring water, mix the resulting syrup (which he spelled *sirop* to be more French) and the Belgian alcohol in exact proportions, and then add Mr. Cohen's vial of essence, drop by drop. After thorough mixing the blend was aged for a day and was then ready for trade use. Ken told me I did not know what I was missing in Leon's Curaçao, and one late summer afternoon, after the business day was over, he, Leon and I assembled in the Placement Office for my initiation. Lily Cups were used. What I estimate to be about two ounces of Leon's compound were poured into each cup. Unfortunately one could not sip one's liqueur; it had to be bottoms-upped before it began dissolving the Lily Cup's paraffin. I knocked mine back without a tremor and, beyond holding my mouth in an O shape for two minutes, gave no evidence of the shock I had sustained. And then the blessed alcohol took hold. I don't know what I wouldn't give—my soul, perhaps—to be able to re-experience the effect of the first of all the drinks in my life. All my tensions and anxieties dissolved, anything was possible, every problem had a solution, and euphoria—a word I didn't know then—suffused me from nave to chaps, and farther. I can remember saying nothing and doing nothing; I was merely content—oh, so content—just to be. Leon, being abstemious and thrifty, recorked his precious bottle and the party was over. Gradually and painlessly my euphoria wore off; I returned to reality without a bump.

What puzzles me now is, Why didn't I have an immediate desire to repeat this delicious experience? That I remember it so vividly after fifty years must argue that I remembered it no less vividly the day after, yet it was a matter of weeks, perhaps of months, before alcohol again passed my lips. It just didn't occur to me. Obviously, alcoholics are made, not born.

*   *   *

I lived now, in Boston, by myself, my undergraduate friends having taken off on careers that led them far away. Sometime or other I had spotted a classified ad that said "Single room available for man in doctor's apartment." I took it. It was a nice big room in a somewhat ratty apartment house right on the clashing crossroads of Boylston Street and Massachusetts Avenue. The doctor's apartment was big, and his housekeeper, dressed in nurselike white, showed me the room, directly across the hall from the doctor's office. He and his housekeeper lived somewhere in the rear, where I never penetrated. When some time later I met the doctor, he turned out to be a pretty scruffy type and an abortionist, or at least a part-time abortionist. One of the apartment's two phones was in my room; if, of an evening, the doctor and his housekeeper were both out and the phone rang persistently enough, I would answer. Oftener than the law of averages would allow, the voice was of a distraught young female, who would swiftly hang up when I said I was not Dr. Arnold. And on several occasions it would be a Boston newspaper reporter wanting to know if such-and-such a story involving the doctor were true. I was always surprised by the unenterprisingness of these newshawks; when I said I didn't know, I just lived there, he merely said thanks and hung up without even asking me who I was. Nevertheless, I grew wary of answering the phone if it was unduly late at night.

My principal recollection of those days was lying at night, alone in a comfortable double bed, and in tears. I had fallen violently in love with Rose Lawson, my secretary, and didn't dare make the slightest gesture toward her. She knew it, and she made the most of it. She liked me, it was plain, but that was all, and although I don't think she had any conscious desire to hurt me, her feminine nature was incapable of resisting the cat-and-mouse situation with which I had presented her. So while continuing to be a loyal and highly efficient secretary, she became also a flirtatious tease, and how long this went on, I mercifully don't remember. But it was due to get worse before it got better. One day another girl, the frank-and-wholesome type, stopped me in the hall. "Why do you waste your time mooning over Rose?" she asked me. "Don't you know she's Ken Reid's girl? And why don't you pay some attention to *Susan?* *She's* got a crush on you." (Note to the reader: her real name was not Susan.)

The first part of the conversation was so devastating that I scarcely heard the second part. That evening I snooped through a big hall window to see if it could be true about Rose and Ken. It could; it was: there they were walking hand in hand toward the Kendall Square subway station. In numb misery I watched them disappear. All I can remember about the rest of that evening was going alone to a Boylston Street restaurant to have dinner. The waitress brought what I ordered. I could not touch it. After I had stared at it for twenty minutes the waitress came to ask "Is everything all right?" I could not risk speech but I could nod. In deference to her I lifted one forkful, choked on it, paid my bill, and went home. This was the end of the world.

• • •

So I was a man of sorrows. But I would conduct myself with dignity before I—before I what? Hanged myself? Went off to seek my fortune in the Transvaal? In the office I tried to treat Rose with a new cool correctness, which she instantly observed. "Are you mad at me, or something? Have I done anything wrong?" Oh, no. Oh, no indeed. So Rose, too, began to observe a cool correctness, and the atmosphere in the office began to become intolerable.

Some days later, Ken Reid, as innocent as a babe of what I was suffering, or that I was suffering at all, said, "Why don't you and Leon and I have dinner and make a night of it?"

We did. Leon's place was far out on Beacon Street in Brookline, but there, after dinner, we went. A full bottle of Benedictine and another of Curaçao awaited us there and this time we could sip from glass water tumblers, not gulp from Lily Cups. I hadn't set out to get drunk because I didn't know what getting drunk meant. But two jolts of liquor had a magical effect on my battered emotions and for the first time in my life I drew the familiar equation of the uninformed: if two drinks make me feel like this, four drinks will make me feel double-better, and six drinks will make me a superman at least. All three of us got more or less drunk that evening, but it was only I who got looping, cockeyed, pissyass drunk. I thought the curve of intoxication just went end-lessly up, and on one of my frequent trips to the john I remember gazing at myself in the mirror and saying, "Oh, it is *glorious* to be so drunk!"

And at that precise moment it was. When it came time to go home Ken and I left together for the long walk to the corner of Boylston and Massachusetts Avenue, and I experienced a little difficulty with balance. This increased. Euphoria, which had been fading fast, vanished, leaving me just plain staggering drunk. Ken steered me into a cafeteria and got black coffee for both of us. I drank two cups, blindly, and when we got out of doors again, I was suddenly, violently, and continuously sick. Fortu-nately we were on the edge of the Fenway, and Ken got me to a park bench to recuperate. My first drunk was a full-spectrum drunk, for now I had a Class-A crying jag, and with a candor I never could have found in sobriety, I sobbed out the whole story that unwittingly involved him and Rose and me. He put his arm around my shoulder. "The same thing, the exact same thing happened to me three years ago. That's why I went to India." And thus he comforted his drunken, brokenhearted "rival."

• • •

Next day I was not well. Not only was I experiencing my first alcoholic hangover; I think I might have had a touch of malaise just from drinking that much flavored sugar syrup, even uncomplicated by Mr. Cohen's alcohol. Yet I must be truthful: the yammers were worse than the nausea. That day and the next I spent in bed, and when I faced the world again, I felt like, although I did not resemble, Algernon Charles Swinburne after a hard experience. (Who was that lodger who had rooms under Swinburne's and who remarked that Watts-Dunton, attempting to get the poet safely home after an evening given over to indul-gence, "sounded as if he were trying to lead a horse upstairs"? Ah, well, no matter.) But my colossal first drunk did have a virtue: my feelings about Rose were now out in the open. If I were a man of sorrows at least I was no longer a man of secret sorrows, and this was an improvement. Moreover, Rose com-pletely changed her attitude toward me. "I think," she said, "that if I weren't in love with Kenneth Reid, I might be in love with you, but I am in love with Kenneth Reid." There was some balm in that.

The story of Rose Lawson and Kenneth Reid is that in due course they were married and lived happily ever after. Literally. This was more than happened to me.

21 · ON GETTING UP COURAGE, OR, ALCOHOL DISMISSED

My FIRST EXPERIENCE with full alcoholic intoxication was enough to last me for quite a while. I have no idea when I had my next drink, except that it was after an interval measured in months, not weeks, and the next time I touched Leon Keach's Benedictine, if that's what it was, I had learned caution and abstemiousness. I was due to forget them again—and yet again—but not for some long time.

Rose was gone, and after a while I got over her with that ease that always surprises the fatally lovesick. But the girl problem remained . . . . What was it that Wholesome Florence had told me about Susan? That Susan had a crush on me?

It could not be true. Susan was a pretty girl, with nicely shaped legs and dark brown hair done up in the fashion of the day then universally described by knowing males as "cootie nests." She was extremely pleasant and agreeable toward me, but a crush? This was ridiculous.

In the days of, for both sexes, the raccoon coat and the flapping, unbuckled galoshes, I had only the galoshes. A distinction was drawn, in those days, between boys of the "Arrow Collar Type" and their opposites. I belonged clearly among their opposites. I despised and was repelled by my own looks. Tubby, a true friend, glanced at my classbook photograph and likened my appearance to "an Early Christian Martyr with a hangover." I could laugh at the terrible aptness of Tubby's description because it was delivered with affection—but what girl would be attracted by such looks? This was distinctly no laughing matter.

But at least I could be attentive to Susan in office hours. I had legitimate reasons to visit the big office where she sat, almost alone. I made the most of them. She would stop work when I came in, and we would chat for five or ten minutes, enjoyably enough. Then I would leave, and that would be that. I came to want, very much, to ask her to go out with me, but two things stopped me dead. First, I did not know how to frame my invitation. Second, I knew she would refuse. She would do it graciously, to be sure, but inevitably; such a pretty and attractive girl would have a lot of boys dangling around her and could pick and choose as she liked.

As an alternative to suicide, I began to think of how I could issue an invitation to Susan and still make bearable her refusal of it. Well, *The Ziegfeld Follies* was in town. I could buy two tickets some time and then call Susan on the phone and explain that a friend of mine had been taken suddenly ill and here I was with the two tickets he had given me and I just wondered if . . . I wondered . . . I . . . No. I couldn't do it. For one thing, it would have to be a Saturday night, because on weekdays Susan and I were practically next-door-office neighbors, and I couldn't, I just couldn't, pull off this act face to face. I could only do it by telephone, and the telephone dictated Saturday, and of course Susan would have a previous date.

So it was hopeless. But I was desperate. So, for a Saturday evening two weeks in advance (to ensure seventh row, center aisle) I bought the two tickets I surely would later throw away. Then I started to sweat out the waiting time. Nobody gets sick and gives you two tickets to the *Follies* except on the very same day, for my invented friend would obviously be hoping against hope that his temperature would drop enough so that he and his wife could go, after all. So I daren't call Susan too early in the morning. On the other hand, every additional hour of lateness increased the already towering probability that Susan would have been bespoken. Three o'clock would have to be Zero hour.

By two thirty I had given up the whole plan. I could not summon up the courage to go to the phone. For some reason, my doctor-landlord had a coin-box telephone on his office wall; he was out, his office door was open, and I could see the phone. All I had to do was take six steps, insert my nickel (yes, nickel), give the operator (yes, operator; no dials yet) Susan's number, long ago memorized, and make my speech. But could I do it? No, I could not, because another aborting possibility arose in my mind: not Susan, but Susan's mother, would answer the phone and say she was sorry but Susan was out and hadn't said when she'd be back. This would be, if anything, worse than the out-and-out rejection; the test would fail of any result and I would just be left hanging by my thumbs because a second call would have been, for some obscure but absolute reason, impossible.

But when three o'clock came, I went like a sleepwalker to the telephone and, like a sleepwalker, called Susan's number. And Susan answered. This restored me to a near-normal consciousness. I had hypnotized myself into believing that my made-up story was the veritable truth, so I had no trouble at all in making my lie sound convincing. By any chance, would she, could she, with all apologies for the lateness of the hour . . .

"Why, I'd *love* to," said Susan.

I had burst from a prison. Now what did I do with my new freedom?

• • •

Susan's circumstances, like mine, were modest, so there was no nonsense about flowers, candy or taxicabs. (I had never ridden in a taxicab; these were for The Rich.) This was strictly a walking and streetcar job. The *Follies* was fun, I guess, but I was much too preoccupied by being Out with a Girl to pay much heed. And by the middle of Act III I was of course worrying over what one did with the girl after the show. Schrafft's? This did not seem very dashing, but Schrafft's it was, for Susan declared that a chocolate ice-cream cone would be just the thing. Halfway through my soda I almost choked with still another anxiety: in what fashion should I bid her good night? Should I kiss her? I mean, should I *try* to kiss her? Would she be mortally offended? On the other hand, would she be mortally offended if I did *not* try? I knew about girls from reading about them in short stories, but this was of singularly little help now that I was in the company of a real one, who was all soft and pretty and smelled utterly delicious. I knew that Susan, in common with all the other girls of her age, had discarded the corset and therefore *rolled her stockings*, which, to hear the older generation go on, was the last word in depravity, the garter belt not having been yet invented. I knew that girls were straining at their leashes as never

181

before, and that Necking had become a Social Problem. But this was not going to be of any practical help to me during the final half hour that now faced me.

Well, with thumping heart I got Susan as far as her own front porch. As she put her key into the lock and half opened the door she thanked me prettily for the evening. Now or never. I inclined my face toward hers and my lips gave the lightest possible brush on one cheek before, in a flash, she had slipped inside the door and was gone. Had she let it happen or was it just a clumsy accident?

This was going to provide me with tortures of doubt next day, but on the long walk home I was exhilarated. I had succeeded, in the words of the immortal George Fitch, the creator of Siwash College, "in steering a girl from home and back without bumping her into a freight car," and this, briefly, was triumph enough.

• • •

I have not overdrawn my twenty-three-year-old quaking timidity in the whole arena of girls. This bespoke, of course, the deepest feelings of insecurity, unworthiness and inferiority running through every layer of my psyche. (There's another word that had no currency in the 1920's; an older man once asked me what it meant; I didn't know, and neither did he.) This being so, I am eternally puzzled to know why I was able to conceal these feelings in my working life. In fact, the word "submerge" is better than "conceal"; in my job I had the most comfortable feelings of knowing what I ought to do, and knowing how to do it, unhampered by feelings of doubt or indecision. Indeed, as I look back on things now, it seems to me that I splattered my young ego all over the pages of *The Technology Review* Nobody ever called me down for it; in fact, Tubby and Lobby both rather encouraged it. An extremely dignified body, the Institute's Alumni Council, held monthly meetings all of which I reported, always with high irreverence, in the *Review*. I think an occasional member would complain to Lobby to the effect "that kid has gone too far this time," but Lobby always upheld me and I never ceased, although I am sure that if I could reread any of those brash reports today I would blush over their downright cheek. In other words, an extremely timid and shy person

182

coexisted in the same body with an extremely brash and assertive one, and I don't quite see how that could have been. Nor how it continues to be, for at age seventy-plus it still does.

• • •

The longer my *Review* job went on, the happier with it I became. It was downright fun, staying at my office typewriter until perhaps two in the morning, pounding out copy, whether of news items, signed articles, those Alumni Council reports, or Class Notes. But the happiest time each month was when, loaded down with a mixture of late copy, galley strips, line cuts, halftones, page proofs and dummy, I would set out for Lynn, Massachusetts, and the printing plant of Perry & Elliott.

Nowadays one would go from Cambridge to Lynn by whizzing over some superhighway. In my time it was not so easy. A complicated streetcar ride brought you to North Station. The Boston & Maine then lugged you to Lynn, but if you had just missed a train, it might save time to take the narrow gauge—the Boston, Revere Beach & Lynn R.R.—for your walk to the Perry & Elliott plant was about the same distance regardless.

Perry & Elliott was a Monotype shop: a small one, with two keyboards and four casters, a row of six flat-bed Miehles, some old-fashioned job presses, and a composing room to match. The job of final make-up could be much better done with me in the composing room than me in Cambridge, for fitting problems could be met on the spot, with no delay. Hangers, widows, a bad break on a runaround: at first the head comp would come to me with a proof showing the trouble, but later he began paying me the compliment that I, like he, could read type right to left and image-reversed and we would settle a problem in his alley, not at a desk. We ran a tight typographical ship. Not even a journeyman compositor or a two-thirder would dream of allowing a widow (a less-than-full-length line) as the top line of a column. More than that: less than three full lines at the top of a column before the short line that marked the end of a paragraph was bad typographic practice; if the type broke that way we'd alter the copy accordingly. (Letter- or wordspacing was a tabooed way to get out of such a fix.) Hyphens at the ends of two consecutive lines? In a hard pinch, maybe yes. But in three consecutive lines? Never. And we (I mean the comps as well as myself) used to

183

examine every page for "rivers"; wherever we found one, we would break it up, no matter what the cost in word-fiddlings or time charges.

The pressroom fascinated me no less. The superintendent showed me how to fold a sixteen-page sheet wet from the press; I was snobbish-proud of this learned ability. The superintendent and I used to confer over the scheduling of presses for the *Review* forms: he would come to me to say that if I would drop my work on page 44 long enough to give a final O.K. on page 67, that would mean that Eddie Gannon could lock up form number five, for which he would have a press waiting in about half an hour. Eddie Gannon was the best stoneman in any shop, anywhere; that was an article of faith in the Perry & Elliott plant. Always providing he was sober. Sometimes, when he would come back from lunch white-faced and stunned-looking (he never staggered, so you couldn't judge that way), a colleague would lead him gently home and his assistant would take over. But there were times when Eddie would have a drop—the merest drop, mind you, with the noon meal—and these were the times when danger lurked. Locking up a sixteen-page form of Monotype in a chase so that every piece of metal is bull tight against its neighbor in a plane that would have to satisfy Euclid is not a casual job like piloting a jet. An eight-page form, maybe, but Eddie should not have gone for the sixteen-pager of the May issue. He did, though. The form stood all the tests on the stone and then was upended for its trip to the pressroom on the two pairs of little steel wheels that trundled it.

Midway on its journey without warning it buckled and exploded, scattering tens of thousands of pieces of type metal all the way into the front office. It was as shocking a thing to see as the collapse of a ten-story building—and it took two days of weekend double time to go all the way back to galleys and slowly duplicate everything that had been lost. But it was done. Nobody—outside the front office—blamed Eddie Gannon in the slightest; it was just one of those things. And triple time was triple time.

• • •

I got to be very fond of the composing room and pressroom gangs at Perry & Elliott—particularly the former. These tough guys, with minimum educations and that maximum fondness for alcohol and fornication that seems to permeate the printing and publishing trades from top to bottom, were ungrammatical in speech and so foulmouthed in language as to make a union plumber wince, but they were a lot more literate than the average high-school English teacher. Years of setting copy and handling type had given them their own set of merciless and free-spoken values. "This guy's fulla shit," Jim MacKinnon, the head comp, said to me about the notes of a certain class secretary, and he was right. Jim hadn't been consciously reading at all; he'd been transferring type metal from galley tray to page make-up, and had come to a correct, if incidental, conclusion. God knows how many million ems of type Jim had handled during his thirty years in composing-room alleys, but I think his fingers told him what the metal was saying, as a doctor's fingers kneading a patient's belly tell him what probably lies underneath. And it was from Jim that I got a compliment I have never forgotten, because it was not intended as a compliment at all, but only as a remark. "Your copy sets close," he told me one night as he tied up a final page. Since then I have seldom written a paragraph without asking myself if it would set close by the inviolable standards of Jim MacKinnon. The Perry & Elliott days were beacon days in my professional life, and I would come back from Lynn to Cambridge after a one- or two-day session, the issue closed, filled with a sense of peace and satisfaction. Except once, but that was later.

• • •

Meanwhile, at last I had a girl. When next I saw Susan after the *Follies* episode she told me she had had a wonderful time, and I was not so chickenhearted that this didn't give me the courage to ask if we could go out again some time. "I'd love to," said Susan.

But I didn't have Susan full time. Susan had a more-or-less official beau, who was a Harvard man and an Arrow Collar Type, damn him; accordingly I automatically relegated myself to second place. Susan seemed to be a little casual about him, and did not refer to him often, but there was no question, he had seen her first.

Susan and I went to the movies about once a week, and of

185

course I saw her in the office every day, and my fear of seeming unworthy or unfit in her eyes fairly quickly disappeared. In this process she actively helped; in the subtle, indirect ways a girl has of telling a boy she likes him, Susan told me that. In our ripening relationship, I continued to pay her every attention and compliment I could think of—yet when we parted after an evening, I never again attempted to kiss her. I was too shy, I told myself, and it was true. But I, too, was playing a game, albeit an unconscious one. And in playing it I discovered for myself what I could have learned from a more careful reading of Shaw's *Man and Superman:* the woman is the wooer.

It's far away and long ago, so I have no recollection of how long Susan and I stayed at arm's length. But I will never forget the moment when all this changed. As I was saying my usual good night to her, she softly and shyly asked, "Why do I never get kissed?" Whereupon our lips met and opened, and we clung to each other in a rapture of young love.

•   •   •

Young love is pretty clumsy. One thing it does not know is how to deal with next day. Last night's kiss had been, for me, the first really shattering collision with sexuality I had ever had. And Susan had certainly acted—but this couldn't be so—as if the same had been true with her. So all I could think of to say next morning in the office was "Are you sorry about last night?" I was rewarded by a vehement shake of the head that said No with an exclamation mark. There was an antidote for this awkwardness, we both knew; it was to be found in repetition. We practiced it assiduously. Where was that Arrow Collar beau? He was real. I had met him. But he did not figure in the present equation.

Before everyone had an automobile and when parents still counted, young love had a hard time finding places of seclusion and was apt to end up in a rear balcony of some movie palace, where the ushers were equipped with flashlights to see that things didn't go too far. This was far from ideal. Moreover, you can't kiss forever without finding yourself, in the chaste language of Floyd Dell, whose first novel, *Moon-Calf*, had recently hit the best-seller list, "on the verge of a more desperate wish." What my body yearned for my lips could not express. Neither could

186

Susan's—directly. But girls are *much* brighter than boys when the boy needs goading.

"Let's run away together," said Susan in the office one bright morning when we were alone there together. And for weeks and months we played this fantasy game of running away, to sceptered isles, to fairy kingdoms, to elflands unknown and hitherto undreamed of. It was our only relief. Meanwhile, I was still living in the distressingly real world of my furnished room in the doctor's apartment at the corner of Boylston Street and Massachusetts Avenue; an ideal place to run away from.

• • •

One night, asleep in the double bed whose single occupancy made me so restless and unhappy, I was wakened by a piercing scream from the rear of the doctor's apartment. It did not sound like a woman's scream. The scream was followed in a moment by a great deal of scurrying, but instead of getting up to investigate, as I should have, I played doggo, never having been in the apartment's rear before, and after a while, I went back to sleep again.

Dressed to face the world in the morning, I opened my door to behold the housekeeper red-eyed and weeping. "Dr. Arnold died in the night," she sobbed. "He had a stroke that paralyzed his chest muscles. Didn't you hear his scream?"

I went to the shabby funeral. The housekeeper said she didn't know what she was going to do, but she had been appointed Dr. Arnold's administrator and as soon as possible she would dispose of the doctor's things and vacate the apartment. This would probably give me about a month to find another room.

Naturally, I had told Susan of the doctor's death, so now I told her of the conversation with his housekeeper.

"I was just thinking," said Susan, who had a seraphic smile, "that if you had your own apartment we wouldn't need to run away."

22 · LIME STREET, or,
HAIR BESTREWN

I HOPE BEACON HILL in Boston will always be a glory. In the 1920's it was in need of reclamation, and was getting it. Beacon Street at its beginnings opposite the State House was always beautiful and more so, house by succeeding house, as it ran downgrade toward the River Charles. Mt. Vernon Street was a close second. Behind it, in the 1920's, things were by no means pristine, but reclamation was going on. (Fortunately a street sign that could exist only in Boston was still there when I last was: "JOY PLACE—DEAD END—NO PASSING THROUGH.") The farther you went downhill, whether perpendicular to Beacon or parallel, the worse the streets got, until, still in the shadow of the State House, you were in a slum of once lovely buildings, first gone to seed and then turned rotten. But whether proud Beacon Street or slimy Primus, so close behind it, all those rights-of-way led down to garish Charles Street, and between this honky-tonk and the river you suddenly came on an acre or so of utter serenity that was still in 1920 pretty much as it must have been in 1890; made a gridiron by streets like Brimmer and Lime, still with gas lamps, and not one of them wide enough for two carts to pass.

I must have been an assiduous reader of the *Transcript*'s classified ads; in any event, my eye one day caught the offering of "1-rm. furn. apt.; kitch., bath, Murphy bed, elev., 3 mo. sublet only; ref. req.; 20 Lime St.," and to that offer I responded promptly. I forget what the rent was, but I could afford it, and having passed the reference test, I would have taken it whether I could have afforded it or not. For here, on this lovely street, was a discreet new apartment house and on its second floor was a handsomely "furn. apt." whose bathroom was a real bathroom, and whose kitchen was a real kitchen with—I don't know why this made such an impression of luxury on me—an electric dumb-waiter. On one of the oldest and certainly the quietest and most sedate little streets of Old Boston tranquillity, I had found—a love nest. I was magnificently portable in those days; two suit-cases held all my belongings, so within a day I had moved into it.

In the 1920's, youth lied to its parents about sex, sexual experiences, sexual experimentations, usually by silence, or as was rarely necessary, by denial. Was this a better system than today's open technique of yes-we're-shacking-up-and-what-are-you-going-to-do-about-it? I have no judgment to pass, but I can report that the knowledge of secret transgression heightened the excitement; the danger of possible discovery did likewise. Susan and I were indeed running away together; geographically not very far; emotionally to Elysium. We were going to bed together; were going to spend the night in each other's arms and find out at first hand what this tremendous experience was like. It was a first for both of us, and it took a great deal of planning. In fact, it already had; but now at last we were ready to move into the action stage. I had no resident parents to cope with, but Susan had—and the ploy of course was "the girl friend" with whom she was to spend that night. (A veritable girl friend existed, and was an accessory before the fact; Susan and I both knew she had ample reason never to betray us.)

•   •   •

When the day of the actual night arrived, Susan and I were both inwardly quaking with fear—not at what we contemplated doing, but at the possibility of something going askew with our plans. No matter how we plotted our logistics, we could not avoid a three-block walk. We would take it separately, of course, and I would carry Susan's bag, but it was unquestionably a girl's bag, *so what was I doing with it in case I met—Who?* If I had been carrying a girl's bag because she had asked me to pick up a pair of ice skates she had left for repair, I would have had no slightest consciousness of guilt. But it was not ice skates in the bag; I knew what *was* in the bag and the knowledge made me as furtive as a dope addict during the three-block walk—in the course of which I met no one whatever. When Susan arrived fifteen minutes later our tension broke. We were alone at last.

Thank God neither of us was disposed to rush things; instinct told us that the more sweet, reluctant, amorous delay, the better. Each of us was much too shy to disrobe in the presence of the other; we took our decorous separate turns in the bathroom. During these early years of the twenties, girls had proved something or other to themselves by discarding nightgowns in favor of pajamas, so it was in pajamas that Susan emerged. Were they just boys' pajamas, or were they girlish and frilly? I have no slightest recollection. My heart was pounding to the point of suffocation, and only two visual memories stand out, never to be forgotten. One was the look of her swelling bosom, freed of the restrainers of the period; the other was the long brown hair that now streamed full to her waist. She came over to me on the divan, sat down on my lap and turned her face up toward mine. We did not kiss, and we did not say a word. But the fifty years that have gone by since that night have not by the slightest dimmed what her face was saying to me. It was saying, among a hundred other things, "This is a True First Time for me, as I know it is for you. If I did not know you are as innocent as I am, I would not be here. Only with an innocent boy would I have the courage to do what I am doing. As it is, I have the faith to put my life and safety as a girl into your keeping, sure that you will not hurt or harm me. But girls are just as desperately driven as boys are to find out what the business of physical sex is all about, so my period of coyness, flirtation and indirection is now at an end. Take me."

Aloud she said only, "Let me get settled in bed, and then you turn out the lights." But I could not turn out the lights right then and there. With Susan settled in bed that long brown hair cascaded over both the pillows and I had to revel in the sight of it, and in the knowledge that this lovely girl was where she was because she wanted love, and wanted it from me. A very small voice, which said, "What are we waiting for?" brought my hand to the light switch at last. If I had it to do all over again I think I would have delayed at least another five minutes, for I was never to see Susan's long hair in lovely, careless disarray on a pillow again. True, our love affair was only beginning, but the rest of what happened that night (and, I grudgingly suppose, other factors, too) filled her with enough spirit of emancipation so that ten days later she had it all chopped off in a twenties bob—thus destroying what was for me the most powerful aphrodisiac in all girls' armory of weapons.

190

• • •

But what did happen that night after the lights went out? It was an unspoken vow between us that although naked embrace was what we both equally desired there would be no act of attempted defloration. The reason the vow needed no open expression was that I was no more eager than Susan that we should try at one leap to jump the awesome distance between complete innocence and complete fulfillment. After all, neither of us knew *precisely* what to do. All I knew was that, sheerly out of considerations of anatomy, the male role had to be the leading role, and I didn't know how to play it. But there was another consideration, too, less crass and more tender. What both of us wanted was physical contact and exploration. Susan wanted to know what a live boy was *really* like; my desire was the precise converse of hers.

And we got what we wanted. The bliss of fondling Susan's breasts and kissing her nipples was four times compounded by the dizzying knowledge that this was what she *wanted* me to do. When I slid my hand between her legs, they opened just enough to let it go as far as it needed to go. It was then that I learned for the first time what the corresponding reaction in girls is to the erection in boys. Meanwhile, Susan's hands were seeking to find out everything they could about me. What inevitably resulted was a night spent in mutual masturbation, which I choose to believe was the usual first step for young lovers to take when both parties to it were full of eagerness and innocence, and anxious to sate the former without doing violence to the latter. When daylight came again Susan and I were full of tenderness toward each other, wholly without regrets and speculating on how soon until it would be safe to plan another Deceit.

The romance between Susan and me was to go on for several years; to have ups and downs, some of them conventional, some of them not; to go deep, and to end, eventually, with some heartbreak, nowhere.

• • •

• • •

The *Review* continued to flourish. The entrance of Susan as a serious element in my life did not lessen my interest in my job; it enhanced it. Nothing was ever going to make me over into an Arrow Collar Type young man, yet without trying I had somehow taken a girl away from another young man of the only type, so I had thought, girls ever glanced at twice. Something had been awry with my self-calculations, but whatever it was, it was pleasantly awry. So, in effect, I had still more time (and energy) for work, and in consequence, worked harder than ever. The *Review*'s first year under its new management had been so profitable that my 70 per cent share had been promptly reduced to something more appropriate, like 50 per cent, but I couldn't have cared less, for by every indication the second year was going to surpass the first.

Lobby was delighted, and although he contributed less and less copy to the magazine and obviously felt that he could take it easier in the amount of supervision he gave it and me, he and I still met for at least an hour in the morning every day in the week, and dined together perhaps twice a week, afterward to talk often half the night, mostly about the magazine. That I did practically all the sweaty work and Lobby was essentially the Front Man did not and does not at all diminish my admiration for what he accomplished, for the *Review* needed a Front Man and he was a suave and superb one, deeply skilled for the kind of politicking that is always necessary in the academic world, and at which I would have been a disaster. And he constantly upheld my hand, so that through those early years we were good friends as well as smooth collaborators. This was eventually to change, but not now.

In fact, during 1924 Lobby and I were getting along so well that we took a transcontinental trip on the Canadian National, from Montreal to Prince Rupert, British Columbia—a five-day journey that we mercifully broke by a long stayover at Jasper Park in the Canadian Rockies. The miracle of the radio was in what seemed like full flower then, for the Democratic National Convention was going through its 103-ballot agonies to nominate John W. Davis, and all the way from Montreal to Winnipeg the loudspeaker in the club car announced that Alabama had again cast 18 votes for Oscar W. Underwood. This in 1924 was the first loudspeaker—as opposed to earphones—I had, I think, ever heard. It was the day of the A battery and the B battery, the word "superheterodyne" was unknown, and it was widely predicted that technology's latest marvel would revolutionize education. Nobody seemed to know what else it might be good for.

Since Lobby and I were both railroad buffs we had a fine time on this transcontinental train that traveled at 25 m.p.h. The reason for this caution was hotboxes. Once you were west of Ottawa you were, almost literally, on your own. My own boyhood Canada having consisted mainly of Toronto and Lake Ontario, I was completely unprepared for the wild, untamed, uninhabited and uninhabitable beauty of western Ontario, where the Canadian National's right-of-way followed the desolate northern shore of Lake Superior for mile upon countless mile until eventually, late at night, the pale, lonely, Godforsaken lights of Fort William and Port Arthur hove into view.

• • •

Susan, Lobby, Tubby Rogers and his wife—these made up most of my small circle. At the very center stood Tubby and his wife. The student-teacher relationship between Tubby and me had all but completely been superseded by pure friendship between an older man (Tubby was eleven years my senior) and a younger. In this transformation Tubby's wife played a most important part. She was, perhaps, only five years my senior. She had an exquisitely beautiful face, which made it all the sorrier that out of love and cooking and eating she had let her once equally beautiful figure go completely to pieces. She was an inspired cook, who memorized no recipes but relied on an infallible instinct. Before her marriage she had been an actress in a minor sort of way; she was not a reader of books, or in any other way the typical wife for an English professor. And, to my slow surprise, I discovered she was intensely shy and, whether as guest or hostess, painfully ill at ease when strangers were around. For the seven years I lived in Boston after my graduation, Bob and Marie Rogers were my closest and dearest friends, yet in spite of being in their home at least one night in every week during the school year, and spending practically every weekend with them during their summers on Cape Ann, I seldom met another soul there except Tubby's father, mother and brothers or Marie's mother and stepfather—no one. But since I, too, was most uncomfortable with strangers, this suited me to a T. Marie and I would never have dreamed of discussing our common failing, but we knew we had it, and I think that was a principal reason why she welcomed me into her home with such warmth. It worried her that I had no girl (when Susan entered my life I kept this

193

a secret), but although she had no candidate to bring forth for me, she spoke of it fairly often.

Tubby was outgoing—one would have thought. In any event, his cutaway and striped trousers were always at the ready, for he was in heavy demand as an after-dinner speaker and augmented his professor's income by constant lecturing to ladies' literary societies in and around Boston-Cambridge, giving the speech-of-the-occasion before conventions of booksellers, and the like. Once I expressed envy for this ability to stand up before a crowd of assorted unknown people and tell them what for.

"Look here," said Tubby, suddenly serious. "As a boy I was the shyest, most withdrawn and thoroughly miserable spectacle you ever could imagine. But before I had reached even your age it was borne in on me that I would have to lay on brass and triple brass if I ever expected to get anyplace at all. I set out to do it; it was torture; but you'll have to do it, too. You're pretty good behind a typewriter right now, but that's not enough. You've got to learn how to stand up and face 'em, and face 'em down. Hideously painful practice—that's all that will do it."

After a while—a long while—the advice began to take. I got my most violent lesson when Tubby let me come to one of the gray-flannel-draped studios of WBZ, Boston, and WBZA, Springfield, one evening when he was to lecture on English Literature before an open mike. These were the days when nobody knew what radio was good for, and nobody paid anybody for anything and the Extension Department of the University of Massachusetts was still able to cling to the idea that radio would be the most powerful tool for education ever placed in its practitioners' hands. Hence Tubby at the microphone.

This evening Tubby strode toward it with languid ease and as he said "Good evening, ladies and gentlemen" he reached into his breast pocket for his notes.

They weren't there.

He *did* have a moment of mild fluster. Perhaps a hundred people were tuned in, perhaps a thousand; who knew?

"I, uh, seem to have forgotten my notes for this evening," said Tubby, snapping back into full control, "so the lecture tonight will be, let us say, uh, extemporaneous." He then swung smoothly into whatever his topic was and talked the full thirty, forty-five or sixty minutes expected of him. When it was all over and he came back to sit down beside me, his brow was only slightly damp. "Goddamn it," he said without much emotion, "I was *sure* I had those things with me when I left the office." I had seen a great demonstration of Aplomb.

• • •

One of Tubby's early jobs after graduation was as a reporter on the Brooklyn *Daily Eagle*. While he was on that job and when, having been fired from it, he had a near brush with theatrical immortality as press agent for Maude Adams, he roomed with another young Harvard man who was an assistant editor of *The American Magazine*. His job, Tubby had told me in my undergraduate days, "was to cut every line of any possible social significance from all stories handed to him." This was obviously a gifted young man, whose heart was not precisely in the work he was doing. Nor was this young man's heart precisely with the world of magazines in general, and when Tubby was wising me up to that branch of the journalistic world I was proposing to enter, he, one day, in his office, burst into song:

"When God the Earth created"

Tubby couldn't quite remember how the music went, but the words accommodated themselves nicely to the tune of "The Marines' Hymn" ("From the Halls of Montezuma . . ."). Tubby started again:

"When God the Earth created
And saw that it was good,
He was naturally elated:
He had done the best he could.
But not to knock Jehovah
Who wisely used His means,
It had to be done over,
By—all—the—mag—a—zines.

"Bill Daly wrote the music for that," said Tubby, "and Jack Reed wrote the words. It was in the *Dutch Treat Show* of 1913."

It was, indeed. I looked it up years later because I wanted to read it entire. It was very, very funny. It gave no hint, of course, that Tubby's brilliant roommate, Jack Reed, was six years later to be metamorphosed into John Reed, author of *Ten Days That Shook the World*, and who lies today near Nikolai Lenin, buried in Red Square, under the Kremlin wall.

195

23 · THE DILEMMA OF BEING MALE, OR, LOVE, SACRED AND PROFANE

It curiously fell to me to reintroduce my elder friends Bob and Marie Rogers to the pleasures of alcohol; they had completely forgone drinking when Prohibition had been imposed. My stories of Leon Keach's Benedictine and Curaçao, home-brewed from Mr. Cohen's gallon tins of Belgian alcohol, had moved Tubby to say to his wife, "Dearest, we *must* be more enterprising next year; we can't go on this way!"—meaning abstinence based on sloth. So, one Sunday evening I brought a bottle of the "Benedictine" to the Rogerses' home, where in defiance of all convention—for Prohibition was ruining the manners and customs of America as well as its morals—we had drinks out of it *before* dinner. Tubby sat his glass down with a crash. "What did you say this horse piss was called?" he asked angrily.

"Please, Bob, not in front of Desirée," said his wife. (Desirée was then about four.) Nevertheless the raw alcohol had a warming effect on his gullet so we all had some more of the horse piss after dinner, and indeed the level in the bottle was noticeably lower by the end of the evening. "Ask your precious Mr. Cohen if he doesn't have some essence for honest gin," Tubby said as we parted.

Curiously, Mr. Cohen didn't. But with my next gallon purchase he gave me a filthy and limp piece of paper on which was written: "Oil of coriander, 2 minims; oil of juniper, 2 minims; oil of peppermint, 1 minim; glycerin, q.v." The friendly neighborhood pharmacist to whom (after a struggle with my courage) I handed this gave me a curious look, but since there was nothing interdict in it he disappeared behind his cage and some moments later emerged with a one-ounce bottle. Whether out of irony, contempt or self-protection I don't know, but beneath the label he had pasted a little blue oblong sticker that read "FOR EXTERNAL USE ONLY."

Thereafter, I abandoned forever Leon Keach's liqueurs and changed my alcoholic diet to gin. Gin-and-ginger-ale; gin-and-orange-juice (the Orange Blossom was the Prohibition cocktail of choice); for festive occasions, gin, grenadine and white of egg, to produce a Pink Lady; gin-and-pineapple juice—there was no limit to the awfulness of Prohibition drinks. So far as I knew, Boston was a city without speakeasies; South Boston was full of beer flats, where near beer was needled with ether, but this was one drink I never drank. I was never in a speakeasy until 1925 in New York; when I came back to Boston and reported on this to Tubby, his response was, "I suppose there must be *hundreds* of such places in New York." (It was an article of faith that during Prohibition New York had "42,000 speakeasies"; never 40,000, never 43,000, always 42,000.)

Unlike her Prohibition sisters, Susan never took a drink; she had no moral objections and even confessed that it was "exciting" to kiss me when I had alcohol on my breath. ("Isn't it exciting when I don't?" I asked her. Was I learning about girls?) But the one time I persuaded her to join me she was so immediately and violently sick that the rest of our sexual lives together was spent entirely without benefit of alcohol. But with the Rogerses and myself it was quite a different story. Drinking together became one of the principal pleasures of our lives. In this the Lord certainly smiled upon us: He brought to our shores, literally, the makings of more than 300 gallons of gin, free, gratis and for nothing—which we shared with nobody. But not until after another appropriate wait.

• • •

The academic year was drawing to a close; so, therefore, was still another publishing year for the *Review*. I had spent my usual happy day-before-closing-day at the Perry & Elliott plant in Lynn, and by nine thirty in the evening the proofroom had asked what its Miss Griswold assured me was its last question. We had been hurrying and I had been working on a set of page proofs so freshly pulled that they were still wet. There were evidences, also, that I had rested my brow on an inky hand. But as I gave myself a rapid glance in the washroom's cracked mirror and was about to scoop out a handful of mechanics' soap to cleanse myself, I looked at my watch. If I didn't stop to wash up, and if I ran all the way to the Boston & Maine station, I *might* be able to catch the 9:47 train to North Station. It was worth a try, so I bawled my good nights and started my race for the train, and won by a hair. As soon as I stopped panting I made for the men's room, but the thin stream of cold water and four successive paper towels brought me no closer to Godliness. "What the hell," I thought; "I'll be home in an hour anyway." And I was, damn it, with an aching heart and my guts churning with self-directed rage and hopelessness.

• • •

When you reached North Station you walked upstairs to the L platform and after a while three coupled street cars labeled "BEACON" would come along. Shortly these dived underground, and this night, carrying me with them, they duly arrived, as they should, at Park Street. The front car in which I rode was almost empty, but at Park Street there embarked a girl in a brown coat who instantly struck me as the most attractive female human being I had ever seen. Eyes, ears, nose, soul and balls all reacted in one mighty heave of longing for this other half of my existence that had suddenly crashed into my consciousness. She sat down on the opposite side of the aisle, two rows in front of me. Goddess. I could get a glimpse of her profile, framed in soft brown hair. Mainly, I could see only her back and shoulders, but they were enough to make me fall in love with her then and there. Shortly, she turned to look the car over and her glance rested momentarily on me. Even as she faced front again my heart was racing.

After Park Street, Arlington; after Arlington, Copley Square; after Copley Square, Massachusetts Avenue, where I would be due to get off. But I didn't *want* to get off; didn't want to do anything except follow this perfect girl to the ends of the earth. She turned backward again. A hideous clamor now rose in my breast: had her purpose in turning been to look at me (it *seemed* so), and if so, *why?* I looked at my hands, filthy with printer's ink. I was conscious of my gray-smudged forehead. Was there also a big blob of ink on my nose? If I had only taken the time to wash up! But if I had, I would have missed the train in Lynn and thus not be on this car. Goddamn Fate!

198

We were stopping at Copley Square now. The goddess girl looked back again, unmistakably at me. There was no hint of invitation in her look, but no hint of amusement or contempt either. But it must be that I was a figure of fun, with a clown-sized blob of solid printer's ink on my nose. Yet wasn't there the thousandth of a grain of possibility that this girl felt the same spring tidal pull toward me that I felt toward her? Wasn't it worth the chancing?

Things now rose to a silently screaming climax within me, for as our car slowed for its stop at Massachusetts Avenue, where I was to get off, the girl, too, arose and stood just ahead of me waiting for the doors to open. In my head I composed a speech: "Miss . . . please don't think me fresh . . . but . . . you're the loveliest girl I've ever seen . . . so may I walk home with you and can we exchange names and addresses . . . (*and be married next week and have a hundred children begotten and conceived in an ecstasy of physical and spiritual passion, and roam the earth together, hand in hand, I loving whatever you love and you loving whatever I love, forever and forever, until death us do part*)?"

I shall be telling this with a sigh
Somewhere ages and ages hence:

Yes, Robert Frost, I quoted that to myself even as I continued to ride home, alone. For I had simply let my Future, my fore-ordained Future, disappear. No speech, not even a clearing of the throat.

When at last I got home to my apartment I went straight to the bathroom mirror. Although my forehead bore its faint gray smudge, there was no blob of ink on my nose. But as for my hands, they were the hands of Esau.

• • •

Next day, my pretty Susan looked frumpish to me. I did not like anybody; not Lobby, not Bob and Marie Rogers. But of course I reserved the choicest loathings for myself. I was the purest quintessence of walking male cowardice. My fear of rejection, my self-projection as a funny-looking guy with a blob of printer's ink on my nose just to make the clown image complete, had paralyzed me. I had been weighed in the balance and been found—shit! Suppose I had been rejected? That would have settled something. As it was, nothing was settled. Nothing would ever be settled and—speaking suddenly of today, the here and now—in truth, nothing has been. The shadows in the life that was still before me were to be the wrong shadows. What was to be worse, the joys before me were to be the wrong joys, the consequences of The Road Not Taken. You think I don't mean it? Think again.

• • •

Searching hard for consolations, I realized that I was now the owner of a secondhand automobile. It was a 1922 Essex. Your great-grandfather may remember it as the one that had the Huntley & Palmer biscuit-box body, with a little bustle of a trunk space sticking out behind, and one of the best four-cylinder motors ever to come out of Detroit. It gave me a much-needed sense of power; it also gave Susan and me a much-needed place to neck, besides the balcony of Loew's State and the side-wheeler steamers that used to scuttle back and forth to Nantasket Beach. This was all necessary because Susan could use the spending-the-night-with-a-girl-friend ploy only every so often. It was Susan's father who in all the innocence of fathers taught me how to drive. It also immeasurably increased my ability to visit the Rogerses over the weekends, driving to wherever on Cape Ann they were staying that summer.

It's hard, even for me, to remember that in those days you drove with the Blue Book of the A.A.A. beside you. There were no directional signs, so until you had memorized a route you referred to the book, which told you to "proceed 1.3 mi., turn r. at white church spire for 0.4 mi., then 1. on Y as far as drugstore . . ." Boston was then unique in having no northern exit except by rail, so you felt your way along Cambridge alleys and streets and Alewife Brook Boulevard until at last you were sure you were headed north-by-east, one-quarter-east, or sufficiently so to head you to the Cape Ann spur and not north to Newburyport. Those days are confusing to remember because along with this primitiveness they did also have motorcycle cops, and the cops, on stopping you, had the same question then as now: "How fast do you think you were going, Mister?" (I guess *Mister* has now changed to *Buddy*.) The answer was also the same: "I wasn't

looking at the speedometer, Officer, I was looking at the road."
But thereafter there was a difference: "Well, you were doing
thirty-five miles an hour on a speed-limited stretch of thirty."
And out came the book of tickets. This happened to me once
when for some reason I was driving Tubby's ancient mother back
to Boston. "Officer, you can't arrest this nice young man!" she
cried in the best traditions of the New England Town Meeting.
And he couldn't, either. The nice young man knew how to fix
a traffic ticket. Obviously we were now in the middle twenties.

Whatever the exact year, Tubby and wife and daughter were
that summer staying at a beautiful beach known as Wingarshiek,
which was then so desolate and lonely that Marie eventually
refused to go back. (The last time I saw it, in the 1950's, ten
thousand cars were parked on it.) One morning, Tubby called
to me in high excitement. Something was obviously wrong. No,
nothing was wrong, but he was sweating like a horse and panting
so hard that I could not hear what he was trying to say as he
pointed toward the sea. The beach shelved so gradually that at
least a quarter of a mile separated the cottage from the high-tide
mark. But as my eyes followed his trembling finger I saw about
a dozen objects, bulky-looking ones, glittering heavily in the
morning sun. Only then did I see what lay at Tubby's feet, what
he had toted up that quarter-mile beach as hard as he could pelt.
It was a big square can with a small screw cap.

"Hooch!" Tubby gasped. "Hurry!" We raced toward the
beach's glitter. Weighing scarcely half as much as Tubby and
being eleven years his junior, I got there first. At least twenty
cans like the one Tubby had salvaged were lying on the sands
in tumbled disarray and over all hung the odor of undiluted
alcohol; one of the cans was leaking.

Further words were unnecessary; we were men of action. I
suppose it must have taken us close to an hour to haul all those
cans up the beach. There were twenty-two of them; the leaking
can, which we left to the last and then cradled between us like
a wounded bird, made twenty-three. I estimated the cans to be
five-gallon capacity. That would make a total—minus the little
leakage that was perfuming the air—of 115 gallons.

But, 115 gallons of *what?* It was alcohol, all right, but was
it potable? There could be no answer to that until a new week
began and I could take a sample to M.I.T.'s Laboratory of Proxi-

mate Technical Analysis and get old Professor Woodman to run it through his tests. Meanwhile the God of Things as They Are decreed that our supply of Mr. Cohen's Verified Gin began to run low, and Tubby became fretful; after all, he'd had a hard day. I was a bit put off myself. As a distraction I began to calculate; *if* the alcohol was potable and unwatered, 115 gallons of it would make at least 345 gallons of gin. Let's see: that's the same as about 1,400 quarts. At two ounces of gin per highball, that's almost 25,000 highballs, and that's enough—.

"For Christ's sake, shut up," said Tubby.

His mood did not improve until the next weekend when I was able to bring the happy news that old Professor Woodman had pronounced the sample I had drawn off from the leaking tin to be 95 per cent American Cologne Spirits, without dilutants or adulterants, that is, the highest grade of commercial market alcohol, ordinarily used in expensive perfumes. We were never able to pick up the smallest clue as to what rumrunner, where, had had to jettison cargo, or what tides in the affairs of men backwashed 115 gallons of it up on Wingarshiek Beach when it did. It lasted a long, long time, but not as long as my first rough calculations had foreseen.

• • •

Susan and I were managing to spend the night together every two weeks or so; that was about the maximum strain the overnight-with-my-girl-friend-story Susan calculated her mother could bear. But I had another apartment now, no longer in as romantic a setting as Lime Street, but at the beginnings of the Fenway, and although spending the whole night together was what we preferred, we could have all the privacy we wanted between 5 and 11 P.M. Gradually, it became apparent even to me that Susan was genuinely in love with me, and that if I were to utter the magic word "marriage," she would chuck her Harvard Arrow Collar boy friend in a flash and give herself without reservation to me. But not before. So although our romance did not wane, it did not wax, either. We had several tempestuous partings, and there even came a time when she accepted an engagement ring from the Harvard lad, and we—or at least I—considered that everything was over. But there also came a time when she went to bed with me while still wearing that ring. This must have been the first time that I asked myself any questions about the essential morality of girls. I was not acting very honorably, myself, I knew; I was letting my balls dictate my behavior—but I was not "cheating on" anyone, as the phrase then went. But perhaps that was only because I had no one to cheat on. What got me was that Susan was such a sweet, gentle girl, and in her heart there seemed to be no guile . . . .

•   •   •

There came an evening that winter when a biology instructor asked me to a party he and his wife were giving on a Saturday night, chiefly for some neighbors in a fairly far-out Boston suburb. I liked this instructor; Tubby didn't. "He's all right, I guess," said Tubby, "but he hasn't got any zing to him. He'll never get promoted but he'll stay here all his life and they'll make him an assistant professor the year before they retire him." I thought Tubby was probably right, but that was no reason for not going to the party. In my 1922 Essex I rattled off and went. The evening was cold and rainy. Cheap cars did not have windshield wipers then, and windshields were in two pieces; in rainy weather you swung the upper glass plate open like a visor and peered through the crack to see your way while the rain slashed at your face.

So it was very nice to arrive at the house near the top of a hill and get into the warm indoors. It was nicer still to be met at the door by the host who already had your gin-and-ginger-ale in his hand. All the other guests were not only near neighbors but couples, and I had a good deal of difficulty trying to keep straight who was married to whom. My hostess turned out to be a pleasant blondish girl. (Why do I still call women girls? She was the mother of three children.) Since I was the only unattached male there she spent a good deal of time pleasantly talking to me. This being a Prohibition party its primary purpose was that everybody of the dozen present should get good and looping drunk; I entered into the spirit of things enthusiastically, and whose wife was mated to what husband seemed to get blurred in other minds than mine. Things got loud but remained decorous; rugs got pushed back and there was some highly inexpert dancing to the music of a little spring-wound Victrola. And after a long while and many drinks, at last it was time to go home.

203

But a problem arose. While we were pleasantly drinking and unaware, the earlier cold driving rain had turned into a major ice storm; in fact those sudden flashes of blue light of which we had been vaguely conscious for the past hour were electric lines snapping under their growing load of freezing rain. All the guests lived only one or two blocks away—all but myself. I had to make it back to Boston, a good half-hour run in sunny, good weather, with an ultrasober driver at the wheel. I had reached the I-can-do-anything stage, so I was all for damning the torpedoes and going staunchly home in my Essex. But the first couple to venture out came back to report that the roads were glazed ice and that anyone who tried to drive even to the bottom of the hill would be a fool, a danger not only to himself but to the public safety, even if coldest sober.

My hostess, whom I had never met until that evening but whom I now called Harriet with easy familiarity, took charge. ("Harriet" is not her real name—it's unimportant to the story.) Nothing could be easier than putting me up for the night. There was a spare bedroom just off the living room, with tiny bath attached. The bed was all made up; she would only have to go upstairs and get a pair of extra blankets, for the night had turned bitter, bitter cold, and that would be that. All I would have to forgo would be a toothbrush in the morning, but there was some Listerine in the medicine cabinet, so wasn't that settled? Her husband chimed in strongly, so it *was* settled. I had the feeling I was imposing, but also that the imposition was inevitable. Harriet came down with the extra blankets and a pair of her husband's pajamas, took a final look around and bade me sleep well. "And don't get up 'til you feel like it. We haven't any set hour for Sunday breakfasts." And thus I went to bed. The wind howled and the windows rattled, but alcohol is a fine soporific.

• • •

During the night the storm abated. At six in the morning I was roused by the creaking of my door and turned to see my hostess enter in her nightgown. "How nice of her," I thought, "she has come to see if I'm warmly covered up." But that was not why she had come at all. Calmly, quietly, as if she had rehearsed this scene for weeks, she slipped into bed beside me, pulled up her nightgown, loosed the drawstring of my pajamas and drew me to her. And it was her other hand that guided mine to the breast that was released from her nightgown.

All this, it seemed, happened in a flash. In an answering flash, I reacted. It was possible, I then and there learned, to experience dismay but have a first-class erection, too, and the dismay disappears first. I kissed her hard, but she was scarcely interested in kisses. She turned from her side to her back and gently pulled me with her.

Whereupon a terrible realization came to me: *I didn't know what to do next.* I mounted her clumsily; all that happened was that joints knocked awkwardly together. Fortunately, the basic technique of sexual intercourse can be imparted in one sentence if the female is doing the talking. In a calm, quiet voice she said, "No, no, put your knees *inside* mine."

So *that* was it; after that I needed only subsidiary instruction, which was more readily supplied; my hostess partner not only knew what she was doing, but what I should do, and gave herself up to Union with complete, and yet controlled, abandon. When my inevitable point of climax came, I withdrew. She moaned slightly for a moment and opened her eyes. In the same quiet voice she had used from the beginning, but this time with a tinge of reproach in it, she said, "Now why did you do that? I was entitled to it."

• • •

Much later in the morning, breakfast was served. It was quite a formal affair. Did I like my toast light or dark? Would I like marmalade? Harriet's husband had the hangover to end all hangovers; lost in his sufferings, he paid little attention to me and less to his wife. Yet despite his obliviousness, not a glance, not a secret look, no recognition of any sort of what had happened between her and me not four hours earlier, passed from Harriet to me. She was merely smiling, gracious, composed, with a pretty concern for the comfort of an unexpected overnight guest, and nothing more. The act was perfect.

Earlier in the morning the weather—the external weather—had changed again. A warmish, pelting rain was fast dissolving last night's ice, and by early afternoon it was safe to drive again. I thanked my host and hostess for a thoroughly enjoyable time, was told that I must come again, and took a cordial departure.

205

My drive back to Boston was somewhat abstracted, and so was the rest of the day. Out of the blue I had run full tilt into a seductress, and had been seduced, in spades. I now had full carnal knowledge of Woman, and in this I reveled, living over and over again in vivid memory the physical act between Harriet and me. I had also learned, in very short time, something of the nature of Womankind. But . . . just what?

24 · NEW ENGLAND WRENCHED, OR, WATERMELON PICKLE

THE TWENTIES had reached, and slightly passed, their halfway mark. Various frenzies rose and rose. Chiefly, these were for the making of money and the consumption of alcohol, but anyone who thinks these were the sole preoccupations of the decade has another think coming. Eva Gauthier, a gifted songstress of the period, provided an important clue to what was happening. She gave, in Boston's Jordan Hall, a recital that required two accompanists, in series. Its first half was standard repertory—Mr. Frederick Perssons at the piano. The second half was jazz (Miss Gauthier was a gifted and "serious" recitalist) and for this a new accompanist was required, a George Gershwin, of whom nobody in Boston had heard, for *Rhapsody in Blue* was still in the future.

This was also the decade that saw The American Theater, thanks in large measure to that new and exciting institution the Theatre Guild, soar to new heights at its little Garrick Theatre in New York. This was the decade that saw Paul Whiteman invade first Aeolian Hall, then Carnegie Hall; that saw Walter Damrosch commission young George Gershwin to compose his second "serious" piece of music, the *Piano Concerto in F*, and play it, the composer at the piano, with the New York Symphony Society Orchestra. It was the decade that saw H. G. Wells's *Outline of History* published and fallen on in ravenous droves by young people everywhere, including M.I.T., who wanted some "integration" of the "fragmented" knowledge they had been fed on campus. It was the decade when "relativity" entered one's active vocabulary, and the name Einstein no longer meant the neighborhood pants presser.

At M.I.T., *some* of the faculty, but naturally few of the stu-

NEW ENGLAND WRENCHED, OR,

dents, were aware that the old Newtonian mechanics, which had served physicists very well indeed for several centuries, had broken down. But the exact nature of the breakdown was obscure, and did not in any important way modify or affect the training then accorded a young engineer. It is hard to imagine today, but in the 1920's a student who was having a hard time in one of the engineering courses, but who was earnest and wanted an M.I.T. degree, might be allowed to transfer to Course IX: Physics*—because it was regarded as one of the two "snap" courses the Institute then offered. (The other was Engineering Administration.) In those days, furthermore, the Mathematics Department was regarded entirely as a service department to the other engineering courses. It was full of able teachers, but, aside from offering a few very special subjects, its job was to pound into freshman and sophomore heads enough differential and integral calculus to make upperclassmen functionally literate in the symbolism of Newton and Leibnitz. In all the Mathematics Department, Norbert Wiener then being too young, there was only one professor thought erudite enough for the higher phases of his subject. He was C. L. E. Moore, inevitably called Dinty. As a physical specimen Dinty was grotesque: more than six feet tall but obese, densely myopic, pigeon-toed, with a high squeaky voice and a few pathetic hairs grown long to be combed over a hopeless pate whence all but them had fled. But Dinty was the nearest thing to a mature scholar that the Math Department had, and when it was announced that Dinty would give three lectures on Relativity, attendance voluntary, the Institute's largest lecture hall was not big enough for the crowds of young people, including me, who swarmed to hear him. *Relevance?* Nobody in the audience had the faintest idea what these new equations were relevant to, or what practical "good" they were, *but something was up*, and we wanted to be in on it.

• • •

Something was up, too, in Boston, New England, the United States and the World, into which, willy-nilly, the Institute was drawn. There had languished in Charlestown prison, since 1921, under sentence of death, Nicola Sacco and Bartolomeo Vanzetti,

* At M.I.T. a Course was a four-year grind leading (hopefully) to your degree as Bachelor of Science; what an individual professor taught was a "Subject of Instruction."

allegedly for the murder of a paymaster of a shoe company in South Braintree. With every passing year, the number of people who believed these two men were going to be executed for their admittedly anarchistic views, and not for a murder they did not commit, grew and grew, and no analyst of this terrible case was more persuasive of the Sacco-Vanzetti innocence than Professor Felix Frankfurter of the Harvard Law School. Yet for legalistic reasons, all motions for a new trial were denied.

But eventually public clamor forced the Governor of the Commonwealth to the unprecedented extreme of appointing an extralegal board to review the case. Perhaps not since Abolition was New England so bloodied and torn with contention as by this case of the shoemaker and the fish peddler; it split families and sundered friends. Since all the world knows its tragic finale, about which God only knows how many million words have been written, my only reason for mentioning it here is that M.I.T. was, at the eleventh hour, drawn into it in a manner to cause practically everyone the utmost dismay. Because, for his final review board, Governor Fuller had picked the president of Harvard University, the president of M.I.T., and old Judge Grant, late of Probate Court. A more incompetent and inappropriate threesome could not possibly have been chosen, and their eventual decision not to disturb the *status quo* was scarcely a surprise. Old Judge Grant was senile. Harvard's Abbott Lawrence Lowell was slowly running down with all the outward dignity of an unwound grandfather's clock. And as for Samuel Wesley Stratton, eighth president of the Massachusetts Institute of Technology, the less said, on any score, the better.* As president of the Institute he was a thickheaded disaster, and it can scarcely be credited that he was a different man as a member of Governor Fuller's board.

• • •

Dr. Stratton had one distinction. It was that he had, in 1901, founded that very necessary institution the National Bureau of Standards in Washington. And until he was "called" to M.I.T. it had been his life. The Bureau of Standards obviously did not deal in ideas, consequently, in the realm of ideas it was not un-

* It is vitally necessary to distinguish between Samuel Wesley Stratton, eighth president of the Institute (1923–30), and Julius Adams Stratton, eleventh president (1959–66). They were in no way connected. The latter, like myself, was an undergraduate during the former's incumbency.

natural that Dr. Stratton was uneasy and unsure. Nor did he compensate for this lack by any outgoing ease or charm. His miserable ineptness on occasions calling for public speech I have never seen or heard surpassed. And it was terribly hard to get an idea through, or out of, his head. He conceived of the Institute as a trade school, and in the seven years of his presidency he almost succeeded in reducing it to just that. To this day the quarrel is not settled as to who among the trustees deserves the major blame for bringing him to Cambridge.

Moreover, Dr. Stratton, sixty-one years old when he took M.I.T.'s presidency, was a bachelor. This was unfortunate enough on a job where a Mrs. President is a social necessity; what made matters somewhat worse was that Dr. Stratton's "confidential secretary" was a moist-eyed young man of full red lips and slightly lisping speech named I forgot what, who was his constant companion. No scandal ever broke into the open as the result of all this, but Dr. Stratton soon found himself an almost isolated man at the institution he was supposed to head, with few friends among faculty, trustees, alumni or students. Cashiering a president of anything is a really tough job, and it took the Institute seven lean years to accomplish the job with Dr. Stratton. In 1930, God sent Karl Taylor Compton from Princeton to M.I.T., where the trustees joyfully elected him president, bumping Dr. Stratton upward to be "Chairman of the Corporation." The Institute had never had such an officer before and felt no need for one then; the widespread hope and belief was that Dr. Stratton would take the hint and resign. This, to universal dismay, he did not do. But his death a year later ultimately solved the tangle. And one good thing did, by accident, come out of the Stratton administration: the chairmanship of the Corporation did ultimately turn into a most useful post. Two friends of mine have since held it: Vannevar Bush and James Rhyne Killian, Jr., and from it have served the Institute and their country with highest distinction.

•   •   •

•   •   •

The Technology Review was outgrowing the facilities of Perry & Elliott in Lynn. P.&E. were persistently unable to make money on the job, for reasons Frank Elliott (an Institute alumnus) was unable to understand, but which I, curiously enough, was able to comprehend at least a shade better for the reason that I was the acquiescing partner in something not wholly honest. Composition was billed to the *Review* at so much per made-up and printed page. Composition not ultimately used ("overset") was to be billed periodically at so much per thousand ems on submission of the galley proofs that attested to its setting.

Well, Jim MacKinnon, the head comp, and Joe Galusha, the composing room foreman, were the very archetypes of the American workingman in their hatred of the Front Office. So every now and again Jim would come to me with a galley tray of Monotyped metal unused for months, and say, "You want any of this goddamn shit any longer? The alleys are getting full up." All I had to do was silently shake my head; a moment later, if I were listening, I would hear a crash of metal into the hellbox and another galley of overset would have gone forever beyond proofing. Let him who hath never condoned wrongdoing by silence be the one to cast the first stone.

On another occasion I took a slightly less passive role in the composing room's conspiracy against the Front Office. Lobdell had, a year or so before, compiled a table of foreign students at the Institute, arranged by countries of origin and courses enrolled in. It was a most intricate piece of hand composition that today I doubt you could get into printing metal for under $500. We never used it. Frank Elliott knew of its existence and was understandably anxious that it be paid for, one way or another. So once in the dead of night I said to Jim MacKinnon, "Jim, I'm never going to use that page." Jim said nothing but returned with the type page on its tray and put it before me. "You're absolutely dead-set certain you're never going to use this?" he asked. When I said Yes, and at his insistence repeated my answer twice, he picked up the tray, tilted it somewhat off the horizontal and then simultaneously removed both his hands from it. There was a shattering crash. "Jeez!" said Jim. "I dropped it." Then he bent to examine it. "It didn't bust enough," he said analytically, whereup he began kicking the fragments around the floor. (Pages with interlocked vertical and horizontal 1-point rules sometimes hold their shape very tenaciously.) Joe Galusha from his foreman's platform observed this tableau. "Now ain't that a pity," he said.

The cost-control system at Perry & Elliott was very good—at least it was amply good to point out the mounting disparity between ems set and ems printed. One day Frank Elliott went storming into the composing room, Joe Galusha told me later, to demand an explanation. "Listen, Mr. Elliott," said Joe, with proper deference, "this goddamn place is getting so full of dead metal some of the boys is complaining. I've given you proofs of every fucking tray I can find. You want to go into the alleys and look for yourself, make yourself right at home; it's *your* shop, and I never forget it."

So Frank Elliott, in his own shop, retired defeated. But he brought his legitimate complaints to me. And here he was defeated, too. With a disingenuousness I had learned partly from Lobdell and partly by myself, I patiently explained that I was powerless: the auditor (there was none) would not pay any bill for overset unless galley or page proofs of that same overset accompanied the bill. If Mr. Elliott would just . . . .

• • •

Well, anyway, the *Review* had grown big enough to attract the attention of the huge Rumford Press, in Concord, New Hampshire, probably the largest magazine printers in the land east of the vastness of R. R. Donnelley in Chicago. They printed the *Atlantic Monthly*. They printed *Harper's*. They printed *House Beautiful*. They printed *The Reader's Digest*—a modest affair in those days but seemingly with growth possibilities. And they also printed, as will later appear in appropriate detail, *The Youth's Companion*. The *Review* was, I suppose, one of the smallest jobs in the shop, but the great Rumford Press wanted it—and got it.

I was sad to leave my friends at Perry & Elliott, from whom I had learned so much, but now I was going to be in contact with a huge printery, with floor upon floor of presses, a composing room that covered acres, it seemed, where there were more Linotype and Monotype machines than I had ever seen before— and everything running in three shifts, twenty-four hours a day, and where the entire business was the printing of national magazines. How was the little *Review* to keep from getting lost in the midst of all this? Very simply. For every job, regardless of size, Rumford provided a customer's representative whose job it was to be just that, and to be aware of the status of everything on that one job—whether engravings, copy, composition, paper, press sheets. It worked like a charm.

Fortunately, it did not work so perfectly that I was deprived of my pleasure in being in the plant at closing time. In fact the pleasure was now somewhat enhanced, for it took the Boston & Maine two hours to drag through Billerica, Nashua, and Manchester before reaching Concord-on-the-Merrimack. Schedules were such that this meant a two-day stay, and *this* meant putting up at the Eagle House, Concord's Waldorf-Astoria.

I wonder what has happened to the Eagle House? I hope it's still there. To persons of my age, or even a score of years younger, it will seem an outrage if some Howard Johnson's or Holiday Inn has replaced it, but I suppose that may exactly be what has happened. For the Eagle House was one of the purest distillations of New England, nineteenth century.

Boston and New England, of course, had been having their own private Depression long before the rest of the country. The textile industry was moving south. The great Amoskeag Mills had gone bust. The great White Mountain resorts flourished only for the rich and only in the summertime. Skiing in America was—I use the word carefully—unknown. So all in all I suspect the Concord I knew in the 1920's was more like the Concord Count Rumford knew than anything the traveler knows today.

But even the Concord of the 1920's was an anomaly. It was a small town but a state capital: seat of the largest body of legislators in the United States. It was hick, but also the home of snooty St. Paul's School. It was full of thriving mechanics and slowly starving farmers. And the Eagle House somehow embraced them all. I can remember with what anticipation I awaited the annual dinner at the Eagle House of The White Mountain Travelers' Club to which a Rumford Press executive had bidden me. I expected an exotic gathering and tales of high adventure on Mount Monadnock or someplace. But The White Mountain Travelers' Club turned out to be the association of the traveling salesmen of that territory, so the evening was not just what I had looked forward to.

On the other hand the Eagle House did once squeeze me in next to a heavyweight celebrity of the period. Its dining room was furnished entirely with eight-seater tables, and the policy was to fill every eight-seater full up before starting on the next vacant one. Everyone was very chummy, in his New England way, and the conversation, when it did not stray to politics or business, was apt to concentrate, in all appropriateness, on the excellence of the Eagle House's hot breads and watermelon pickle. One day, in accord with the head waitress's seating policy, I found myself on the chair next to a most distinguished and handsome gentleman with a flawlessly trimmed Vandyke. This was too much! This was Burton Holmes, who had for years been the country's most famous (with colored lantern slides) travel lecturer. As a small boy, I had heard him lecture in Philadelphia's Academy of Music, on the Panama Canal. Now here I was, not fifteen years later, sharing watermelon pickle with him in Concord's Eagle House dining room. Golly.

• • •

After lunch a Come-One-Come-All poster appeared in the lobby inviting Concord-at-large to attend tonight's Burton Holmes lecture at the town auditorium, *absolutely free*. It appeared that the great man had a new lecture that he was trying out on the dog, and Concord that night was the dog. And it was a very good lecture indeed—except from this distance I can't remember what in the world it was about.

214

25 · PORTENTS, OR,
ONE NEVER KNOWS, DOES ONE?

By now there was coming a time when the *Review* simply had to have more staff. If I could find a literate girl who could be an editorial assistant but who also, pray God, could double at taking dictation and was not too proud to be a secretary when needed, that would be it. I telephoned the Katharine Gibbs secretarial school, which not unnaturally asked for a day or two to ponder the problem. When they called back it was with the standard response, "We think we have *just* the girl for you." So I agreed to see Miss Catherine Carlson the following afternoon.

On the dot of the hour agreed, a pleasant young girl, very blond and with a high facial coloring that suggested her last name was no accident, walked in my door. She was a bit above average height and she put "hazel" down on the application blank for the color of her eyes, which I had not noticed. What I did notice was her voice, which had a sort of whispering quality, yet was extremely distinct. I shall never forget that voice.

Well, Miss Carlson, where have you worked before and what have you done? Nowhere and nothing, she informed me with unabashed directness. She was a Smith graduate but had failed to see why anyone would employ her just on that account so after graduation she had enrolled in Katharine Gibbs to learn the secretarial arts. She had been interested in editorial work since her days on the Smith campus and thought this must be a back-door entrance to it. But she was a brand-new Katharine Gibbs graduate, and this was her first real job interview. She did not lack confidence. "I can spell," she said with a trace of pride. "I'm only slightly above average as a stenographer, but I also think I can write a pretty good letter of my own when I know what the situation calls for."

"I like to be neat," she added. Did I imagine that her glance at my desk top was just a mite critical?

All of a sudden the tables were turned and she was interviewing me. "You were Class of '22, weren't you?" Yes. "You wrote *Tech Show* that year, I think. I saw it in Northampton." Uh-huh. "Weren't you on the *VooDoo* that year, too?" "Look here, Miss Carlson, how come you seem to know all this about me, when we're meeting here and now for the first time?"

Miss Carlson emitted a well-controlled musical laugh. "Daddy used to be president of the Alumni Association," she said. "I've learned about you from him."

For me, this put an instantaneous damper on what had been, up till then, a splendid interview. Harry Johann Carlson, head of the architectural firm of Coolidge and Carlson, had indeed been a past president of the Alumni Association, and during his year in office he and I had had quite a run-in. But that was not what disturbed me. Mr. Carlson was also a life member of the Institute Corporation; I had no wish to hire his attractive and apparently very competent daughter, have her turn out badly, and then be under the necessity either of firing her or of putting up with her. So I brought the interview to an abrupt close with "Well, I'll think it over."

I didn't have to think it over long. Mr. Carlson, not a transplanted Minnesota Swede for nothing, telephoned me next day. He was forceful and direct. "I didn't want my daughter to apply for that job, and I told her so. But I guess you don't know what daughters are like these days; she went ahead and applied anyway. Now: if you hire her and she makes good, that's fine. If you hire her and she doesn't make good, fire her. But whether you hire her or fire her is entirely up to you. I will tell my daughter tonight that I've had this conversation with you, and after this my interest in the situation terminates. Are we clear?"

Yes, we were clear. So two days later I hired Miss Carlson, provisionally, and she worked out very well, staying on at the *Review* two years after I left it. It was, of course, totally hidden from me that I had just hired my future wife.

• • •

• • •

Harriet, my seductress of a few weeks before, had not been slow on the follow-up. It was a brand-new experience in my life to be pursued by a woman. In theory, it sounded blissful; in practice, I discovered, it was not that at all. Not, at any rate, unless

216

you were the kind of male who knew from long and deliberately acquired experience *exactly* how to manage the situation, and I think I have described myself sufficiently to indicate how very far indeed I was from that type.

Harriet called me from home. "My husband's going to be away at a convention for three days," she said. "I'm all alone and I have something very important I need to talk to you about. Please come to see me."

I went. To say that I didn't want to go would be a lie. To say that I did would not be accurate. I didn't know it, but I was in her toils. The "something very important" that Harriet needed to see me about became plain enough when she met me at her door in a negligee. There were a few moments of artificial social remarks, but this demure-looking mother of three, older, but only slightly older, than I, was in reality brassy bold. Perhaps all women were. How should I know?

"Come upstairs," she said. I followed. She peeled off her negligee and made straight for the bed, indicating with a pat of her hand where I should sit down on the coverlet. Harriet had a complete innocent on her hands and thoroughly knew it; indeed I think that was my principal attraction. Her deft fingers began loosening my clothing. There was nothing coy or flirtatious in her manner; nothing whatever.

"I need something tonight," she said. "Do you understand what I mean? I *need* it."

She got it. Whether she got it or whether she took it is too fine a point to argue now. When at length we were both spent, it was plain that Harriet was eager to enjoy indefinitely a delicious languor—and it was just as plain that no such emotion was going to visit me. I was tired, all right, but my real desire was to get out of that bed, where I had cuckolded a friend, and out of that house, where I was a trespasser. It took me about an hour—a very uncomfortable hour—to get my way. Later that night, alone in my double Murphy bed, I dwelt on what Harriet and I had experienced together. But I also reveled in my solitude.

• • •

• • •

Into my office one day, there walked a tall, villainous-looking man who was to change my life completely. Villainous, all right, yet caste was also written all over his long, dark face. He had

217

just dropped in, he explained, because he had seen my name on the door, and that had reminded him that a professor of mechanical engineering had mentioned me to him a few weeks before.

The villainous-looking man introduced himself offhandedly as Harford Powel, Jr., and thereafter I had the most terrible time in following the gist of his conversation. The earnestness with which he was asking me to do something was matched only by the impenetrable vagueness with which he surrounded what the something was. I tried to trick him into giving me some solid information but had little success. "Townsend and Phelan and Clapp and Young all agree you're the man to do it," said Mr. Powel. "It's not often you get such unanimity." Although I was later to discover that this unanimity had occurred to Mr. Powel only on the spur of the moment, I did recognize the names he'd quoted. They were all instructors or assistant professors in various Institute departments, and I did know all of them, although none well. What could they be agreeing about that concerned me? "I'd like to talk this thing over with you *thoroughly*," said Mr. Powel. "Lunch at the Saint Botolph Club Tuesday, eh?"

That seemed reasonable, but beforehand I wanted to consult a less hypnotic personality than Harford Powel, Jr. So I sought out Arthur Townsend, Assistant Professor of Mechanical Engineering, who was an earthy soul. "Harford's the new editor of *The Youth's Companion*," Arthur told me. "He used to be editor of *Collier's*, but he got fired there and Ellery Sedgwick's brought him up to Boston to breathe some new life into the old sheet."

Having been brought up on *St. Nicholas* in my boyhood, about all I knew about *The Youth's Companion* was that its headquarters was Boston. What Mr. Ellery Sedgwick, the great editor of the *Atlantic Monthly*, was doing in this equation I did not know, and Arthur could not enlighten me very far.

"Harford has a good idea," said Arthur, "*I think*. Anyway, he's started this thing called "The YC Lab," which is a page a week on science and engineering, and he's signed me and Clapp—"

"—and Phelan and Young," I put in. "Yes, as 'Councilors,' he calls us," said Arthur. "He pays us fifteen dollars a week for about half a column. He's got a membership coupon on the page and the come-on is that any kid who clips the coupon gets a certificate that says he can ask any question in his head and get it answered by a member of the M.I.T. faculty. It's going good and Harford was over here a couple of weeks ago asking me if I knew any other junior people he could sign up as Councilors. But his page is an editorial mess, so I figured out I knew what he wanted better than he did, and I told him that if I was him I'd go talk to you."

Aha. Now I could have a halfway intelligent talk at the St. Botolph Club. When Mr. Powel discovered that I'd just happened to speak to Arthur Townsend, he dropped most (but not all; there had to be *some* element of mystery in everything he did) of his ellipses.

"What I need," he said authoritatively, "is a man who can edit the page, run the Councilors, keep the boys happy and make sure everything is shipshape. I'm doing the whole thing, and it's been taking more and more of my time. You'd have one full-time secretary to help you with all the details. Excellent woman. Broke her in myself."

A waiter tiptoed in with the custards.

"I can't pay you what I'd be able to pay in New York," he said. "Boston penury, eh? I'm going to write a novel about that, blessed if I'm not.* But how would an extra twenty-five dollars a week sound to you?"

It sounded mighty pleasant.

"I have a full-time job running the *Review,*" I said.

"After hours, after hours," said Mr. Powel impatiently. "Get there at five thirty, leave at seven thirty. Closing days would take a little longer, but that would be all. Mrs. Rodgers would have all your problems arranged for you by the time you got there. Remarkable woman. Has Mr. Sedgwick thoroughly intimidated. Never comes 'round anymore. Best that way."

I liked the idea. "Your title," said Mr. Powel, "would be 'Director of the YC Lab.' I'll put your picture on the cover. We can give that Institute of yours some valuable national publicity." (Mr. Powel was Harvard, same class as Tubby. "Oh, the fat boy who ran the *Advocate?* Fine. Sound fella." Tubby could not remember Harford Powel at all.)

* And he did. He thus antedated his friend John P. Marquand in his discovery of this lode, but was never remotely able to mine it with Marquand's unending success.

"You'll start on the payroll on Monday," said Mr. Powel.

I hadn't even said yes. I couldn't say yes until I had checked with Lobby, and said so. "Furthermore, I'm going to Paris for a two-month vacation in July."

"Then it's settled," said Mr. Powel, rising. "I'll have a desk cleaned out for you."

Strangely enough, it *was* settled. When I broached the idea to Lobby, he was at first inclined to demur until I gave him my solemn promise that I would work no less hard or long for the *Review*. And when Harford Powel called on him to explain how the *Review* and the Institute would both actually gain by the arrangement, that was that. Lobby was something of a hypnotist himself, but Lobby's method was the marshaling of all possible favorable facts into an avalanche of logic. And Harford could make his own turbulent waterfall of non sequiturs roar louder than anything from Lobby. So, on a Monday in April 1926, I took up my duties, part time, as director of Mr. Powel's *Youth's Companion* YC Lab.

26 · AN AMERICAN IN PARIS, or,
40 RUE DE MONTYON

THE RECORDS SHOW that among the Americans in Paris in 1926
(the year of my first trip abroad) were Ernest Hemingway, Gertrude Stein and her brother Leo, Archibald MacLeish, Edmund
Wilson, Kay Boyle and others. Did I meet any of them? I didn't
even know any of them were there, except in the vaguest way.
I had never heard of Ernest Hemingway until *The Sun Also
Rises* was published later in the year. Everyone had heard of
Gertrude Stein; not everyone, of her brother. Much later on I
came to meet, one way or another, a few of these famous ex-
patriates, after the Depression and other forces had driven them
back to their own shores. But in 1926, when the more serious
of them were struggling and striving with their arts, and the
hangers-on were the 1920's foreshadowings of the hippies and
beatniks still to come, I was just a young Philistine tourist, coming to Paris just to "see it" and knowing nothing about anything
if I hadn't read it in a guidebook. In fact, I made a point of
reverse snobbery to cross to the Left Bank as infrequently as possible and never, positively never, having food or drink at the Dôme
or La Rotonde.

• • •

I crossed on the *De Grasse*. Would God I could do it again—all
eight days of it. André Mesnard, who was to be my guide and
friend, if not *always* philosopher, had a last-minute change of
plans and had to follow a week later. So I would have been all
alone had it not been that that indomitable Francophile and
formidable Renaissance man Samuel Chamberlain, was on board
with his wife and then toddling daughter, Narcisse. Sam was
then at the height of his etching and lithography phase—the

221

rest of his illustrious career still ahead of him. Particularly for a genius, Sam was one of the simplest, happiest and most charming individuals I have ever met. I speak of him in the past tense only because I've not seen him for half a century; I hope he lives to be a hundred. He was barely five years older than I but his gifts made me stand in great awe of him; consequently, we did not make very good conversationalists for I could think of very little I thought worth saying to him. In the midst of the very generation that was eternally promising to do great things once the world gave it a chance, Sam never promised to do anything at all: he just went ahead and did it, superbly and with no fuss. I remember the depths of my admiration for this quality.

• • •

That summer day when the *De Grasse* sailed out through Ambrose Channel bound for Le Havre with a cargo of Americans bound for Paris was a flawless day. The sun was warm; the sky a cerulean blue; only faint airs were stirring; there was no sea. The afterdeck of the *De Grasse* was crowded and gay; the orchestra played "Valencia," and white-coated stewards moved deftly about, bearing trays laden with *legal* alcoholic drinks, not made from Mr. Cohen's one-gallon tins, nor even the windfall of Wingarshiek Beach, but from some noble distillate of . . . well, I ordered an Orange Blossom, the only cocktail I knew. It tasted delicious and its effect was divine. I ordered another and yet another. Heaven drew closer; I was content merely to *be*. Out of all the world's riches, I wanted nothing more than what I then and there had; this exquisite feeling of contentment. Getting blithely stinko could, and did, wait for evening. A serious panic did break out on the evening of the sixth day: the bar had run out of Pol Roger 1920. Except for that, eight days was too short.

• • •

In the second-class compartment on the boat train bound for Paris there sat two men. One had red hair and went to the Yale Law School. The other one was I. We faced two girls. I fell violently and instantaneously in love with one: Professor Irving Babbitt's daughter, on whom I had never laid eyes before. She did not return my love and I can think of *one* comforting reason why: I never voiced it. I merely sat in stony, miserable silence through what seemed a very long train trip. And of course I never saw her again. I never saw *anybody* again except Red, the Yale Law School boy. I never did get to know Red's last name, but that did not prevent us from having an adventure together.

• • •

Red and I had parted, we thought forever, when we were off-loaded that evening in the Gare de St. Lazare. I had been desperately practicing the first words of *operative* French I would ever utter, which were the directions to the driver of my taxi: "*Onze* Avenue Mac-Mahon." To my amazement they did not cause Gallic shrugs, they did not call forth a stream of anti-Americanism—they simply worked. In the Splendid Hôtel, 1 Avenue Carnot, just off the Etoile, the *ascenseur* of course did not function, but I was soon in a room from which I could see the huge Citroën sign flash on and off on the Eiffel Tower, and the glory and wonder of being in Paris quite overcame me. Far below, I could see a hospitable-looking *zinc* where my French proved adequate to produce a ham sandwich and a beer, although not idiomatically.

This was living. Here I was on my own, getting along quite nicely and encountering, so far, neither confusion nor any of the anti-Americanism that was supposed to be rampant in Paris that year.

Since my banking and mail headquarters was the Bankers Trust Company in the Place Vendôme, it was not unnatural that I would often find myself near the Café de la Paix, and one afternoon I bumped into Red there, by himself, with a fairly tall pile of saucers in front of him. He greeted me like a long-lost brother and I greeted him like one. "It must be hell to be a Frenchman in this town and want a piece of tail," said Red, who had observed that the girls were making their exclusive plays to the throngs of Americans and leaving their compatriots to fend for, by, and with themselves. But we pursued the subject of sex no further. Instead Red suggested we go to the theater, and somehow we had no trouble at all in getting seats for that evening for the Casino de Paris. Doubtless we paid scalpers triple super-prices for them, but the franc was in its deepest postwar trouble that year, so Americans *were* rich. Red was rich, *I* was rich. The French nation of purveyors had not yet, in 1926, incredible as it seems, caught on to the basic workings of foreign exchange.

Red must have been a year or so older than I; at any rate, he was in charge of the evening. Our seats were beautiful and on the aisle, and just before the curtain went up on the performance where we were to see, naturally, Mistinguette and Maurice Chevalier, I saw Red in earnest conversation with a seal-like young man in the aisle. Red leaned over to me: "He says the intermission is very long, and wouldn't we like to go and see some dancing girls instead of just waiting around. I said sure. O.K.?" Of course. O.K. This was unlike Boston, New Haven, or even New York, but why had we come to Paris, after all?

The instant, the very instant, the curtain closed on the first act the young man was at Red's side. "Pssst." He ducked and wove, we behind him, through the crowds in aisle and lobby and hustled us into a taxi that had obviously been waiting for us alone. The taxi made some deft twists and turns and in just a few moments we were in front of a lovely house on a lovely street near the Opéra. *Quatorze rue de Montyon.* I shall never forget that address. Only when we mounted the well-scrubbed steps and the conventional mulatto maid in the conventionally immaculate uniform opened the door to us did it burst on me that we had been led by a pimp to a whorehouse—a whorehouse *de grand luxe*, however, to benefit wealthy Americans. The large lobby floor had subdued lighting and soft carpets; the Madam who greeted us was conventionally huge and conventionally red-haired. She could not have been more—well—solicitous. *"Bonjour, messieurs, montez en haute,* yes?" She indicated a graceful spiral staircase.

The second floor was a trifle more functional. We were ushered into a large brightly lighted room where some vacant chairs stood about. Red and I were the only—what shall I say?—guests. A mechanical piano against one wall was operating, *mezzo forte*, in 4/4 time. Then Madame (I have to add the terminal *e*: she deserved it) clapped her hands and a set of double doors opened. Through them came a parade of naked girls. A hundred was my first estimate, but as the years have gone by I have revised this down to fifteen or twenty. They were of every size, shape and variety; some of them were obviously veterans; others, to judge from their breasts, were comparatively unused. Pubic hair ranged from the most feminine of strict triangularity to slightly shaggier types. They paraded before us in a slow procession, and one, perhaps for contrast, perhaps because she caught cold easily, wore a short, diaphanous green scarf about her shoulders.

The preliminary rules of the house were obviously very strict. The girls kept three feet away from us, and any suggestion of physical contact was wholly forbidden. The girls could do anything they wanted with their eyes: from "You are the true love for whom I have been hopelessly waiting all this time" to "Boy, what a good time I could show *you*" to "You wouldn't violate my innocence, would you, you great big all-conquering male?" to "Why don't we cut out this crap and get started?" Their mouths could suggest anything from tenderest motherhood to a faint—very faint—suggestion of cocksucking. It was obviously impossible for them to walk without their inbuilt feminine grace, but any suggestive pelvic movements were utterly barred. This was a mannequin show, and all that was missing was clothes. The girls made two rounds; then, on a signal, all the girls filed out of the room.

Madame's English, like my French, was functional only. "I have *nice* girls," she said. "All good. Nice cunt, nice twat. Which would the gentlemens like? Pick *any*."

But the gentlemen were petrified. Apparently this was not a wholly new situation, for champagne was brought and the suggestion made that perhaps the gentlemens would like to reflect and perhaps confer. Madame and the pimp engaged in subdued conversation. Red and I continued petrified; we were also wholly at a loss how to handle our situation. If either one of us had *not* been scared out of his wits it's possible that neither of us would have seen Act II at the Casino, but this was not the situation.

Shortly the girls re-entered and their tableaux were repeated with slight variations. The piano had now been silenced; perhaps it was a distraction. But Red and I continued petrified, the smiles of utter fools frozen on our faces. At length Red, the lesser coward, indicated to the pimp that we thought we ought to be leaving now. "*Ah, non, messieurs!*" came from Madame. It was not the protest of a balked proprietress, but rather the anguished wail of a mother for two dead sons. The pimp took the news in a somewhat different spirit, and there were further conferences with Madame. It seemed that such a situation had never before arisen in all Madame's long experience; some adjustment would have to be made. Eventually it developed that if we would buy champagne for all the girls the incident could be considered closed, not without sorrow, of course. The ritual was strictly carried out; two bottles of Pol Roger 1920 and the necessary goblets appeared by magic, and we all raised our glasses to one another. Madame's spirits were restored; the girls displayed just the right degree of ruefulness; only the pimp sulked. When cordial good nights were said, he deserted us without a word.

"Goddamn it," said Red, "we've probably passed up the best and cheapest piece of tail we'll ever be offered."

I'm sure he was right; the state of the franc was such that the two bottles of Pol Roger had cost us $2.40. But our brush with sin had cost us more than money; it had cost us pride. Life had walked right up to us and said "Come for a Ride" and we had been too frightened of Life to accept. It was too distasteful and degrading to talk about further.

> *A flower there is, that shineth bright,*
> *Some call it mary-gold-a:*
> *He that wold not when he might,*
> *He shall not when he wold-a.*

I thought of this verse from Bishop Percy's *Reliques* as I dejectedly undressed at the Splendid Hôtel after our night was over. My scrotum was drum-tight with residual excitement, but my penis was still shriveled with fear to not much more than a protruding button. In the dark, in the warm and solitary bed, it reasserted itself with a wild and throbbing erection. I tried hard to get my mind off masturbation, knowing that the ecstasy and relief of the orgasm would be followed by the deepest feelings of depression. And they were.

27 · CANONS AND CATHEDRALS, or, EVENSONG IN VERSAILLES

Everything considered, I had a most peculiar letter of introduction to present when I got to Paris. It was to the Reverend George Crocker Gibbs. And it was not, as might be supposed, from my father or other ecclesiastic. It was from H. E. Lobdell of M.I.T. And *this* was because the Reverend Mr. Gibbs had started life as a civil engineer.

Young Gibbs lasted scarcely longer as a civil engineer than I as a chemical one, but his career took an even stranger hop. After being graduated from M.I.T. in 1900 he had felt the call to enter Andover Theological Seminary, and soon after he was an ordained Episcopalian priest. He remained a bachelor, as quite a few of the High Church clergy do, and he never manifested much interest in purely parochial work. He was famous for years as the highly efficient and dearly loved secretary of the Seamen's Church Institute in New York; then after many years of tenure, he suddenly became Canon of the American Pro-Cathedral in Paris. No combination of job with man could have been more perfect.

George was famous among M.I.T. alumni for the very reason of his career switch, so on the *Review* I had heard a great deal about him without ever having met him. He was famous for his gregariousness and his conviviality. And because he was a bachelor and openly liked the society of the young, there were, almost everywhere, the inevitable speculations about his sex life. Here it is sufficient to say only that George Gibbs was a most unusual clergyman, and that Paris was a city much more suited to him than the New York in which he lived and worked so long.

When I first met him he was a tall, vigorous man in his middle forties, with a well-thatched skull and a face that was good-looking in a craggy sort of way. He had a deeply booming voice, yet with the faintest trace of lisp in it—somewhat as Churchill had. He spoke his French without making the slightest effort to make it sound anything like *la langue de Molière "Av-noo Praise-daw Will-son"* was plenty good enough direction for a taxi driver whom he wished to take him to the causeway named after the late American President.

When I presented my letter to George, he fell on my neck with joy. When André arrived in Paris, a few days later, George fell on his neck, too. George fell on everybody's neck—he loved his fellow man not because it was his Christian duty but because he just couldn't help it. And to André and me he made a most practical suggestion. Why didn't the two of us move into his *pension*, where, he happened to know, there was a large double room recently vacated. This is how André and I came to spend two gorgeous months at 26 Rue de Lubeck.

The Rue de Lubeck was a little backwater of a street near the Place d'Iéna. The right bank of the Seine, the Trocadero, the Bois, the Etoile, were thus all within easy distance. The *pension* itself was slightly ramshackle but the two arms of its L shape enclosed an enchanted French garden—not a blade of grass, but flower beds, pearly white gravel, overhanging trees with seats carpentered around their trunks, and a seductive dotting of white garden tables and chairs all about. To sit in this garden after lunch on a warm sunny day and dawdle with one's cognac—this was heaven.

The duties of the Canon of the American Pro-Cathedral did not seem to be at all onerous, at least not on weekdays. George wore his canonicals only on Sundays or occasions of state. He paid a great many calls, but somehow the settings were almost always cafés, where George was in ordinary dress, caned, gloved and spatted as any *boulevardier*.

The question of religion did eventually come up between George and me. (André was French and therefore outside George's domain, but I was pure American, a member of his own sect, and relapsed at that, so I was the fairest of fair game.) Would I come to evening prayer this Sunday? I'd think about it. Well, think about it *now*. Don't push me, George. Will you come Sunday after next, when *I'll* be officiating? I'll try. What do you mean, you'll *try?*

• • •

But George and I had discovered that there was, alas, a bond between us stronger than religion. This was alcohol. George loved to drink. So did I. So, of course, did André. But André's pattern of drinking was completely different from George's or mine. André's was highly ritualistic, slow, deeply savoring, and always—*almost* always—to the accompaniment of food. When he reached a certain mild degree of euphoria he would stop, not out of self-denial but because there was in him some circuit that would switch off at a certain point. He had had all he wanted, thank you, and nothing could induce him to take another drop until tomorrow. But in my circuits and in George's there was no such switch, or, if there was, its *off* setting was much, much higher up the scale. One did not get plastered in Paris, as one did in Boston and New York, because the elements of sin, secrecy and scarcity were absent. But one could get *blotto*—that was the word of the year—and if one were George or myself, one did. If one were André, one did not.

Thus, André was outraged at a proposal from George that I accepted with enthusiasm. George had simply suggested that some evening we start at the bottom of the Rue des Martyrs, have a different drink at every café we came to, and see how far up Montmartre we could get. "Barbarous, simply barbarous!" said André, who dissociated himself from the project with deep Gallic scorn.

So, on an appointed evening, George and I set forth together. We did not get off to a very good start, for at our first café something prompted George to order a sherry cobbler and, by the prearranged rules of the game, that had to be my drink, too. Now a sherry cobbler, which I doubt any modern bartender has ever heard of, was an inferior drink at best, being sherry, not of the first rank, festooned with fruits. The waiter was a very long time at the bar and what he eventually set before us were two vases. "*Mais c'est une salade, n'est-ce pas?*" said George. Whether it was his accent or the sentiment expressed I do not know, but a minor wave of anti-Americanism did then break out, and to make matters worse, there was not enough sherry in the sherry cobblers to raise us to the level of even the mildest elation.

We made up for all this at subsequent stops, of which I remember four or five. George grew confidential. "This business of being a clergyman has its drawbacks," said the Canon of the American Pro-Cathedral. "I don't care much about women, though," he said reflectively. "Liquor's *my* weakness." He must have made other confessions that night, and so must I. But all of them got lost in the subsequent alcoholic fog. Neither of us remembered anything about getting home. André did, though. "You were both pigs," he said, and would not elaborate beyond saying that in a letter to his father he had said of *"cette fripouille* d'Hodgins" that *"il boit comme un trou."* The idea conveyed that I was a bottomless pit. Well, at that time, I thought I was.

•   •   •

George eventually played his trump card in the matter of religion. "If you'll come to the evening prayer tomorrow," he said earnestly, "I'll turn my collar around afterward and go down to Versailles and get drunk with you." The bargain was struck. Versailles, in the moonlight, was never more beautiful. It was so beautiful that we did not get very drunk.

George may not have cared very "much about women" but he was not indifferent to them. On another alcoholic occasion we had ended up where one did, in those days, at three or four in the morning—at Les Halles. I was slowing down, but George, although the elder by far, was still going strong. In the little restaurant above the markets there was dancing to a tinny orchestra and the space for it was L-shaped. George picked up a pliant girl and whirled her out of my line of sight. They were gone for a long time, and when the music stopped, George came back with a look of deep satisfaction on his face. *"I felt her all over,"* said the Canon, in a devilish whisper.

Perhaps it was that same evening that George and I commandeered a carriage to drive us through the Bois for half an hour of early-morning fresh air before we turned in for what we called "the night." In the placid carriage, I fell asleep. When I awoke there George's arm was about my shoulders, and as I swam giddily to consciousness, I heard him say, *"Dear* Eric," whereupon he leaned down and planted a gentle kiss on my brow. And that was the nearest approach to an adult "homosexual" experience I ever had.

I think there must be a sort of man who is not unduly driven by his balls and thus is seldom led to focus his emotions strongly on a woman or women, but who is nevertheless full of love that he diffuses widely among his fellow humans without particular regard to the sex they belong to. And I think George Gibbs was such a man. May he rest in the peace he deserves.

• • •

• • •

The year 1926 was, until then, the year of the greatest American tourist influx into Paris. It was, by and large, a youthful influx. As I try to recall this distant time I find myself left with two impressions: Paris seemed repelled by Americans but also fascinated by them. The repulsion was all too easy to understand. France itself was having a very hard time that summer: the government fell four times as Briand (twice), Herriot and Poincaré played musical chairs with the premiership. Totally unlike today, only the most sophisticated *hôteliers* and *restaurateurs* understood why all Americans seemed so filthy rich: it was because the franc was plunging toward its all-time postwar low. Seen from the other perspective, things were crystal-clear: I made daily visits to Bankers Trust on the Place Vendôme, and drew against my letter of credit the smallest number of francs possible to see me through a day of riotous living—because tomorrow a dollar would buy still more francs. The franc did not sink by the day or even the hour; it sank by the minute, and I can remember watching the register board at Bankers Trust one day, until, eventually, it registered the franc as worth 1.8 cents American. I promptly bought five dollars' worth, whereupon there outpoured on me all the franc notes I could stuff into my wallet. Since a dinner at an extravagant restaurant might cost five hundred francs, at a quite good one, one hundred francs, and at a *bon coin*, ten francs, it was easy to see why even I could afford almost anything. I tried to spend my untold wealth as unostentatiously as possible, but it is still hard for me to forget how good the *paysan* dinner André and I consumed at the Bon Bock, *vin compris*, for thirty-six cents for the two of us, was.

Madame, who presided over the *caisse* of the Bon Bock, was puzzled by this, since we did not *look* like millionaires, but not resentful: possibly André and I had a good thing going in the

White Slave traffic with the Argentine, in which case more power to us, and would we not come back again and again?

But a certain number of our American compatriots and contemporaries had taken to unhappy examples of chauvinism, like pasting 500-franc notes on their luggage along with the hotel and travel stickers. The French saw absolutely no humor in this, and all of us from Les Etats-Unis suffered somewhat in consequence. Yet in all that Paris summer the worst thing I remember happening to me was when a taxi driver, hitherto a stranger, drove dead slow along the curb from the Place du Tertre beside me muttering obscene hatred. I could understand not one word, but the intent was clear. So in return I merely opened my own lungs and let come forth all the corresponding things I could think of in English. This proved to be a satisfactory arrangement until, at length, he turned off into a side street.

• • •

I suppose I was protected, in some measure, against displays of anti-Americanism by André's almost constant presence at my side. Although we had been schoolboys in Philadelphia and New York, André, born in Paris, was American only because Walter Damrosch had brought his father, a first-prize bassoonist, from the Paris Conservatory to play first chair for the New York Symphony Society Orchestra. Although André was exactly my age, his pate in 1926 was beginning to be shiny bald and he had cultivated, as second nature, a very European beard. His English was as unaccented as mine, but his French was pure Parisian, as were his looks and his soul. School and college years in the United States had Americanized him without taking away a jot of his Frenchness. Thus, when when we toured not only the streets, monuments, institutions and museums of Paris, but the châteaux of the Loire and most of the major cathedral cities, I had by my side, in all literalness, not only a friend, a guide, but also a buffer state.

A climax to our conscientious tour came in Reims. The Hôtel Univers was directly opposite the railroad station. Not knowing that, we hailed a taxi; we gave the driver our destination whereupon he solemnly made a wide U-turn, stopped in front of the hotel and just as solemnly collected his tariff.

It was about nine in the evening and the dining room was

deserted. But the *propriétaire* was delighted to see us. No less were we delighted to see him. He was a huge, portly Frenchman who wore a porous-knit shirt and whose trousertops came up almost to his armpits. He was rubicund, shiny and as jovial as Santa Claus, with a beard and mustaches that were masterpieces. Somehow, while we toyed with glasses of sherry (André toyed; the verb for me would have been slightly different), he confected a huge and exquisite omelet, and he and André had a long, complex and very knowing conversation about whether Avize or Mesnil would be the perfect bottle to accompany it. I forget which was decided upon, but at any rate such was the *ambiance* of everything that we had one of each.

And then, the moon sailing in a sky of ragged clouds, we set out to see the ruins of the cathedral. American money had already done much to restore its perfect beauty, but in the moonlight the profanation of the two west towers seemed even more dramatic and seizing in the intestines than by daylight the next morning. The two of us stood there, not *quite* sober but far from alcoholic, and thought thoughts we could not put into words.

Next morning André vowed a vow that summed up his feelings. "I'm going to come back here next year, on exactly the same day, at exactly the same hour, and repeat this experience down to the smallest detail."

"Don't!" I begged him. "Please don't. It won't work. This is not said selfishly because I won't be with you. But there will be something the matter with the omelet, and there will be scaffolding on the cathedral towers. Worst of all the proprietor will have lowered his trouser band and shaved off his mustaches. Things like this cannot be duplicated."

But André was stubborn, and in 1927 he carried out his vow. And everything I had predicted came true.

• • •

André, by then being an instructor in French at Columbia, could and did cross the Atlantic every summer. But I didn't know when my next chance would come. Perhaps never. And I was resolved that I was going to see London as well as Paris before I died. So ten days before our joint holiday was to end, I said goodby to André, to George Gibbs and to some other friends I have not brought into this narrative, and crossed the Channel.

For some reason known only to God I had booked myself into a Temperance Hotel—the Hotel Thackeray on Great Russell Street, spang opposite the British Museum. My brief stay in London was typical of the compound my adult life was becoming: deep happiness combined with deep loneliness, in an inseparable amalgam. My girl-hunger had not left me in Paris—far from it!—but there had been distractions enough in Paris to keep it in the relative background.

"I'm afraid you're going to find things a bit on the dull side," said the Englishman who sat opposite me in the Pullman on the boat train from Dover to London. (Like a well-briefed traveler I had said not the frigidest word to him; he opened a conversation the moment I put down my prop newspaper.) "Tomorrow's August Bank Holiday, you know."

I hadn't known, of course. And London was about as closed up as any human aggregation could be. I didn't care. From the moment of my alighting in Waterloo Station I had been seized by the most vivid attack of *déjà vu* I have ever experienced—and it did not wear off. I walked and walked the streets of London and used my wretched Hotel Thackeray quarters only to rest so that I could walk some more. These walks were random, not organized. What endlessly delighted me was the incredible Englishness of the English. The British Empire was close to finished, of course, but no one knew that yet, least of all the British; London was still the capital of capitals of the terrestrial globe.

The vast concentration of whores in West End London came to me as a complete surprise. I liked it. It gave me a sense of sin to be solicited, and the English opening gambit of "How do you do?" I found charming. I never responded, but hygiene, not morality, was my inhibitor. Fortunately, the girls weren't too seductive to be resisted. And I was so far from being any man-of-the-world type that the idea of picking a girl up, talking to her over dinner, and then just paying her off, never occurred to me. By that I mean precisely that it *did* occur to me but I could not imagine myself in the role. Why not, I wonder?

So I got lonelier and lonelier, and thought to myself O, if the social system were only arranged so that you could go up to a lovely girl and without offense introduce yourself and carry her off just for companionship, if she were willing, how much more endurable the world would be. (The social system *was* arranged that way, but I didn't know it, and besides, it took nerve to make it work, more nerve than I had.) One evening, in Shaftesbury Avenue, I saw a beautiful girl approaching. There, I said to myself, is the perfect example of what I mean: if there were *only* some way I could meet a girl like this one, and not some used-up prostitute swinging her handbag.

Then, as we drew abreast, the lovely girl said, "How do you do?" I was so utterly flabbergasted I just kept on walking.

28 · LEAP ACROSS THE CHARLES, OR, THE YOUTH'S COMPANION

WHEN I FINALLY got home from Europe, I discovered that the generous Harford Powel had continued my twenty-five dollars a week completely through my absence, so my European summer had cost me substantially nothing at all. It was evident that Harford wanted me around, and I felt correspondingly complimented.

Susan and I had the happiest of reunions and promptly resumed our sexual practices. And my life was no longer complicated by Harriet for I had finally got up the courage requisite to telling her that however physically gratifying our relationship had been, I simply could not go on with something that involved adultery and cuckoldry both. God knows how I put it, for I am sure I did not use those words. And God knows where I found the courage to take this decisive step. Not until later did it occur to me that a year or two before it had taken all the courage I had to start on a romantic path with a woman and that now it was taking all the courage I had to bring an affair to a stop. Women, I was to reflect later, had me over a barrel. Getting close to them, having an intimacy develop, eventually going to bed with them, this was not a climax except physically; in other, manifold ways it was just a beginning. Pandora's box was at last open, but . . .

• • •

In the *Review* office that fall Miss Catherine Carlson was joined by another editorial assistant, one Jim Killian, a just-hatched alumnus of the Class of '26, who had been editor of the student newspaper, *The Tech*. So not only did the little *Review* office house me and my unsuspected and unsuspecting wife-to-be; it also housed the future Dr. James Rhyne Killian, eventually to

236

be president of the Institute, scientific adviser to Presidents of the United States, and chairman of the Institute Corporation. *Who's Who* today takes five inches to list his honors and accomplishments, but he took his first upward step when he succeeded me on the *Review* in 1927. This was probably sooner than he expected. It was sooner than I expected, too.

Lobby and I had continued our friendship throughout what was now close to five years. But it had always been something of a wary friendship on my part; partly because I am such a wary person; partly because—that old curse—he seemed fonder of me than I was of him. But I did deeply appreciate the confidence and enthusiasm he invested in me; there was no question whatever that he was boss, but he displayed the very best traits of the boss: if I had done something unwise or foolish he would defend me 100 per cent in public; only in private to me would he say, if he thought so, that I'd been off base. In short, he never once failed to uphold me. Of this I was highly conscious and, for it, highly grateful.

And all of this came to a sudden end one Sunday evening of lashing rain while Lobby and I were mired together in a taxicab that was trying to take us to dinner at a professor's home in a far-out Boston suburb.

• • •

It was really a terrible edge-of-winter night to be out. Our first taxi had blown a tire at the precise peak of an icy-driving rain squall—and we were in suburban mud when it happened. We were both pretty wet by the time we had paid off our drenched and cursing driver, phoned our hosts that we would be good and late, and then, through God's surprising and erratic mercy, found another cab.

But none of this had stanched our conversational flow and as we got into our new cab Lobby asked, "How's your crazy friend Harford Powel on *The Youth's Companion?*"

I answered that he was crazier than ever (which he was). Then I added, gratuitously and innocently, "He keeps giving me advice about my future career."

"Like what?" said Lobby.

"Well, just yesterday he said to me, apropos of nothing at all,

'Never go to New York for a salary offer of less than ten thousand a year.' "

A thunderous silence fell. We had obviously reached the end of *that* conversational line, but unaware that all lines were down, I tried one or two other minor topics. Silence. Then the cab at last reached the front door of our destination and that particular tension relaxed. The four of us spent a pleasant but slightly formal and restrained evening, in which it was noticeable, to me at least, that Lobby addressed not one word to me. When it came time to leave there was hell's own time about getting a taxi, although the storm had somewhat abated, but eventually it was got.

Our long ride back to Boston, Lobby's and mine, was made in total silence. If I had been a more outgoing or an opener personality, I would have said, "Lobby, what did I say that offended you?" or, still more honestly, "What was there about my quote from Harford Powel that made you go blackout on me?" But I wasn't this kind of person. I was the kind of person who said, to himself, "All right, you son of a bitch, if you're going to play insulted with me, I'll damn well play it with you." So frigid silence prevailed on both sides, broken only by curt good nights as we took leave of each other. Our friendship, our collaboration, everything, had suddenly ended as the result of one innocuous-seeming sentence.

• • •

Next morning, Lobby sent for me. This in itself was unusual because the ordinary routine was that Lobby would amble into the *Review* office at his own pleasure. This morning, sitting in his assistant dean's office, he was a fat, dark thundercloud.

"I've made up my mind," he said, "that whoever is going to run the *Review* next year, it's going to be full time, without any chasing back and forth across the Charles."

I immediately and violently saw red. "I have been running the *Review* full time," I said. "What you call chasing across the Charles has been afterhours activity, to which you've made no objection for the past year until this morning. What's changed you?"

"I don't like your attitude," said Lobby.

"And I don't like yours," I said.

"Look," said Lobby, "I'm not kidding myself that the *Review* without you will be the same magazine as the *Review* with you, but I'm prepared to accept the consequences."

"Fine," I said. "We have a contract that runs until next July. Do you want to cancel it now or let it run its course?"

"We'll let it run its course," said Lobby.

• • •

And those were the last words we spoke directly to each other for more than ten years. This placed a considerable burden on the then fledgling Jim Killian, for whatever Lobby wanted to convey to me he conveyed through Jim, and I used Jim in the same way. But it all stood Jim in very good stead for later. After he succeeded me in 1927 he edited the *Review* for twelve years, until his meteoric rise in the worlds of education and M.I.T. began in 1939—triggered by the departure of Vannevar Bush from M.I.T.'s vice-presidency to become president of the Carnegie Institution of Washington. It was then that Jim became executive assistant to President Karl Compton and his genius for administration became evident.

I used to spend a good deal of time wondering *just* why all friendship and intimacy between Lobby and myself came to such a sudden, not to say explosive, end. It was obviously triggered by my casual and perhaps not even very tactful quotation from Harford Powel about not going to New York for any offer of less than $10,000 a year—in those days a goodly sum. One thing Lobby and I had never discussed was my future. I had never thought very specifically about it, but in whatever vague thoughts I had had I had somehow placed myself in New York; in whatever event, I never pictured myself growing old as the editor of *The Technology Review*, nor, even, growing old in Cambridge or at M.I.T. And Lobby had never discussed the subject with me, one way or another. So I was left to conjecture that perhaps Lobby had interpreted my Powel quote as a veiled hint that I would not be averse to leaving him and the *Review* at my own pleasure, and he had resolved then and there that it would be at *his* pleasure, particularly now that Jim Killian was on the scene. Or, perhaps . . . .

Years later, I got a tiny retrospective peek at the me of those days as seen through another pair of eyes. The eyes were Susan's

We were due to part "forever" at last in 1928, she to marry
the lad from whom I *could* have taken her. But in another sense
we never completely parted at all because for many years I used
to telephone her or even occasionally see her whenever I visited
Boston from New York, and we would have long, nostalgic talks.
During one of those, in an outburst of frankness that must have
come at least ten years after our relationship had ceased, she
said, "I was so in love with you, *but you were so ambitious.*"

That remark shook me up for several reasons; the only one
to be recorded here was my complete incredulity at being thought
ambitious in my twenties. But Susan knew me better and more
intimately in those days than any other human being, so I was
pretty much forced to take her assessment as correct. But if I
was ambitious, I was not conscious of it; I *was* conscious of working very hard because I wanted to be thought good at my job.
I held the image of my father constantly in mind—not to emulate
his virtues as a human being but as an awful warning of the
possibilities of failure, and of the fate that lay in store for those
who were vague, or imprecise, or not constantly on the alert
against the dangers of leaving undone something that should
have been done, against being unprepared for the unexpected.
So my constant inner state was a state of Anxiety, with a capital
A; yet this inner state was eternally perceived, by a girl who
knew and loved me, as Ambition, also with a capital A.

• • •

I never said a word to Harford Powel about my rupture with
Lobdell, or that as of the summer of 1927 I would be leaving
the *Review.* After all, it was his innocent remark that had been
the cause of the blow-up, so I felt sensitive about discussing it
with him. And I think also a matter of pride was involved. Had
I been fired? The record would be very ambiguous on that point.
Lobby had not fired me, but he had said, with provocation his
intent, that "next year" the *Review* was not going to be edited
by anyone working in his spare time for *The Youth's Companion*
or anything else. It was an ultimatum, and I had rejected it.
Discussing this with Harford might make him feel that I, by
refusing to give up my association with the *Companion,* had
placed him under an obligation.

But I think some version of the story must have leaked out

to Harford from some other M.I.T. source, for in the late spring of 1927 he said to me one day, quite casually, "Well, Reverend, I think you ought to make the jump across the river and come with us full time." (A curiously formal man, in some ways, was Harford. His favorite greeting to me was "Hello, Reverend" when he was at ease; but when he had his executive manner on, it would be "Cut twenty lines of this drivel, Hodgins." He never called me by first name.)

I asked him what job he was proposing for me and he promptly answered "Managing editor." Since this involved quite a bit of internal shuffling it was obvious this was no sudden whim of Harford's. We shook hands on the deal there and then, whereupon it gave Harford the greatest pleasure to yell at his secretary for the "big" dictionary so that he could look up every meaning of "manage." He went into loud guffaws of wild Welsh laughter when he discovered "to cause persons or animals to submit to one's control"; "to bring over to one's wishes by artifice, flattery, etc."; and finally "to contrive cunningly." "There you are!" said Harford. "There's your job all laid out and defined. Now go figure out how you're going to fill it. Contrive cunningly!"

•   •   •

My last months on the *Review* were scarcely pleasant, but they went by. Lobby's attitude toward me in no way softened. But as a sort of farewell present an ambivalence appeared. Through Jim Killian, Lobby sent word that I was to have nothing to do with putting the last issue of the summer, or of my tenure, to press. I hit the ceiling. Even as a very young man Jim Killian was tactful and soft-spoken. "This is not punitive," he said. "I'm in a spot. I can't discuss it, but Lobby isn't being punitive. You'll just have to take my word."

I did, and when the final issue came out I discovered the reason for my exclusion from it. My picture was on the cover, and inside there were graceful words (written by Jim, I think, BUT AT LOBBY'S DIRECTION AND APPROVAL, YOU WALLOWING DISBELIEVER) of appreciation for my five years of service and hearty good wishes for my future. I wrote Lobby a rather formal note about it, gave Jim all my good wishes for *his* future, shook hands warmly with Miss Catherine Carlson, who would now be Jim's assistant, and took my departure.

29 · THE ABDUCTED CHILD, OR, $20,000 HEART BALM

The Youth's Companion in 1926 was almost 100 years old and properly boasted itself as "the oldest magazine of continuous publication in America." The pretensions of *The Saturday Evening Post* to have been founded beforehand by Benjamin Franklin were utterly without foundation. Ben had founded *The Pennsylvania Gazette*, from which, after various discontinuances and transmutations, had sprung the *S.E.P.* Throughout much of the nineteenth century the *Companion* was *the* magazine of mass circulation in the country, read assiduously by the light of candles, of whale-oil lamps, of kerosene lanterns in the outlands, even possibly by gaslight in the cities, by families when reading was, with certain other exceptions of course, the only recreation—certainly the only quiet, solitary and *approved* recreation. The *Companion's* moral tone was high and it was edited to be read not only by youth but by every member of the family. Its editorial home had always been Boston, and as it grew and mightily prospered it moved to successively more and more spacious and elegant quarters. In the 1920's there were three or possibly four buildings bearing its name, chiseled imperishably into stone. It was published by the Perry Mason Company—an entirely synthetic name, for there was never a Mr. Perry or a Mr. Mason connected with the publication—and I have often wondered whether this synthesis was the source of Erle Stanley Gardner's famous and infallible defender of falsely indicted murderers.

Whether or no, the Perry Mason Company moved into what was to prove its final palace—if not its final home. The Commonwealth Avenue edifice (it was no mere *building*) was appropriately outfitted with solid bronze elevator doors, solid mahogany balustrades and the like. In the basement lay the great presses.

In the late teens of the century the Perry Mason Company began to feel an unaccountable economic malaise. Eventually a radical decision was made by Mr. Kelsey, president of the company. The *Companion* would junk its own presses, growing rapidly obsolete, and, distasteful as it seemed, negotiate a contract with a "commercial" printer. It chose for this honor the Rumford Press, in Concord, New Hampshire. Rumford was delighted: here was a fine fat contract. A new enormous modern press would have to be built to take care of this unprecedented job, but that was more than all right. Hands were shaken on a deal.

The Perry Mason Company was still riding very high, despite this annoying financial dyspepsia that would not quite go away. If it was going to move its manufacturing operation to Concord, good sense dictated that it move its circulation department there, too. Architectural plans were drawn up for an appropriate Doric temple to house this operation, and it was then suggested by Mr. Kelsey that the Rumford Press and the Perry Mason Company join hands in financing this structure. Rumford made agreeable noises about the proposal but suggested, just as a preliminary formality, mind you, that it would like *its* accountants to take a casual peek at the Perry Mason books. Of course this was a little crass, but Perry Mason gave assent, as any gentleman was bound to do under the circumstances.

Some forty-eight to seventy-two hours later a frenzied exchange of telephone calls flashed back and forth between Boston and Concord. The information conveyed was simple and stark: even by accountancy methods considered modern a lustrum in advance of the stock-market crash, of the fate of Kreuger and Toll, and all that was to follow, the proud Perry Mason Company was "technically" bankrupt.

• • •

In the dust arising from this then incredible debacle certain facts are still obscure—but certain others were painfully clear. The Rumford Press was stuck, and stuck good. It had invested hundreds of thousands of dollars in new equipment for the *Companion*, which was already being printed there, and this investment had to be protected. And editor Ellery Sedgwick of the *Atlantic Monthly* owned the majority of the Rumford Press stock. It was thus that Mr. Sedgwick, against all his instincts and desires, came to be the proprietor of *The Youth's Companion* and the owner, if that is the word, of all the assets and liabilities of the Perry Mason Company.

• • •

By the time Harford Powel had arrived on the scene a series of almost incredible circumstances had been uncovered, as if archeologists, digging into a mound of dust, had discovered something resembling Angkor Wat, but without its style. As an example: The Perry Mason Company had discovered, many years before, an Eternal Verity that still confronts all magazine publishing everywhere, no matter how wildly successful—it is easier to get a subscription out of somebody who has subscribed before than from someone who hasn't. In other words, renewals come cheaper than new subscriptions. This must have been an exciting discovery in the 1880's or whenever it was made, so many decades before market research or readership surveys had been invented. But whenever it was, Perry Mason, the company, made an error in deduction of which Perry Mason, counselor, would never have been guilty. Upon a correctly observed fact it built the Policy that helped, by soft, gradual degrees, to wreck it; since renewal subscriptions were more inexpensively obtained than new ones, it would concentrate its future efforts on this easy circulation market and let the more difficult one go hang. Since the *Companion*'s renewal rate was very high this seemed to be a perfect example of the Boston-prudent. But time *does* pass, and people *do* grow older, so when Ellery Sedgwick had the magazine crammed down his sagging throat *The Youth's Companion* had scarcely any youthful audience at all, but a fanatically loyal readership among hundreds of thousands of grandfathers and grandmothers who had been subscribers since *their* childhood. The old Perry Mason Company was not unaware of this, but its solution to the problem—in case anyone considered it a problem—was merely to alter its editorial policy to conform to the tone of the incoming mail.

• • •

Thus it was that when Harford Powel began his laudable attempts to make the magazine appeal again to Youth, his efforts were crowned with thorns. The incoming mail changed to a flood of whining complaint and senile abuse from the magazine's ancient subscribers; cancellations and nonrenewals poured in; and the real Youth market, long invaded by *The American Boy* and *Boys' Life*, responded only feebly. "When I took the magazine over I swore I would never put a penny into it," Mr. Sedgwick had cause to say to me in bitterness a few years later. He did, though; he had to, and it galled his soul.

• • •

Mr. Sedgwick was a strange, incalculable man. With a ragged mustache and a manner at once sullen and explosive, he did not remotely resemble any stereotype of what the *Atlantic*'s editor might be supposed to resemble. His fondness for loud checked suits led Frederick Lewis Allen, later to become his rival on *Harper's*, to a sentence in a Profile on Mr. Sedgwick that *The New Yorker* regrettably decided not to print: "Mr. Sedgwick's appearance gives the impression more that he is dressed for Atlantic City than for the *Atlantic Monthly*." But what an editor he was, and what a stable of writers he assembled, at a maximum of $150 per piece! When Freddie Allen took over at *Harper's*, he began to raid the *Atlantic* stable by offering fifty to seventy-five dollars more. Mr. Sedgwick blandly refused to meet this competition; he let writer after writer go to Allen and *Harper's* and just built up a new and perhaps even better stable of his own. He was the one editor I ever knew who would read anything regardless of its physical form. If something came in written on butcher's paper with a blunt stick, he could somehow tell by snuffing it whether it had something of value and more than one was the pearl he pried out of the most bedraggled and unpromising oyster. He could be hoaxed, and occasionally was, but most of the long chances he took paid off.

In 1926, my first year under his publishing roof, he announced with great fanfare The *Atlantic Monthly* Prize Competition for the best first novel of a hitherto unknown author—the prize being $10,000 in cash, guaranteed publication by Little, Brown and serialization in the *Atlantic*. Lo and behold in 1927 up turned a horse-faced Canadian lady, Mazo de la Roche, with *Jalna*. The whoopla in Boston was tremendous and serialization started with a bang. But as *Jalna* went on, Mr. Sedgwick began to grow sick of it, so thoroughly that he threatened to drop it in its mid-career. The Business Side persuaded him against this, eventually, but nothing could prevent him from printing later installments in smaller and smaller type. For Miss De la Roche this was the making of her fortune; she milked the *Jalna* theme for more than a dozen books, estimated total sale, two million. But there were no further *Jalna*'s in the *Atlantic*. Mr. Sedgwick had had it.

• • •

• • •

"Like most American men of letters," wrote Harry Hanson, "Mr. Powel was once the editor of *Collier's* magazine." That was how he began his review of Harford's first novel, *The Virgin Queene*, which I, then with a great interest in typography, had designed. This was in 1928, and Harford had pretty well turned the editing of the *Companion* over to me. He knew it was dying; I thought it could be saved. The eventual climax was little more than a year away.

When I say that Harford Powel was a deeply kind man—which he was—I don't mean to give the picture of a quiet, beneficent, passive dispenser of kindness. Harford was a *roaring* personality, who was extravagant in his self-praise, but also in the praise of others. He would dictate endless streams of promotional copy for *The Virgin Queene* to the Advertising Department of Little, Brown, which did not always appreciate them. In these would occur without a trace of blush or self-consciousness such assertions as "the three greatest advertising copywriters in America today are Bruce Barton, Harford Powel, Jr., and Raymond Rubicam." But once when he was dictating some promotion copy for his novel I suddenly heard as I was passing his door, "The book was designed by that eminent Boston typographer Mr. Eric Hodgins."

I protested. "Harford, for God's sake, please—"

"Shut up!" he roared. "If I say that six more times you *will* be!" His life was built on such assumptions. He was a very bad editor, in my youthful opinion, but he was a great teacher of editing—very often by inadvertent demonstrations of exactly how not to do it—but I consider that by his faith in me, and his advertent or inadvertent guidance, he gave me my true start in my career.

246

Harford gave me my first lessons in cynicism, which I needed badly. He had announced in the *Companion's* pages The Great Junior Fiction Contest, open to boys and girls of etc., etc. I forget what the prize was, but the response was colossal. The Reading Department, which Harford had neglected to consult in advance, simply dumped, unopened, all envelopes addressed to "Junior Fiction Contest Editor" into old-fashioned peach baskets and relentlessly sent them up to the main editorial floor. I have no idea how many there were, but I remember having to pick my way through them for several weeks, for Harford paid them no attention at all.

He made it a habit, once or twice a day, to stroll out from his private cubicle to my desk, in the unprotected open, usually polishing the briar bowl of the pipe he seldom smoked with the tip of his aristocratic nose. "You have been worrying about the Junior Fiction Contest," he announced. As a matter of fact I had ceased worrying about it something like three weeks before, but to Harford an interruption of three weeks or thirty seconds in a conversation were as one. He picked up our three-week-old exchange as if a mere telephone bell had severed it.

"I will let you in on a great secret," said Harford. He lowered his voice to a house stage whisper. "The winning manuscript is in *that* basket." He pointed to one with his pipestem.

"Do you mean—?" I said.

"Yes," said Harford, striding back to his office.

Next morning *that* basket was on my desk; all others had disappeared. Also on my desk was a succinct note from Harford: "Pick best three from among these and submit to me. I shall be final judge. HPjr."

I did as I was told. For a while, a little while, I felt qualms but they went into reverse when I decided that Harford's method was not only as good as any, but *better* than any. It had just been a little surprising at first.

• • •

Between his days on *Collier's* and *The Youth's Companion* Harford had indeed been a copywriter for Barton, Durstine and Osborn in the days long before it became known, through its strange amalgamation with the George Batten Company, as the "B.B.D.&O." of today. How great a copywriter Harford really was, I don't know, but he was certainly an idolater of Bruce Barton and quoted him constantly, as if he had been Jesus—a confusion that seemingly arose also within Barton himself.

The year 1928 was a momentous year at 8 Arlington Street for many reasons, not all of them publicational. For one thing it was rocked to its foundations—and so was a lot of Boston, for that matter—by a scandal that would have been more typical of the nineteenth century than the twentieth. It was so wildly improbable as to be comic—to those not directly involved—and as I remember it today it seems more like a bad dramatic invention of Sir Arthur Wing Pinero's than the real thing. But it was the real thing, all right.

Mr. Sedgwick's "business partner," so referred to by the great man himself, was a tall, genial, bald-pated Scot by name of Mac-Gregor Jenkins. Mr. Sedgwick's Sanctum, long and ornate, gave on Arlington Street on the second floor of No. 8; Mr. Jenkins' office, of identical size but a bit more Spartan, was directly above. Mr. Jenkins made the perfect business chief for the *Atlantic*; he was cordial, approachable and gracious of manner. He used to write a little, too; small essays for *House Beautiful*, then also a member of the Atlantic Monthly group of publications, called "Bucolic Beatitudes," signed "Rusticus," which might begin—in fact one *did*—with the invocation "Blessed be the Pig . . .," for in his nonbusiness hours Mr. Jenkins was a gentleman-farmer slightly north of Boston. He was in good demand as an after-dinner speaker, and he shone at this difficult art. He never said anything of particular importance, but he wasn't supposed to. He was the kind of speaker who relaxed his audience right away, for his manner was easy, bespeaking long experience. He had a fund of apt and nonstock anecdotes to warm up with, and he never needed a single prompting note in front of him. *Urbane* described him exactly. I never knew him well, obviously, being a young squirt one-third his age, but the path from elevator to my desk led me past his always open door, and if he was looking up he never failed to bid me a smiling good morning. He was an in-the-office-on-the-dot-of-eight-thirty type, which was why he was always there first: regularity seemed to be his life's touchstone.

But all was not what it seemed. I had once briefly met *Mrs.* MacGregor Jenkins in some fashion now forgotten and had wondered, idly, how he could stand it. The answer was, as later transpired, he couldn't.

One morning, many months later, Mr. Jenkins was not in his office. His distracted secretary didn't know where he was—this was no business trip. He wasn't in his office next day, either. And it was to turn out that Mr. Jenkins was never to be in his office again. *Something* had snapped and MacGregor Jenkins, the genial, urbane, charming business head of the *Atlantic Monthly*, totally at ease as "Rusticus," essayist for *House Beautiful*, had without a word of warning deserted his wife of many winters and run away—literally run away—with a chorus girl—a literal chorus girl! And—also literally—he was never heard from again. Lawyers obviously entered this extraordinary equation somewhere, sometime, not only on behalf of Mrs. J. but also on behalf of Mr. Sedgwick, who was, like Ophelia before him, the more deceived. But Boston Society, to which the Jenkinses definitely belonged, merely reacted as it had from time immemorial when such situations, once in a blue moon, arose: it just closed ranks and pretended that no such person as Mac-Gregor Jenkins had ever existed. No. 8 Arlington Street of course rocked and buzzed, and Harford Powel went around for days with an evil look in his glinting eye, as if he knew something he was damned if he'd ever tell, but whether he really did I really don't know.

• • •

We were also in the election year 1928. Political conventions were held earlier those days—in June—and the campaigns were intolerably long. This one, having been prefaced by Calvin Coolidge's enigmatic utterance, "I do not chose to run," was Hoover *vs.* Smith. It was one of unparalleled bitterness and the issue of Catholicism made it more so. Mr. Sedgwick, Boston Brahmin though he was, was a Smith man notwithstanding, and from afar I got my first glimpse of *creative* editing, as it would now be listed today in college catalogs, I am sure. Having signed up Al Smith for an article later to be titled "Catholic and Patriot" on why Catholicism should be no bar to the White House, he sought out an author, whose article he would publish prior to Smith's, strongly deprecating the possibility of Smith's election. He found him in a lawyer named Marshall. *His* article appeared and such was the *Atlantic*'s influence in those days that the Marshall article all but set the country aflame. What had hitherto been a whispering campaign was now in the wide open.

Uncle Ellery let a couple of months go by before he published the powerful Smith rejoinder, and by this time it seemed as if the country was waiting for the issue to appear as the country now waits for a known and coming TV high news event. So, at any rate, did it appear to E. A. Grozier, publisher of the Boston *Post*, always by far the city's worst-looking newspaper but also in those days far the best and most enterprising. The *Post* dispatched a reporter to Concord, New Hampshire, where the *Atlantic*'s run was coming to an end at the Rumford Press, and where, with the aid of enough whiskey, he suborned a night watchman into handing over a premature copy of the *Atlantic* containing the Smith article. Thus, one day before the *Atlantic*'s scheduled on-sale date, the *Post* broke the story all over its page one.

Mr. Sedgwick in a towering fury was a terrible sight to see, and this day must have been one of the towering furiousest he had ever gone through. The child he had, singlehanded, if that expression is permitted, conceived, nurtured and reared had been stolen from under his nose. No one dared go near him for hours. Privately, as time wore on, his fury must have abated somewhat, for the wire services of course instantly picked up the *Post*'s story and spread it all over the country, including points west of Pittsfield, where some people might never have heard of the *Atlantic* before. But publicly he never allowed his fury to descend any lower than a supertruculence, and when he could get his breath he sued the *Post* for triple punitive damages for willful, deliberate and malicious invasion of copyright.

When after a long time the case came to trial, I attended as many sessions as I could and was fascinated at watching the Law in action. When the decision was handed down it was anticlimactic and curious, both. The judge ruled that the *Atlantic*'s lawyers had erred, in that the action should have been brought in equity, not in law. But, His Honor added, if he had heard the case in equity he would probably have found for the plaintiff. Mr. Sedgwick had another seizure when this verdict was announced, but by the seismographs it was a relatively minor one.

Eventually the case was settled out of court, the *Post* getting itself off the hook by a payment of $20,000 to the *Atlantic*. Mr. Sedgwick had the check photostated and framed. It hung, the pretty thing, on a corridor wall just outside Mr. Sedgwick's office. If I know my Boston, I'll take any reasonable bet that, more than forty years later, it's still there.

30 · LAUNDRY EVERY THURSDAY, OR, THE HONEST WHORE

IN SEPTEMBER 1927, in its one hundred and first year of publication, *The Youth's Companion* changed from a weekly to a monthly publication. Nothing that Harford Powel had tried to do—and he had tried every editorial trick he knew—had been successful in making the *Companion* answer its helm and regain its once profitable course. He had indeed changed its contents and style to make it once again live up to its title, but he lacked the courage or the resolution or the skill or the luck or whatever was needed to do it wholeheartedly enough to rid the magazine of its awful wholesomeness; the "Divine Smell" still lingered on, from every page. The all-type cover of that September issue (copy by Powel, design by Hodgins) had some noble prose on it, issuing from Harford's typewriter, mixed with heavy clouds of pipe-tobacco smoke and some really horrible obscenities. It eventually emerged, in part, as this:

> . . . The world moves forward. All of us must move forward too. Progress is the law of life. *The Companion* now has the opportunity to print more [of everything], and in addition there is space to give you a full-length book in every issue . . . . From its foundation *The Companion* has been dedicated to happy and successful living, and to leadership of youth, illuminated by wholesome respect for religion and for the old-established ideals of the American home. To these great ideals we dedicate the still larger and finer issues of *The Youth's Companion* which are to come to you.

• • •

In a nutshell, that was the whole damn trouble.

• • •

The editorial department of the new monthly, against which a terrible outcry arose from the seventy-five-year-old subscribers, was a small but strange mixed bag. There was Harford, editor; there was me, managing editor. Very roughly the division of labor between us was that Harford was in charge of the fiction, some of which he bought, a lot of which he wrote himself with or without collaborators, and I was in charge of the nonfiction, writing some of it, commissioning the rest. I was also in charge of the various departments and also of make-up and production— two problems that could not have interested Harford less. I had enlisted my friend and classmate Malcolm Johnson as art editor, and, in effect, the two of us put out the magazine as Harford grew more and more remote from its problems of the everyday, and more and more interested in promoting his book and other aspects of his career.

• • •

Malcolm Johnson was an M.I.T. classmate whose *Weltschmerz* sufferings made mine look like a bad case of the sniffles. On graduation he promptly took off for China, the Standard Oil Company having in those years been on the hard lookout for young technical-school graduates willing to pledge themselves to five years of service in the Orient. Malcolm so pledged, and between 1922 and 1927 I would receive sporadically semi-illegible but still obviously heartbroken letters from him. China was then being riven by its contesting warlords, only one of whom was named Chiang Kai-shek. It was certainly in a letter from Malcolm that I got my first political assessment of the future Generalissimo—"that horse-thief . . ."

Well, anyway, Malcolm served out his five years and came home quite unchanged, except that he needed a job. Malcolm was tall, personable and multigifted, and his return, Shanghai to Boston, coincided with the minor upheaval at 8 Arlington Street that had made me managing editor of the *Companion*, one of whose innumerable pressing needs was a new art editor. I mentioned Malcolm to Harford Powel. "Well, hire him, hire him!" said Harford, whose mind, as usual, was on other things. So I did. And everything worked out very well for a long time.

253

• • •

But as time passed, I became the Man of Sorrows. Susan and I had parted at last, and my sufferings were very real. I would never find another girl, of this I was irreversibly convinced. Very well, I would bury myself in My Work. This was quite sensible as well as ultraheartbroken, for it was more than high time that I started work on an aviation book for which Ted Weeks had so flatteringly offered me a contract. In lonely splendor I started pounding the typewriter in the Cambridge apartment in which I now lived.

Now to make everything 10 per cent worse, Malcolm had found a splendid furnished room on Marlborough Street, hard by 8 Arlington Street, and the occupant of the adjoining room was a very pretty and quite informal young girl whose name was Helen. Helen and Malcolm not so slowly came to be seen in each other's presence much more often than contributed to my peace of mind. The scenes I envisioned taking place on the secluded top floor of whatever-it-was Marlborough Street between Malcolm and his beautiful Helen did nothing to make me feel less bereft. But there seemed nothing to do save devote myself to my typewriter.

• • •

One evening, while I was doing just that, there came a furious knocking and kicking at my front door. I opened it to behold Malcolm and Helen. Malcolm was stinky. (I deliberately use a word of the period; in more modern usage he was *stoned*.) As for Helen, she was feeling quite, quite happy, but was under complete control. I had to make a quick mental switch from broken but indomitable author to convivial host, but aided by Mr. Cohen's alcohol this proved so surprisingly easy that my next ambition was to get as drunk as Malcolm. In this I failed— Malcolm's head start had been too long—but not by much.

After a while the three of us found ourselves curled up on the floor with a deck of cards, playing a game John Scarne (*The Odds Against Me*) would never have recognized as poker. Things were getting a little contentious, but not dangerously so, when suddenly an emergency arose: we had run out of ginger ale! Mr. Cohen's alcohol was still ample in its gallon can, but so firm was the Prohibition ethos of gin-and-ginger-ale that one without the other was unthinkable.

"I shall go out and find some ginger ale," said Malcolm, passing from the contentious to the heroic with the greatest of ease. He was taking on quite an assignment for by now it was very late at night; Malcolm would probably find no store open this side of Harvard Square. But undaunted he strode out into the night.

• • •

Left alone, Helen and I, still on the floor, fumbled with the pack of cards. We must have found *some* topic of conversation while Malcolm was on his dogged trudge, but I remember nothing until I was brought up as by a pistol shot. Helen had just said, "If he only wouldn't come back we could have some fun."

So she wasn't his girl at all! She was open stock! Moreover she couldn't be much attracted to Malcolm, for he and she had unlimited opportunities for sin, yet here she was handing me the boldest-eyed and most explicit Proposition . . . .

And I could not credit the evidence of my senses. I need only have said something like "Well, since he *is* coming back, how about a quick practice round, and what are you doing tomorrow night?" Or I needn't have said anything at all, just manhandled her to produce at least the beginnings of the fun she had in mind. I did neither. I merely smiled, as if I had heard a conventional social remark that needed no reply, and Helen—the one repulsed—merely made a smooth transition to some other subject. And when Malcolm *did* come back, with one quart bottle of ginger ale (he had started back with two, but one had somehow hit a fire hydrant in passage), everything went on as before, ending in mild alcoholic chaos.

• • •

I saw Helen only once again, six months to a year later, and not under circumstances when any fun could be had. We were in separate automobiles that had been stopped, side by side, as a Boston & Albany freight train rumbled by the crossing. Helen chanced to see me first and cheerily called my name. Then the caboose went crashing by the crossing, the traffic was unblocked, our cars sped off—and I never saw Helen again. Yet to this day she is responsible for the poignancy with which I remember the last two lines in a poem, "Grandmother's Song," by Margaret Widdemer:

The only things I'm sorry for
Are those I didn't do.

For were I destined to sleep with 1,000 girls (which I wasn't) I would still always be one down.

• • •

More than half a century later I was having a ceremonial breakfast with an old male friend, Nicholas Samstag. It was only a short time after I had been quite ill.

"Well," said Nick, "how the hell are you, anyway?"

"Pretty well, considering," I answered, "except that ever since I've got back from Phoenix my eyes have been watering so that I can scarcely read."

"And how are the spirits?"

"All right, except that I'm full of this insane senile wish to lay every attractive woman in the country before I die."

Nick adjusted his necktie. "Well," he said thoughtfully, "now I guess we know why you're crying."

But back to the past, quick!

• • •

Harford, Malcolm Johnson (later to be executive vice-president of Doubleday) and I were the *Companion*'s "new" and almost total editorial staff. Of the throngs that used to populate its former impressive offices, only two oldsters remained: Harry Chapman, the editorial writer, and Mr. Wood, the incredibly ancient proofreader. Harry Chapman had been writing the *Companion*'s short and numerous weekly editorials and various pieces of filler for years, and he was a master of compact, concise, clear and pointed prose. They weren't *about* anything, of course; under the old management it was almost as if they were forbidden to be. Chapman could and did turn out reams of this stuff, textbook models of how to say nothing gracefully. Harry Chapman was a master of his craft and so long as the *Companion* was a weekly he was a busy master. But now, all of a sudden, his work load had been quartered. But Harry seemed no less busy inside his little private coop of an office than he had been before. We wondered what he was doing—and we soon found out. One day when I turned the corner into his coop he gave a guilty start and tried with arms and hands to cover what was on his desk. Politeness dictated that I should seem oblivious, but I couldn't help seeing what I had seen: this master writer of homilies to the young of the purity of mind, body and soul had a girlie magazine in front of him and had been diligently and inexpertly copying, with the same pencil used for his editorials, one of its more toothsome and curvaceous photographs. So *that* was how Harry Chapman spent his now idle time. I giggled to myself but I wouldn't have told on him for the world. Poor Harry! He was so fed to the teeth with bogus piety that he had to find some sort of what Dr. Kinsey was years later to call "outlet." That he was able to resist rape in the Public Gardens I took as a sign of stout fiber indeed.

But one such catch-in-the-act did not stop Harry, nor did many, although they never abated his consciousness of guilt. Harford caught him at it a few weeks after I had, and Harford's reaction was quite different from mine. It was high indignation—not moral indignation, obviously, but indignation at "that damned old hypocrite." He went on about it at great length. "I wonder what Mr. Kelsey *does*," Harford ruminated, speaking of the deposed president of the Perry Mason Company, to whom Mr. Sedgwick had felt himself forced to offer office space for purposes unknown. Harford's speculations on what the elderly, dignified Mr. Kelsey "did" soared freely into realms familiar enough now, but using words and describing acts publicly impermissible even in the 1920's. Meanwhile, for all the rest of the *Companion*'s days, Harry Chapman did his official work with all his accustomed skill, and continued his interim activities with guilt unabated.

• • •

Mr. Wood, the proofreader, was quite a different case. He was so old he doddered, and his comprehension of the world about him was dim to the last degree. *Anything* could confuse him. His eyes were rheumy and he worked with the stub of an unsharpened pencil never more than two inches long, with which he made wavering and uncertain marginal marks. Yet, despite all this, Mr. Wood was not only a good proofreader but an absolutely top-notch one. He had been reading *Companion* proof for more than forty years, after all, and all his powers were failing one by one except the power to catch any sort of error, in sense as well as type, in what lay before him. What is the reverse of "intention tremor"? Mr. Wood had it; his hands trembled violently *except* when he was applying his stub pencil to a galley strip.

A remarkable thing about these two elderly men was that they never manifested any resentment toward any of the young upstarts (Harford, the senior of us, was forty) who were now their bosses. *They* had once been seniors in the most solidly established and dignified magazine publishing house in America and now their world was upside down, diminished, shriveled and reversed right-for-left. A certain remoteness, indeed a certain frank disdain would have been more than understandable. For all their peculiarities they were men enough to accept what an inscrutable God—He was certainly inscrutable—had sent.

• • •

Meanwhile I was writing a book. Edward Weeks, later to be Mr. Sedgwick's successor as the *Atlantic*'s editor, but then a pale young curate who was Mr. Sedgwick's assistant, was also in charge of the Atlantic Monthly Press, whose titles were in effect chosen by Sedgwick-Weeks, but were published and distributed by Little, Brown & Company. (A long and tangled tale lies behind the beginnings of *that* arrangement, still existing today.) Ted Weeks had come to me with the idea that I could write a popular history of aviation. The year being 1927, this was a splendid idea, for Lindbergh had flown the Atlantic, solo, just a few months before and the United States was in a ferment of excitement about aviation. Looking backward to 1927 it is a bit difficult to see why the Lindbergh flight aroused the hysteria it did, for the Atlantic had been flown before, one way or another. But Lindbergh's flight had been the first solo flight that had not crashed on landing, had landed precisely where it was supposed to, and had been accomplished by a modest young man of twenty-five. That was enough.

I had no qualifications for writing an aviation history, however "popular," but few things are as stimulating as someone

258

else's placid assumption that of course you can do something or other that had just never before entered your head to try. That assumption was what Ted Weeks supplied me.

Yet it was quite a few months after his proposal before I did a lick of work on this flattering suggestion, and when I began it, it was because Susan had brought our five-year romance to an end. We had gone out as usual one evening in my 1926 Essex and headed for "the reservoir," that placid body of water whose quiet roads were nightly jammed with cars in which the young unmarried couples of the twenties necked and necked and necked. But this was to be my last trip to the reservoir, ever. "Jim wants to marry me, and you don't," said Susan, using that forthrightness with which women put the chips on the table at last. I had known for a long while that this time was bound to come, for once, long, long before, she had said, "*What* do you want that you haven't got in me?" and I had been unable to answer the question. I deeply wanted and deeply needed Susan's love, but the words "Will you marry me?" I could not force across my lips. I had wanted to have my cake and eat it, too; thanks to Susan's patience and forbearance I had succeeded, but now, without reproach, without bitterness, but also with an inflexibility that could not be mistaken, she was bringing a long young-love chapter to a close.

I drove her home in wordless misery; thereafter I was to see her a few times more, but this I did not know at the time. My life seemed blasted and empty without her, and it was to distract myself that I finally began on the book Ted Weeks had so long ago suggested to me.

•   •   •

I *did* have one asset for the job, after all; that was access to the Treasure Room of M.I.T.'s Vail Library, which had in it all sorts of things I needed and hadn't known I needed until I came on them. It was here that I gained my first rough knowledge of how one went about putting a book together.

"Mr. Weeks seems to have a great deal of enthewsiasm, no doubt delewded, about your manuscript," Mr. Sedgwick said to me on one of those days he deigned to speak. And it was Mr. Sedgwick who gave the book its title, *Sky High*, which I thought awful at the time. But when the book came out, in 1929, and was a success, I am glad to say Mr. Sedgwick and I had parted forever.

• • •

Later in 1928 Harford summoned me to his office. "You will find Miss Manning a very good secretary," he said. "My advice is to keep the Jonathan Brooks stories running, and remember, you have to keep after Sol Metzger hard to get his copy in on time."

"Harford," I demanded, "what is up?"

"I am annunciating you my successor," he said. And that's just what he was doing. But not for a few days did Mr. Sedgwick send for me. "And now, Mr. Hodgins, I think your chance has come," he said.

One of the many things that puzzle me as I set down these words is that my memory of myself is of someone who was perpetually meek, and this doesn't go with the cheeky things I have more than once done. Mr. Sedgwick was proposing to make me an editor in chief, but he was not saying anything about a raise. So I did. Mr. Sedgwick impatiently, as if the matter was in very poor taste, said, "From five thousand dollars to fifty-five hundred dollars."

Now for some reason I have maddeningly forgotten, *The New Yorker*, itself then only four years old, and I had been having a correspondence, and Katharine Angell, only later to become Katharine White, had written me (I can't account for this for I had never then even sought to be a contributor; I think I must have paid a call on her about Tubby Rogers), saying that the magazine needed "a sort of managing editor" and would I be interested? I had always thought, then, that Katharine Angell *was* the managing editor, and only when I was much older and wiser did I realize I was being offered the job that later went by the office name of "the Jesus." I would have lasted at that job about two weeks—the apparent average—but since I didn't know that then, I had no hesitation in telling Mr. Sedgwick about it: at least it was bona fide and in writing. Mr. Sedgwick's impatience rose, but so did the money—by another $500, so that at age thirty I had my own magazine, was writing a book for which I *think* I got an advance, and was making $6,000 a year. Harford, on leaving his office for the last time (in high glee; he was obvi-

ously delighted to give up editing—again—and go back to advertising—again), presented me with a copy of *In His Steps*, duly
inscribed "To Eric F. Hodgins, on his assumption of the Moral
Guidance of American Youth."

• • •

American Youth didn't know the half of it. I think Harford
must have been the first editor of *The Youth's Companion* ever
to take a drink. And I am sure I was the first one to take a number
of drinks and get drunk. By the standards of those Prohibition
times I drank moderately—that is to say, too much. Boston was
an extremely curious Prohibition city, for I was never aware of
so much as *one* speakeasy. Such drinking as Boston did, which
was a lot, seemed confined to its clubs and its homes. Such, at
any rate, were my two loci.

Some time after my parting from Susan the odd thought must
have occurred to me that what I needed to improve my physical
and emotional tone was *exercise*. At any rate, I began playing
badminton—furiously—at a Boston club and succeeded, after a
long while, in rising from the bottom of Class C (there was no
Class D) to Class C's upper third. Never mind; it was splendid
fun. Pretty well matched with me was a genial Irishman named
Harold Kennedy, who lived at the club, and who was New England advertising manager for *McCall's* magazine. He had quite
a job on his hands for those were *the* days of the primacy of
the women's magazines. *Ladies' Home Journal* led the pack, with
Woman's Home Companion hard behind. *McCall's* was in third
place, with *The Delineator* (of which Theodore Dreiser had been
editor at one time!) and *Pictorial Review* bringing up the rear.
(*Good Housekeeping*, known in the trade those days as the Book
of Common Prayer, was excluded from the rank list because of
its different trim size, which would have inconveniently made
it Number 1 in number of advertising pages carried.)

Since Hal Kennedy and I were players of about equal inepti-
tude, we liked to be opponents, whether in singles or doubles.
And after our exhausting games and sessions in steam and shower
rooms a group of us would inevitably find ourselves in Ken's
room, where an upended steamer trunk was forever yielding up
pints of bootleg bourbon. When ice and Boston tap water were
added to a two- or three-ounce slug of this liquor, the full glass

261

would develop a creamy head, not quite as deep as on today's beer commercials, but deep enough and thick enough to be—momentarily—disconcerting. But three or four of these would produce a feeling of euphoria such as a subsequent heavy dinner would not put down. And night after night after night, I would drive home from the club to my Cambridge apartment (garage in immediate rear) without knowing how I got there. God was with me, all right, because on not one of those many occasions did I as much as scratch a fender. In other words, I was experiencing blackouts and not knowing their considerable significance.

I was, however, vividly aware of the gorgeous Boston newspaper headlines that would result if the editor of *The Youth's Companion*, which remained a heavily revered Boston institution until the day of its death, should be picked up for driving under the influence of liquor. I deliberately avoid the blunter term "drunken driving" because I was able to steer an arrow-straight course, obey all signs and otherwise conduct myself as if I were sober when I was not. My lapse of memory would worry me extremely when in the morning, for example, I would find my car precision-parked in its garage stall and would strive vainly for the recollection of my drive home. I took a curious but effective means of avoiding such confrontations between my two selves: when I got home at night I would write a half-sheet account of what I had done between badminton and bedtime. When I woke up the next morning, there it would be, the handwriting neat, the sentences telegraphic, as I had intended, and no hint anywhere of bootleg liquor excessively consumed, except by my own careful notation. But what was more remarkable, the reading of the account of the night before *instantly* recalled everything I had done. And I had done nothing out of the ordinary except, of course, take so much hooch aboard that my memory failed. The pattern of my drinking, I am trying to say, was abnormal but in an abnormal way.

• • •

It might also have been thought a little odd by the *Companion*'s subscribers, by Mr. Sedgwick, and perhaps even by the eccentric, cynical, Boston-hating Harford Powel that the *Companion*'s new editor lived in a one-room Murphy-bed ground-floor apartment, rent fifty-five dollars a month, between Central and

Harvard squares, right next to a whore. What's more, I saw her regularly once a week. But here I admit that I am playing for effect, for what just went through your mind wasn't so. In fact, I hate to call such a nice, wholesome-looking and impeccably sanitary girl a whore, except that that was her avowed, self-designated trade. I was a curious mixture of innocence and debauched guile in those days and I was a next-door neighbor to Miss X for a long time before I tumbled to her profession. Our meetings were always on Thursdays. Since I was out all day and she was in all day, our joint laundryman would leave my laundry in her care; when she heard me come home, she would open her door and with the friendliest of greetings hand me my blue box. For a long time I took her for a district nurse, or equivalent, for she was always dressed in a white uniform, white stockings and white shoes, and our Thursday meetings never varied from this blameless and antiseptic ritual.

But above me, in Modern Manor, built forty years ago and still standing, a U-shaped building enclosing a pleasant court, lived a young graduate student, whom I'll call Patrick R. Patrick was sexually adventurous, so it was not long before he patronized Miss X. In fact, I think it was through his patronage that I first tumbled to Miss X's true vocation. She must have been extremely adept, this pleasant wholesome girl I had first taken for a little sister of the poor, for Patrick, during the next four or five days after his session with her, went about looking listless, pale and wan. I was not in Patrick's deep confidence, but somebody was and he reported to me that, in effect, Patrick had had momentary doubts he would ever emerge alive. He had further reported Miss X as saying, "If I ever find a man who can really satisfy me, I'll get out of this business like *that*"—with a snap of the fingers.

Patrick, for all the prowess he liked to boast beforehand, was obviously not that man. Some months thereafter I was waked in the middle of the night by a commotion next door, whose nature was unmistakable. Bedsprings were jangling. (They had never jangled before; in fact the quietude from next door had been one of the reasons why I had always found it so difficult to equate Miss X with whoredom.) Not only were the bedsprings jangling; the very floor was creaking—and more than that, there drifted (*drifted?*) through the party wall the unmistakable cries of a woman in the highest throes of sexual ecstasy.

All this, I need hardly add, was extremely difficult for a young man, solitary and unshriven on a Murphy bed next door in the middle of the night, to bear without the arousal of the highest degree of lust and envy. But along with my carnal thoughts there ran a parallel stream: "Miss X has met her match at last!"

And so, I think, she must. Next Thursday evening the same smiling wholesome girl in white handed me my laundry as always before, but at two the next morning another Homeric sexual bout took place. (The male must indeed have been the strong, silent type; I never heard a sound I could attribute—directly—to him.) And then at last there came a Thursday when I merely found my laundry in front of my locked door. Miss X had apparently not only met her match but kept her word. I never saw her again. Patrick seemed to take the news ruefully but yet with a measure of relief. I think his masculine pride had been egging him on to ask for a return match at the same time his body was expressing grave doubts that he could come through it.

31 · FAREWELL TO BOSTON, OR, A NEW LIFE

ONE THING THAT Harford Powel had to contend with, before I succeeded him in 1929, was editorial suggestions from Mr. Sedgwick. I did not. I was granted this immunity not because Mr. Sedgwick reposed any special confidence in me, but because by now he was thoroughly sick of the *Companion* and its problems. But by Harford's testimony I was spared a vast deal. When the great editor of the *Atlantic* tried to project himself into the inspired salvager of *The Youth's Companion*, the results were simply awful: suggestions for a "Tommy Tinker Page" and the like. When economics forced the *Companion* into once-a-month frequency, Mr. Sedgwick's basic reason for having taken it over in the first place disappeared: the Rumford Press was no longer equipped to handle the job. Anyone connected with publishing knows, although no one knows *why*, a publisher with a printing plant (an almost vanished breed, now) insists that even if hell freezes over and the product of the presses goes for a loss, the *plant* must show a profit. Samuel Butler's dictum "It is cheaper to buy milk than to keep a cow" was never truer than here. Not only was Rumford now ill-equipped for the *Companion* as a "job," publishing *ethos* firmly and incomprehensibly dictated that the Rumford books must show a profit on the *Companion* as a job; hence it was in no state to meet price competition from an outside printer. Mr. Sedgwick, who must have been torn twenty ways by the need for making the decision, just plain took the *Companion* away from Rumford and signed a two-year contract, later to be dishonored, with the Charles Schweinler Press in New York. The result was a considerable improvement in typography and design, the use of color in illustrations for the first time, and a radical overhaul in four-color cover

265

design. This last, Fate decreed, was to lead me to my eventual future.

I think I was able to make some improvement in the quality of the magazine's text, but dwelling on this would be pointless now: I can think of few authors, still living or recognized, whose names would be familiar in the 1970's. Like every editor I had my staff problems, and one of them nearly landed me in a bad mess. To my delight one day, there arrived addressed to me a story by an unknown author that was eminently printable. I bought it, scheduled it, scanned it in galley proof and was about to put it into the next issue's layout when by the sheerest good luck I picked up and thumbed through a copy of *The American Boy* out two months previously. There was the same story. I had bought a line-by-line plagiarism and only by the greatest luck had I not printed it. The author was well known in juvenile fiction circles, so I promptly wrote him of what had happened, and *almost* happened. The letter he sent me made me tear my hair. It couldn't have been nicer. But after thanking me for writing him and congratulating me on my narrow escape from embarrassment or worse, he went on: "What beats me is how a plagiarist of one of my stories can come so much closer to getting one published in your magazine than I can. After receiving routine rejection slips from the *Companion* for over a year I not unnaturally gave up."

I investigated and it was all too true. All magazines receive daily mountains of trash; to cope with it all they have to maintain a Reading Department that is supposed not only to dispose of the trash but keep an eye out for a possible emerald among the peanut shells. For some reason the author, who should have known better, had merely addressed his manuscripts to "Editor," which caused the mail room to siphon them off to the Reading Department, which reflexively returned them. It is always disconcerting to reflect how many times this sort of thing may happen without anyone knowing anything about it.

• • •

Things had been all too different with the *Companion* of the nineteenth century, as first Harford and later I were to discover. Among the assets of the Perry Mason Company when Mr. Sedgwick took over was a massive manuscript inventory carried at

a value of $1 million. It was impossible, even in 1929, to recon-
struct what was going through successive editorial minds as this
mass of wordage slowly accumulated. Each manuscript was
folded into a square manila envelope. Each had been read successively by three editors, who recorded their opinions, in handsome
penmanship, on half sheets of different-colored paper. It was the
duty of one editor to write a fifty-word summary of story plot
and of the two others (the summary job was rotated, of course)
to criticize, analyze, weigh pros and cons, and, eventually, vote.
Each editorial criticism had to end with one of two words, set
apart on the final line: "Yes" or "No." It was permissible to
modify "Yes" with "Possibly"—*provided it did not occur on the
final line;* under the same ground rules "Probably" could hedge
a "No." True mystification for the 1920's examiners like Harford
or me entered when two out of three, or perhaps three out of
three, editorial opinions ended with "No" but a cashier's stamp
would say "PURCHASED" at such and such a date and figure. It
must have been that the tricolored half sheets expressed the opinions of undereditors and that someone in the Sanctum Sanctorum
(this ancient phrase must have had a true applicability) had
reversed the lower decisions. How many thousands upon thousands of unused manuscripts were in the vaults only God knows,
and Mr. Sedgwick may have kept the consoling thought in the
back of his mind when the assets and liabilities of the Perry
Mason Company were rammed down his gullet that perhaps gold
would be discovered in these mountains of words, if not publish-
able gold then perhaps antiquarian gold—for the purchase dates
of some manuscripts ran back not just to the 1890's, but the 1880's
and some perhaps to the 1870's. But Harford had done a thorough
mining job and no Mother Lode was ever discovered. The largest
nugget he turned up was a Jack London story, not of top quality.
Harford published it with all the whoopla at his command, but
its audience was unresponsive. Harford also uncovered an early
indiscretion of Mary Roberts Rinehart's and a piece of genuine
juvenilia from Henry L. Mencken. Harford used to tell entertain-
ing stories about his threats of blackmail against the Sage of Balti-
more and the sum he would exact for *not* publishing the story,
but the Sage, shrewdly guessing that the *Companion* readership
would know much less about him than about Jack London, could
not be induced to go above one dollar for hush money.

• • •

It's now about a century since the earliest unpublished *Companion* manuscript was purchased. For the next fifty years the inventory grew and grew as the ratio of manuscripts published to manuscripts purchased declined. In the age when Baudelaire and Rimbaud seem dated, try to imagine what a manuscript written for *The Youth's Companion* in the 1880's was like, and you will fail. They were no less unpublishable in the 1920's. I can only account for the vastness of this literary junk pile if I try hard to imagine how proud and prosperous the *Companion* was in the decades before I was born, and how it must have looked down, from its Boston eminence, on such Johnny-come-latelies as Cyrus Hermann Kotzschmar Curtis, who didn't establish the *Ladies' Home Journal* until 1883 or buy *The Saturday Evening Post* until 1897. Before the twentieth century began, the Perry Mason Company was invincible—that must have been it. The element of *timeliness* in magazine publishing was yet to establish itself; therefore nothing would grow stale, and the value of the steadily growing manuscript inventory would probably *increase*.

• • •

Well, in the late 1920's the properly concerned auditors of the Atlantic Monthly Company would periodically visit first Harford and later me on the subject of that inventory. Nobody had the financial guts to write it down. I don't know what Harford told the auditors about the inventory but I suspect, without malice, that he double-talked them into thinking it must be worth something. Harford was innocently good at double-talk, and in any event it was not hard to double-talk auditors in those days.

But I was no good at double-talk, though I have always wished I were, and when the auditors visited me I felt compelled to take a flatter line: the inventory was not worth one red cent. "But surely there is *something* of publishing value in this great accumulation?" No, by the publishing standards of the day there was not one line.

• • •

It may be that I cut my young editorial throat by this evaluation of what had so largely taken place before I was born. I don't know when Mr. Sedgwick decided in his own mind to cut and run so far as the *Companion* was concerned; possibly he didn't either. He did let me make all my fall and winter editorial commitments for 1929–30 before there began to be the slightest whisper that he was thinking of getting out from under—which was far from cricket. But Ernst & Ernst, or someone of equal financial foresightedness, had told him in June or July of 1929 that whether he understood a Consolidated Balance Sheet or not, he had better get rid of *The Youth's Companion*. In view of what was going to happen three or four months later in the stock market this turned out to be one of the soundest pieces of advice a firm of accountants ever gave a client, but it was bitter medicine for everyone at the time. Ironically, the *Companion* met its end with more advertising pages on its books and with a sounder, solider circulation than it had had within a decade, so in that sense the magazine went down with its flag flying. It went down nevertheless, for Mr. Sedgwick had sold it to its principal competitor, *The American Boy*, published in Detroit, and its issue of September 1929 marked the end of its century-odd history. My memory tells me, perhaps erroneously, that Mr. Sedgwick got $80,000 to $85,000 for the Perry Mason Company and all its worldly goods—which did *not* include me or Malcolm Johnson or the Messrs. Kelsey, Chapman or Wood. It is tough to lose your first command, but the erratic and unpredictable publishing business is full of stories more poignant than the *Companion*'s demise, even if I did not think so at the time. I had as much as accused Mr. Sedgwick of bad faith in his behind-my-back dealings, and he had given me the indignant back of his patrician hand, so whatever was going to become of me, it seemed most likely that Boston held no further publishing opportunities and that the decade that had begun for me there in 1919 was coming to an end, almost to the month and day.

• • •

Two jobs got offered to me when it became known that I was out of one. First, Daniel Longwell, then of Doubleday, Doran, had been alert enough to notice a change in the *Companion*'s covers and contents as viewed on New York newsstands and he offered jobs to both Malcolm Johnson and me. I remember a long session at the Garden City Hotel with Dan and a silent,

269

shy young man whom Dan called "Oggie," without having bothered to give me his last name, in which Dan tentatively offered me $10,000 for certain not clearly specified duties in the world of book publishing. Oggie later turned out to be Ogden Nash, who had yet to publish his first unique contribution to poetry:

I sit in my office at 244 Madison Avenue
And say to myself "You have a responsible job, haven't you?"

My other job offer was less of a surprise but more fantastic. The McCall Publishing Company had just purchased, for $3 million, the Consolidated Magazine Company of Chicago, whose properties were *Red Book* and *Blue Book*. My Irish badminton and drinking friend, Harold Kennedy, was being recalled from Boston to be *Red Book*'s New York advertising manager. He had the notion that I would make a good advertising salesman and he was then and there offering me a job at that, and thought he could guarantee a salary of $8,000 a year. I was flabbergasted at the idea.

Fortunately, I had some time in which to make up my mind. Dan Longwell was willing to wait for an answer, particularly since it was August and he was leaving for vacation. As for Ken and *McCall's-Red Book*, the transfer of power was not due for a month at least.

• • •

Whichever way I decided, it was in the cards that I was to leave Boston. Correspondingly, another question became suddenly quite urgent. The quiet (although not sedate) courtship that had been going on between Catherine Carlson and me had not been diminishing. Contemplating a new and unknown future, with job offers but no job, I came face to face with the problem: Can I bear to part from this girl or can I not? If I cannot, how does she feel about me?

On this latter question, I was not without some guidelines. Catherine and I had been carrying on exactly as all young people in the twenties were accurately reputed to do: that is, we took the fullest of the advantages afforded by Model A Ford runabouts, remote parking places and sexual drives released by a hip flask full of warm bathtub gin. In short, we were well and happily accustomed to intense love-making, nor did the next day bring rebound emotions; instead, it made us look forward all the more intensely to still another evening with more of the same. Catherine was just technically "proper" enough to do nothing overt to incite me, but if submissiveness can be called wholehearted, that's what Catherine's was. In short, her mother would have been horrified. (The young of the 1920's did not rebel at the "hypocrisies" of their elders; they merely emulated them.)

So there was no doubt that Catherine was "my" girl. But neither of us had ever used the word "marriage"; there was no implication of obligation on either side. Most young men in the twenties didn't particularly want to get married and the then current view was perfectly summed up by one of my rogue classmates: "I'd be scared to death to ask a girl to marry me for fear I'd meet someone I liked better tomorrow."

Any fear like that was rapidly fading from my mind. But neither Catherine nor I were mentioning that within a week to six weeks I would be saying goodbye to Boston.

To a second-rate English poet and playwright I owe the instantaneous end to any doubt about my future with Catherine. As we were driving along a twisting Cape Ann road one day in bright sunshine, I had some strange necessity to speak of the author of *Hassan*. And I miscalled his name: "James McElroy Flecker." And Catherine, beside me, said in her quiet voice, "Elroy, darling, not *Mc*Elroy." And then and there, suddenly, and on an occasion I shall never forget, the feeling surged through me, "I love this girl; I love her with all my heart."

That night, lying side by side on a Gloucester beach, I summoned up all the resolution that was in me: "Would you marry me if I asked you?"

"Ask me and see."

• • •

• • •

Of the two jobs that had been offered me, the one I thought most likely to be congenial was also the one that carried the higher salary. So I chose the other. In later years, I rationalized this seeming perversity by saying to myself that my choice lay between continuing to be an editor but leaving magazine journalism or staying with magazines but ceasing to be an editor. That *was* the choice, all right, but I doubt if it had presented itself

271

that clearly in my mind at the time I made it. I think I was more influenced by the fact that in going with *McCall's-Red Book* I would have an enthusiastic and understanding friend as a boss and by Harford Powel's awesome view of the other offer. "Be warned," he intoned, "the Doubledays are *excremental matter*." I don't know what the Doubledays of that era had ever done to Harford to deserve this unqualified judgment, but there was no question of the passion with which he made it. And so I cast my die with Harold Kennedy and *McCall's*. But as it was to turn out, all roads lead to Rome.

• • •

Meanwhile, I was calm and happy, happy even in nursing the grudge I held against Mr. Sedgwick, with whom I had a final acrid exchange of correspondence. His last letter to me enclosed a check and the phrase "this would seem to satisfy your contention," although I now forget what, or which among many, my contention was.

Catherine and I were spending our weekends together on Cape Ann—she with her father, mother and younger brother near Gloucester; I with Tubby Rogers, his wife and daughter at Rockport. Over the years we had both become widely acquainted with that granite promontory, Cape Ann. (In its metropolis of Gloucester, Clarence Birdseye was making his final, successful experiments with quick-frozen foods.) Sitting together one morning on a jagged ledge of rock, with the sea roaring in our ears and the gulls wheeling overhead, I proposed to Catherine that we should ratify our engagement by going to bed together. (After all, we had already done everything else but.) And she agreed. Not until well after our marriage did she confess she had been shocked. (Despite her four years at Smith, she had been, after all, born and brought up in Newton Centre, and the firm name of her architect father was not Coolidge & Carlson for nothing.) But she agreed, and I picked up no faintest hint of reservation in the manner of her agreeing.

• • •

So to bed together we went before that week was out. We *probably* fortified ourselves with some alcohol, but certainly not very much. It was a thoroughgoing sexual success. "Be gentle with me; it hurts, but don't stop." This was my first intimation that Catherine *was* a virgin. Looking back on youth now, I think there is a good deal to be said—on strictly psychophysiological grounds, not moralistic ones—for a girl's not giving up her virginity until she is *quite* sure that she wants her partner for more than passing physical reasons, and is as sure as she can reasonably be that he is acting in what was once quaintly known as good faith. Certainly this act of defloration forged a bond between Catherine and me the like of which I was never to experience again. In the later years of my life, virgins were to be in very short supply. In fact, I never met another.

• • •

In Rockport there is a straight and narrow spit of land, piercing the water of the harbor, scarcely fifty feet wide and perhaps an eighth of a mile long—Bear Skin Neck. Today it is a hideous tourist trap and pedestrian traffic jam, full of tiny souvenir shops, tiny other items of the fake-picturesque. But when Catherine and I were young it was not picturesque, fake or genuine. It was merely tumble-down. It had perhaps two dozen shacklike, tiny two-story houses—refuges for honestly starving painters or writers, with or without talent. A house of two stories, and about twelve feet wide, with the merest trace of any modern convenience, could then be had for five dollars a week or twenty dollars a month, and demand was sluggish. I rented one of these for the month of August 1929. Downstairs was the living room and kitchen; upstairs was the bedroom. That was all. In the August weather it was suffocating and smelled of hot dusty matting and crumbling roller blinds.

I had rented that house to have someplace to read page proofs of *Sky High*, now scheduled for fall publication, and it became a haven for Catherine and me. When I suggested that the house would be equally convenient for proofreading and love-making, Catherine said, "Could we? Oh, *could* we?" and now it was suddenly my turn to be the conservative and conventional one. I had resolved that this girl and I would not have sexual intercourse again until we had exchanged vows—in the sight of God, if no other company. In the hot, close little bedroom we became, by mutual declaration, and in our own eyes, man and wife. Then, and only then, did we reconsummate our marriage. (The formali-

273

ties of the Church were not to enter our arrangement for living until July of the following year.) Meanwhile, there were many things for Catherine and me to do—including proofreading!— before I was to take off for my part of our future in New York. The prosperity of America was on the verge of being shattered, and the future for Catherine was to be short indeed, but mercifully we had no slightest intimation of these things as I ended the decade of my Boston years on the conventional day after Labor Day, A.D. 1929.

32 · EDITOR INTO SALESMAN, OR, THE SMILE AND THE SHOESHINE

WHEN I SHOWED UP for my first day's work at 230 Park Avenue, the then new New York Central Building into which the McCall Company had just moved, my friend and now boss Harold Clark Kennedy greeted me with enthusiasm but also with embarrassment. He had only just arrived himself, the offices were chaos, and he had not only nothing for me to do, he had no place for me to sit. I spent the rest of the day, the week and indeed the year wishing for my past life. I felt I knew something about the editorial side of the business from which I was now excluded, but I knew nothing about how to be an advertising space salesman, and what was more, I now passionately did not want to learn. But it was too late for those thoughts now. When I had been the *Companion*'s editor I had gone on periodic junkets to advertising agencies in New York, Philadelphia, Chicago, St. Louis, *et al.*, but these had been carefully prearranged by the advertising department, and agency men, in general, gave courteous attention to editors talking about the high plans and unique virtues of their magazines. So I was not wholly unused to talking to "Plans Boards" and their like in the agency world; but after all, at such meetings I had been pre-set-up as a personage, and the fact that I was youthful was an asset, not a liability, for someone editing *The Youth's Companion*. In Boston I had taken to wearing spats to emphasize that I was Somebody, but now I was spatless, stripped of dignity, and inwardly quailing at the prospect of visiting the advertising manager of the Ace Comb Company and pleading with him—or whatever you did!—for a column of space.

Meanwhile, since after a week I still had no place to sit in the office, and nothing to do, Harold Kennedy began inventing activities that would not only get me out of the office but out of New York. It was some time before I tumbled to the shrewdness of what he was devising, and some longer time before I appreciated it, but when at last I came to, the appreciation was very great. Against my will I was learning a few things about magazine publishing from a view not ordinarily accorded mere editors.

The first trip Ken sent me on happened to be the kind that I liked: it was to the McCall printing plant in Dayton, Ohio. Since I had begun collecting printing plants, as some people collect stamps, at the age of twelve, when I first watched the speeding presses of the Philadelphia *Times* on Chestnut Street, this was splendid, and I spent two days watching all phases of the McCall production operation. Nothing had changed much in printing technology between 1911 and 1929; nevertheless, watching all its crashing metal going through its variety of paces remained for me still the greatest fun in the world.

• • •

The McCall printing plant, larger than ever, is still in Dayton, Ohio. But Dayton, since 1929, has lost one other institution that it still possessed then. That was Orville Wright. He was not only still living there; he was in the telephone directory. When I called his number, the surviving father of aviation answered his own phone in a hesitant voice; with the brashness of youth I asked for an interview. Had I been older I wouldn't have dared to use a completely cold and unheralded approach to so eminent a man, but I just didn't know any better. So Orville Wright, a shy man living in a slightly shabby house whose roof leaked on the rainy day I saw him, talked to me for several hours and out of the notes I made I much later wrote a Profile for *The New Yorker*.

The Dayton citizenry seemed quite unconscious not only that a celebrity but an Immortal was living among them; they seemed to regard Orville only as the survivor of the two brothers who used to run a bicycle repair shop and had monkeyed around with flying machines. I remember a story my friend Edward Warner, first head of M.I.T.'s Department of Aeronautical Engineering.* had told me of a Dayton farmer, while actually seeing

* And, in the Coolidge Administration, first holder of the sub-Cabinet post of Assistant Secretary of the Navy for Aeronautics.

Orville in the *Wright Flyer* several hundred feet in the air above him, saying to Wilbur, "There ain't no sense fooling around with that thing, Wilbur, because it's agin nature to fly, and besides, if anybody ever does, it won't be anybody from Dayton."

• • •

The day after my interview with Orville Wright I got a telegram from Ken in New York telling me to arm myself in Dayton with the names of all individual *Redbook* subscribers (*Red Book* had just become *Redbook* under McCall management) to be found in Galion and Sandusky, Ohio, Erie, Pennsylvania, and Rochester, New York, and come back to New York via those cities, in which I was to conduct as many personal interviews with subscribers as possible and report fully on what I found. This must have been one of the earliest "readership surveys" on record and it could well have been one of the most worthless.

Galion, Ohio, was my first stop. It was a miserable little town of about 9,000, with the manufacture of road machinery and burial vaults as its chief industrial props. Maybe *Redbook* had fifty subscribers there; maybe I succeeded in seeing fifteen; if I did, that was a big percentage. There was no city map and no public transport of any kind; I simply had to get sailing instructions from a friendly druggist, who wanted to know, in an amiable way, what I was up to, and why all the street addresses I wanted were in "that" part of town. A day of footsore tramping told me a great deal I had never suspected about magazine subscription procurement methods. The wife of a brakeman on the Big Four Railroad summed it up for me: "Listen, mister, there's goddamn little reading gets done around here, let me tell you, me busy with the kids all day and when the old man comes home all he wants to do is put his socks up and not fool around with no magazine."

Why had she subscribed, I wanted to know. "A fella came 'round," she said darkly.

It was the same everywhere, in every city. The fella who had come around was almost always, essentially, the same fella; a fella from the door-to-door canvassing operation of the Crowell Publishing Company, which had methods all its own for club and other bargain cut-rate subscription offers, made by a gang of kids under the supervision of a hardened door-to-door huckster. I did come on one enthusiastic cover-to-cover subscription reader.

EDITOR INTO SALESMAN, OR,

Yes, she read all the fiction, all the articles. Looked at all the ads, too. It was handy in the waiting room, and all the girls liked it, too. Unfortunately, this gratifying response was not of much use to either advertising or editorial departments; it came from the thoroughly genial Madam of a whorehouse.

•   •   •

Back in New York, I reported to Ken, who wished the results of my microscopic survey had been different, but was not really cast down or surprised. This had been for *my* education, even if I did not yet know it. And Ken had another course planned, slightly less grueling but no less instructive. I was to spend two days in New Jersey in tow of a newsstand and retail-outlet checker for the S-M News Company, independent rival of the American News Company, which in those days distributed almost all magazines published except *McCall's* and a small handful of others.

This, too, was enlightening. "In this business, the retailer is the lowest form of animal life," said my mentor. "Just stick with me, an' you'll see what I mean."

I did. We started out in Jersey City and Hoboken (the latter then briefly enlivened by Christopher Morley, needled beer and his "Black Crook" company), then on to Paterson and Passaic. Even in 1929 these were all dreadful cities; it would be impossible to choose between them for which most deserved the designation of *anus mundi*. We hit Newark and Trenton, thence on to Atlantic City. The routine was always the same at the newsstands, the drug and candy stores, the stationery shops, and all the other kinds of dives where magazines were on display. The retailer usually could not remember what his draw was (how many magazines the company had allotted him); therefore the number he had left gave him no clue to how many he had sold. It was my mentor's business to check up on all this; rearrange, at his own pleasure, the way the magazines were displayed, putting the S-M products on the front line and dumping everything else as far out of sight as possible; warn the retailer that his draw would probably be increased next month so he'd better pull his socks up, etc. Since a rival checker from American News had already rearranged everything to *his* advantage, or would soon, the retailer felt deeply put-upon. And he was indeed a battle-

278

ground, for the objective of all magazine publishers was to de-
crease newsstand returns to as close to zero as possible. There
was, for example, a technique known as "eating" copies, my men-
or told me, whereby certain unspecified persons of low moral
character would slip something or other under the right tables
here or there that would make it more profitable for certain out-
lets to destroy copies than to pay postage to return them for credit.

Ah me, the things I had *not* learned in my Boston cloisters.
During the Depression that was yet to come, it was not unduly
out of the way for hundreds of thousands of magazines to be
printed, assembled, bound and then immediately thrown into
a convenient river. A.B.C. Net Paid circulation guarantees had
to be met, after all; the penalty was rebates to advertisers and
a colossal and long-enduring loss of face . . . . I certainly
learned quite a lot about the business I was in during those two
Jersey days.

Coming back alone on the train from Atlantic City to New
York, I solaced myself by finishing my copy of Ernest Hemingway's *A Farewell to Arms*, and felt a terrifying sense of despair
in the final pages when the girl, Catherine Barkley, dies in child-
birth and Frederic Henry goes out into the cold night alone.

• •

• •

The McCall Company, and its president, Mr. William Bishop
Warner, had bought *Red Book* and *Blue Book* at the absolute
top of the 1929 bull market, and, as it turned out, had thus acquired the privilege of losing $1 million a year for quite a few
years thereafter. *Blue Book* presented a few problems; it was the
acknowledged best of the fiction pulps in the heyday of the pulps
and carried almost no advertising except for rupture cures and
correspondence schools. *Redbook* was a different matter altogether. In advertising as in circulation it was the firmly entrenched third in a field of three. These were the so-called "general" magazines (as distinguished from "women's"); among
them, Hearst's *Cosmopolitan* (under the editorship of Ray Long)
stood in the unquestioned front rank. Long had corralled almost
every big fiction name of the twenties, including Hemingway,
Maugham and Cobb. Crowell Publishing had *The American
Magazine*, and neither the editorships of Merle Crowell nor Sum-

ner Blossom had yet done anything to lessen the head of steam given it years earlier by that extraordinary man John M. Siddall who was second rank only to George Horace Lorimer in giving prewar America what it thought it wanted. The *American* stood a strong second to *Cosmo*, as I learned I should call it in my new trade. And then there was *Redbook*.

Redbook was edited by Edwin Balmer, who had been two years in the saddle when Mr. Warner bought him and moved him to New York, and he was destined to remain in the saddle for twenty years more. So clearly he couldn't have been as mediocre as I thought him. He *did* have the misfortune to be the successor to Karl Edwin Harriman, who deserved to rank with Lorimer and Siddall among the great instinctive discerners of What the Public Wanted. Balmer was as fast and prolific a writer of third rate fiction—some of it in collaboration with a then mild young man named Philip Wylie—as I ever knew, but great editor he was not.

• • •

Harold Kennedy, my boss, was outwardly plump, genial and relaxed. Inwardly he was a tense, concerned and worrying man these inwardnesses would periodically break through into bout of depression that, in the nature of his job, he had to be at deep pains to conceal. Occasionally he would let go with his true feel ings to me, because of all his staff, I knew him best due to our Boston days together and because, also, we had become close friends. Into all this bargain he had the job of keeping *my* spirit up; the rest of the staff were all salesmen with long years of experience in how to deal with insults, indifference, frustration and disappointment. It never came easily for anyone, I slowly grew to know, but these veterans had at least learned the art of rolling with the punches. Up to now, in my professional life at least, I had never had any real punches to roll with.

Now I had plenty. I wish Arthur Miller had written *Death of a Salesman* two decades earlier; that line about "riding on a smile and a shoeshine" sums up the emotional agony of those who aren't supposed, in the eyes of the comfortably deskbound to have any emotions at all, let alone any agonies. I must have seemed an odd fish to my veteran colleagues. I was owl-eyed and cadaverous in those days, and I was busy writing two book and contributing to *The New Yorker* at the same time I was peddling space for *Redbook*. But we all had in common the knowledge that we were supposed to be the revenue producers for a magazine that was then on a heavy downgrade. So novice and veteran alike, we were united in adversity. One of the hardest-bitten but most successful of the McCall salesmen, who shared the same big bull pen, summed up a lifetime of space selling: "I never got an Order in my life; all I've ever got was the Cancellations." It wasn't said with any particular bitterness, but it was a great capsule truth just the same; when you came in with a fat order it was because your Vice-President-in-Charge-of had paved the way; when the same advertiser canceled his whole schedule, the Front Office wanted to know what *you* had done to lose the account.

Ken was a sentimental Irishman. He knew of my engagement to Catherine, so when he was assigning the staff its varying out-of-town territories to cover, in addition to their city accounts, he gave me Connecticut. Thus, after I had spent three or four days calling on my territory, I could wind up in Boston for the weekend and then take *The Owl*, the New Haven's crack all-sleeping-car night train, back to New York in time to be at work Monday morning.

It will amaze readers in the 1970's to realize what a proud railroad the New Haven once was—"the finest short-haul railroad in America." On nights of heavy traffic, *The Owl* often ran in three sections, each sixteen or seventeen cars long; long before the invention of the roomette some of its cars were solid corridors of single rooms as well as the conventional drawing rooms and compartments. Three all-Pullman extra-fare day trains were also needed in addition to the humbler transports that also carried day coaches—the *Knickerbocker*, the *Yankee Clipper* and the *Merchant's Limited*. Of these, the proudest was the last; two diners were supplied to ensure no waiting, and the senior conductors, ambassadors all, bowed slightly when they took your tickets, and wore swallow-tailed coats. On those weekends when I was not Boston-bound for *Redbook* I would catch the *Merchant's* at 5 P.M. on Saturday* and Catherine would be watching for me

---

* Saturdays, yes. The five-and-a-half-day work week persisted until the days of the New Deal, when "Share the work" was one of the N.R.A.'s prescriptions for unemployment.

at Boston's Back Bay Station at 9:45, her little Model A Ford runabout waiting to take me out to Newton Centre, where, after her parents had gone to bed, we would behave outrageously.

. . . The ugly little parking place where that Ford runabout once stood waiting became, in the later years when I still had occasions to visit Boston, the most nostalgic spot in my universe.

• • •

In handing out accounts to salesmen, the fair-handed boss tries to give everyone as equitable an assortment as he can; to each a mixture of good accounts already running, hard nuts to crack, steady, loyal customers, hopeless dogs, easy marks, dangerous characters, Indian-sign artists, bearers of false witness and plain sons of bitches. Ken was the fair-handed boss personified, but he never made the slightest concession to the fact that I was a novice salesman. "How can I?" he wanted to know. "Just go in there and start pitching; that's all anybody can do. I've given you some of the same accounts for *Redbook* that Walter Biery handles for *McCall's* because he's an old-timer and a good guy and you can pick up some tips from him. And I've given you Bristol-Myers, which has a twelve-time Ipana contract for page one facing inside front cover; just don't *lose* it on us, for Christ's sake, that's all."

"Watch your step when you go call on Miss Fairburn," Ken said to me on the verge of my first visit. But he would not elaborate; he only made matters worse by saying, "If you take her out to lunch you can have the rest of the afternoon off." And a giggling conspiracy of silence descended on the whole office when it became known that I was, indeed, going to have lunch with someone I'll call Miss Fairburn, the agency's space buyer, in a day or so.

By twelve-thirty on the day of the lunch I was trembling violently when I presented myself at the agency office to ask for Miss Fairburn. And when I was shown into her office, Miss Fairburn was trembling violently, too. But the etiology of our tremors was different. Mine came from fear. Miss Fairburn's came from the biggest hangover I had until then ever seen anyone, man or woman, endure. Her hands shook; her body shook; her voice shook. It was evident even to a young lay eye that Miss Fairburn, now past the best years of a woman's life, was a lady drunk, and, it must be, of long standing.

Well, the mystery was not only cleared up but an evident course of action was made clear. "If you're ready for lunch, we could go right now," I suggested.

"There's a speakeasy on Forty-Eighth Street . . ." said Miss Fairburn tremulously. There were 105 speakeasies on 48th Street, I was sure, but it was obvious Miss Fairburn was a homing carrier pigeon; all I had to do was follow in her train. "I'll have a double French Seventy-Five made with brandy," said Miss Fairburn to the waiter before the chairs had stopped scraping in. I had never heard of a French Seventy-Five before and don't to this day know what was in it besides the brandy, but with an infallible instinct I was sure Ken would admire later, I uttered two languid words: "The same."

After the first two drinks Miss Fairburn stopped shaking; after the third her outlook on life grew as healthy as Dr. Norman Vincent Peale's; after the fourth she got down to business with a bang. Despite the A.M.A. and A.A. I swear the breed exists, rare though it may be, and that Miss Fairburn, like two or three others I have met, belonged to it: people who can't function at all when sober, but who not only think they're wizards when they're full of booze, but *are* wizards. At the end of lunch I scarcely knew where I was or who I was, but Miss Fairburn was in full control; she thanked me cordially for a very interesting time, graciously hoped we would meet again soon and helped me— I needed it—into a taxi. Then she walked, alone and straight as a die, back to her office, where, beginning at about 3:15 P.M., I am convinced she did a good day's work. As for me, the taxi took me home to my one-room Murphy-bed apartment on 35th Street, where, after phoning Ken to mumble that I had had a wonderful lunch with Miss Fairburn and we understood each other perfectly on all points, I fell asleep with all my clothes on. Dear old Ken; how thoughtful he had been in telling me I needn't come back to the office after lunch.

• • •

Dear old Ken, indeed; he's been dead now for thirty years, but he was a true teacher and a devoted friend. He was a bachelor in those days, and once told me what he thought was the truth about himself: that there were only four things in life he was interested in—eating, drinking, sleeping and fucking. It didn't happen to be true, but it was his conviction. He was a devout

Catholic, and like so many of his kind his attitude toward his religion and life baffled me. By virtue of our long Boston association I was his confidant as well as his employee; it was as the former that he used to tell me about some of the complications of his life. Not unnaturally he had a girl friend; not unnaturally they would go to bed together more than occasionally; not unnaturally these lapses from morality would have to come up in the confessional, for Ken was strict with himself in his observations of all his Church's rituals and practices. According to Ken, his parish priest at first admonished, prescribed penance and gave absolution. But as, time after time, these lapses continued undiminished, the confessor priest became sterner and instructed Ken that he must not only stop this particular Sin, but "avoid those temptations or occasions" that might lead to Sin.

"Father, I'll do my best, but that's all I can promise," Ken reported himself as saying. The best turned out to be none too good, and the day arrived when the confessor came to the end of his rope and refused to shrive Ken. This put him into a real sweat. "Jesus Christ!" he said to me later. "I had to spend all Saturday afternoon and go all the way out to Far Rockaway before I could find a priest who'd grant me Absolution!"

• • •

The dizzying slide of the stock market that began in September and culminated in the panic day of October 29, 1929, did not begin the Great Depression, as many people now think; it merely heralded it. Advertising linages, for example, held up well through all of 1930 and most of 1931; it was only thereafter that everything began going to pieces.

I think my total assets in 1929 must have been around $3,000 in a savings account, but Ken's state was very different. In addition to his other qualities he was consumed with ambition for money and power—neither of which he ever achieved. Throughout all of 1929 he had been pyramiding all the McCall stock he owned, and when the Crash came he was simply wiped out, and worse. He owed debts he could not possibly pay. My little $3,000, secure in a savings bank, suddenly became Wealth—Wealth, when personal insolvency had suddenly become epidemic. So although Herbert Hoover was technically right—at and for the time—when he said "the business of the country is fundamentally sound," the country's mood, particularly in New York, was the blackest of the black.

• • •

One night at home, late in the evening and late in 1929, I decided I could stand the life of an advertising space salesman no longer. I made half a dozen trips to the phone to call Ken, ask to see him, and then and there tell him I would have to quit: I couldn't take it any longer. And half a dozen times I turned away, caught in an emotional cross fire because, even though I could not stand my life, I did not want to let my loyal friend down.

But the seventh time I did not turn away; by now, desperate, I called his number.

"Mr. Kennedy is not at home," said the switchboard operator.

"Can you tell me when he'll be back?"

"No, indeed I can't," said the operator. "He was taken to the hospital in an ambulance just twenty minutes ago."

33 · J. WALTER THOMPSON, ADVERTISING, OR, NEW LIGHT SHED ON THE BILL OF RIGHTS

THE EMERGENCY that had taken Ken to the hospital was a bleeding gastric ulcer. He was a sick, sick fellow, worn down by his personal financial disaster, by his responsibilities as an executive and the absolute necessity for the unfailing "smile and shoeshine" that must be maintained not only outside with prospects but inside with staff. Fornication and liquor were, as they remain today, excellent short-term solvents for assorted anxieties, but in the end they fail, they fail.

And they failed Ken badly. He was kept in the hospital a month at least, and when he came out it was as a pale and wan individual who had lost more than thirty pounds and was living on his nerve. He had, as a matter of fact, damn near died, and his post-hospital regimen accorded very badly with his psychological make-up, for he was a lusty fellow and the prospect of living on a diet of tea and dry toast, with occasional assorted fine-strained mushes, held for him little appeal. Alcohol was, of course, absolutely ruled out. So was "any excessive activity," which Ken grimly interpreted as the end of any necessity for further trips to seek Absolution in Far Rockaway. Thus deprived of three of the four props on which he had insisted his life was based, the fourth prop—sleeping—also collapsed. Fortunately any form of barbiturate could then be purchased without a prescription and a judicious dollop of phenobarbital was indicated anyway. But Ken's ulcer persisted like a sleeping volcano for a long, long time, and even a sea voyage did very little good. It was two years before he was back to full normal.

• • •

Under these circumstances, I had lost my opportunity to quit. My sales record was nothing to brag about, but it wasn't hopeless, either, and of course I eventually got over, as everyone eventually does, the initial stage fright that was so paralyzing in the beginning. Ken set me some hard tasks. He was determined that I should find some way of battering down the door of Stanley Resor, then head of J. Walter Thompson. Mr. Resor's secretary was equally determined that I should not. "You sit down," said Ken, "and write him a letter telling him thus-and-such." Thus-and-such turned out to be Ken's contention that Mr. Resor's refusal to see me was in effect a denial of my constitutional right to free speech, peaceable assembly and several other items guaranteed under the Bill of Rights. It wasn't *quite* that, but it was almost that. Having nothing to lose I wrote Mr. Resor roughly along those lines and two days later was amazed to get a call from his secretary saying that Mr. Resor would see me at 11 A.M. on the next day.

"I don't often get a letter like that," said Mr. Resor, who seemed rather puzzled that he had. At any rate we chatted amiably for half an hour, and thereafter he was accessible to me. The moral of this tale is that I never sold Mr. Resor a line of space, and no evidence existed, direct or indirect, that any J. Walter account was in any way swayed toward *Redbook*. But Ken didn't care. He felt a Principle had been established: the Principle that no agency head, however exalted, could consistently and persistently refuse to see a magazine representative, however humble, without accountability. And the experience did me some good too. I discovered that I could, within reason, write my way into seeing just about anybody I wanted. The process might be long, desperately trying on the nerves and patience, and the success, if it came, empty—but it *could* be done. The business of letter writing on *Redbook*'s behalf was destined to be important to me, as time went on, and was eventually to be one of several wildly diverse factors that led me back to an editorial path once again.

I hardly learned a single principle of the art of selling and don't know many to this day. I *did* learn, and early, too, that logic was among the very weakest tools of the trade, and that the Overwhelming Argument was no good either because among the hard-bitten men of the agency and advertising worlds it simply did not overwhelm. The space buyers were the only ones interested in costs per page per thousand net paid, or the alleged quality, characteristics or make-up of your circulation, and they were daily so deluged with various active sales appeals that they regarded you through hooded eyes and in a silence they rarely broke unless for some discomfiting remark. As for the account men, when you got to see them, the only prayer, usually silent, that went up from them was "Please, for God's sake, don't bore me." So one tried not to be a bore. I remember with affection a Mr. Beatty of the then firm of Newell-Emmet, who "had" the Chesterfield account. The first time I called on him I was full of zeal to talk about *Redbook*'s virtues for Chesterfield. He was a thoroughly cordial man, with a reputation for amiable eccentricity, and on this morning he did not want to talk about *Redbook*, Chesterfields, or any aspect of publishing or advertising at all. He wanted, for reasons of his own, to talk about endocrinology.

So we talked about endocrinology. "You know," he said, "the medical profession is getting too damn clinical about everything. They're always going 'round diagnosing this patient as a hypothyroid or that one as a pituitary disfunction; that a man might just plain be a horse's ass never occurs to them." Not all our talks were so easy to set down, but of one thing I am sure: we never talked about advertising, publishing or cigarettes. An instinct told me that this, with Mr. Beatty, could be a way to lose an account. We didn't lose it.

• • •

One of my accounts in those days was Life Savers, accurately described by its founder, Ed Noble, who had yet to become a powerful man, as "a whimsical little business." Space salesmen had other descriptions, for as the Depression began to deepen, the Life Saver advertising department developed a highly logical and strenuously cursed policy. It would wait until some magazine, with its closing date upon it, still hadn't sold its back cover—the most expensive space unit in any magazine. As everyone in magazine publishing knew (except that two young men named Luce and Hadden hadn't known it when they began publishing their "newsmagazine" a few years earlier), you just didn't go to press with a blank back cover, nor with a black-and-white ad, either. Anything less than a four-color ad on the back cover was, in the magazine world, more shameful, shocking and disreputable than indecent exposure in Macy's window. So Life Savers used a tempting bait. When it knew that a magazine was up tight to closing with a back cover still blank, it would step forward with the proposition that it would fill the blank back cover with handsome four-color plates, but would pay only the rate-card price of an inside black-and-white page. And many were the premium pages it picked up by this maneuver.

I used to enjoy calling on Life Savers; the plant in Greenwich, Connecticut, smelled delicious; Mr. Bates, the advertising manager, and Mr. Hardy, his assistant, were pleasant though deadpan: they made me do all the talking. And since the running time on the New Haven to Greenwich was an hour, one call used up a whole afternoon. I think I must have made a trip a month to Greenwich, made an impassioned speech there to Mr. Bates or Mr. Hardy, and then taken the train back, having accomplished absolutely nothing.

I did this for two years, always coming back with a roll of gratis Life Savers but nothing else. But then there came an afternoon that began like all the others and ended quite differently. As I unlimbered my briefcase, Mr. Hardy said, "Don't make any spiel today; I'm going to give you an order." He then thrust into my incredulous hands an AAAA standard order form for six four-color back covers at the full card rate. As soon as I expressed my gratitude, trying hard to make it sound less intense than it was, I telephoned the news to Ken. "You wouldn't joke about a thing like this, would you?" he asked, "Because in that case I'd break every bone in your body." I assured him of the occasion's utter solemnity. As a result, when I got back to the New York office we had a celebration so vast that I remember nothing about it.

Of course this story has a tag. The Life Saver plates duly arrived at the Dayton plant, were run, billed and paid for, at full rates. No sooner had these pleasant formalities been accomplished than there arrived a cancellation of the remaining five covers. Apparently Life Savers had no intention at all of running those six covers; Mr. Hardy was, in effect, making me a present of one just for being a good boy. Who says there is no sentiment in business? Up to a point.

• • •
• • •

But the best friend I ever made in my advertising years I had the luck to make all by myself. I called on him in early 1930 because one of my Connecticut accounts was the Phoenix Mutual Life Insurance Company and in *McKitterick's Guide*, the handbook of every space salesman, it said, after a multitude of other details, "Agency Man: Bill Strong." The agency was B.B.D.&O., and William McCreery Strong was the account executive—a title he detested. Phoenix could in those days advertise "How to retire on $250 a month." (The campaign continues to this day but with a revision in the figures.) Since the account was running in *Redbook* I had no need to do anything but pay a courtesy call on the "agency man," but it turned out to be a unique pleasure. Our first meeting was formal enough, but by the second and third we knew that we were friends, with many common interests, which specifically *excluded* advertising and everything connected with it. Bill was a Princetonian who wished at the time that he were F. Scott Fitzgerald too. Like so many gifted collegians before and after him he had sought out the agency world as one where he could exercise his writing talents for good money and then, later, make good an escape into what was yet to be called "creative writing." But Bill, after almost ten years in the advertising world, had not yet made an escape; and about the time we first met, it must have been beginning to dawn on him that he wasn't going to. (He never did.) It is a tough emotional fix to be good at a job and profession you dislike, and this was precisely the fix Bill was in.

Bill was enormously tall and prematurely bald. On the surface he was merry, and had a sense of humor that sprang equally from indignation and from self-depreciation, but the better I got to know him the more I realized how corroded with unhappiness he was. But that was not quickly apparent. Messrs. Barton, Durstine and Osborn were all then alive and at the height of their powers, and Bill's aversion toward his job was fully and mysteriously equaled by his loyalty to his top employers.

• • •

In those days when there was nothing prouder than the ocean liner, except the shipping firm that had a fleet of them, B.B.D.&O.

was the agency for the French Line, and Bill was the account executive. Since one of the passions of Bill's life was travel, he could really put his heart and soul into the French Line account, in a way that Phoenix Life could never lay claim to. And then— B.B.D.&O. lost the account. Bill was disconsolate for weeks. Not only is an account executive on the spot to explain why *he* had lost the account, but the French Line was particularly dear to him. It was a long time before he stopped bemoaning his loss.

And then, one day at my *Redbook* office, I got a letter on the stationery of the French Line, which was to the eye the very epitome of the come-on form letter, complete with salutation that didn't quite match the body type.

> DEAR MR. HODGINS:
>
> Come with us to the sun-drenched Caribbean. Enjoy two unparalleled weeks of utter peace surrounded at every hand by luxuries of food, drink and sport which only the French—

I was about to toss the letter into the wastebasket when some inner sense warned me that some sort of bomb was about to shatter the rituals of direct-mail composition. I was right. The letter went on to a final paragraph:

> And now, one thing more. By special arrangement, the French Line has secured permission to permit fucking on the decks. No more stumbling down a staircase. No fumbling with a stateroom key. Just whip it out and ram it in.
>
> Yours very truly,

Bill had thus relieved his agony of soul. He had some leftover French Line stationery in his desk and had used it for altogether the most enticing form letter that never got mailed in quantity. He, like myself, was a minister's son, but underneath a bland exterior that far outdid mine, there raged a volcano of assorted bitternesses, contempts and hatreds for the world-as-organized that I, once again, could not match, although I could come reasonably close.

Shortly after the French Line letter episode, Ken took away from me all my Bill Strong accounts. We had become "too friendly" and in the trade that meant that I had become incapable of ever selling him anything again.

34 · *NIKISCH IST TOT*, or, FIRST FLIGHT

In 1930 I sold my first long piece to *The New Yorker*. It was called "Steam Song" and was my first Reporter at Large acceptance. The prewar *Bremen* was newsworthy then for she had just captured the Blue Ribbon for speed in Atlantic crossing. So all the newspapers had sent reporters down to her dockside where they interviewed, besides the passengers, the Captain, the Purser and the Chief Steward—but not a word about the Chief Engineer, his vast engine room and the four triple-stage turbines that were her true claim to fame. So the next time the *Bremen* visited New York I got permission to board her at Quarantine and to absorb the noise and steamy hot oil smell as she made her way dead slow to her berth. To be in the engine room of a huge liner as she is docking was, forty years ago, just about as far out as you could go for excitement. I wrote the piece, the first time, as a Profile of Herr Leitender Ingenieur Gustave Hundt, and Katharine Angell rejected it. I rewrote it as a Reporter and, lo and behold, it was accepted. I got a huge sum for it—something like $200—and this tipped the balance. When I sold another piece—on Tubby Rogers—to the blessed Mrs. William Brown Maloney, editor of the really tip-top magazine that the *Herald Tribune* once published every Sunday, I felt I had enough security and earning power, stock-market crash or not, so that Catherine and I could be married—formally. And on July 5, 1930, we were, in a tiny little Episcopal Church in Newton Centre. Catherine's father had given her the choice of a "big" wedding or a present in cash of the amount the "big" affair would set the unfortunate man back. She, with my frenzied concurrence, chose the latter. My father, whom I had not seen in his canonicals for a long time, assisted the Rector and pronounced that part of the ceremony known as the Betrothal. "I could feel the chancel shake," he said afterward, a remark I could have done without, for although I had been the typical terrified bridegroom and my violent tremors had been responsible for the chancel's instability, I thought I had myself under better external control. With the purchased connivance of Catherine's younger brother, we sneaked away from the small reception as soon as we could, and Drawing Room A on the *Twilight Express*, Boston to New York, served us as our first indubitably legal wedding couch. We were deliriously happy at the beginnings of a marriage we imagined as lasting into our twilight years.

• • •

We had no honeymoon problems of any kind. Thanks to the moralities of the twenties we were experienced sexual partners, and what we now reveled in was that all necessity for deceit or furtiveness was behind us. We now had society's permission to do what we had been doing anyway, and we made the most of it.

We had no lesser problems, either. Since the *Schnelldampfer Bremen* had been largely responsible for the excess funds on which we had accepted the economic dare to get married, we would sail on her to Germany, where neither of us had been, traveling as slowly as we could. Thanks to Ken's generosity we had three weeks to go from Bremerhaven to Munich, with stops at Berlin, Leipzig and Nürnberg, and then streak back for Paris, Cherbourg and the voyage home on the *Bremen*'s sister, the *Europa*. The Weimar Republic still stood; it would have amazed us, as it did amaze all equally uninformed Americans, if we had realized that in barely two years the buffoon of the abortive Munich beer-hall *putsch* of a few years before would become Chancellor of what was to become known as the Third Reich and the stage would be set for Armageddon. All Catherine and I knew was that we wanted to have a glimpse of Mit-Europa and this would not only be romantic but would have its practical aspects, too, for I had further writing designs on the ships of the North German Lloyd.

We had to travel second class, of course, but that turned out not to matter at all. To my great surprise a second-class steward, from whom I would have expected nothing but the most rule-bound rigidity, said, "You have evening clothes. Let me show you the easiest place to cross the barrier into first class." So although we ate and slept second class, we traveled first. What was more, we had frequent cocktails in the really luxurious quarters of Herr Leitender Ingenieur Hundt for I wanted to find out about his thirty years at sea. His office was filled not only with handsome furnishings of all sorts, but opposite his desk was a fascinating wall covered with dials and gauges that told him at a glance how every piece of machinery in his engine room, ten decks below, was functioning. But this was the one thing he didn't want to talk about. Instead he pulled innumerable scrapbooks from his bookshelves. "Fancy-dress ball!" he would exclaim, dozens upon dozens of times, pointing out his portly self in all the guises he had assumed on all the Gala Nights on all the ships he had ever served. It was not what I had come after, but Herr Hundt's commands to his private steward, "*Drei mehr* Manhattan cocktail," whenever glasses were empty, made the time swim by. The month was July, the mid-Atlantic weather was balmy, the seas were smooth, even the second-class food was good, and, all in all, the voyage was an idyll.

• • •

The international relations between America and Europe in the time of which I am writing were very much, *mutatis mutandis*, what they were in the 1960's. With our former foe, whom we had likened to Attila's Huns scarcely a decade before, we were now on the most cordial terms; between La Belle France and America there was snarling enmity. So Catherine's and my trip through a land stigmatized as the very seat and center of barbarism could not have been smoother or more delightful. On our first night in Bremen we dined in that most famous of rathskellers, which even in 1930 bore to young American eyes and ears an atmosphere still medieval. To pass the open door of a private dining salon and observe a room at which enormous priests sat about an enormous table, eating and drinking enormously, somehow suggested corruption or at least high intrigue, and was very pleasant.

I had gone to Germany armed with several letters of introduction. It was in Berlin that I presented most of them; in the course of this I met an authentic Fiend-to-be of the Hitler regime. Having published one book on aviation I was resolved to write another, and my friend Edward Warner, of M.I.T., but now editor of *Aviation*, supplied me with a letter to a Herr Milch of Deutsche Lufthansa. (Europe in 1930 was about a decade ahead of the United States in commercial flying.) Herr Milch was a small man, as innocuous-appearing as his name, and with gentle, quiet, deferential manners. He was the soul of courtesy. Anyone who came to him recommended by the distinguished Herr Geheimrat Doktor-Professor Warner could have anything it might be in his poor power to bestow. Pray, what were my wishes? Well, Herr Milch, my wishes were only two: a conducted tour of Tempelhof Field and a look into any picture archives of Deutsche Lufthansa as such an unofficial American author could have access to.

But of course! Herr Milch's only disappointment was that my requests were so easy to grant; he had hoped I might have had something to challenge his powers further. (In the light of history, I'm damn glad I didn't!) He had enjoyed reading my book on aviation; regrettably there did not seem to be a German edition but luckily his English was adequate.

Well, Herr Milch and I got along famously. I had a fascinating look behind the scenes at Tempelhof, and a whole squad of archivists at Lufthansa deluged me with material. Obviously, in giving me his letter of introduction to meet Herr Milch, my friend Ed Warner knew that this was the man who could deliver the goods.

He certainly could. He and I parted forever on a July day in 1930, and the next time I heard of him, the whole world heard of him too. He was by now Colonel-General Milch of the Luftwaffe, and Hermann Goering's chief executive, whose psychopathy in the last days of World War II outran even his chief's. That mild, polite little man. And a Fiend.

•   •   •

Bremen had preceded Berlin, where in addition to Herr Milch and Lufthansa I had visited that vast printing and publishing establishment Ullstein Verlag, the finest thing of its kind in Europe and perhaps anyplace before World War II. Since the Ullstein family was Jewish, Hitler's accession meant that within two to three years after my visit their property would be wrenched out of their hands—and, ultimately, join the rest of

1945 Berlin in rubble. But here, too, in 1930, despite my slight credentials, I was given a warm welcome. In the British Isles, post-World War I, the visiting American was accorded a stiffly proper reception; in France he was treated with freezing hauteur (and street insult); but in Germany, the touring American was somehow welcomed as a friend. This mysterious cordiality went all up and down the social ranks; it applied to the police, the *Gepackträger*, to that all-powerful hotel factotum *der Portier*, to pedestrians, to businessmen—and to Herr Milch.

To two wedding trippers like Catherine and me, absorbed in each other and cloaked with the really terrible ignorance that afflicted all Americans in those days, the Germany we were traveling in might as well have been Yucatan for all we understood its problems. It wore, it seemed to wear, a cheerful outward face. The pale ascetic Dr. Brüning was peaceably and without apparent difficulty ruling the Weimar Republic. The horrors of inflation were over and the reichsmark was an apparently solid currency. Business was depressed, but business was depressed at home, too, and in fact all over the world. But it hadn't affected us, and somehow it wasn't going to. Two more superficial and uninvolved travelers than my bride and I it would have been hard to imagine. We did what tourists were supposed to do, and little more, whether we were in Leipzig, Nürnberg or Munich. Catherine had a habit that I deplored the lack of in myself: she was a diary-keeper. Ever since her teens she had written a brief page a day in an ordinary desk diary—and if I had access to those pages now, I would remember vastly more than I do. What impresses me today, with shame either to ourselves or to our American education, was the literary wasteland that existed in both our minds, stretching all the way between Goethe and Heinrich Heine and Thomas Mann, except for school-child poems. Musically we were a good deal better off, but the nearest thing to a cultural exchange during the enchanted journey occurred between a rubberneck *Wagen* guide and me in Leipzig, in which it was mutually covenanted and agreed that the great Arthur Nikisch had in the previous century for a while been musical director of the Boston Symphony, about which I could claim some superficial knowledge—*"Aber Nikisch ist tot." "Ja, Nickisch ist tot."* A similar discussion of Dr. Karl Muck was attempted but broke down.

Munich, I think, was the high point of our trip. The names of all these cities stand for something terrible now: the Munich capitulation, the Nürnberg Trials, the slaughter of Berlin, but in 1930 the War to End War had been won more than a decade before. Never more than in 1930 were Americans Innocents Abroad.

•　•　•

Neither Catherine nor I had ever been in an airplane. This was not at all peculiar; commercial aviation had barely begun in the United States. The gifted Bill Stout, whom I later had the privilege of knowing pretty well, had already produced that nerve-wracking boneshaker the Ford Tri-Motor, and a company then known as T.A.T. (Transcontinental Air Transport, a progenitor of T.W.A., which *used* to stand for Transcontinental & Western Air) had, in collaboration with the Pennsylvania Railroad, inaugurated a rail-air transcontinental service—air by day, rail by night.

But long before 1930 Europe had been laced with airlines and Herr Milch's Deutsche Lufthansa was a flourishing carrier. So we decided that we must put the capstone on our trip by flying from Munich to Paris. *That* would give us something to boast about when we got home. We booked passage; it wasn't hard. Even the European public had not yet taken to the air with any mass enthusiasm.

Nevertheless, the Munich airfield had considerable bustle to it. The all-metal airplane was by no means in universal use, but the Lufthansa fleet did consist entirely of all-metal Junkers. But there was a distinction between them: some of the Junkers had two engines, some only one. The airfield was, for Germany, a rather informal affair. I remember that the two of us stood around for quite a while before our flight was ready. There was no enclosure, and no place to sit down, but from some sort of elaborated pushcart I bought a small *Reisenflasche* of brandy, from which we both extracted some of the Dutch courage we needed for the high adventure. When our flight was at last announced, lo and behold, we had drawn a single-engined plane, at which discovery I promptly took another pull on the *Reisenflasche* (Catherine disdained a second; she was almost always the calmer of us), and thus it was with a certain euphoria that I followed my bride up the ramp. We sat on opposite sides of the aisle for the best of reasons; the passenger capacity of the plane was seven. Years later I saw a picture of the type of plane we flew in; by then a whole case of brandy never would have persuaded me to go near such a primitive Puffing Billy of the air.

We were due to touch down at Stuttgart, Karlsruhe and Saarbrücken on our route to Le Bourget; since the roar of the single engine sounded extremely healthy and the sky was a cloudless blue, my euphoria grew without any further necessity for the *Reisenflasche*. Flying itself became a wonderfully exhilarating experience. Catherine and I exchanged happy glances, and I observed with a certain mild contempt another American tourist in the seat before me who seemed to be totally absorbed in a copy of *The Saturday Evening Post*—except that he was holding it upside down. As for me, I was totally at ease.

I have no idea of the height at which we were flying, but the trees had individuality. Ahead of us I saw something that looked like the edge of a huge quarry, or something. How interesting, I thought, *everything* looks from the air. The edge of the quarry passed behind us, and I looked for new features of the terrain. Suddenly, we were struck by a tremendous downdraft that put us into a free fall, the like of which I hadn't in my innocence known existed. *Everything* hit the ceiling, and stayed there, it seemed, for an eternity. When things were finally straightened out Catherine and I managed wan smiles. And our enthusiasm for flying was not enhanced when after our touchdown at Karlsruhe the skies changed from blue to black and we landed at Saarbrücken in a violent thunderstorm, which kept us grounded there, on the Franco-German border, for two hours. We had had our first and—as it turned out to be—our last airplane flight together. And I have never liked flying since.

We had only a day in Paris and then the boat train took us to Cherbourg. The solidity of the *Schnelldampfer Europa* as she waited for her passengers in the roadstead seemed deeply reassuring. We had a violent passage home, but we didn't care. We would now take up true domesticity together.

35 · "BE A SNOB," OR, THE 10,000 CLIPPINGS

To THIS DAY, the injunction "Marry the boss's daughter" is everywhere familiar. Few people can get the whole cynical quotation right. It is *"Be a snob,* and marry the boss's daughter." And fame being what it is, almost no one remembers who said it. It happens that it was my teacher and beloved friend at M.I.T. Tubby Rogers who said it, and the manner of his saying of it helped Catherine and me to get married, for I was able to make—and sell—a short story of it. But no artifice of mine could improve on the facts as they were.

Tubby was in great demand as a speaker. So I was not surprised that the graduating class of 1929 asked him to be the star performer at its class banquet—the last time the seniors ever got together except when, a day later, the majority of them would receive their diplomas. Tubby by then had taken off with his wife and small daughter for their summer place in Rockport, and as he later told the story to me, he cursed mildly as he flung his evening clothes into the suitcase he had to take along for the filthy hour's ride on the Boston & Maine's Gloucester branch, which would land him in North Station. On the trip he wondered idly what he would say to the kids, but being a twenty-year veteran of this and similar occasions he languidly decided to postpone thinking about his topic until dinner was in progress. It was not up to him to be solemn; the Baccalaureate Sermon would take care of that in spades. His only obligation was to bid the boys an affectionate and, if possible, graceful goodby, and wish them well in their lives to come. And no such speech would be complete, of course, without some friendly words of advice on how to meet the world.

So when the student toastmaster said, "And now it is our privilege to hear, unfortunately for the last time, from Professor Tubby Rogers," Tubby did what was expected of him. He made his speech. His audience applauded him strenuously, as was usual. Tubby changed back into street clothes, shook hands all round and dozed through most of the train trip back to Rockport.

"Anything special happen?" his wife inquired.

"Nope," said Tubby, who, being tired from the train trip and the noise of the banquet, soon went to bed.

Shortly after midnight the telephone rang. It was the Associated Press. Was he correctly quoted in the lead story in the Boston *Post*, which had bannered "TELLS BOYS, 'BE SNOBS!'" Tubby, completely unaware that he had done anything more than play horse with the hard-work-and-lofty-ideals theme, could scarcely collect himself. Nor did he have much time to. The U.P. and I.N.S. were equally eager for verification, quotes and amplification. So was *The New York Times*, which quite understandably trusted nobody but itself. What with one thing and another, Tubby's telephone rang all night, and before next morning was far along, the small Rogers seaside cottage was as thick with reporters as if there had been an ax murder. On Sunday, June 2, 1929, there was scarcely an American newspaper that did not carry the story. In the next few months a blizzard of 10,000 newspaper clippings descended on Tubby from all over the world—praising him, denouncing him, passing every manner of judgment on him. The random nature of journalism was never better illustrated. City editors understandably don't send reporters to cover college senior dinners, but the canny Boston *Post*, which was once the city's most enterprising newspaper, had early spotted Tubby as a phrasemaker and had sent a student staffman to cover—just in case. Since Tubby had made his whole speech up out of his own head as he went along he was somewhat hard-pressed to make it part of his Philosophy of Existence or to compare his Rationale of Education with John Dewey's, as he was being constantly asked to do for the next half year. He was that precious thing, the born teacher, not the theorizing pedagogue, and the whole thing became a crashing bore to him in a very little while. "The only consolation," he told me, "is that I've been able to quadruple my lecture rates at women's clubs."

• • •

Catherine had begun preparing to be a bride in a very business-like fashion. For example, she had gone to cooking school before our marriage, so the burned biscuits, the leaden dumplings and the prolapsed soufflés of the radio and the comic strips were never among our troubles. She did suffer from what every intelligent girl suffers: housework. Here she was, a Smith graduate and not only that but one with enough gumption to go to secretarial school afterward so that she could have a business career. And she had gifts as a writer. But there were always the beds to be made and the marketing to be done and the dishes to be washed; there just wasn't any escaping any of those things. Catherine had thrown her destiny in with mine, and the days when the husband was the master and the wife was the unquestioned and unquestioning slave were over, but no new but equally unambiguous arrangement had arisen to take its place. (As I write this forty years later, the stage wait continues, but with disquieting off-stage noises.)

• • •

It was a sudden and temporary parting that made us realize all over again what we meant to each other. The occasion of our parting was, curiously enough, the *Schnelldampfer Bremen.* My piece in *The New Yorker* about her engine room had stirred up a good deal of interest, and among the significant places where that had happened was the American offices of the Norddeutscher Lloyd. Would I not like, they wanted to know, to take a round trip on her, first class, and write a book about her and her sister the *Europa*, in the same fashion as *The New Yorker* Reporter piece? They mentioned a fee that seemed attractive, particularly since the month was May of 1931 in the now deepening Depression. Might I, I asked, take my wife along? But assuredly! . . . except that there was a small technicality. Under the rules of the International Shipping Conference, she, unlike myself, could not be carried free. Although we could have a double cabin on A deck, no small matter in the month of May, the Lloyd would have to charge for her passage—minimum charge, of course, but charge. So here was a hell of a mess; the minimum charge for Catherine's round trip would come to substantially the same amount as my fee for writing the book! And since we were paying for our furniture, and my absence from *Redbook* would be without salary, despite Ken's best endeavors, the only two alternatives were clear—give up the whole project or go alone.

Catherine was a good sport about it, as she was about everything, but as the day of my departure approached, her spirits began to droop. I was to be gone two weeks, the *Bremen*'s then incredibly short round-trip interval, and during my absence, Catherine would go back to Newton Centre to stay with her parents. "But it's not *home* anymore," Catherine said, and suddenly burst into tears. In those days the two ships sailed at midnight— and from a Brooklyn pier as far distant from Manhattan as Coney Island. Catherine and I, together with our friend André Mesnard, took the interminable taxi ride together. Catherine was speechless with misery. Part of me knew that some of her misery was caused just plain by being left behind while I was going off on a jaunt—a money-making jaunt, but a jaunt. But another part of me knew that Catherine did not want to be parted from me for even a fortnight's time. As for myself, I was in an odd state, at once excited by the prospects ahead of me, but at the same time cast down by the picture of Catherine looking as if she were seeing me off to a war from which I would never return.

Never, so much as that night, had I wished to be Rudyard Kipling. As soon as the gangplanks were drawn back I was escorted to the bridge, via the chartroom directly behind it, whose lights went out the instant the connecting door was opened. We had not yet cast off but the atmosphere was electric with tension. The helmsman was at his wheel. Junior officers stood stiffly by engine-room telegraphs and every other piece of equipment imaginable. In most un-Germanic fashion Captain Zeigenbein was violating one, and I suspect two, of his own rules. He was smoking a cigarette and had with him a countesslike lady, exquisitely coifed and attired. But the touch I liked best was of the jovial and relaxed man in an Irishman's cap and somewhat rumpled business clothes who looked much less nautical than I. When a red light on the pierhead changed to white, a junior officer bellowed *"Alles klar"* and the man in the Irishman's cap said casually, "All right, let's go." He was the docking pilot, and it was his seven-minute job to see that the *Bremen* safely cleared her pier, safely tacked into midstream and safely made her turn toward open water. All of this he did with a police whistle and megaphone to signal any of the four tugs that were churning at the *Bremen*'s hull, and with a few casual remarks about propellor speed, which would be translated into peremptory German orders from Captain Zeigenbein to an *Unteroffizier*. His job accomplished, the docking pilot shook hands, descended hundreds of feet to one of his tugs, and that was that.

The great ship was now under the guidance of another civilian. This one wore a beret and a checked suit and was the Sandy Hook pilot, whose job was to get through the curving buoys of Ambrose Channel, which he did, languidly, laconically and very carefully . . . . It was hard to go to sleep that night.

• • •

It was the utmost good fun to have the run of the whole ship, from the kitchens to the cargo holds. Did I wish to see how alert the fire brigade was? My conducting officer smashed the glass in an alarm box with his fist. Within seconds, three men converged on the spot. *"Etwas ist los?"* *"Nein, nein, nichts los."* *"Nichts los?"* It was explained that this had been a demonstration.

And it was in this fashion that the *Bremen* and I made our way to Plymouth. I had a delightful cabin on A deck—equipped for two, of course—and cursed the rule whereby I could not afford to have taken Catherine with me. My plan was that I would debark at Plymouth, go to London for four days and then meet the *Bremen* again after she had plowed her way through the North Sea to Bremerhaven and arrived again at Plymouth. The timetable worked perfectly. Whenever I have been in London I have walked and walked and walked. Then I have gone back to my hotel so that I could rest until I could walk some more. And that's what I did this time.

It was well that I had done most of my work on the eastbound trip, because westbound was a wretched compound of storm and fog, and we were half a day late in arriving again in New York. But such were those simple days that I could, and did, boast that I had made a round trip to Europe in fourteen days—and people's eyes widened in surprise at such a feat. That last half day was simple torture, for from Nantucket on we ran in deep, dense fog—and I got an intimate firsthand glimpse at how tense experienced master mariners get under such conditions.

• • •

On the cavernous and resounding pier Catherine spied me before I spied her, but only by a split second. Then we did not embrace; we collided. By the time we were conscious again of our surroundings the customs inspector had, I don't know how long before, chalked his X's on my bags without even asking me to open them. He knew where my mind was, and Catherine's too, and it was not on smuggling.

Whereas the taxi trip *to* the pierside a fortnight ago had been an eternity, the trip *from* it to 54th Street and First Avenue was over in the blinking of an eye and we didn't give a damn what the driver, cops, stray pedestrians or anyone else thought of us. The arrival at our apartment marquee, the paying of the fare, the carting of our luggage, the elevator ride to the twelfth floor—all these demanded a few moments of desperate dignity. But once secure inside our own threshold, we didn't even try to make it as far as the bedroom.

36 · "BROTHER, CAN YOU SPARE A DIME?" OR, "NO"

THERE HAD BEEN, Bill Strong told us, in advertising circles in the year 1930, the wry joke that when the history of our times came to be written, what we were going through "would be known as the Great Depression of 1934." As 1931 slowly edged toward 1932, it began to seem more and more as if this were to be no joke at all. Catherine and I, with no money to lose, were among the most fortunate of young people, and I was even glad, occasionally, and in an odd way, that I was a "salesman"—people who held that title were naturally among the last to lose their jobs. I even had a $1,000-a-year raise; it was due to be nine-tenths wiped out when in 1932 "everybody" (which meant *almost* everybody) at McCall's took a 10 per cent salary cut. But that was nothing. Catherine and I and Bill Strong and his wife, Betty, were now closely sealed in the bonds of friendship and did almost everything together, along with our then bachelor friend Dick Leonard. The city, of a winter's night, was grim. The apple sellers shivered over their baskets on every street corner. Edward Angly's book *Oh Yeah?*, a compendium of the asininities uttered by men in high places, was a wild best seller. But *if* you had a secure job, and *if* (as was becoming increasingly difficult) you could momentarily turn your mind away from the miseries all about you, it was possible to have a good time in 1932–33. For one thing, *there were no crowds*. Would you like to go to the theater on the spur of the moment? Just pick your play; there would be two—or four—good seats at the box office, and your patronage was appreciated. Was it a cold, rainy night and did you want a cab (at fifteen-cent drop and five cents a quarter mile)? Two or three drivers would jostle fenders to be the first to reach you. At the newly built Waldorf-Astoria, the feed line for cabs began on Park Avenue, turned east on 49th

Street, turned again on Lexington, ran north a block and then doubled back on 50th. Cops were stationed there for two reasons: (1) to keep the tail of the line from overrunning its head and (2) to break up fistfights between drivers battling to keep their places. Was it summer? Jones Beach was new, vast and conspicuously underpopulated. Only an occasional traffic light stayed your progress to or from. Reservations for restaurant lunch or dinner? Don't be silly.

It was a buyers' market for everything. If you priced something in even the proudest shops, and then honestly decided you didn't want it at *any* price, you might be in for a hard time, for the salesgirl almost literally grasped your lapel and said, "Just a second! Let me ask the Buyer!" Then she was breathlessly back with authorization to clip 10, 15 or even 20 per cent off the price tag. Cigarettes were two packs for a quarter. I cannot remember the price of a speakeasy drink or meal for the ultrastrange reason that Catherine and I were never in a speakeasy together. Young marrieds in our price class did not go to speakeasies; we did our drinking at home. Not only did bootleggers have business cards and multicolor catalogs; the city was awash with "Cordial & Beverage" shops. In their show windows there were a few flyblown bottles of grenadine and *lots* of ginger ale. Also some bottles of orange- and lavender-colored liquids, suggesting to the well informed that somehow Curaçao and Crème Yvette were exempt from the Volstead Act and could be purchased inside. But you seldom went inside; you phoned and said, "Send me over a couple of bottles of gin," and the husky but friendly gangster's voice said, "Yes, *sir;* what apartment?" It was the age of Courteous Service; the day of the dime tip.

• • •

Of course there was another side to the dime. *Now* magazine advertising was affected in earnest; so was circulation, which despite new heights of desperate chicanery began failing to meet guarantees; rebates were in order. Yet the publishers were of a stability Gibraltar-like compared to the advertising agencies. "Pedlar and Ryan let go fifty men last Friday"—this sort of talk was all over town and a lot of it was true; if a huge account changed agencies or lopped off three-quarters of its schedules, what else was there to do?

306

This was about the time when John Sterling, Vice-President in Charge of Advertising, called a joint meeting of the selling and promotion staffs of *McCall's* and *Redbook*. *Redbook* had been hemorrhaging much more rapidly than *McCall's*, and a principal reason was that *McCall's* was a woman's magazine but *Redbook* was a "general" magazine. And what *was* a "general" magazine? In the face of a total ambiguity from the editorial department, should the salesman try to sell it as a man's magazine (advertising copy made amazingly little attempt to appeal to men in the 1930's) or as a woman's magazine (where the competition was murderous) or, *somehow*, as both?

John Sterling's favorite expression when a knotty problem was to be faced was "We're all going to lock ourselves in a hotel room and not come out until we've got this thing settled." Part of this statement was literal; a large hotel suite was reserved and arrangements for ample food and drink were made with room service and bootleggers. The sales proconsuls had been summoned from Chicago, Detroit and the West Coast. And the problem was posed: How, in what fashion, was *Redbook* to be sold?

• • •

In the weekly letters I had been writing, on Ken's orders, to a list of several hundred advertisers and prospects, I had chanced on a phrase that I had tossed off lightly and thought no more about. But a sales colleague on *Redbook* had a sharper eye for the main chance and said "Boy, what an advertising campaign you could write around that!" I hadn't known that it was loaded, but when Ken agreed strongly with my fellow salesman Dick Whitney, and with John Sterling's meeting getting closer, the three of us formed a plot. I would write three pieces of advertising copy around the theme and present them at the meeting. But there was a catch: copy without an accompanying layout, no matter how rough, can be singularly nonconvincing to the ear—and John Sterling's stern instructions were that *Redbook*'s problems were to be discussed with no advertising agency whatever prior to his meeting. Ken's Jesuitical mind found a way around this. "Go to Strong's home as his *personal* friend," he said. "Tell him not to ask any questions, but just get one of his art directors, as a *personal* friend, to make some tissue roughs for these three pieces of copy." He reached into his pocket. "Here's fifty dollars for subway fare," he said.

When the locked-hotel-room evening came, Ken had my copy and the tissue roughs in his briefcase. The arguments, almost theological in their blend of subtlety and ferocity, went on for at least two hours. Should we sell as a man's magazine or as a woman's magazine? Now my chance line, which I might have thrown away if Dick Whitney hadn't seen something in it, was simply: "The Shadow of a Man Stands Behind Every Woman Who Buys," and I must say that Bill Strong's *personal* art-director friend had done three fine jobs of depiction for the copy. So when Ken, who had kept suspiciously silent during most of the evening, thought the right time had at last come, he opened his briefcase, displayed the layouts and asked me to read the copy. It quelled the argument absolutely, for both sides took it as being what they had wanted all along. So the evening was a triumph, as I was able to tell Catherine when at last I got home, for the forces of truth and justice. And I was able to tell her something else, too. I was able to tell her that John Sterling's final announcement of the evening was that we were all going to take a 10 per cent salary cut. But I didn't really care. As the meeting was breaking up, I felt I had to deliver some sort of remark to John Sterling about the barefaced defiance of his no-agency order. "John," I said, "I *did* have to get a little professional help from a personal friend with these things." John's forte was that he played everything *piano*; he was widely regarded as the most dangerous low-pressure salesman in the business. "Yes," he said, "I rather thought so myself. I think I could even guess where it came from. But under the circumstances I guess there's no harm done."

• • •

• • •

It had been on a train coming back from Greenwich and another, as I thought, futile visit to Life Savers that I had casually read of the collapse of the Credit-Anstalt in Austria. Now it was a year later and Herbert Hoover was fighting for his political life. Those who have read and remembered Mr. Hoover's subsequent autobiography will have been struck by his unique explanation of the cause and persistence of the Depression: it had

308

been imported from overseas, beginning with the collapse of the Credit-Anstalt, and unlike the action taken against the European corn borer, there was nothing effective the great United States of America could do about it. To this theme Mr. Hoover reverted many times during the course of the desperate economic and political year 1932. The Republicans had renominated him because there was nothing else they could do; the Democratic Party had nominated Franklin Roosevelt in Chicago, and in his acceptance speech the words "new deal," without caps, were heard for the first time. And throughout the long hot summer of 1932 (campaigns lasted from June to November then) the mood of the country grew blacker and blacker. This was the first campaign in which that still modern miracle the radio played any significant or important part, not just in compiling election results but in the presentation of the campaign. Calvin Coolidge's voice was heard, nation-wide, for one of the last times; it was not inspiring even to lifelong Republicans. As for the wretched incumbent Hoover, he seemed to be speaking out of, and into, a past century. His vast fatigue was also evident in his every speech and he constantly referred to the "Hoot-Smalley Tariff," which he defended to the death. "Grass would grow in the streets," he told city dwellers; "your produce will rot in your barns," he told the farmers—whose produce had already long been doing that—as a consequence of Protectionist repeal. As for the businessmen of the country it was increasingly popular among them to say "What this country needs is a good dictator"—whatever they meant by the adjective. My friend Henry F. Pringle, who had the year before won a Pulitzer Prize for his book on Theodore Roosevelt, had made a terrifying compilation of what American men of supposed brains and substance were saying about what ought to be done with and to the American *political* system while of course leaving the *economic* system severely alone. Henry had broken into magazine journalism on Condé Nast's *Vanity Fair*, along with a beautiful and brainy girl then known as Clare Boothe Brokaw.

• • •

Election Night, 1932, was, for me, one long sustained experience in rapture; so it was for Catherine, for Bill and Betty Strong, and for Dick Leonard. We listened enchanted as almost every mossback in the Republican Party was swept off his Senate seat or out of the House. The Depression was not to lighten for a long time after this, and the approaching year 1933 was to be a grim one for the world, for the country, and for me, personally. But on this November night of 1932 we all thought that a new era had begun. That it was in many ways destined to be worse than its predecessor was a fact still mercifully hidden.

37 · CATHERINE

IT HAD NOT BEEN HARD to make the transition from Boston to
New York, for New York as much as any place was my home.
It was infinitely harder to make the transition from Boy Editor
(with spats!) to a space salesman. But in the years of 1930 to
1932 I was sustained by Catherine. With her help and encouragement I had managed to become a salesman, of an odd sort, to
complete the writing of two books, and get myself published occasionally in *The New Yorker* with "Talk Stories," Profiles and
Reporters at Large, all at the same time. When Harold Ross,
after sitting on it for an infinitude of time, finally published
my brash Profile of Orville Wright, I felt that I had arrived
somewhere.

A rift in the lute suddenly occurred in late 1931. Bill Strong
at the end of an evening of rummy (*gin* rummy was still far
in the future) turned serious. "Look," he said, "we're all just
about the same age and I can't imagine anything ever affecting
our friendship. We've been married couples for almost two years.
Why don't we deliberately plan to have kids at the same time
so the little bastards can grow up together?"

Bill's tone was light but his mien was serious—and it seemed
a most attractive idea. The four of us discussed it for a while,
or to be painfully accurate, three of us did. Catherine fell suddenly silent and I could see, to my then only mild consternation,
that her face had gone white. So I fell silent too, and when Bill
and Betty Strong went home, Catherine began preparing, still
silent, to go to bed. Something was wrong and I was bound to
ask what it was. "I don't want to talk about it," she said, and
the "it" was something much larger than anything I grasped
that night.

With all the enthusiasm of an advertising man *malgré lui*,

Bill came back to the subject at our next session of cards; this time Catherine pointedly left the room. When we were again alone she burst out "Tell him to stop talking about this! Tell him so he won't do it again!"

But why, I wanted to know, wasn't it quite a good idea? "I'm not ready," said Catherine; "I'm just not ready." There was no mistaking her deep agitation and distress.

• • •

It was easy enough to tell Bill that I thought the subject should be deferred for a while. It was much more difficult to explain to him, or even to myself, *why*. But with the topic dropped, Catherine's spirits came back to normal and all was again as it had been since the happy wedding day. But the business of attempting to plan your life strikes me today as an exercise in sublime futility. You can plan 2 per cent of it, maybe, and it's probably your bounden duty to strive as hard as ever you can toward this maximum—but the other 98 per cent *happens*. Life ain't neat. And it happened to Catherine and me.

We had been married about a year and a half by the end of 1931. We were not too ignorant to know about things like diaphragms but we were both much too shy to mention the subject to a doctor of medicine. Our method for population control was simply postcoital douche, nor had it failed us.

Or, suddenly, had it? Catherine missed a period in late March or early April of 1932 and was mildly depressed. But such things occur, so we waited for another interval to elapse. It did, and nothing happened. "Come on," I said to my golden girl, "you're tired and run down. Let's go to Atlantic City for a long weekend of bracing salt air." So we did, and had a slightly subdued good time. But as Catherine was getting ready for bed the second night, I had a clear and complete view of her lovely female body, and the areolae of her breasts were unmistakably darkened. "Darling," I said to myself, "you're pregnant."

Back in New York it was obvious Catherine must consult her doctor. The Aschheim-Zondek test was a very reliable indicator for suspected pregnancy in those days and perhaps still is, but in the 1930's it somehow took the lab a long time to make its report. One morning just after breakfast, the telephone rang and Dr. Lewis wished to speak to Mrs. Hodgins. Catherine listened for scarcely a minute and fumbled to put the phone back on its cradle. Then she staggered to the nearest chair. "I'm pregnant," she said, with all the voice she could muster, which was scarcely any voice at all. She was shaking with panic.

•   •   •

My day at the office was correspondingly not very lighthearted. I confided the situation to my sentimental Irish boss. "Don't worry," Ken said. "We're going to find the goddamnedest best obstetrician in New York and that'll be that." Ken's own doctor was the distinguished internist Dr. William B. Rawls, who unhesitatingly recommended Dr. Hallie Mayo Ratliff as just the right man. Guided by some instinct, I looked him up in the mammoth Directory of the American Medical Association. He looked fine. He belonged to all the proper professional societies, and best of all he was "Clin. Prof. Obs., Poly. Post-Grad. Med. Sch. & Hops." I interpreted "Clinical Professor" to be the man who, directly under the head of the department, did the teaching, demonstration, and the great majority of the hard deliveries. So I went to see Dr. Ratliff and found him a pleasant man whose office turned out to be only a few blocks from where Catherine and I lived at 405 East 54th Street. I explained to him Catherine's panicky fear, and he was most reassuring. "That's a lot more common than most people realize. As a matter of fact this business is really half physiological and half psychological. I'll give your wife my first available appointment as soon as she asks for it. It's always good to get a case so early as this."

•   •   •

But would Catherine like him and be reassured? The answer turned out an unqualified Yes to the first half of the question, yet she continued not to be able to speak much above a whisper, and her mouth was still so dry with fear that she could barely choke down the little food she tried to eat. Things went on that way for some three months. Although Catherine had talked about wanting children before we were married, it was crystal-clear that she spoke the truth now when she said "I'm not ready."

One evening of her deep depression I took the bull by the horns and not without difficulty said, "Answer me truthfully. Is it an abortion that you want?" She shook her head in misery. I was glad, for although I didn't believe in sin, I thought *that* would

313

be a Sin against the Holy Ghost; we were happily married and I loved her deeply and felt I had every evidence that she loved me. And there were no financial problems. If Catherine were to be a willing mother then I was fully prepared to be a willing and happy father. Couldn't she tell me what the terrible trouble was? "I'll never make it," said Catherine.

That was a climax after which things grew easier, somehow. Catherine's spirits rose thereafter; she began to be able to talk and to eat almost normally. I relaxed—a little. But I went to see Dr. Ratliff again, sometime in September, to make my own report.

"Your wife is a fine, healthy girl," he said. "She has a good pelvis, and her abdominal measurements are exactly in accord with her calendar. And she's had no dizziness? No morning sickness, even? She hasn't reported any." I agreed; except for the psychological reaction, this pregnancy was completely uneventful and was to stay so. Only one thing: During a rainstorm Catherine had stumbled and fallen in the street, but picked herself up without difficulty.

"But afterward she had no pain or cramps or bleeding or anything else unusual?" asked Dr. Ratliff. No.

"I could take her to Doctors Hospital or about anywhere else when the time comes, but I'd much prefer her to be in Polyclinic. We have a fine team there, you know. The hospital's in a poor neighborhood, so we get a lot of tough cases there: women who've had absolutely no prenatal care and then get dumped on the doorstep practically in labor, and we've never even seen them before. So we have a very alert team; we have to. Of course, if you want a *fashionable* hospital . . ."

I said he could save his breath, except that I'd like to go and see Polyclinic.

"By all means," said Dr. Ratliff. "They'll be delighted. The sixth is the obstetrical floor." As we parted he gave me two mimeographed sheets of instructions: pack the hospital bag at least a month in advance and include the following things (long list). Dr. Ratliff had, after all, been in practice twenty years.

• • •

At Polyclinic they were indeed delighted to see me: here was a *customer*. In the 1970's, with hospitals bulging and the desperately ill parked in hallway cots, it strains memory and credibility close to the breaking point to realize that in the absolute Depression sump year 1933 most hospitals were more than half empty. The Polyclinic obstetrical floor was emptier than that. Women weren't having babies—or at least if they were, their husbands couldn't afford hospital care. So Miss Smith, the very pleasant day nurse in charge, was actually doing a selling job on me. "Come and look at the nursery first," she said. "In all New York you won't find a finer one than ours." Through the thick plate-glass windows I beheld a lovely room, sparsely sprinkled with pink and blue cherubs. Those that were squalling you couldn't hear.

"When's your wife due?" Miss Smith asked.

"Sometime in January."

"Let me show you some of our rooms. Here's one I'm *sure* she'd like." Miss Smith opened a door marked 603. The room was very nice. The number is to remain engraved on my mind for the rest of my days. "I can mark it reserved in her name right now, if you'd like. What's your address?"

So, three or more months in advance, that had all been taken care of.

As the weeks wore on, Catherine became almost like her old self—almost but not quite. She was wearing becoming maternity dresses but when the inevitable bulge began to appear she was not elated, as I had been told women usually were, at this evidence they were fulfilling their biological destiny. Instead, she was somewhat depressed. "It shows," she protested.

One evening, much later on, Catherine voluntarily brought up the whole subject, almost for the first time. "I've changed my attitude," she said. The elation I felt was short-lived: "I'm not afraid for myself any more; now I think the baby will never make it."

There was some parapsychology at work here, too deep for me. Outwardly things were much more normal. "Pregnancy becomes you, Mrs. Hodgins," said Bill Strong one evening. And indeed it did. Her fair hair shone; her high complexion glowed; she was the picture of health. That Bill Strong had dropped the idea of simultaneous parenthood, and was never to bring it up again, made me both sad and angry, but both these emotions I felt I had to suppress.

315

• • •

I thought occasionally still of the litany ". . . all women in child-birth, all sick persons, and young children . . ." but I had ceased to think about it very much. After all, this was the twentieth century. Also a new kind of worry had entered my mind. Anyone who thinks that "crime in the streets" originated in the 1960's has another think coming. There was plenty of it in the 1930's, but of a wholly different kind. First, the gangsters and racketeers of Prohibition, and their triggermen, roamed the streets more or less at will; holdups and armed robberies flourished in the complaisant Tammany Hall administration of Jimmy Walker. Catherine and I once watched helpless from our twelfth-floor apartment window while two gunmen across First Avenue shot down a cop and left him dying on the sidewalk. Furthermore, the city was full of despairing men, driven by total destitution to do *anything* to gain as much as fifty cents.

Catherine's Time was coming in mid-January, and as the date approached, a second anxiety arose in my mind. It was that her pains would begin in the small hours of the morning, during a blizzard, and we couldn't get to the hospital. The other was that our taxi would be stopped and robbed—not at all an uncommon occurrence. I could do nothing against the first contingency save deprecate it; against the second, I had a plan. I would have fifty dollars in my pocket—a large 1933 sum—and if we were held up I would instantly hand it over and explain things to the thugs; in my imagination they would understand and let us go. I was centered completely on the goal of reaching the hospital safely: once there, I felt worries would be over.

• • •

Early in the morning of January 19, Catherine woke me in alarm at about 2 A.M. "I'm all wet, and I'm frightened," she said. I knew enough to know that the amniotic sac had ruptured, so I straightaway called Dr. Ratliff. "Get her to the hospital now; I'll phone ahead so they'll be expecting you."

So Zero Hour had come. We got dressed and got downstairs and discovered God was good; although the streets were rutty with old snow, they were passable, and at 2:30 A.M., there sat,

316

right in front of the apartment entrance, a lighted and empty taxi; the driver had been there for about four hours, he told us, hoping for a fare. So the first worry dissolved. Ten minutes later the second one had vanished too; the trip had been bouncy, but no footpads had appeared and we were safe in front of Polyclinic's entrance. I heaved a vast sigh of relief as the elevator took us to the sixth floor; I remember being somewhat surprised but in no way alarmed that Catherine needed a wheelchair. She was soon in 603's bed and I, by invitation, took a chair inside the nursing station; the Depression had made hospital routines pretty casual. Soon a young resident came in in answer to a call from Dr. Ratliff. "No, sir," I remember hearing him say, "she is not in labor; that is correct, she is *not* in labor."

I forget what I did with the hours until 8 A.M.; Catherine had been mildly sedated and was drowsy so the best thing for her was to leave her alone. By 8:30 Dr. Ratliff had examined her and came out to see me. "Things are moving very slowly. My advice to you is go home and get some rest. There won't be much point in coming back here until evening—maybe around six."

So I left but I didn't go home. I knew I couldn't sleep and I had no desire to take off my clothes and lie down. I walked aimlessly along 50th Street and found myself abeam the Roxy Theater, whose doors had just opened at 9:30. I suddenly knew what I would do: I would blow seventy-five cents for a loge seat and go in and rest there in the dark until the show started. I may have broken all records for continuous attendance, for I didn't leave there until after 4 P.M.—and of what was on the screen I had no faintest idea.

I was back at Polyclinic by five thirty. Still very little progress. Catherine was awake but somewhat confused by sedation. "I can't understand why I'm not home getting dinner," she said—and then suddenly vomited.

Dr. Ratliff appeared and looked Catherine over. Then to me he said, "Go out and have a *leisurely* dinner. There won't be anything doing here until around nine o'clock at the earliest." He proved a most accurate prophet. There was nothing doing until nine thirty. Meanwhile, I had tried to have a leisurely dinner at Beefsteak Charlie's, across the street. At 9:45 there was a flurry around Catherine's room and in a little while out came the stretcher with her white-draped figure. Following were a resi-

317

dent, the anesthetist and Dr. Ratliff, who gave me a cheery wave: "It won't be long now."

• • •

• • •

"*How* long?" I wanted to know of a passing nurse. "Oh, about half to three-quarters of an hour." The conventional period of chain-smoking had now arrived. The wicker-chaired alcove for expectant fathers was off one end of the corridor that provided entrance to Room 603; at the extreme other end were doors marked "Delivery Room A" and "Delivery Room B." There another corridor made an L with 603's; in the corner of the L stood the nursing station. But unless you poked your head around the fathers' alcove, which I did frequently, there was nothing to see, except, through one window, the blank winter darkness of mid-West Manhattan, mixture of speakeasy and slum.

It grew to be more than half an hour, and more than three-quarters, but there was no sign of activity, anywhere. I was the solitary occupant of the fathers' alcove. With increasing frequency I peered down the corridor toward Delivery Room A. The past-due minutes grew to fractions of an hour, and then to still larger fractions. I had taken to lighting a cigarette, taking two shallow puffs, snubbing it out and instantly lighting another. It was getting to be pretty hard going, this business of waiting, with no one even in view to ask a question of. Why had Catherine been in Delivery Room A for almost two hours now? As I looked at it, its door suddenly burst open and a nurse emerged, running full tilt down the other leg of the L. She must have been gone no more than thirty seconds when, still running as fast as she could, she was back again, the delivery-room door slammed behind her. This was scarcely reassuring. I think I must have slumped into one of the alcove's wicker chairs in an effort to control my shakes; in any event I cannot account for the next twenty minutes to half an hour. In this interval it must have been that Catherine's stretcher had been wheeled back to Room 603. But in whatever never-never land I had temporarily been, I snapped back to reality when I saw Dr. Ratliff, still in his whites, come down the corridor toward me. My instant impression was that he looked drained and exhausted. But his first words were reassuring: "Well, everything's all right," he said. My

318

trembling began to subside. "But we had a close call," he went on, "and for a while I was afraid we were going to lose the baby. It was the kind of situation where if this had been a home delivery we'd have been *absolutely* out of luck." The italics were his.

I did not know where to begin asking questions, except that I wanted to know, Is Catherine all right? Yes, she is, said the doctor. "But things went very slowly, and of course it was a dry birth, as we say. The baby's heart rate began going down so low I had to make it an operative delivery." I thought of course he meant a Caesarean section. "No, no," he said. "No surgery. I reached in with my hands, turned the baby around and took him out by his feet. It's called a version."

My heart lightened again. Only later did I realize that the conventional first question—"Boy or girl?"—had been completely skipped over and that only Dr. Ratliff's use of the masculine pronoun had made me aware that Catherine and I were now the parents of a son.

"Because it was an operative delivery your wife will be in shock when she comes to, so you won't be able to see her for two or three hours, but at least you can relax." Then he left me to change his clothes. Just as I was wondering what to do with another two to three hours of nothing, a nurse invited me into Delivery Room A to see my infant son get weighed. He set a husky mark: eight pounds twelve and three-quarter ounces. This established, and with my spirits completely rebounded, I telephoned Boston to tell Catherine's parents that they had a new grandson and all was well. I didn't go into further details.

No sooner had I received their drowsy but fervent expressions of love to all than *I* had a telephone call. The charge nurse said, "There's a friend of yours, a Mr. Strong, down in the lobby. He can't come up here, but you can go down to see him, and he says he has a bottle of Jersey Lightning with him for celebration." This was a total and delightful surprise. In the first place it was now 11:15, rather late at night for Bill. That Bill was toting a flask of applejack was even more surprising, for alcohol interested him almost not at all.

In the lobby we embraced each other; Bill pulled the cork and I took a mighty slug of applejack direct from the bottle. Bill followed with a more decorous sip, and we both settled down

319

on a hard oak bench to watch the sluggish night life of the Polyclinic. A well-dressed but roaring drunk was dragged in by three friends, presumably to be put to bed after a heavy enough dose of paraldehyde to knock him out. Two cops brought in a workingman in painter's clothes, holding a dripping bloody rag to his right eye. Emergency room.

Despite this traffic and the applejack, time, the minimum two hours of it that must pass before I could hope to see Catherine, passed very slowly. I could not believe that the hands of my wrist watch could seem so unmoving. But Bill was resolved to stay with me until this had happened, even though this might be at 1:15 A.M. or even 2:15. On the dot of 1:15 I excused myself from Bill and made for the elevator. The orderly on duty looked me over casually and said, "I can't take you up until you give me a check for seventy-five dollars."

Was I going crazy? What had I heard? I managed to ask what this was about. "The doctor has ordered a blood transfusion for your wife," said the orderly. With a shaking hand I managed to write the check. I knew just enough about such things to be aware that the need for a transfusion after a delivery was anything but a good sign. I managed to tell Bill what was going on and to say, "A transfusion in obstetrics—that's rockets at sea." Then I went to the sixth floor.

• • •

• • •

Dr. Ratliff, now in his street clothes, met me at the elevator door. "She's not doing so well," he said. "The uterus isn't contracting properly; that's why I've ordered a transfusion."

I staggered as if he had struck me a physical blow. Simultaneously, two other blows struck. All the bureaus and tables had been moved out of Room 603 and were in a disorderly pile across the hall from its door. I knew why. It was to make room for the blood donor's cot.* Only my death will obliterate the memory of this sight. And at the same instant I heard Catherine's normally quiet voice. It cried out in agony the single word *"Oh!"*

I had to be put someplace, but that was easy. A private room,

---

* It may be necessary to remind younger people that in 1933 there were no such things as blood banks. A transfusion was then an emergency operative procedure and that was that.

next door to the nursing station, had so long been unoccupied that it was being used for some sort of experimentation; it still had a bed and chair but the whole bureau top was covered with an elaborate assemblage of laboratory glassware. The charge nurse led me into it and then broke all the rules by giving instructions that Bill Strong should be brought up to join me there.

The compassion of the nursing staff that night stood sharply out against the callousness of the night orderly who, representing the Administration, had demanded seventy-five dollars as the price of taking me to the sixth floor. (Somehow, in hospitals then as now, no matter how desperate the emergency, *someone* never forgets the Money Angle.) One or another of the nurses would drop in for a moment's call from time to time; it was obvious that the whole sixth floor was mobilized in Catherine's behalf. Later, Dr. Ratliff appeared for a brief moment; of him Bill Strong demanded "some sort of sedative" for me. "I mustn't stay here," the doctor said; "I've got to be with her."

At that moment a nurse came in and I overheard her whispered remark: "Dr. Ratliff, the second donor is on his way." They both left the room together, and I was again alone with Bill. In due course another nurse arrived with a two-ounce glass of something for me. It had as much effect as so much distilled water. So, for that matter, had the applejack. I knew for sure now, if I hadn't known before, that things were in a state of desperate emergency. I dropped to my knees against the bed and prayed, feeling devious and hypocritical as I did: I had not paid any tribute or attention to God for twenty years; now I was suddenly asking His Divine Intervention. As I rose again my eye fell on that laboratory glassware and a wild urge went through me to send it all crashing to the floor with one sweep of my arm. I suppressed the urge, and was often to wonder later what would have happened inside me if I had not. Terror and rage were so mixed up within me that there was no distinguishing between them.

Dr. Ratliff came in again, briefly, in about half an hour. "I don't hear anything," I said vacantly. "No," he answered. "I've had to give her quite a bit of morphine; she's terribly restless." He left again. Later I was to learn that an uncontrollable restlessness is a prime accompaniment of massive hemorrhage.

Duly (I didn't know what time it was by now) another nurse came in. I was beyond speech. "How is she?" Bill Strong demanded. "I think she's just the tiniest, *tiniest* little bit better," said the nurse. Here was the first straw to clutch. It was wispy and sodden, but I clutched. And again I prayed, and again that crushing feeling of hypocrisy overcame me: this scoffer who was I, suddenly appealing to an Almighty because I was face to face with an Ultimate.

The everlasting minutes kept dragging and dragging by. Another nurse came in, bearing, unbidden, another two-ounce glass of liquid. "Dr. Ratliff wants you to have this," she said. I wanted it to be hemlock, but it wasn't. Bill Strong was now as numb as I. We had been sitting silent, looking at the floor for I don't know how long when Dr. Ratliff entered the room for the third time. When he spoke his voice was very low. "Now, Mr. Hodgins, you've got to be very, very brave." I looked at him and forced a question past my lips. "You mean it's all over?"

A century elapsed.

"Yes," he said, "it is."

• • •

And yet the compensations of calamity are made apparent to the understanding also, after long intervals of time . . . a mutilation, a cruel disappointment, a loss of wealth, a loss of friends, seems at the moment unpaid loss, and unpayable. But the sure years reveal the deep remedial force that underlies all facts. The death of a dear friend, wife, brother, lover, which seemed nothing but privation, somewhat later assumes the aspect of a guide or genius; for it commonly operates revolutions in our way of life, terminates an epoch of infancy or of youth which was waiting to be closed, breaks up a wonted occupation, or a household, or style of living, and allows the formation of new ones more friendly to the growth of character. It permits or constrains the formation of new acquaintances and the reception of new influences that prove of the first importance to the next years; and the man or woman who would have remained a sunny garden-flower, with no room for its roots and too much sunshine for its head, by the falling of the walls and the neglect of the gardener is made the banian of the forest, yielding shade and fruit to wide neighborhoods of men.

—Ralph Waldo Emerson, "Compensation"

• • •

In Mount Auburn Cemetery, Cambridge, Massachusetts, there is a stone with lettering designed by her architect-father that reads: Catherine Carlson Hodgins ✝ 1903–1933. Behind it lie her ashes, and it is my hope that when the appropriate time comes, space can be found for mine to lie beside them. The infant she bore, never knowing she had, never knowing whether son or daughter, is now a man older than I was at his birth; happily and successfully the father of a son and a daughter.

In Catherine's tragedy there were four major sufferers. First and foremost was my son Roderic, for the loss of a mother is the heaviest psychological blow a child can sustain. Next came Catherine's father and mother, for the loss of a child is the hardest psychological blow parents can suffer. This leaves me, properly, last, for I was the only one of the four involved to whom was given at least the theoretical chance to compensate, to rebuild and reshape my life. That I made a hash of the job is neither here nor there: the *possibility* existed.

I don't know why I never took my immediate agony to a psychiatrist; I knew the breed existed, few of them as there then were. I suppose I must have thought they were on hand to deal with people who had become disconnected from reality rather than those who were suffering from too much of it. Although I knew the words of Emerson's essay "Compensation" from school-boy days, I could not carry the tune. What help I got came from amateurs and friends, some of them very wise. I remember the eloquent sentences of a much older man: "Look, the volume is closed. It was a lovely volume, but now you should place it reverently on your treasure shelf, instead of which you've got the binding torn off and the pages scattered all over the floor." He was quite right, but I was not ready for cure by metaphor.

• • •

One of the most awful things about the days and weeks of 1933 that followed was that I could not weep: I was dry-eyed as a stone. Also, a large steel ball was lodged right in the middle of my chest; it was difficult to force speech upward past it or food downward below it. But soon I made a discovery. If I had always been fond of alcohol I had used it as most other people do; and if I used too much of it, as I more than occasionally did, the classic reaction occurred: I threw up and the celebration was over. Now I began to use alcohol in quite a different way—as a drug. Two cocktails at a speakeasy favored by the *McCall's-Redbook* staff and the steel ball began to dissolve. I didn't want company, and I couldn't have stood conviviality, so after the two cocktails the bartender would sell me a pint of "rye" the color of blackstrap molasses, and with it I would make for the hotel room I had gone to live in after I had dismantled and abandoned forever the apartment where Catherine and I had lived. In the solitude of this room I would pull the cork of the rye bottle with my teeth, tip the bottle up, and let three gurgles down. I had my typewriter with me, and on it I would begin to write letters to Catherine just as if she were able to receive them, and keep it up until I could no longer hit *any* of the right keys. Then I would settle down with the bottle in true earnest, and soon a moisture—a blessed moisture—would come into my eyes. At the next stage, tears would begin rolling down my cheeks and I would by then have achieved a certain measure of "relief"; but my true objective was to drink until I was racked with sobs, so racked that I would have to put a pillow over my head so that I would not be heard. After some indeterminate time I would go to sleep. When I waked up in the morning, my eyes would be red but dry, the steel ball back in the middle of my chest and the rye bottle empty. I would then have a glass of milk for breakfast and go to the office. It was *a* way of life. Physiologists may wonder—and so do I—that I could stand it. It could not continue, and it did not, but I cannot remember how long this phase lasted. Alcohol was to do many things for and to me during the ensuing years, but one thing it was never, never to do again. In my future there lay hospitalizations from alcohol, one case of D.T.'s from alcohol, suicidal impulses from alcohol, near-death from alcohol—but *nausea* from alcohol? No, never again.

38 · SHARING, OR,
"EIN MAGAZIN VOR DER KRIEGSPFAD"

I WAS BACK at the *Redbook* office a week after Catherine's death, except, of course, that I wasn't there at all. "A fixation, deflection or deficiency in the power of attention"; that's the nonclinical dictionary definition of neurosis, and my power of attention was affected on all three counts. It was fixed on Catherine, it was deflected from everything else and its deficiency was almost total. People would come and talk to me, and I would nod as if I were listening. And I thought I was, except that if they paused to ask a question I would realize I had no faintest idea of what they had been talking about.

After the night of his birth, I did not see my infant son again for more than a week. I could not formulate any idea of how to cope with the problems of a home destroyed at the very moment that had been thought to be the true beginning of "family" life. Catherine's father and mother wanted to take the baby, and I asked myself, fruitlessly, if there was any other solution. There was, of course, but I could not face it. It was that I should return alone to the home Catherine and I had made together, hire a nurse and a housekeeper, and take my infant son to live with me there. When, overwhelmed, I made the decision against this and agreed that Catherine's father and mother should take the baby, God alone knows, and no one else ever will, whether I did the wise, right and proper thing or its reverse. But so it was decided, and the one passionate desire I had was to dismantle—no, to *wreck*—the apartment where Catherine and I had lived. It was years before I gained an insight into why that was so overwhelming a desire. It was one of the few, the very few, things I really learned from psychoanalysis.

325

• • •

Meantime, Roderic Carlson Hodgins, age eight days, was no longer in the Polyclinic Hospital. Later in the day of Catherine's death, I had, at the urgings of the friends who rallied round me in Bill Strong's apartment, signed a number of papers in blank, and above one of my signatures Catherine's closest friend and fellow Smith alumna, Emily Judson Hooper, had written a letter to the Polyclinic Hospital authorizing herself and her husband to assume custody of the baby and place him under the care of her own baby daughter's pediatrician at St. Luke's Hospital. This had been accomplished while I was in Boston, Harold Kennedy at my side, at Catherine's funeral services.

Now, back in New York, "Hoop" (the inventor of the "Hoop-erating," which all students of advertising and marketing history will remember), his wife, "Judy," and I were in a taxicab to-gether, northbound to St. Luke's, so that I could have my first real look at my infant son. I remember that taxi ride quite well, for an interesting reason. I insisted that Hoop and Judy take the broad seat while I perched on one of the jump seats at right angles to them, my back leaning against the left-hand door. (Taxis carried seven passengers then, when there were no pas-sengers.) All of a sudden the taxi had to make so violent a swerve that the latch of the door against which I was leaning burst open, and instead of sitting up I was suddenly horizontal, the lower half of my body still in the cab, my chest, shoulders and head hanging face up over the cobblestones of First Avenue. It was a terrifying experience—but not to me. Hoop and Judy lunged for my arms and hauled me back into the cab, now stopped, then paused to catch their breath and mop their faces. It was I who felt no trace of fear, and whose pulse rate did not flicker. My emotions were dead. I remember only a vague disappoint-ment that I had not been pitched out of the cab and effectively run over by a following truck.

• • •

At St. Luke's the pediatrician, a Dr. Stevens, whom Judy had enlisted, led me to my infant son, still behind plate glass. "He has something of a birth injury," said Dr. Stevens, "which is why his head and neck deviate to the left, but all his reflexes

326

are normal. I'll go inside and demonstrate what we call the Monkey Reflex."

Anyone can demonstrate the Monkey Reflex on the newborn, but you have to have your nerve to try, and it is wise to be an M.D. The doctor simply touched his two rigidly outstretched forefingers to the baby's fists, which uncurled to grasp them. Then, with those forefingers, the doctor lifted the baby into the air, the baby clinging to the fingers, literally for dear life.

Dr. Stevens discussed the plans for moving the baby to Boston, but it was Judy and he who did most of the talking. During the several years that stretched into a long and seemingly black thereafter, I was to make biweekly trips to Boston and watch my young son, in the care of his grandmother and a nurse, slowly grow up. He had the benefit, in Boston, of the Dr. Spock of his day, Dr. Dick Smith, who one day gently took the baby's head between his hands and twisted it slowly to and fro. There was heard a tiny click—and thereafter the baby's head stood upright on his shoulders.

• • •

In New York, my days as a salesman were slowly, thank God, drawing to a close. The Shadow Campaign was having a good effect on *Redbook*; if it wasn't increasing linages (which by now were plummeting for everybody, except for those impudent kids at ten-year-old Time Inc.), it was at least making *Redbook* talked about in agency circles and to an extent that was beginning to make the *McCall's* salesmen sore. A deputation of them waited on Vice-President John Sterling with the request that the *Redbook* campaign be stopped, but Sterling ruled that the magazines must compete just as vigorously as if they were not jointly owned, and that was that.

But then another threat to the campaign arose. It was a highly complimentary threat but a heavier one: *Saturday Evening Post* salesmen, obviously on instruction, for space buyers reported they were all taking to carrying proofs of the *Redbook* ads in their own kits, hauling them out in front of The Prospect and saying "This tells the right story; the trouble with it is that it's signed by the wrong magazine. It *really* applies to the *Post*." This was an attack from a new salient, and very hard to counter; the only consolation was that now the salesmen for the *Ladies' Home*

Journal were just as sore as the *McCall's* peddlers. All this I would have enjoyed immensely if only I had had anyone to share it with when I went home at night.

Something else that needed sharing occurred to the Shadow Campaign that year: it got translated into German. A prewar German magazine devoted to advertising, typography and other allied arts up and published an article about the campaign—*"Ein Magazin vor der Kriegspfad"* ("A Magazine on the War-path")—photoreproduced some of the ads in English and rendered a few more into the language of Goethe, where, I must say, they carried the air of unassailable authority that only German black letter can convey to someone who can't read it well.

Perhaps it was this—it could have been anything, so far as I cared—that shifted me out of selling and made me, for a brief period, promotion manager of the McCall Company, responsible for *McCall's* as well as *Redbook*. Bill Strong and I devised between us a new campaign for *McCall's* based on an idea that seemed vigorous and relevant at the time, but now seems so tired, out of date and silly-from-the-beginning that I can't bring myself to mention it. And besides, my tenure as promotion manager was extremely short.

• • •

• • •

By now, my tears over Catherine were exhausted. But some months later something else happened to reopen the wound, and to raise all over again the haunting and unanswerable question: Did it *have* to happen? Although I could never bear to see Dr. Ratliff again, I did pay a long call on his chief, Dr. Ross McPherson, head of the Department of Obstetrics at Polyclinic and thus Dr. Ratliff's immediate superior.

"Your wife died of hemorrhage shock," he said. He spent two hours with me discussing Catherine's case, with which he turned out to be intimately familiar, and the upshot of it all was that her death had been unavoidable—"It was in the cards." Then why, I wanted to know, had Dr. Ratliff asked me the question "Did she have any sisters?" only *after* the battle had been lost and we were both staring at the floor in the room filled with

328

the laboratory glassware? Dr. McPherson was obviously taken aback by this one, so despite the earnestness and deep sympathy with which he treated me I was still left asking myself the question, "Have I been told the truth?" So I sought out a Dr. Walter Dannreuther, who had no connection with Polyclinic, but who happened to be President of the American Board of Obstetrics and Gynecology. Despite my being a complete stranger, asking him for information on something he knew nothing about at first hand, he received me, and I encountered a distinguished man with an ice-cold personality. Curiously, that was just what I needed, for with my friends I had been wallowing, but there could be no wallowing with this man. He asked me questions about Catherine's case and answered them as if we were talking of something that had been a textbook case in 1800. Curiously, it helped. Toward the end, he warmed up about 2 degrees. "*Every* pregnant woman represents a potential major surgical risk," I remember him saying. Although there was not much consolation in that, he diverted me better by telling me some of the strangenesses of Chance in his profession. "For example," he said, "as a fledgling doctor my very first unsupervised case was the delivery of *triplets*. Well, my principal teacher had been old Dr. Blank, who had delivered thousands and thousands of babies and hundreds and hundreds of twins. And after he retired he would travel miles at his own expense whenever it was rumored that a multiple birth might be expected. But he died at eighty without ever having seen triplets born—and I got triplets on my very first case. That's the kind of business we're in. You've got to expect *anything*."

• • •

There was consolation here—up to a point. But what had reopened the issue of Catherine's tragedy was that in mid-1933 the Commonwealth Fund had published the results of a five-year study of Maternal Mortality in New York and of who was to blame for figures far inferior to most of Europe's. The startling— and to me horrifying—conclusion of the study was that the attending physician was the culpable person in 67 per cent of the deaths, the other 33 per cent being distributed among midwives, nurses, the patient herself or "others." Thus was revived all the torturing doubt I had: *Was someone to blame?* I don't know what

I would have done with this information if I had ever been able to come by it; if there had been culpability, and it had been establishable, surely this would have been new salt in the wound. Even as it was, I had two fantasies: in the first I would murder Dr. Ratliff in his office and then call the police; in the second I would murder him and then turn the gun on myself. It was obvious that I needed psychotherapy pretty badly, but as I have recorded, I did not know where or how to turn to it. This was to come later—much later.

• • •

Meanwhile, another and conflicting personal problem was presenting itself—sexual starvation. For weeks and even months after Catherine's death I believed I would remain unmarried and chaste ever thereafter—a thought just about as healthy as my fantasies of murder. Since I was thirty-three when I made the "vow," it will not be surprising that I was thirty-four when I broke it—and I do not mean to give the impression that my chastity lasted a calendar year, either. It lasted, in fact, less than six months.

The girl was Anne (whose real name was not Anne but that name will do here). She made her solicitude for me quite evident, and one evening when for once I had had all the solitude I could stand, I asked her out for dinner. We dined and then went from speakeasy to speakeasy, getting ourselves gently, quietly but thoroughly plastered. I think our evening must have begun at 7 P.M.; it is somehow given to me to remember that it was about 3 A.M. when I brought her to her apartment door. We had embraced in taxicabs, the darker corners of speakeasies and such other havens as the evening afforded, and I was aroused—for the first time in what seemed like many months. So, I felt alcoholically convinced, was she. So I did not propose or intend to go home now. Anne proposed that I should. There began a sexual struggle. It went on for an hour or more, and to compress it all into two words, I won.

The acrobatic night turned out to be the beginning of a two-year intimacy. Anne later explained what I was too inflamed to realize at the time—"You know what men think of girls they can push over the first time they try." But as a matter of fact, I didn't. Never in my life before had I "pushed" a girl "over";

330

never in my life was I to do such a thing again. Other things, yes—but not that.

• • •

The picture of me as a quasi rapist has its comic aspects now; in fact, it did then, in view of my soberly correct and slightly shy and formal manner in the office. If *I* was a whited sepulcher, I reasoned, everyone must be. I wondered about Mr. Warner, Balmer, and even little Donald Kennicott, who, like me, bore an associate editor's title on *Redbook* but actually spent most of his time editing *Blue Book*.

• • •

• • •

Meanwhile, I couldn't go on in the office, not as I was going. One of two people took mercy on me. It was probably Ken but it *might* have been Francis Hutter, secretary of the company, with whom I had, through sheer accident and good luck, struck up an acquaintance. However it came about, Edwin Balmer came into my office coop one day to ask me, officially, to come back to the editorial side of the business and become an associate editor of *Redbook*. He was obviously acting under instructions, for our acquaintance had been merely a speaking one. Nevertheless, his invitation was cordial, and whatever was happening, I was not being rammed down his throat. Let me assume, without knowledge, that it was Mr. Hutter, for as one of the small handful of people with the McCall Company in those days who had any spark of interest in him, he deserves some description.

Francis Hutter was an Austrian who had fled Europe on the eve of World War I and landed in this country with the conventional single dime in his pocket and the equally conventional no-word-of-English. But he had been a printer of considerable sophistication in his native land and he held several patents of no small value, which made a number of entrepreneurs anxious to Berlitz him with all possible speed. Mr. Hutter was the aptest of pupils; very shortly he knew his English, although it stayed heavily accented and the pronunciation of *th* remained forever beyond him, but it was superadequate for the expression of any ideas he had, which were many. His printing presses and processes were of unique value to the McCall Company, for in the teens of the century, when its magazine was a blasted little thing selling for a nickel when the *Ladies' Home Journal* cost a full dime, the real source of its solvency lay in its pattern business. When properly managed, the dress-pattern business is an ideal hedge for a publisher who owns his own presses, for demand runs countercurrent to the general flow; in 1933 the further purchasing power declined the more women bought McCall patterns from which to make their own clothes.

Warner, president; John Sterling, vice-president; Francis Hutter, secretary; these were the only officers of the company in the Depression days, and only Mr. Hutter's side of the business was free of gnawing problems. Mr. Warner loathed Mr. Hutter—but there were those presses and those patterns. Unique at the time to the McCall's patterns was Mr. Hutter's "inventive difference"—patentable difference, profitable difference: the printed-on-the-pattrn allowance to be cut away as the woman used the pattern and cut out her fabric; it was this that made Mr. Hutter (barely) endurable to Mr. Warner.

• • •

Mr. Warner was tall, thin-faced, utterly proper, and, at a guess, highly constipated. Mr. Hutter was eccentric, voluble, and unquenchably lewd in thought and deed. He paid attention to the magazine part of the business when it pleased him; when he did, he would drop in on anyone without regard to rank or importance. He wandered into the *Redbook* advertising bull pen one day, and seeing the desk opposite mine unoccupied, sat down at it. "I dreamed ze ozzer night I was having sexual intercourse wiz an angel who had two waginas," said the secretary of the company to the novice space salesman, for openers. "And when I told my doctor he said, 'Ah, now we really know your idea of heaven.' " I offered the information (doubtless gleaned from the *National Geographic* when I was a Philadelphia schoolboy) that here on earth one need only be a kangaroo to experience Mr. Hutter's dream as a matter of reality.* He did not know this and was enchanted. He solicited my views of the transmigration of souls, and went on talking to me, his outward mien earnest, his every expressed thought lubricious in one startling

* The male kangaroo's penis is bifid; his mate's vagina has a septum.

way after another, for more than an hour. Not a word was spoken about publishing or advertising.

"Hutter spending that time with you, with everyone looking on," said a colleague afterward. "Boy, that's worth two thousand dollars a year to you right now." It wasn't, though. It did mean that the secretary of the company and I had mysteriously fallen into some sort of rapport. "What did he talk about?" my colleagues wanted to know. "Policy," I said, implying that the details would have been a breach of confidence, which, in a sense, was true.

Once every month or two Mr. Hutter would drop in for one of his aimless but always fascinating chats. When, then, I moved over to the editorial side of *Redbook*, he was far from a stranger to me. Things were now becoming so bad that even Mr. Warner was persuaded that some radical redesign of the magazine was called for. Otis Wiese had drafted the services of a then almost unknown young man, Henry Dreyfuss, to lift *McCall's* face, and the results had been good. Mr. Warner called Balmer, myself, and the new art editor, Sid Hydeman, into his office. John Sterling was also there, and then in strolled Mr. Hutter, whether by invitation or not I did not know. Mr. Hutter strolled where he pleased.

In those days, *Redbook* opened with an Inspirational Editorial by Bruce Barton. This was followed immediately by an eight-page insert, on coated paper, of beautiful girls, artfully and variously posed by the best sex photographers then to be found. Mr. Warner questioned the continuing worth of the section; coated paper, after all, was a heavy expense item. A silence fell, broken by Mr. Hutter. "I do not zinks," he said in his mildest tones, "zat ze importance of zeez aids to masturbation can possibly be over-emphasized." Mr. Warner turned inaudibly green, and shortly after prorogued his parliament, nothing having been settled, except by Mr. Hutter. And Mr. Hutter *did* cheer me up.

• • •

• • •

Nevertheless the editorial and art departments went hard to work to give *Redbook* some new dress and new content. The Dayton presses were redesigned so the front of the book, after the portfolio of girls, whose aid, on reflection, was considered important enough to offset the cost of coated paper, could consist of spreads each one of which could carry a second color. If the rotation of second colors was decreed for the first three spreads in a certain order, then that order could not thereafter vary. Hydeman and I knocked ourselves out pasting up a new dummy, lovingly slip-sheeted with tissue, and admired our handiwork. (Roughs and dummies always look better than the finished product; this is one of nature's laws.)

The morning came when *we* invited Mr. Warner to view our efforts, and in due course the great man sauntered in. He leafed through the whole book without saying a word. Then he went back to the beginning and started again. This time he mumbled somewhat. He was a great believer in the squelch as an instrument of executive control, so this time he applied it. He didn't like the dummy. Some pages he seemed not to disapprove of, but some others he flipped rapidly over, saying, "No, no, no!" Eventually, as with tongs, he dropped it back on Hydeman's desk, and made off—no suggestions, no specifics, just general disdain. Whatever wind had been in our sails before, they were empty and flapping now.

"Goddamn *him*," said Hydeman when Mr. Warner was safely vanished.

"Did you notice," Hydeman went on, "that every time he came to a blue spread, *that* was when he got sore?"

I hadn't noticed. "Well he did," said Hydeman. "I kept track. *Why*, do you suppose?"

I had no idea. Neither had Hydeman. He dropped the dummy listlessly on the desk and heaved a deep, deep sigh. "Maybe he got stuck with a hundred thousand pairs of blue underdrawers when he was with the J. L. Hudson department store in Detroit."

It was as good an explanation as any.

• • •

• • •

My, the difference it makes when your job shifts from selling to buying. The world of the so-called literary agent has a very efficient grapevine, so the word that somebody new was installed as an associate editor at *Redbook* reversed all of the last three years' polarities in a hurry. From trying to arrange lunches with reluctant advertisers and their agents I was suddenly shifted into the lunchee; some agent always had a hot new young writer who was exactly what *Redbook* needed and wanted. Once in thirteen blue moons this would turn out to be so. But at least it was interesting to observe the various techniques of approach the different agents used; they varied, of course, all around the compass, from the uninhibited use of phony social charm to the elaborately indifferent take-it-or-leave-it-and-see-if-we-care attitude of those who had been in the business long and had so many "properties" securely tied up that the attitude was genuine. Some agents would make genuine, conscientious and studious efforts to match manuscript to market; some were utter dopes about *any* manuscript until the subject of Money came up for discussion, whereat they became downright brilliant; some thought that the black-tie "literary" dinner was the route to *empressement*. These last I went to all the pains I could to avoid; I knew that solitude was bad for me, but that was what I wanted just the same.

• • •

Of the various literary agents I had to deal with, only a few remain in my mind, and these usually for odd reasons. Helen Everitt, then of Curtis Brown, was far and away the most intelligent and the most charming. My cause for remembering Jacques Chambrun was *not* because he was the son-in-law of Pierre Laval, but because he must have spent a fortune on typists, for every manuscript he ever submitted was pristine, in a pristine cover, suggesting thereby that you were the first to have seen it. But the agent I have cause to remember best of all was one Ben Wasson of the American Play Company, who one day visited me with a very dog-eared manuscript indeed.

Balmer and I had instituted in *Redbook* what we first called "A full-length Novel, Complete in this Issue"—even as Harford Powel had done when *The Youth's Companion* went monthly. We printed it on pulp stock at the extreme back of the book, with its own "cover" and the text rubricated with fake woodcuts or the like. It was full length when we bought it, all right, but by the time Donald Kennicott, on whom such chores fell, had finished cutting it, it was more likely two-thirds full, or in extreme cases not much more than half full. These novels were usually dogs to begin with, for book publishers were not then keen about what they called "one-shot serialization" of anything they thought had a real sales chance as a hard-cover book.

Some friends of mine had genially said, "Look out for Ben Wasson; he's a burglar!" But Ben bore few aspects of the burglar as he came in on a June morning with the extremely bedraggled manuscript of a novel, which looked as if it had been all the rounds twice and been turned down everywhere. And this was surprising indeed for the title page bore the name of an author far from unknown. "I thought this might just fit in nicely for your monthly novel," said Ben. I knew we could not afford what Ben would ask for it; despite what its tattered appearance confessed, I knew he would ask plenty.

I said I'd read it within the next few days, and when I did, I found myself in the midst of the best murder mystery I had ever in my life read. The manuscript was quite long and in addition to being fascinating was one of the most salacious pieces of prose I'd ever read up to then. Maybe that solved part of the mystery of why it hadn't found a ready magazine publisher. At any rate, these were the disadvantages I stressed to Ben before I told him, guardedly, that I liked it. "The price is twenty-five thousand dollars," said Ben.

My heart sank because I knew what I would have to say. "That's that, I guess. Our budget for these pieces is four thousand dollars, and Balmer will cut my balls off if I go to forty-five hundred dollars; I will, but that's the limit, and it's a shame."

"It certainly is," said Ben, in high dignity. "I wouldn't even convey such an offer; it would be an insult."

On that note we parted, and I was genuinely sad. I had read what I thought was a masterpiece of its genre, and it was beyond my reach. That was on a Friday.

On Monday morning Ben was on my phone. "I happened to talk to our author over the weekend," he said, *"and much to my surprise* [italics his] he was somewhat interested." Here he had to pause to clear his throat. "I wasn't aware of it but it seems that his cash position is a little tight right now, and if you could have a certified check for five thousand dollars in my hands soon enough to get to the bank before three P.M., one-shot serial rights to the manuscript could be yours."

"It's done," I said, not knowing whether it was done or I was fired. As soon as I'd hung up the phone I rushed in to Balmer.

336

"Edwin, I've busted the novel budget by one thousand dollars but please sign this requisition *now* and call up Brower [the company cashier] and put the heat on about the check certification. Then give me hell later." When I told Balmer what was up, he did all I pleaded, and did not give me hell. Mr. Warner, to whom all things both great and small eventually found their way, did, in a public corridor. But I didn't care. With the deposit of the certified check *Redbook* had successfully launched the long and profitable career of *The Thin Man* by Dashiell Hammett.

39 · HENRY ROBINSON LUCE, OR, BY WAY OF BROOKLYN

THE FAMILIAR COMBINATION of accident and coincidence that plays an almost daily role in life stepped up its pace as the dreary, awful year 1933 began drawing toward its close. But this time the combination led me into the major part of my professional career and the most significant associations of my life. A strange combination of forces in Paris, Berlin, Prague, and Brooklyn, New York, were to lead me into meeting Henry R. Luce, a decade after he and Briton Hadden had founded *Time*, The Weekly Newsmagazine. The path could not have been more roundabout.

In mid-1933 there one day came to my desk an article bearing the title "What Life Would Be Like Under a Dictatorship." This was timely not only because Hitler had been Chancellor for six months but also because nobody in the United States knew very much about him or about Nazism.

The article I now had in front of me was graphic. Its author was Guy Hickok, who was—and this must sound quaint now—Paris bureau chief for the Brooklyn *Daily Eagle*. He was not only a first-rate journalist; he had also the power of a good fictioneer. So he opened his article with an imaginary scene in the offices of *The Saturday Evening Post*. The "Whumpsy Party" was now in total control of the United States and the *Post*'s editor, then George Horace Lorimer, had just seen fit to publish an article that the Party Leader found not to his liking. Whereupon a gang of young Whumpsies, in whipcord uniforms and appropriate leather puttees, forces its way into Mr. Lorimer's presence, gives him a good physical roughing up, ransacks and vandalizes his office, and after a long interval leaves with the dark admonition that he'd better think twice before he committed such a heresy again.

Edwin Balmer liked the story as much as I did, so we bought it. But once we had scheduled it Balmer grew apprehensive. Talking in his machine-gun bursts he began voicing the fear that Hickok's vivid opening might offend George Horace's dignity, which was indeed granitic. Finally he could stand it no longer and strode into my office with a great idea. "Now this fellow Luce on *Time*—he's a young man. You know him?" No. "Well, no matter. Why don't you write him a letter and send a copy of the Hickok piece with it, and ask if we can substitute him and *Time* for Lorimer and the *Post?* Nice publicity; he could probably use it."

So ordered, I did just that. Several days passed, and then when my phone rang, a gruff voice greeted me. "This is Harry Luce. Funny coincidence. Friend of yours was talking to me about you just the night before I got your letter. You have lunch with me at the Cloud Club [atop the Chrysler Building] day after tomorrow?" I said I'd be delighted, but could we have the permission I'd asked for? Impatiently he said, "Sure, certainly, go ahead," and hung up with a bang.

• • •

Accordingly we met, and I encountered a young man with thinning red-blond hair, a stammer (the *m*'s and *w*'s were the letters that stuck in his throat), a plodding-through-snowdrifts gait, and an intensity of gaze and manner that were new to me. I have sought for a *Time*-like phrase to describe him, but sandy-shaggy was the best I could come up with. He was thirty-five, a year older than I. We exchanged no pleasantries about the weather; it was instantly obvious that if I had said it was a nice day it would have annoyed him since he had formulated no opinion about this, not having noticed. He studied the menu impatiently and barked his order. The instant that I did the same, he started in. "Well, the friend who spoke to me about you was Dan Longwell of Doubleday." I privately thought this was damn nice of Dan, since Dan had offered me a job with Doubleday four years earlier and I had turned him down. Rejected suitors usually give the permanent backs of their hands to such ingrates, but Dan had obviously done just the reverse of this and given me a fine build-up, although I had scarcely seen him since. But I kept my mouth shut; it was clear Mr. Luce was going to direct

339

the conversation. "Know anything about *Fortune?* Ever read it?" He plunged a fork into something he had not examined and waited for an answer. "Yes, Mr. Luce, I do, as a matter of fact. Your Mr. Alan Jackson sent me a letter in 1929 telling me about plans to publish *Fortune* and saying my name had been given him as a possible contributor and asking if I would like to call on him." I brought my sentence to a close there, not adding that a loving friend (it was Malcolm Johnson) had told me at the time that a letter from Alan Jackson indicated that I was considered Class B; that Class A prospects had gotten a similar letter, but from Luce himself.

"Well," said Luce, "go on. What happened?"

"It all petered out," I said. "I saw Mr. Jackson. I remember he showed me something called 'Trial Signatures Number Five' and suggested that if what I had seen appealed to me, why didn't I come back in a few days with a list of what I considered appropriate story suggestions." I paused, and it was obvious my tempo was too slow for Mr. Luce.

"Well, go on," he said. "What happened then? Did you come in with a list, or what?"

I saw I must speed up. "Yes, I did. I came back with a list of about twenty suggestions and Mr. Jackson went over them one by one. Of about half he said 'I don't think that's down our line' and about the other half he said 'We're already working on that,' so my list simply evaporated and that was the end of that."

Luce had a grunt that simply cannot be rendered into the Roman alphabet; you came to learn that it indicated impatience, displeasure or both. He issued one now.

"Well!" he said, post-grunt. "I guess that didn't leave you feeling very enthusiastic about us."

Incomprehensible Fate had delivered into my hands an ace, and now I played it.

"I admit that I was quite disappointed," I said, "but I began reading *Fortune* when it came out, and I felt very much honored when I found my name in an article I read in last December's issue."

"What?" said Luce. "What article? How come?"

I felt I could now afford to take my time. "It was in an article called 'Obsolete Men.' It had a lot of material taken from a book I wrote in 1932 called *Behemoth*. The article never mentioned the book, but it did refer to Hodgins and Magoun."

340

Luce put down his fork. "Did *you* write that book?" Obviously he had either read or skimmed it, without noticing the title page. "I kept telling Arch MacLeish he was using too much material from one source but he said 'But that's where the best material is.' Well, I'll be damned." This was my first knowledge that it had been the Great MacLeish who had quoted me; all *Fortune* articles in those days were unsigned.

I have never been particularly astute commercially, but this time I knew for sure I was in a sellers' market, so for the rest of the lunch I had the good sense to keep pretty quiet.

"*Fortune*'s come to the point of needing two managing editors," Luce said, "and I'm tired of being the other one. You know Mac Ingersoll?" I didn't, despite having been a contributor to *The New Yorker* when he was *its* M.E.; I had known only Ross, Katherine Angell and Wolcott Gibbs. The Ralph Ingersoll who was later to found *PM*, was, at the time of my lunch with Luce and for quite some years thereafter, known as Ralph McAllister Ingersoll and very proud of his genealogical connection with Ward McAllister of an earlier New York's Four Hundred. But the McAllister ornament went into an old attic trunk when the Proletariat came marching in.

Luce went on. He described to me *Fortune*'s problems and philosophies, subsequently to be so well set forth in *Time*. It made a fascinating story to me, coming as it did from its creator, here opposite me in person at the lunch table. I had never met a journalistic *creator* before; even the great Ellery Sedgwick of my Boston days had inherited the *Atlantic Monthly*, although, pre-Luce, he was probably the greatest creative editor of his day.

Suddenly Luce came to a halt. "Well," he said (most of his spoken sentences began with "Well" or "Hey"), "think over what I've told you. If you're more than fifty per cent interested you and I could have another lunch, with Ingersoll, maybe. If you're less than fifty per cent interested, that would be that."

I was about 225 per cent interested, but I kept my finger pressed down hard on my squelch button and after an abrupt goodby we parted.

I went back to my *Redbook* office in a high state of excitement, not all of it pleasurable. I had just met the most interesting man in all my encounters, and had apparently made a favorable impression on him. The hint was strong that maybe he was going to offer me a job if I took the further step he suggested. I had a contempt for my work at McCall's, and, what was more important, all my surroundings were a constant reminder of the personal tragedy I had suffered in January of that miserable year.

On the other hand . . . on the other hand, I had security where I was. I had been with McCall's for four years and I had been successful there. My boss had recommended me for $10,000 a year and was indignant when William Bishop Warner, then McCall's president, would allow only $9,000. In 1932, with the Depression steadily growing worse, everybody took a 10 per cent cut, which put me back to $8,100. Still . . .

• • •

I wrote Mr. Luce a polite note of thanks for lunch and found some cautious way of indicating that I was definitely more than 50 per cent interested in whatever he was thinking of. In consequence, Messrs. Luce and Ingersoll and I had our projected lunch. I well remember the day for many reasons, among which was that it was the day after Election Day, 1933; first anniversary of what F.D.R. had done to Herbert Hoover, and the day the newspapers bannered the news that Republican Congressman Fiorello H. La Guardia had clobbered Tammany Hall for the mayoralty of New York. But I can't remember that we spoke a word about politics beyond a remark of mine to my hosts: "I think it's only proper I should tell you that politically I incline toward the Left." Luce did not even grunt, and he certainly did not cross-question me, for I could scarcely have forgotten it if he had. A Luce cross-questioning was an unforgettable experience, as I was later to learn. Instead he faded into the background as much as Harry Luce in his nature ever could to give Ingersoll a chance to look me over. When he re-entered the conversation it was to raise the always delicate point of money: "Do you want to tell us what you'd expect in the way of salary, or what you're making now, or anything of that sort that would be helpful?"

A sudden wave of economic courage came over me, from where I don't know. I knew beforehand that the question was bound to come up, but I had gone to lunch without the foggiest idea of how I would answer it. So of the three of us I am certain I was the most surprised when I heard my voice saying, quite calmly, "From what I've gathered about the job and its responsibilities I should think it would be worth something between fifteen and twenty thousand dollars a year." I was conscious of a lightning-flash glance that passed between Luce and Ingersoll, but all Luce said was "Well, that gives us a sort of bracket on things, anyway," so the adrenalin supply continued its most unusual flow through my blood stream, and I took the initiative: "Are there provisions for stock options or anything like that?" I got a snap of an answer: "Not until a year of satisfactory service at a minimum." Shortly after, Luce ended the lunch, again abruptly. "Well, let's break up now and we'll all go back and think it over. I may get in touch with you in a week or so."

• • •

I walked back to my office in a what-have-I-done daze. I knew now for sure that I liked Mr. Luce enormously, Republican or not. My own veiled confession of non-Republicanism had not fazed him a bit. My outrageous bid to approximately double my present salary had produced *some* reaction; although I did not know what it was, at least it had not broken up the lunch in disorder. Of Ingersoll, I didn't know what I thought. From his facial expression I judged him to be a dull sort of fellow. I was only later to learn what a mistake *that* was.

By next day my adrenalin supply was all gone, and I spent the next seventy-two hours in a turmoil, one moment hoping ardently that the next ring on my phone would be Luce; the next, equally ardently hoping it wouldn't be. I had spent eleven years in the magazine business by now. I had resigned from one job; my second job had been shot from under me. Now I was in my third, and about to be offered—or else *not* offered—my fourth. If the offer did come and I accepted it, it would mean a jump across the widest puddle I had ever attempted. And I had lost the wife whose love and counsel would have strengthened and advised me; she had been dead not yet a year, and my mind's automatic reflex—"I *must* tell Catherine!"—had not yet been completely extinguished by the jagged fact that there was no longer any Catherine to tell.

• • •

In November's second week the call came from Luce. "Could you be in my office at eleven tomorrow morning? There are a couple of things I'd like to discuss." I could indeed, but next morning it turned out there was only one thing to discuss.

"We'd like to have you come with *Fortune*," said Luce, "and my frank purpose now is to persuade you to come at the lower salary figure you mentioned, and not the higher."

He was about to go on, but I interrupted him. I was not in awe of him—yet—his reputation was still smallish, and besides, he was wooing me. So I broke in on him. "Mr. Luce, I'm enormously complimented and attracted, and if by any chance my answer has to be No, I assure you that the decision will not turn on a matter of money." It so happened I meant it.

"Fine," said Luce. He had apparently expected something more extended from me and was relieved that he wasn't going to get it. "As a matter of fact," he said, "Ingersoll gets only sixteen thousand dollars, so you can see . . ."

At the time, I did not give that remark any very full faith or credit; I took it as a perfectly acceptable business fib. Not until almost two years later, when I succeeded Ingersoll as managing editor and thus came into possession of the budget sheets, did I have to eat my thoughts. The *Fortune* editorial payroll for the year 1933 was headed by "Ingersoll, R. McA., Man. Edit.—$16,000."

• • •

This last interview with Luce took a bare ten minutes. "How soon can you make up your mind?" I asked for a week, and got it. It was a terrible week. I had to confide in someone, but I didn't know who. I also had to tell my boss, *Redbook* editor Edwin Balmer, that I'd had a flattering offer from Henry Luce through a chain of events he, Balmer, had unwittingly started. Balmer and I were on good terms but had never been particularly palsy. But now he turned gratifyingly partisan. "I don't want to lose you," he said. "We've got to get you some more money."

Well, God knows he tried. But I was in an awful state. My impudent courage of a few weeks before had vanished completely, and in its place there flowered a week of rankest cowardice. I formed the pusillanimous conclusion, which fortunately I kept secret from everyone, that if the coldly genial Mr. Warner, sitting in his enormous Mussolini-like office down the hall, would raise me to $10,000, I'd offer Mr. Luce my heartfelt regrets, stay with

McCall's, continue to be thoroughly miserable on all fronts but—secure. Who knew what the inside of Time Inc. was really like? Certainly not I. I was ashamed of the decision I was making; nevertheless I was making it. And Balmer, by suddenly coming through with an offer of extraordinary generosity, reinforced it. "Look, I'm going to see Mr. Warner personally about this thing. As a matter of fact, they're paying me more salary than I need. I'm going to suggest to Mr. Warner that he cut me a little and boost you. That way it won't make a nickel's addition to the editorial budget."

I had never heard of anything so generous, and said so, yet at the same time I did not like it. I expostulated with Edwin Balmer, protesting his kindly plan. If he succeeded in it I would put myself under a feeling of perpetual obligation.

On two counts I might well have saved my breath.

Balmer dropped in on me a day later. "I didn't get as far as I would have liked with Mr. Warner," he said, "but he wants to see you himself."

So the Moment of Truth was approaching. It was typical of the "techniques of executive control" of those days that despite four years with McCall's I had never before been in Mr. Warner's office, except as a sightseer invited by his secretary when he was out of town. But now, today, I was there by his invitation—nay, his command—and seated beside his desk.

I had a few reasons for not respecting Mr. Warner very much, but the deep seat of my carefully concealed disrespect was that, again typical of the 1920's, his preparation for being the head of a large publishing enterprise was that he had been an executive of a large department store—J. L. Hudson, in Detroit—where, the bitter Sid Hydeman had previously speculated, he must have been stuck with 100,000 pairs of blue underdrawers. In short, he didn't know a single damn thing about editing or publishing and was thus the diametrical opposite of Henry R. Luce. So I considered myself a pro and Mr. Warner an ignorant outsider—*amateur*, meaning lover-of-the-game, being much too complimentary. But I also realistically knew that he was the Admiral and I, at very best, was a lieutenant commander, junior grade. One is respectful.

"I understand," said Mr. Warner, looking at me with his cool blue eyes, "that you have received an Outside Offer."

345

I said, "Yes, sir."

"I don't know what Mr. Balmer was thinking of in recommending a salary increase, because both he and you should know that under the present economic circumstances, to speak only of them, it's quite out of the question."

Curiously, happily, my inner tensions began to unwind.

"Many of our better men have received Outside Offers, from time to time, but practically without exception they have preferred to remain with our clean-cut McCall organization."

At that I relaxed completely and was delighted to realize that the word "horseshit" was echoing and re-echoing in my mind. Mr. Warner had just made for me the decision I had been too cowardly to make for myself. To my discredit I think I said something like "I understand." *What* a liar! The McCall organization was about as clean-cut as a rip in the seat of the pants.

Mr. Warner shifted his gaze to one of the windows that gave him the whole northward sweep of upper Park Avenue. "It is only fair to tell you," he said, "that anyone who leaves our organization never comes back."

That did it. My calm was completely restored. "Thank you very much, Mr. Warner," I said; "I don't think that leaves anything more to discuss." I bowed my farewell.

Compared to my previous mood, I was now walking on air. As soon as I made my report to a regretful Edwin Balmer I telephoned Harry Luce to say the die was cast. We made another appointment to talk practicalities.

Word of firings or leavings gets about offices pretty quickly, so it was only the next day that Otis Wiese, then the boy-wonder editor of *McCall's*, six years my junior, damn him, poked his head in my doorway. Otis, although highly successful and totally secure at *McCall's*, had his own reservations about Mr. Warner and his Clean-Cut Organization and felt no constraint in expressing them. "I hear you're leaving us for Time Inc.," he said. I nodded assent. "Gee, that's *swell*," said Otis. "Did you have to take much of a salary cut to do it?"

I said it was nothing substantial. *What* a liar!

40 · PROHIBITION'S END, or, CHILDS RESTAURANT RISEN

THE FIRST QUESTION Harry Luce wanted to know of me was, obviously, when I would report for work. It was now more than halfway to the end of November 1933. I said I'd like to take a month off between the ending of my old job and the beginning of my new one.

"Where would you go?" Luce asked.

"To Europe," I answered.

"Well, with winter coming on, I imagine you'd pick the Southern Route?"

I allowed how that would make good sense, although my plans were so vague I hadn't really thought about it.

"In that case," said Luce, leaning back in his chair, "you'd be going to Italy, and that would be just fine—because *Fortune* is planning a single-subject issue on Italy sometime in the spring and you could be a sort of advance man if you felt like it."

I said I felt like it. The results of that lighthearted remark were not to be revealed to me until later, some time later, nor was I yet acquainted with all the computerlike qualities of the admirable Luce mind. For the moment, that was merely that.

Meanwhile, I had a telephone call from Ingersoll. "I've got a sour manuscript on my hands. Could you take a few hours off and see what you can do with it?" Wow, I said to myself, I've certainly got myself hooked up with a fast-moving organization that overlooked no bets. I was yet to know the half of it. But I told Ingersoll I'd be delighted to try. At least it would afford me some distraction, which I badly needed. I had been getting myself pretty drunk every night of the week ever since Catherine's death, but was still capable of working hard every day. And the rewrite would give me some practice, as well as some insight, into the workings of *Fortune* Editorial.

The manuscript was a corporation story (one of Luce's many inventions in *Fortune*) on Simon and Schuster and it was brought to my *Redbook* office by its *Fortune* staff writer. This was my first contact with a *Fortune* writer, and it was a shock, because he was a courtly Virginia Gentleman, Old Style, dressed in black broadcloth with a square-cut vest. But this was not the shock; the shock was that this courtly Old-Style Virginia Gentleman was about twenty-five years old. Green Peyton was his masthead name but he was the younger brother of Charles Wertenbaker. The brothers had decided, not wholly amiably, to be differently identified. Young Mr. Peyton wrote a rolling and somewhat oratorical prose, so I had no difficulty in seeing why Ingersoll had found it inappropriate to its subject: the then hard-driving firm of publishers who had come up from nowhere, within a decade, first via crossword-puzzle books and then on to seeming smash successes with everything they laid their hands on. What the story about them needed was an infusion of some *excitement* about their then unparalleled achievement, and this I set out to supply. It wasn't hard, and after two or three days and nights of work—still on the *Redbook* payroll!—I had my rewrite finished. Since *Fortune*'s December closing date was upon it, I thought it a good idea to call its office, although since it was close to eleven at night, I assumed, in my vast ignorance, that it would be shut tight. Instead Ingersoll himself answered in a flash; when I said my draft was finished and asked when he wanted it, he said "Instantly!" It was only a five-minute walk from where I was to where he was, and when I showed up on the fifty-first floor of the Chrysler Building I was flabbergasted to find every desk occupied and all lights blazing. It was editorial high noon. I had been going to press for more than ten years now but this degree of intensity was unknown to me. Later I would come to accept it as routine, but on this late-autumn night it was new to me.

And I made a swift and sweeping reassessment of Ingersoll. As a manuscript editor he was swift, sure, incisive and decisive. Much has been written about *The New Yorker*'s Harold Ross as the Great Editor, which of course he was, but with manuscripts he was a fumbler. At least he was with mine. "It gets

348

sort of fuzzy in here," he would say, indicating an imprecise spot somewhere between pages 17 and 21. Not so Ingersoll. He knew precisely what he thought from sentence to sentence and paragraph to paragraph. Within half an hour he had read my draft and covered it with marginal scrawls—"Good"; "Dull"; "Hit it harder"; "Kill"; etc. I asked Ingersoll when he wanted me to rework it. "Right now, for Christ's sake," he said. So I sat down at a secretary's typewriter outside his office and went to work. I finished about 2:30 A.M.

• • •

That should have been the end of the evening, but the Lord ordained it otherwise. The night of December 5, 1933, was surely one of the strangest in New York's—and my—history. Every one of those 42,000 speakeasies was dark, locked and shuttered. Not an illegal drink was to be had. The reason was of course that Utah—the necessary thirty-sixth state—had abolished the 18th Amendment by ratifying the 21st—and Prohibition fell instantly dead. The owners of those speakeasies, seeing the event coming from afar, had naturally all applied to the state for legitimate liquor licenses. Until these came through, $1,000 would not have bought an ounce of gin for the first week of December.

I was just reconciling myself to the fact that not even December 5 was *de facto* Liberation Day in the speakeasy world—the only liquor world I knew—when I heard my name loudly, even desperately, called as I came out of the Chrysler Building at 42nd and Lexington. I turned about to behold my old friend C. E. Hooper (from whose "Hooperating" so much of the measurement of "popularity" has sprung). He was running—not walking—toward me. He was carrying two bulky suitcases and sweating heavily on this night, and on his face were mixed expressions of apprehension and despair.

"I've just missed that goddamn night train to Battle Creek, Michigan," said Hoop. He could say no more for the moment and I uttered what I could in the way of comforting noises, which did not include the thought that this might not have been so bad as catching it. Hoop was in no mood for jesting. "If only we could get a drink," said Hoop, who had a three-hour wait for the milk train. In our fifteen-year speakeasy conditioning it never even occurred to us that previously nonspeakeasy establishments, whose license applications had been the first approved, were as open as open could be. We turned about and discovered we were standing spang in front of a Childs restaurant whose plate-glass window bore an enormous sticker proclaiming "cocktails"! Hoop and I stared at each other while thoughts without words raced through our minds. To have the first legal alcoholic drink in—Childs! It could not be. On the contrary, it obviously was going to be! Hoop and I gave each other long looks and then with backs braced and luggage divided entered the restaurant where among the porcelain-topped tables we loudly ordered "Two Scotch and sodas."

Whether or not that was what we got I don't know. The establishment was not well prepared to furnish what it had advertised. The glasses, of a shape made popular years ago by Nedick's Orange Drink, were filled with snowy ice; the remaining space was filled with a liquid unmistakably amber if viewed *just* so. Three of these in rapid succession failed to produce any threshold of sensation at all familiar. Giving up, we crossed the street to Grand Central. I was in a quandary: I could not desert my desolate friend, but what was there to do instead? The enormous commuters' bar of the Hotel Commodore, demolished in 1920, was in far from good order to celebrate Prohibition's end; in fact Childs was giving it real competition. But a certain number of train travelers had been more farsighted than Hoop. They had bottles. They were at the stage where they were brandishing them, and such was man's love for his fellow men that night that suddenly Grand Central Station became a bacchanalia. I think it must have also been that bootleggers, their profession absolutely shot, went about toting gunny sacks of rotgut for what the market would bring . . . . It comes back to me, hazily, that Hoop missed the milk train, too, but it doesn't come back to me at all how I got back to my hotel room.

• • •

My next meeting with Time Inc. individuals was strange indeed, and caused me more than momentary wonder at what the hell I had gotten myself into. I was to be briefed on my duties in Italy as advance man for that forthcoming one-subject issue of *Fortune*, its first ever. My two briefers—we met in a nearby restaurant-speakeasy—were Allen Grover and Laird Golds-borough. To Grover, tall, handsome and cordial, I took an instant liking and we later became good friends. He was something or other on *Fortune;* I didn't know what. Toward Goldsborough, deaf, lame, softly and interminably didactic, I conceived an instant dislike that was to deepen continually thereafter, but at least I knew who he was: foreign news editor of *Time* and the man who would go to Italy for the *Fortune* issue after I had returned. What I could not know was how strangely these two strangers felt toward each other. Like all new boys at school I had assumed pre-existing solidarities, and after that lunch I spent a lot of useless time trying to fit Grover and Goldsborough together—useless because they didn't fit at all, knew each other only slightly, and were not personally cordial, to say the least. But with that strange lunch as my only background, I sailed for Naples on the *Rex,* pride of Mussolini's fleet, in early December 1933.

• • •

The *Rex* proved to be a splendid foretaste of Fascist Italy. She was huge, pretentious and completely fourth-rate. Form was everything and substance nothing. Completely by coincidence, as I was descending one wing of the Grand Staircase I spied an old acquaintance descending the other. He was Lieutenant Commander Fitzhugh Green, U.S.N. (Ret.), whom I had known because he had been one of my most reliable and satisfactory contributors—of sea stories, naturally—to *The Youth's Companion.* This bleak December afternoon, after we had exchanged greetings, expressed our mutual surprise at this meeting on the central platform of the Grand, etc. etc., Commander Green, like an old salt, turned to the huge ornate barometer that hung on the wall behind us. Its needle pointed dead low; a metallic peg prevented it from falling any lower.

"What could be more like a wop ship," said Commander Green; "its barometer is busted."

But as that night and the next two days were to prove, the barometer was not busted. We were not even abeam of Nantucket Light when the weather the barometer had accurately foretold hit us.

> *When the ship goes* WOP *with a*
> *wiggle between*
> *And the steward falls into the*
> *soup tureen*
> *And the trunks begin to slide—*

—that was how it was, except that the *Rex* didn't only go *wop;* she developed at the same time a roll that seemed to a landsman like 20 degrees at least, and it was more than once that I wondered if this elephantine, rococo-refitted cattle boat would ever reach Naples hull down. She did though.

41 · SEE NAPLES AND DIE, OR,
INNOCENCE ABROAD

THE YEAR STILL BEING 1933, with trade and business close to an absolute standstill abroad as well as at home, the hotel in Naples greeted an in-funds American with unashamed delight and installed me in a room with a balcony and classic postcard view of the Bay. Vesuvius itself elected to issue thin plumes of volcanic smoke. But I was alone and unhappy, and my first night in Naples did not lighten my mood. My last act after preparing for my solitary bed, of more than ample width for two, was to take a pee and flush the luxurious, abundant toilet.

Whereupon, it would not stop flushing. I tried all the tricks I knew with toilets of American origin whose sense of proportion or time has deserted them. They did not prevail. There was no emergency control valve to turn to *Off*. I pressed wall buttons to summon *garçon* or *valet de chambre*. They were the souls of sympathy but *il signore* could see . . . Momentarily I thought I was in luck when I made telephone contact with someone at the front desk who spoke good Cleveland English. But his verdict was the same: The situation could not be resolved or even considered until morning when the . . .

So that first night in Naples, with a moon riding high and glistening on the waters of the Bay, with Vesuvius still glowing faintly in the background, I spent upon my bed with that toilet roaring in my ears and thinking, in despairing dejection: *"This is the story of my life;* whatever I do, wherever I go—outward trappings favorable but some fatal or tragic or ridiculous turmoil ruining my true peace."

Actually, I was somewhat oversorry for myself that night. I had work to do in Naples before I went on to Rome, and before that, even, Anne would arrive in Naples on the *Conte de Savoia* at my explicit invitation for sexual and other forms of companion-ship. We had been forced to travel on separate ships because she had confessed our liaison to her boss, a devout Catholic, who had, out of some mingled fear of God and company scandal, in-sisted on this curious concession to convention. What she and I did on dry land was up to us, but he somehow stuck on being even a third party to shipboard sin.

So in Naples in the meanwhile I sought out Time Inc. stringers and other working journalistic stiffs, Time Inc. then having not a single correspondent in all Europe (or even in Washington, D.C., for that matter), and picked up what tips I could here and there find. And *of course* I went to Pompeii, and *of course* I climbed some of the lesser slopes of Vesuvius, and *of course* I went briefly to Capri and to Ischia. And when Anne arrived, we spent a whole day and night in bed together before I resumed other activities. By now, the toilet had been cured of flushing.

I owe myself, if no one else, an explanation of how I was living my life those days, with my wife not quite a year dead. I was drinking hard, and screwing hard *and* working hard, and I don't know how I did it. It is difficult indeed to keep three such ac-tivities in proper balance but I did it—for a while, a fairly long while as I look back on it now. Not one day of reckoning, but several, were in eventual store for me, but not for a while. Mean-while I drank enough to blur the reality I could not face, but not so much as to interfere with the physical pleasures of sex. This is a line you can walk in your twenties and thirties—but not, alas, far beyond.

• • •

Naples was mostly the "vacation" I had planned between jobs. But by the time I got to Rome I realized that I had come to the end of my leisure. Almost forty years later there is not much point in recording my impressions of Mussolini's Italy, except to wonder if Italians still confuse "we have done it" with "we are thinking of doing it"—whatever the "it" may be. This self-deceit was rampant under Fascism—but is it also a national char-acteristic? Two American things stood out in Rome: the utter incompetence of the American Embassy, even in giving you the correct street address of the Italian Foreign Office; and by startling contrast, the high professional excellence of the Rome correspondents of the U.S. newspapers. Even the Hearst correspondent, "Billy" Emmanuel, had to lead a semisecret life; there were those who regarded him as inimical to the Regime. Arnaldo Cortesi of *The New York Times* didn't *quite* extend diplomatic recognition to anyone from Time Inc., but other top performers more than did: Wallace Deuel of the Chicago *Daily News* and Paul Cremona (a Maltese) of *The Christian Science Monitor*. These men were not Hot Flash artists but thoughtful, reflective and downright scholarly men, observing at first hand a phenomenon that they could not fully persuade their U.S.-based bosses to accept as really existing. From Deuel, Emmanuel and Cremona I learned an enormous lot, and from them or through them I commissioned about a quarter of the articles we would later edit in New York. Count Ciano, Il Duce's son-in-law, received me with the highest affability and was the source of absolutely nothing. "*That* information is unfortunately not available but is there not something *else* we can do for you?" It turned out that all the something elses were also unfortunately not available, but I did leave with an enormous and quite American-looking organization chart, in English, explaining how the Corporative State was supposed to work. Since it was supposed to work that way, it *did* work that way; there was no brooking this official position. But it is surprising how much loot one can pick up in several weeks of gumshoeing around, and when I came home it was with a heavy load of material—some of which the official Italians were indignant later to see published.

• • •

Anne and I debated how we should spend Christmas Eve in Rome, other than in our usual pursuits. In our ignorance we made for St. Peter's, only to discover it dark, empty and unwelcoming. Then somehow we learned that *the* church for Christmas Eve was Santa Maria Maggiore. Thither we went, to discover it jammed to its ecclesiastical gunnels. We stood on the cold stone floor, enchanted by the sights and sounds of a Christmas Midnight Mass in full swing, and at the reverent throng that packed us in. On Anne's other side stood a handsome Fascist officer, dutifully murmuring and crossing himself as occasion called for. But Anne was manifesting unease, and in answer to my querying glance she leaned close and whispered in my ear, *"He's pinching my bottom."* We changed places and I gave Il Duce's legionnaire a pointed glance; he answered with a slight shoulder shrug and a tiny suggestion of outspread palms that quite clearly said, No harm in trying; how was I to know? We left slightly after.

• • •

We felt that what Anne's boss didn't have to see, he didn't care about, so we made the homebound voyage together on the *Rex.* But I remember very little about it. To save time we traveled from Rome not southward to Naples, but northward to Genoa, getting there at 8 A.M. It was in a bar there, I think, that for the first time in my life I took that most sinister of all indulgences, a drink-in-the-morning. The effects of one double weeski-soda were so enchanting that I had another. Only someone who has done a similar thing can know how totally different and indescribably finer (at the time) are the effects of alcohol at 8 A.M. than at 5 P.M. I walked up the gangplank in a beautiful alcoholic haze and from the top deck of the *Rex* (now, of course, transmuted into the Queen of the Seas) watched the Genoa harbor slowly recede and disappear. I wasn't tight; I was just having an experience with Absolute Beauty, and it's too bad that the phrase of the 1960's "turned on" was yet to be coined or that "psychedelic" was not in any vocabulary, for that was my state. And I stayed in that state, not drunk, but on the farthest outward rim of sobriety, for most of the voyage. It's a neat trick if you can do it, and just then I could do it. I remember Anne's concern at my lack of concern for what I was doing, or for her, but she was a gentle, gentle girl, and there was little she could do about it. I failed to see a distinction between us; Anne liked to drink, and drink a good deal, as seemingly everyone did in those days, but she definitely knew when she had had enough, and I didn't. Later, much later, I was to learn from Richard Peabody's book *The Common Sense of Drinking* his pragmatic distinction between "alcoholic" and "nonalcoholic" drinking, no matter how heavy the latter. For the nonalcoholic, "a night's sleep is the definite end of an alcoholic occasion" but for the alcoholic it is merely "an unusually long period of abstinence." So the voyage came to an end, and so did my jag, and I was in good shape to report for my new job.

• • •

The editorial schedule for *Fortune*'s March issue had been posted; the story heading the list was "European Munitions: Hodgins-Luce" and this was my first acquaintance with the story that was destined to give me the biggest break of my editorial career. But before I could find out anything about it, something else confronted me: Ingersoll had another "sour manuscript" on his hands, and it was going to be my job to alkalinize it. (I had been hired as Co–managing editor, but my first appearance on the masthead was as associate editor and I stayed that way until in September 1935 I succeeded Ingersoll as M.E.) The sour manuscript was again a corporation story, the subject was the U.S. Rubber Company, and its original writer was a strange person indeed, and up to then *the* master of this new journalistic form—on the masthead as E. D. Kennedy. But Ingersoll found much to criticize in the manuscript, and after calling me next door to his office—*Fortune* had just moved lock, stock and barrel to the Chrysler Building's fifty-second floor and everything was in physical chaos—to explain in great detail what he wanted done, and getting my brash assurance that I thought I could do it, he summoned Ed Kennedy to join us.

Ed Kennedy was a little fellow, and about as unprepossessing as a human being could be. He sidled into the office where Ingersoll told him, with a bluntness that seemed to me brutal, that the story was being turned over to me for rewrite but that Ed should stand by for any necessary help. Kennedy received the news without demur or protest, made a few routine remarks to me and sidled out again. Ingersoll's brutality in taking a story out of a veteran's hands and giving it over to a rank newcomer shocked me, but it was obviously necessary for me to catch on as quickly as possible to the way things were done in this strange new world. But I did ask Ingersoll, "Are there many hurt feelings around this place?" Ingersoll gestured with his pencil and said, "There goes the Number One Hurt Feelings around here right now." A foreboding of office politics and feuds came over me—a foreboding happily *not* to be realized for some five years.

• • •

As with the Simon and Schuster story, Ingersoll's comments on the manuscript and how it should be rearranged were so

357

definite and explicit that I was able to follow them, even though I didn't *quite* know what I was doing, and a day's hard work brought the story around to Ingersoll's liking. This was fortunate, for that night was closing night. Since the story was late, Kennedy and his researcher on the story, plus two proofroom girls, one of whom was the darling Louise Wells,* and I piled into a seven-seater taxi and took off for the Jersey City printer. Here, working with galleys and page proofs on which the ink was still wet and smeared at the touch, we closed the story. This was heaven; I was back in my element, back into the days of *The Technology Review* and the composing room of Perry & Elliott, Printers, in Lynn, Massachusetts. So even the up-and-coming Time Inc. did basic things, like going to press, the same way I had learned to do them with a little 5,000-circulation magazine a decade before. Before 1934 was over I was to see the dawn come up like thunder over 200 Communipaw Avenue, Jersey City, more than once. This was only the first of such occasions, and a happy one. Ed Kennedy, who had every reason to despise and resent me, treated me instead like a colleague. It turned out, to Louise Wells's delight, that I didn't know how to spell "colossal" (I doubled the *l* and singled the *s*). The brass Linotype mats clinked and rattled from their big magazines above, down that diagonally moving belt into the assembler; the operator pressed down his casting lever, the spacebands wedged the line to justification length, the casting wheel made one revolution—and another line was born. From somewhere in the far distance came the roar and rumble of the presses.

* A major omission in Time Inc.'s official history, since she then headed not only the proofroom but also the Research Department.

42 · GETTING GOING, or, THE DOGS OF WAR

Fortune WAS A SUCCESS when I joined it—a roaring success. The meagerness of its staff and its other resources in 1934 seem incredible now. There were six writers on the staff, headed by Arch MacLeish, who already was the winner of one Pulitzer Prize (for *Conquistador*). The staff watched how *Konzertmeister* MacLeish was using his bow, and in their several ways took pointers from the master. In addition to MacLeish and Ed Kennedy, there were Charles Wertenbaker and his previously described brother, Green Peyton. There was Wilder Hobson, a smooth rhetorician in English prose but without much substance to his writing, since his true interests lay in playing the trombone and in jazz. That bearded gadfly Dwight Macdonald, whose chin whiskers then were golden brown and who *must* have prided himself on his resemblance to pictures of Jesus Christ, which was considerable, was on the masthead, but not then writing, since Luce had assigned him to the Experimental Department. And then there was an incredibly shy young man whose very gestures stuttered when he tried them as aids to the speech he could barely articulate, but whose prose on paper was beautifully the precise reverse. His name was James Agee. He was unknown, and it seemed likely he would always remain so, for his most intense desire was to fade into the background and, in the words of Owen Johnson, "not annoy the cows." But he was a protégé of MacLeish's, and through MacLeish he had published the conventionally slim book of verse *Permit Me Voyage* as part of the Yale Younger Poets Series. If it is not a collector's item now it surely will be sometime. (I can and do take some pride in an editorial critique I rendered on a *Fortune* story on U.S. Ambassadors: "I think the text is pretty indifferent, but the writer certainly got going when he did the picture captions." Only later did I learn that the text was written by John S. Martin, momentarily on leave from *Time* for the purpose, but that the picture captions were the work of Jim Agee.)

• • •

That was the staff. We were able to borrow from *Time* occasionally and once in a blue moon we were able to use something from an outside contributor, but usually this was something special like "The Legal Opinion"—a curious form sired by Luce, out of the New Deal. The wholesale Roosevelt-inspired "alphabet agencies" raised many brand-new legal issues for businessmen (the one word was also a Lucemphasis), and it was Luce's idea that getting an eminent and expensive lawyer to write an opinion that might cost a corporation executive $5,000 or more and giving it to the executive in *Fortune* for one dollar might be a bargain he would appreciate. It was.

In fact, the Luce inventions in *Fortune* were so copious that we had almost every journalistic thing our hearts could desire except enough competent staff to carry them through. There was the corporation story of which I have spoken. It was the only thing I ever heard Luce boast of: that *Fortune* had turned the searchlight of journalistic inquiry onto this prime factor in American life a full two years before Berle and Means had got around to publishing *The Modern Corporation and Private Property*. There was the recapitulation story, which said to the reader, in effect, "Some months ago you read a lot in the newspapers about the X Situation. It didn't hang together very well, and after a week or so the whole thing fell into oblivion, unresolved. *Fortune* will now undertake to straighten it all out for you." It was a brash approach, maybe, but in the 1930's it was also new. Today *The New Yorker* frequently cashes in on the same formula with its "Annals of————." The excitement in and about *Fortune* in those early days was that we could and did write about anything we pleased, so long as, most of the time, we could put some dollars-and-cents figures into the story.

• • •

• • •

To cope with the richness of the Luce journalistic innovation in *Fortune*, Thomas Maitland Cleland had created a design of classic beauty, inexhaustible typographic ingenuity, and production problems just a hair's breadth short of impossible to meet. He also left behind his protégée, Eleanor Treacy (who was later to become my second wife), as art editor. All the world knows of Margaret Bourke-White's initial contributions to *Fortune* illustration, but the names of such other innovators as Russel Aikens and William Ritasse of Philadelphia are strangely absent from Time Inc.'s official history. Good journalistic photography combining art and point was rare in those largely Bachrach-Kodak days. The Leica camera was barely on the market and Kodachrome had yet to exist commercially. Yet we used a lot of color photography—yielded up by ten-pound "single-shot" cameras, infinite lab work, carbro prints and a lot of prayer. Sometimes the results were good; sometimes they were horrid. We were on a technical frontier here, and sometimes we pushed too hard.

Cleland's design called for all illustrations, including color, to be printed in sheet-fed photogravure on antique "wild wove" paper. This was fine, for gravure illustrations showed no half-tone dots and did not require the use of slippery, glaring, reflective coated paper. But the gravure of the day was not adequate for the printing of type, which had a faint out-of-focus disembodied look, and no sense of bite, or impression, for the good reason that there was none. So Cleland blithely specified good old letter-press relief-plate printing for all text. Moreover, since gravure illustrations always showed a fuzzy edge, he demanded 4-point rules, in letterpress, surrounding all pictures. The results were twofold: not only did every illustrated text page have to go through two presses, of different kinds, but all art and artwork decisions had to be made before the writer had finished his first draft. So the illustrations had been chosen, the page layouts made and the gravure press would be turning before the managing editor had had even one preliminary glance at the manuscript for which the illustrations were being printed. It sounds wild, and it was wild, but Tom Cleland was a wild man and he had us locked into a beautiful and unimitatable design that drove us crazy every month. Oftener than not our luck would hold, but when it didn't the result was expensive disaster in junking and rerunning sheets, remaking layouts and in effect starting all over again.

When I first saw how *Fortune*'s color gravure was printed I couldn't believe my eyes. Three old German Olympia presses were hooked up in series, and the sheets came out of the first press to be seized by the next, and then the next, and were then trucked to the letterpress department for text printing. How we ever achieved register I just don't know—and sometimes of course we didn't.

• • •

• • •

In January 1934 the "European Munitions" piece was my assignment, and Harry Luce called me down to his fifty-first-floor office in the Chrysler Building. One reached this by going through "the Library," a room about fifteen feet square on whose oaken shelves there rested all the reference books Time Inc. then possessed.

"About a month ago," Luce explained, "I was having a talk with Norman Davis* and he said there was one hell of a story to be told about what's going on in France and Czechoslovakia. He said there was a French family—knew its name as well as his own, on the tip of his tongue but it kept escaping him—that as good as controls the biggest munitions racket anybody ever heard of. That's what started me off. Ingersoll's got Hamill [Katharine Hamill, then of *Fortune*'s six-girl Research Department] at work on it, so you pick it up from there. I'll be your editor."

Hamill and I had our first talk. In those days on a story like that *Fortune* worked from secondary sources and Hamill had already turned up some startling facts, of no circulation in the United States, from *Crapouillot* and from an English outfit, The Union of Democratic Control, in London. I went downtown to interview Norman Davis and suggested (thanks to Hamill's efforts) that the name of the French family that had been on "the tip of his tongue" was the ancient family of François de Wendel. "*That's* it!" said Ambassador-at-Large Davis, and I always thereafter suspected that the name had never escaped him at all but, veteran diplomat that he was, he was damned if he was going to utter the name first—to Luce or to anyone else.

My old friend from *Redbook* days Guy Hickok of the Brooklyn *Daily Eagle* now re-entered my life in a most important way.

---

* F.D.R.'s Roving Ambassador and a former Under Secretary of State.

362

We lunched and I told him what Hamill and I so far knew or were working on. Does this accord with what you know from your Paris post? I wanted to know. "It sure as hell does," said Hickok vehemently. Would he, I asked, be willing to write me as long a memorandum as he could about the whole situation? He said he'd be delighted, and I apologized that all I could offer him for fee was fifty dollars. "That's all right," said Hickok, "you'd be surprised at what the thrifty French habits I've picked up have taught me can be done with fifty dollars." For the brief but vital parts Guy Hickok played in my life, he has my eternal gratitude.

From Hickok and Hamill I learned simultaneously that Dodd, Mead had in galley proof a book that the authors, H. C. Engelbrecht and Frank Hanighen, were planning to call *Merchants of Death*. I called Hanighen to ask if *Fortune* could "rent"—that was my word—the galleys, once again for a fifty-dollar fee, and on this basis I got them. With this raw material I started to work. The writing came easy and within a week I had a draft I was ready to show Luce. I don't think I was particularly anxious about it; more curious, perhaps, to see what this strange, gruff-but-gentle, patient-but-impatient editor would do with it. I knew he would not flay it—not because I had confidence in my draft, but because I had confidence that Luce was just not that kind of editor. And in this I was even righter than I knew.

"Well," he began, "this is pretty fair, but it needs quite a lot of work." We then went over it page by page, looking for his big X's in the margin, the points at which he would then painstakingly explain what he thought was lacking. Then and there I learned that once you were able to follow his occasionally difficult line you thereby discovered that he had unraveled a knot for you, given you an essential splice or handed you, gratis, a whole new ball of yarn. One secret of his touch was that no matter how much or how little he did for your manuscript, in his eyes *you* remained the author; he didn't want it any other way.

• • •

The Lord, or Someone, must have been guiding my typewriter; I worked like a dog for three days, trying to meet or match Luce's trenchant points. The revised manuscript wound its way through the typing department and landed on the various appropriate desks. *This* time when Luce sent for me I really trembled; I had either passed or flunked and I hadn't the faintest idea which. So Luce's words of greeting were the sweetest music of my career: "Well, I congratulate you; very competent job." Many things were later to be said by many people, not all of them favorable by any means, about "Arms and the Men"—the title I gave the piece, from Bernard Shaw, out of Virgil—but nothing ever equaled, in my mind, Luce's one-sentence commendation. At Luce's instructions I sent the manuscript to Ambassador Davis and to Allen Dulles, at that time a high-ranking member of that mighty legal firm Sullivan & Cromwell, later calling on them for their criticisms. The Ambassador remained true to his calling. Smiling a smile that was cordial, enigmatic and bland all at once, he said, "That ought to do it," and bade me good day. Allen Dulles was slightly more specific, for anyone later destined to head the C.I.A., saying, "I *hope* you're right; if you're right, it's terrific."

"Arms and the Men," prepublication, also accounted for my first significant meeting with Archibald MacLeish, who suddenly popped his head in my doorway, the manuscript in his hand: "If there's anything to reconcile me to working for Time Inc., this is it," he said. Over a lapse of thirty years plus, I cannot guarantee this as a verbatim quote, but that was its import—faintly puzzling to me then, to become clearer as years went by.

• • •

• • •

I well remember the night we closed the final proof on "Arms and the Men," for it was January 20, 1934, the first anniversary of my wife's death. I silently dedicated the piece to her memory and got to bed at about 2 A.M. My emotional state was mixed, as it so often was, and is, for on the one hand my mind was melancholy at the memories of what I had lost, but on the other I was giving thanks that at last I had found work that absorbed me, and in which I could lose myself as I had never been able to do at McCall's.

In 1934 *Fortune* had a circulation of slightly under 100,000. Already the magazine was far ahead of any projections made for it, for its beginning circulation was just over 30,000 and Luce himself was firmly on record as saying that 50,000 subscribers within five years would be double-success: the magazine would be profitable and it would also have fulfilled its publishing mission, for it was Luce's belief that that was the maximum number of people in the United States of those days who were "entitled," I think his word was, to read *Fortune*, or at any rate the idealized *Fortune* in his own mind, from which the actual month-to-month magazine was always falling short. But a magazine with a circulation of under 100,000 is still a smallish magazine, so the press run took just over thirty days, and so a closing date of January 20 meant a publication date of February 25 for the issue dated "March."

• • •

When the March issue, with "Arms and the Men" as its lead piece, came out, all hell broke loose. Today the article is as out of date as a lady's hat of the same era, but in 1934 it burst as a startling revelation of what was going on in Europe amidst an international tangle of such institutions as Le Comité des Forges in France, Krupp in Germany and Schneider-Creusot in Czechoslovakia, to name only those. What the article asserted was that

> . . . there is at the moment in Europe a huge and subversive force that lies behind the arming and counterarming of nations: there are mines, smelters, armament works, holding companies, and banks, entangled in an international embrace, yet working inevitably for the destruction of such little internationalism as the world has achieved so far. The control of these myriad companies vests, finally, in not more than a handful of men whose power, in some ways, reaches above the power of the state itself.

There was no question; the article shocked the U.S.A. and produced *no* political lines of cleavage. The spectacle of isolationist Senator William E. Borah of Idaho and internationalist Nicholas Murray Butler, then president of Columbia University, thumping the tub for the same article was certainly an odd one, but it occurred and reoccurred.

I think the reason for the national shock created by the article lay in America's intense innocence—yes, true innocence—in the mid-thirties of this century. We had had our Robber Barons, we had had our "malefactors of great wealth," but we had cured

365

everything by the Sherman and Clayton acts, and we had Made the World Safe for Democracy; subsequently the Depression had shown us that many of our Captains of Industry who were not fools were Grand Larcenists—and still we were innocent America! We were still incapable of taking in the vastness of the mendacious and supercynical hypocrisies of double-dealing, European style. A less idealistic and more brutal America has now gone Europe one better, but in 1934, with the outbreak of World War II still a lustrum away, we could not credit it.

Meanwhile, "Arms and the Men" was being widely circulated and reprinted in America and being roundly denounced in Europe. There was a good deal of New York speculation as to who the author might be, since *Fortune* followed for many years the English custom of journalistic anonymity. Next to Luce's own prepublication encomiums, I think I most treasured *The New Yorker*'s impudent announcement, "we hereby award it the Pulitzer Prize" (the world-famous Time Inc.–*New Yorker* feud was not to break out for another year or so). Still, nobody knew who wrote it, except that *The Nation* decided that Arch MacLeish had written it and had named him to its National Honor Roll for having done it. How *The Nation* decided this, I do not know, but I do know that Arch was more upset about the misattribution than I. He promptly wrote *The Nation* a letter of correction in which, however, I first discovered that this gem of a man was a flawed gem. After disclaiming authorship, but before handing it over to me, he could not resist saying, "Naturally, the article had my full approval," thereby implying with delicate modesty and restraint that he'd had *something* to do with it. And he hadn't had a goddamn thing to do with it!

Neither this nor anything else interfered with the friendship that grew up between us, but I liked Luce's postpublication attitude toward me much more. He dropped into my office one morning while the hubbub was still rising to say, "When it gets about that this was your piece somebody or other may try to take you away from us but I hope you will believe that it would be in your own best interests to refuse." I would no more have thought of leaving Time Inc. or *Fortune* than exploring Mars, so I tried to convey, roundabout, that I was complimented, in effect, to be declared a fixture so soon. But being overdelicate with Luce, or beating around the bush, was never a passport to his esteem,

366

so all he said, gruffly again, was "About the question of a possible stock deal you raised while we were still in the talk stage about you—there's no need to wait a year. You can have two hundred shares whenever you want to buy them." I wanted to buy them right away and did. It was the only good investment I've ever made in my life.

• • •

While I got the praise, Luce got the lumps. Various French officials, resident in this country, wanted to see *the* editor, in various moods of menacing suavity or frank outrage. He dealt with them all. One day he called me to his office to show me a letter, on the crackliest and engravedest bond, from the American legal representatives of Les Petits-Fils de François de Wendel, who considered themselves particularly traduced by an article based on *un documentation controuvé* (*"controuvé"* being a particularly insulting word). The letter alleged numerous libelous errors and ended with the threat of legal action. It was all most impressive. Then Luce showed me his reply. Of it I remember:

> DEAR MR. SO-AND-SO:
>
> If you will put your allegations of error into formal and specific written record I assure you *Fortune* will take them into fullest account and make any necessary corrections and amends . . . .
>
> As to your last paragraph, I never discuss lawsuits.
>
> Yours very truly,

There was a rocklike quality about "I never discuss lawsuits" that told me a lot about the editor in chief of *Time* and *Fortune*.

• • •

Another thing that began to delight me with *Fortune*, in addition to the electric excitement of the place, was the absence, *then*, of office politics. Let me not paint too idyllic a picture. The *Time* boys had their intramural vendettas, but there were scarcely enough of them in those days to make up street gangs of any respectable size. They regarded us on *Fortune* as interlopers, and pretentious interlopers at that. We in our turn simply ignored them and read their weekly sheet sometimes with admiration, sometimes with fury or contempt. When I later became M.E. of *Fortune* and still later its publisher, it remained a source of fury to me that *Time* would so seldom pick up a story from *Fortune;* if *Fortune* ran a story the newspapers picked up, as happened more and more, the newspaper clip would find its way into *Time*'s now growing morgue and then *Time* would pick it up, which merely compounded our *Fortune* fury. But as families went, Time Inc. could in 1934 be described as a happy family, with wronged children constantly running to Poppa with complaints, but which Poppa straightened out by banging heads together.

Or so it seemed to me. My own office life was completely happy because I had been accepted without jealousy or new-boy hazing; in fact the pitifully small staff's attitude seemed to be that here was a new hand that could take charge of a story and put it to bed, and thank God for that, since it correspondingly lightened, by a fraction, their own desperately heavy loads. By that same token the news " 'Mitch' Davenport is coming back" was greeted with cheers. I had never heard of Russell Wheeler Davenport before and I didn't know what he was coming back from, but we were to have, as things turned out, strangely intertwined careers, a great and dear friendship, a vast falling out, a complete reconciliation, and a final, dramatic parting when he suddenly died in 1954. But this was still twenty years in the future.

Meanwhile, back in the present, I was busy being Ingersoll's deputy. He treated me generously, and gave me some of his dirtiest jobs to do, which is one of the things, after all, a deputy is for. My job as "associate editor" had settled down to being twofold, or maybe three. In the first place, I became a staff writer, like everybody else. But I also had the job of rescue man. When Ingersoll decided he was stuck with a manuscript on which the assigned writer had reached the end of his rope, he would turn the story over to me for the dirty job of superseding the writer and redoing the piece—usually to Ingersoll's marvelously detailed and appropriate criticisms. Only later did I discover that this brilliant and gifted journalist-editor could not, himself, write prose worth beans. His self-assigned and self-written story on *The New Yorker*, which we published in August 1934, and which was to be the unheralded start of the lasting Time Inc.–*New Yorker* feud, was a thoroughly second-rate job.

Although Ingersoll and his wife of that period, Elizabeth ("Tommy") Carden, were deeply kind to me, and I had yet to develop my aversion to Ingersoll, he was not popular with his staff. There is, and should be, no such thing as a popular managing editor; the best he can hope for is a little grudging admiration, and that's in the nature of things. But the feeling was widespread among the staff that Ingersoll was a tricky customer. It was often said of him, with variations, "If there were two equally effective ways of reaching the same objective, and one of them was straight and aboveboard and the other underground and devious, Mac Ingersoll would instinctively choose the latter." I didn't then agree, but before too long I came to.

Ingersoll bore a cross. He was the most spectacular sufferer from the common cold there ever was, and thereby he granted me a series of opportunities that were to serve me well. Before I had been with *Fortune* five months, Ingersoll was so stricken with one of his bouts that he had to take three weeks off for a Southern sunshine cure, so for the May 1934 issue I was acting M.E. It was invaluable experience, particularly since, by Luce's decision, I was to be M.E. for the Italian issue, now scheduled for July, thus permitting Ingersoll to leapfrog from the June to August issues and try to get caught up, for God's sake. I think I must have served four or five times as acting M.E. before I finally succeeded Ingersoll as official managing editor in the summer of 1935.

43 · "FERT   FERT   FERT," or,
THE CORPORATIVE STATE

IT WOULD BE NICE and pleasant and conventional to be able to report here that my personal life was progressing as well as my professional one, but the exact reverse was the unhappy fact. I was still deeply involved with Anne and she was a sweet and gentle companion, but I wasn't in love with her. I wished I could be, but I wasn't. I still spent a great many evenings, and nights, with her, full of alcohol and quarrelsome, yet somehow still able to "enjoy" sex and withal able to be at work, right side up, next morning. I had, at least, abandoned any drinking until the cocktail hours, but then I made up for lost time. The eternal mysteries were two: I was able to work, and work well, under a really crushing load, in spite of the gross abuse I was giving my psyche and my soma; furthermore nobody in the office ever seemed even remotely to know the private struggle for life and sanity I was undergoing. I confided in no one.

And this was not the full extent of my personal entanglements. I had gradually slipped into a strange *ménage à trois* relationship with the Elsons. Val Elson was a charmer; Jack, her husband, now dead, was a newsman of the highest gifts, although his name was not well known outside professional circles. I had known Val since my *Redbook* days, for she was a contributor, and she did not know I was a widower; since I never spoke of my wife, she made the natural assumption that I was a carefree bachelor. At first the husband-and-wife-and-me combination was pure and delightful friendship, with the obvious yet unobserved snake-in-the-glass being alcohol. We all liked to drink and it was one of the things that bound us together. Alcohol was eventually to cost Val's husband his life, after they were divorced, and to put Val into a sanitarium twice, for a year each time. I got off by far the lightest, but also far from unscathed.

(Once again, I've used fictitious names for the Elsons for reasons the reader will understand.)

In the beginning, everything was delightful. We liked to play parlor games. High on alcohol, but with our wits still sharp enough, we invented a game we called "esoterica," and despite Jack's connections with radio broadcasting in its golden age, we didn't know what we had. What we had was the germ of *Information, Please*, which later independently occurred to Dan Golenpaul, who *did* know what he had, and who lined his pockets with it for the years it flourished on the air, with the omniscient John Kieran, F.P.A. and Oscar Levant as panelists and Clifton Fadiman as moderator.

Imperceptibly, Val and I felt the terrestrial magnetism of sex. We tried to govern it, but there was no means of weightlessness in 1934. Val sometime later confessed to her husband, who took it with surprising calm, because, as neither Val nor I then knew, *he* was in love with someone who was not Val, and thus was not only placid about what was happening, but, I think, subtly encouraged by it. After what seemed, and may have been, months of struggle against it, Val and I inevitably went to bed. It was hell for Val the next morning because Val was a devout Catholic who had committed a mortal sin. But it was bad enough for me for—this may sound odd—I had a stern puritanical conscience whose reproaches were unbearable. Yet there I was, self-involved in an adulterous situation and two-timing Anne, and using alcohol as the solvent for what I had involved myself in. Eventually, of course, the whole impossible situation broke down with a crash, but not before it grew deeper and worse.

Meanwhile, I kept on working, harder and harder, at the office.

• • •

• • •

It must have been around May 1934 that Harry Luce and I had a curious lunch together. (He was calling me Eric by now, and I fell into the habit, without self-consciousness, of calling him Harry.) The lunch was curious because Harry was musing over the problem: What is *ever* going to bring the Depression to an end? The Depression had affected little Time Inc. not at all, but although the New Deal was now more than a year old there were still millions upon millions of unemployed, and this, at the time, was a heavy reason for Harry's anti-New Dealism: it hadn't solved this colossal problem. He wanted me to do a *Fortune* story on Unemployment, which I later did, but that article was not what was absorbing him this day. I brought up the 1921 Depression, which still remains the steepest, sharpest break in stock-market and other prices that U.S. business has ever experienced. The reason why it's all but forgotten now is the incredibly rapid recovery from it; by 1922, things were all but normal again.

"All right, all right," said Harry impatiently, "that's just the point. The auto industry helped pull us out of *that* one. But what's going to pull us out of *this?* The men's clothing industry, for God's sake? *What?*"

I made some mention of T.V.A. and Rural Electrification, but both these things were so new and so mixed up with ventures like the N.R.A., the F.E.R.A., the A.A.A. and other things still of doubtful efficacy or constitutionality that when Harry snorted at them as too local, too experimental or too something-or-other-else, I had no very strong case to put up. Housing? Here was something dear to Harry's heart, but how was it ever to be pulled out of its hopeless mire? I mentioned something, which sounds now, and probably was then, irrelevant, about the nationalization of the railroads. "That wouldn't produce much of a yip out of me," said Harry, "but what the hell has it got to do with solving unemployment?" I had to admit it had no bearing on the subject at all.

I don't remember what *Time*, the Weekly Newsmagazine, had to say about Spending, the issue that was driving the 1934 businessman up the wall, but I also don't remember the Harry Luce of those days ever joining in the deafening chorus, still antiphonal to Herbert Hoover's "We cannot squander ourselves into prosperity" or denunciations that came from editorials everywhere about Spending or Planning, the two dirtiest words in the businessman's limited economic vocabulary of the thirties. Harry never liked F.D.R. much (or vice versa) but he always, at least when I heard him, based his fundamental criticism of the New Deal squarely on the proposition that it had barely touched the then rock-solid problem and issue of massive unemployment. He was still saying this in 1937, and he seems to have been right.

But the point I am trying to get at about this 1934 lunch is that Harry and I ended up absolutely stumped on what would ever get the U.S. economy going again. The first diesel-electric locomotive was about to take to the American rails, nylon had been invented by the brilliant genius of one Wallace Carothers of Du Pont, television was struggling to be born but seemed to be breech-impacted, plastics were progressing well beyond the Bakelite stage, and so on. We knew these things, in a sort of way, but they added up in our minds to little more than zero. In short, two men, one with a soaring imagination, the other with the remnants of a technical education clinging to him, spent two hours of hard thought about what would get the American industrial machine running again and had come up with nothing. So the only thing to do was go back to the office and start getting out another issue. At least there was no dearth of things to *write* about.

• • •

It was about then that Laird Goldsborough got back from Italy and there began a series of conferences in Harry's office about the Italian issue. I got my first really close look at Goldsborough and intensely disliked what I saw—and heard. This put me into square opposition with Harry—an opposition that I was either too new, or too lily-livered, or both, to voice. (The really wild office opposition to Goldsborough did not break out until his views on the Spanish Civil War began to be expressed two or so years later.) Luce was on record that Goldie had a *"unique* mind" (italics Harry's) and God knows he had. Its uniqueness lay in its really great powers of sophistry. He could turn anything into its precise opposite before your eyes, and he seemed to take an almighty delight in this power. To give the devil his due—and as a true devil Goldie deserves it—he was an excellent *short-run* journalist. By short run I mean two things: (1) he was capable of thinking about next week or next month but not about next year; (2) although his writing for *Time* ("curt, clear, complete" used to be a promotional phrase) was technically excellent, his writing in anything but the short form, at which he was a master, was simply—to my intense surprise—no good; he could not build and sustain a long narrative, as could MacLeish or Davenport or Wertenbaker—or Dwight Macdonald. He could, however, and did, talk endlessly, interminably, in excellently connected sentences, with the quiet, almost whispering voice of the very deaf; like so many people who perpetually seem *about* to come to the point, he was very difficult to interrupt. In personality he can be denominated in only one way: he was a horse's ass.

One morning, six or seven of us were in Harry's office listening to Goldie's long, long account of his travels and discoveries; Luce was leaning back in his chair, taking it all in and not cross-questioning. At last Goldie reached a point of explaining that whereas the action of a certain *Podesta* (roughly a mayor) in a certain city might superficially seem to have been anti-Democratic, closer examination and reasoning could reveal it to be, in purest essence, the very embodiment of the Democratic ideal, because—

Here Luce suddenly snapped upright in his chair. "All right, Goldie, it's horseshit," said the editor in chief.

Shortly, but not immediately on this account, the meeting broke up, and I walked back to the *Fortune* office with my new friend Allen Grover, who had known Luce much longer than I. "You know," he said, "I've never heard Harry use such a word before." He shook his head in wonder. And in the course of the next twenty-five years, *I* never heard Harry use such a word again. He could be and was appropriately and sometimes volubly profane, but this remained forever his only venture into scatology within my hearing and despite some pretty heavy provocation.

• • •

This small anecdote may illuminate a slightly larger surface. Although Harry preserved, protected and defended Goldsborough far beyond the point so many of us thought was reasonable, proper or even decent, he was *not* Goldsborough's dupe as it is now often fashionable to believe. Goldsborough was an out-and-out Fascist; Luce was not. For the *purported* aims and ideals of Fascism Harry had a certain hankering, which he could not wholly suppress. Harry's whole intellectual life, in a sense, was a vast effort to make everything somehow fit into and relate to everything else. Harry's mind was organic. The Hegelian Corporative State that Mussolini had put together on paper looked to be organic; everything *seemed* to fit with everything else; and this is my personal and perhaps erratic explanation of Fascism's early appeal to the then thirty-six-year-old Luce. The desire to make everything relate to everything else is an early yearning for most thoughtful young people, but push it far enough and it suddenly becomes a No-Go Proposition. I was never able to make up my own mind whether Luce eventually stopped pushing against the Immovable Object or whether he kept up the struggle to the end of his life. I think I do feel sure that the younger Luce, if not the older one, would have given a hell of an argument to G. K. Chesterton's proposition that "there is no connection between a triangle and the idea of pink." *Yes, there is, if you just hunt hard and long enough:* this, I think, would have been Harry's attitude. It is an exhausting attitude, but it is also the best possible set of mind for the journalist and, as the readers of the daily papers know, very, very rare.

Mussolini's 1934 Italy had another appeal to Harry, too, and this was expressed in the brief contents-page foreword he wrote for the July *Fortune* the day before we put it to press:

> . . . No 100 per cent journalist can be more than a few per cent Fascist, which is to say, he is by definition non-Fascist.
>
> But the good journalist must recognize in Fascism certain ancient virtues of the race, whether or not they happen to be momentarily fashionable in his own country. Among these are Discipline, Duty, Courage, Glory, Sacrifice.

These were noble words. They did, of course, turn their backs on certain ancient vices, momentarily fashionable in Il Duce's country. Among those were Repression, Dictation, Castor Oil and Assassination. To this extent, Goldsborough had done his work pretty well.

• • •

But in other ways Goldsborough had done his work pretty badly. I think it must have been even more of a surprise to Harry than to me that the man whose writing for *Time* pleased him so much couldn't write extensively in a style up to the standards that *Fortune* was then demanding. At any rate, when Goldsborough had finished the first draft of his article "The State" (meaning the Italian State, not the Corporative State, which was the subject of another piece), Harry followed the peculiar course of bringing Goldsborough to my office so that I could say to both of them at once what I thought of the draft. Once again I was on a spot. I was still New Boy at *Fortune*, but I was also, by Luce's personal direction, the managing editor of the issue. So I had to speak my piece, but obviously I had to use whatever diplomacy I had in doing it. By luck, I hit on some right words. "I think the thread is spun but the cloth is not woven."

Luce quickly responded. "Yes, that's it, that's the trouble so far." He turned with the utmost solicitude to the author. "Goldie, get yourself a few days rest in Atlantic City or somewhere, and when you come back we'll go at it again." Goldie limped out of the office, obviously not liking me any better than I liked him, and Harry stayed momentarily behind. Even though we were now alone he lowered his voice. "Goldie's not strong physically, you know. That deafness and that lameness come from his having had scarlet fever when he was a boy. But it didn't touch him here," said Harry, gesturing toward his forehead. I wasn't sure I agreed, but Harry was speaking as a compassionate man, from a heart he wasn't supposed to have, and the only appropriate thing to do was nod. I nodded.

• • •

Before the Italian issue finally went to press it involved everybody in the office except Ingersoll and, I think, MacLeish. "Journalism consists in writing for pay on matters of which you are ignorant," Sir Leslie Stephen once said, and he, who fathered *The Cornhill Magazine* as well as Virginia Woolf, should have known. There's a bitter, ineradicable truth at the center of this possibly facetious nineteenth-century remark, and never since I came on it have I been completely able to get the taste of it out of my mouth. I tried my hand at rewriting Goldsborough. Luce got in his licks. The result was a strange amalgam, and not bad—but ah, Sir Leslie. The article I had commissioned from Wallace Deuel in Rome on the Corporative State was splendid in its exposition of the myth-state and was better still when Luce himself purged it of its occasional journalese. The prize example of Sir Leslie's dictum was a successful and uncriticized piece on Fascist Finance. Allen Grover studied and restudied until he was blue in the face the lire economic figures and studies that Goldsborough or I had swiped or commissioned in Rome and then undertook to pound their significance into the head of Wilder Hobson, who couldn't have cared less. But under Grover's stern instruction, Hobson turned out a lucid, persuasive piece of prose on a complex and obscure topic—not one line of which he could, or wanted to, remember three weeks later. Jim Agee turned in a fine piece on Roman Society and its complex fornications based on facts furnished by I-still-won't-say-who. In 1970 it is impossible for me to realize that Dwight Macdonald and I collaborated on anything thirty-five years ago—yet we did, on Italy's Agriculture and Industry. We all worked like dogs, night and day, and exhausted ourselves, and yet at the time it was great, it was vast fun. Luce would come back in the evenings, not to stroll among the slaves, as people like T. S. Matthews would strive to convey, but to take off his coat, roll up his sleeves, and go to work, wherever his skills were needed, in Ingersoll's vacant office, next to mine. He disdained the telephone and when he needed something he simply bellowed—usually "HORN," to summon that incredible little girl on the *Fortune* research staff, Florence Horn, who had been detached from all other duties six months before to do nothing except work on the issue now about to go to press. Luce set himself tasks—even menial tasks like writing captions. When he wanted me he would merely yell "Hey!" since I was only next door. And I discovered that Luce, like lesser editors or writers, had no abiding confidence in his writing until he had tried it out on somebody who gave it approbation. One piece of loot we had brought home was a fine color photograph of Signore Marconi, inventor of the wireless, long ago, and now resting on his laurels in a resplendent uniform. This militarylike figure of a scientist turned statesman fascinated Harry, who spent almost all one evening fussing and fussing at writing a worthy caption to go under it. About 11 P.M., when he thought he had what he wanted, he yelled "Hey!" for me, and when I appeared, he said, "How does this strike you?" Then he did not read, but rather declaimed:

A SENATOR, NO LESS
. . . is this handsome engineer: His Excellency Grand Councilman Guglielmo Marconi, the man of wireless, and the best that Fascism can muster up in the way of a man of intellect. Mussolini was in an awkward spot when he determined to found a Royal Academy. For Italy had scarcely a dozen men of art or intellect that anybody had ever heard of. (Croce, the philosopher, Ferrero,

the historian, Pirandello, the dramatist, d'Annunzio, the poet, would about finish the list of those transatlantically visible.) Likewise they were practically all anti-Fascist and still are. Luckily for Mussolini most of them had been made Senators before Fascism, and so he could pass them over by a quaint ruling that no Senator could be an Academician. The Academy was then filled with second-string intelligentsia. But who was to be President? Marconi was pro-Fascist, but he too had been made a Senator. So Mussolini made a new rule that the President of the Academy could be a Senator. Marconi has been President ever since.

Harry never heard of Professor Claude Shannon's Information Theory, formulated while he was a member of Bell Labs, highly complex, based on the binary numbers system and regarded by some scientists as the most important scientific statement since the Quantum Theory. And in the 1930's I think Shannon was yet to formulate it. Yet Shannon, scientifically, and Luce, pragmatically, were working toward the same end: the reduction to an absolute minimum of Redundancy in communication. And Harry was a master of his end of things. In one of Wilder Hobson's manuscripts the author had been guilty of the phrase "and so, to repeat . . ." This was too much even for one of Harry's big marginal X's; he printed angrily in the margin: "Make your emphasis come from STRUCTURE, not STATEMENT." I have lived to carry that around in my mental vest pocket ever since. It's so much easier to do it the wrong way.

• • •

As it was bound to, closing day arrived. I remember being in the office at 9:30 A.M. As fast as one crisis was settled, another arose. Finally, in early evening, seven of us piled into a taxi bound for Jersey City, complete with semifinal proof, dictionaries, whatever reference works were portable, our unresolved crises and a bottle of Scotch. It got to be midnight. It got to be 2 A.M. It got to be 3 A.M. Three A.M. is the point of absolute sump in the psyche. We were exhausted. But by 4 A.M. we all felt better. The bottle of Scotch was not for carousing purposes, and from it I took not one drop. It was for the benefit of the proofroom, whose members could keep themselves going by taking, with no loss of acuity, one tiny sip every three-quarters of an hour. The season being late spring, the skies began to lighten early and before 5 A.M. the east had begun to glow. Still we were not finished. Mary Grace of the proofroom looked at the roseate sky and then at the whiskey bottle and with a shudder thrust it out of sight, still three-quarters full. Now that it was morning the idea of a drink was repulsive. No alcoholic, she.

By 9:45 A.M. we were closed, dizzy and a mite hysterical. *But* we were closed, and said good night to the puzzled composing room day shift, which had arrived for work some two hours before. A taxi took us back to our various homes. I remember when I got to mine it was 10:30 and I had put in a twenty-five-hour working day. The first thing I did was to mix myself a stiff drink, and then two more. But these were *not* drinks-in-the-morning; these were last night's drinks deferred. Having taken them, I took off my clothes and went to bed—to sleep about fifteen hours.

•   •   •

The Italian issue, when it came out a month later, was a success—except in Italy. I was worried about what still seemed an overenthusiasm for Il Duce clinging to it, but a letter from Wallace Deuel in Rome reassured me a good deal:

> I think you have done a damned good job . . . . You have offended the finest sensibilities of not only all good Fascists but also several not-so-good Americans . . . . The few Americans I know who frequent what is called Roman society say the number is in what they call bad taste . . . . You undoubtedly know that the Embassy quarantined the copies you sent for us. The delicacy of American diplomats would be more impressive if accompanied by equal comprehension in other respects.

Since Deuel's letter and other sources indicated that Rome considered Goldsborough, postpublication, a vile *anti*-Fascist, I was able to indulge in a wide, evil, private, ear-to-ear grin. I don't know what Goldsborough thought. I doubt he and I exchanged more than three sentences during all the remaining time until his death.

•   •   •

For the cover of the issue, on which this will be my last word, that sterling artist performer Antonio Petruccelli had designed

379

a cover based on the Great Seal of the Italian State—done in gold and black. At its bottom, arranged in a semicircle, were the Italian words *"FERT FERT FERT."** One morning my mail was gladdened by a letter from Paul White, then the brilliant head of C.B.S. radio news who might have succeeded in establishing a unique and *sui generis* independent radio news-gathering service in the 1930's had not the newspapers threatened to de-list all radio programs if C.B.S. took such a step. But this was not what was on Paul White's mind in the letter before me. "I enjoyed your Italian issue," he wrote, "but I wish to call your attention to three typographical errors occurring on the cover . . . ."

---

* The word seems to mean "bear," but some expert in heraldry will have to explain its significance in the seal.

44 · GENERAL FOODS, or, 17,000,000 ON THE DOLE

Without exaggerating or falsifying I *could* paint my year A.D. 1934 as a succession of triumphs. I had come to a new job with the most exacting journalistic taskmasters in the United States, and on my very first assignment I had knocked the ball clean out of the park for a grand-slam homer. Then, after five months' experience, I had demonstrated that I was capable of managing the most complex magazine then being published anywhere. I had all but doubled my salary. Coming from "the outside" into a nest of prima donnas, I had been accepted, without effort on my part. Because I could and did perform well at the typewriter I had all sorts of emergency or last-minute jobs flung at me after others had failed at them, and I did not fail.

Why, then, as this year of unbroken successes drew to a close did I attempt suicide?

I pose that question to myself, and here and now, as I attempt to answer, I'm not sure what I am going to say.

• • •

But to start the attempt: In the first place, I had no home. Catherine's death was now a year and a half gone by. In retrospect I can see clearly now that I had a *duty* to perform. The duty, which was not only to myself but to my baby son, was to set out on a conscious, deliberate—and perhaps even announced—search for a new wife, and with her help build a new home. I did nothing of the sort. Although working my head off at the office and actively consuming large quantities of alcohol by night, I was, as psychiatrists would view it, being completely passive about that not unimportant consideration, my life. I did not wear my grief about Catherine on my sleeve. I did something

381

far worse—for everyone. I wore it as a hair shirt.

In the beginning, I had wanted desperately to talk to Harry and Elizabeth Carlson about their daughter, and in the beginning I had tried. But very soon after her funeral I became aware that these two granitic New Englanders were never even going to mention their daughter's name in my presence again. They never did. If I did, the subject was deftly changed. Their rock-bound code obviously said, "We intend to keep our heartbreak from you; in return, kindly keep yours from us." So I did. Catherine's parents outwardly showed me every kindness and consideration. Inwardly, it was a different story. I have only to ask myself today what would *my* emotion be toward the husband of any daughter of mine who might meet with the same end as Catherine's and the answer comes crystal-clear: hate.

Conscientiously, I took the train to Boston every other weekend to visit my young son. His grandparents, his grandmother particularly, poured out on him an overcompensatory excess of love—far beyond what would have been normal for any child their very own. I watched this with some alarm—and had no idea what to do about it. I even had difficulty in seeing my baby *alone*, for God's sake. By the time he had reached the playpen stage (when he could hoist himself to his feet but couldn't solve the problem of how to sit down again), I wanted to get down on the floor with him and, in effect, tell him he was my little boy and I loved him. But his grandmother's almost constant presence inhibited all this; she seldom or never left us alone together and I somehow could not find the right phrasing with which to ask this devoted woman to leave me alone with what was fast becoming *her* little boy.

• • •

So I can scarcely say that my Boston visits were much of a success for anyone. Back in New York I would use my combination of hard work, alcohol and sex to dull the sharp edges of emotional problems that, to me, had no solutions. Among other things, my son would grow up confused about *me*. Since it would seem to him that he had the standard couple of male-female older people with which all children seemed to come equipped, who was this third party—myself—who also seemed to have some claim on him? In due course, this confusion indeed arose.

One of the things that every friend had said to me after that January night of his birth was "Don't blame the baby!" I answered "Of course not." And in the sense that I avoided him, rejected him, or that thoughts of *real* blame went through my mind, I did not. But did I, just the same? When my thoughts went back to that January night, I asked myself, "What was the emotion that made you want to smash every piece of glassware in the room where you had been waiting?" Was it grief? No, it was *rage:* rage that I had lost a wife and had instead a helpless infant on my hands, whose mother, just to make everything as involuted as possible, had not wanted to bear him! So in due course years later this matter did come up when it became obvious that regardless of what *I* thought, my son thought I blamed him. It remains a mystery to me how I forecast with such accuracy what was likely to happen, and still did not see my obvious path of duty: bury the past, seek to marry again, have another child at the earliest possible moment, re-establish a home, re-establish myself as a husband and father. *Perhaps* I did see that path, but certainly I did not follow it. Instead, I stood still, waiting for further events to overwhelm me. Which, of course, eventually they did.

• • •

I flew into a frenzy of work in the summer and fall of 1934. The theory of *Fortune* was that every writer on its staff should be capable of turning out one good major story per month for eleven months of the year—and on the twelfth month he rested. Some few—I was among them—could actually do this. Arch MacLeish could, except that his compact with Luce was that he got twelve months of salary for nine months of work (later reduced to six). It was a good compact. Arch was not only the best but the most efficient writer in the shop. He arrived every morning at 9 A.M. on the dot, wrote (or thought) steadily all day long and left at 5:30, with reams of copy behind him. Most unpoetlike. Jim Agee could do it—if he were watched like a hawk so that he would not disappear into some private dreamland. That incredible little man Ed Kennedy could also do it if he managed to ride over the perils of alcoholic excess. Ed was a deeply gifted writer, and a real souse—not just a hangover-in-the-morning type, but a disappear-for-five-days type. As for the rest of the staff, it varied widely in its gifts, some of which were great, but it was homogeneous only in its unreliability. It could come through magnificently or fall flat on its face, and from issue to issue there was no telling which it would do. The parade of gifted men who joined the staff for four or five months and then re-signed or had to be fired was a Grand Army of the Republic of Letters. The ability to write well and the ability to write well against deadline pressure are, unfortunately, two widely different gifts. MacLeish himself had sponsored for the staff a deeply gifted man, Schuyler Jackson, a fellow poet. He had a flat, sad face, with a flat, sad mustache. His prose was beautiful—as good as Agee's any day—and he did not disdain journalism; he just didn't understand it. You didn't just create a set of images; you had also, like Homer, to tell a story. This somehow eluded Jackson—and deadline pressure did awful things to him. We struggled mightily with and over him, for he had gifts we badly needed, but when the struggle at last failed, it was MacLeish, his sponsor, who diagnosed the incurable trouble: "He just can't bear down; his pelvis is too narrow."

• • •

Well, apparently my pelvis was broad enough, whatever other endowments I lacked, for although the story-a-month pace was grueling (most *Fortune* stories averaged more than 10,000 words in those days), I could keep up with it, and even gain on it a little bit. It was this, I think, that led Ingersoll to suggest that I take two solid months and in them write two major stories, to appear in the same issue: the issue of October 1934. One was to be the lead story on Unemployment, which then idled 17,000,000 workers; the other was to be a corporation story on General Foods. This double hitch meant that I had to run two researchers simultaneously, one working in Washington, the other in New York. It meant that I had to be interviewing the frail and idealistic former social worker Harry Hopkins, as the head of the F.E.R.A. (Federal Emergency Relief Administration), in the one place, and pompous horse's asses like Ralph Starr But-ler, advertising sultan of General Foods, in the other. It turned out not to be easy.

Of the two stories, of course, Unemployment had the larger theme, but General Foods turned out to be much the harder journalistic nut to crack. The reason was simple enough; in Washington everyone was eager to tell you (his version, of course) about everything. In New York, General Foods was eager to tell you nothing at all. And in the 1930's, General Foods was a particularly, perhaps even uniquely, interesting company.

For one thing it was one of the largest and last of the pre-Crash mergers, put together in the Coolidge Era out of a bunch of, by today's standards, little "independent" food companies. The keystone in its arch was the Postum Cereal Company, which had waxed fat indeed on Post Toasties, Grape Nuts, Postum, and other brainchildren of that mountebank C. W. Post. Then it had reached out for the Genesee Company, which for a long time had had a very nice little thing going in Jell-O. Maxwell House Coffee once had no higher ambition than to beat out Chase & Sanborn in annual sales, but its membership in the growing General Foods family changed all that. Half a dozen other small companies made up the rest. Just before the Crash GF had bought the patents, good will and everything else salable of the little Birdseye company from Clarence Birdseye, a simple, genial hick from Gloucester, Massachusetts—who just *may* have been the last one-man inventor in history, for all by himself he had cracked the problem, which had defeated hundreds before him, of how to refrigerate foods for long preservation and then have them taste like anything when they were later thawed and cooked.

Until Clarence Birdseye came along—and for quite a while after, too—"cold storage" appropriately relegated to second class or worse any foodstuff to which it was adjectively attached. When GF bought out Birdseye, the firm of Goldman, Sachs and Company came forth with the statement that "the Birdseye patents could be capitalized at a billion dollars." That turned out to be a haunting statement, for the "frosted foods" division of GF just couldn't seem to get off the ground—and the whole country wasn't worth a billion dollars. A quarter century later this turned out to have been an understatement.

The fundamental question the GF story had to answer was: Did the old-time premerger consolidated net profits of the constituent companies add up to more before the merger or less? In short, how good a business idea had General Foods been? But there was no answering this unless I could get from GF a breakdown of profits by divisions. So I asked for it. "Good God, we don't tell our own stockholders *that;* why should we tell you?" said Verne Burnett (brother of Chicago's Leo), public relations vice-president of GF.

"Because I so very much want to know," I said.

Verne Burnett was a genial man, so he grinned. "I'm afraid you'll have to come up with a lot better reason than that," he said.

Well, I *had* to defeat him; otherwise I wouldn't have any news to break. In thumbing through past GF annual reports, I came on an illustrious business name. The name of a vice-president, it came back to me, who had resigned suddenly from GF as the result of a "policy disagreement" and was now executive vice-president of a big advertising agency. I didn't know him, but Bill Strong did. Would Bill help me? He would and did, so in a few days I was in the big man's office. I represented my call as for general purposes only, but after twenty minutes or so I admitted to a certain interest in the divisional profit breakdown. "That's a state secret," said my new acquaintance. "But I could give you a rank list. Would that be a help?"

"It would be much better than nothing," I said, trying for just the right amount of pathos.

My new friend began a slow recital. In the midst of it he succumbed to a sudden attack of self-induced boredom.

"Aw, what the hell!" he said, and began scribbling on a pad. It took five minutes. "There," he said. "Those are last year's divisional profit figures. Fuzz them up a little bit and for Christ's sake don't tell anyone where you got them."

I gave my oath, which I am still keeping. As soon as I got back to the office I copied my informant's handwritten figures on my typewriter, and, after fuzzing them up a bit, tore his sheet into careful and minute shreds. I was no more eager than he to reveal my source. The fun was going to come when I presented my manuscript to GF for their prepublication checking and criticism.

It came, all right. Verne Burnett was a skilled pro at his job, so he did not explode at the manuscript. He was just terribly, terribly pained that anyone in whom he had reposed such confidence as he had in me should have resorted to whatever rotten, dirty, low-life methods to obtain figures that were, in the last analysis, not correct.

I, too, was pained; hurt to the quick by his characterization of my methods as questionable. As to the breakdown figures, I had merely introduced them as "extremely reliable estimates." If there were errors and GF wished to correct them with officially sanctioned accountancy reports, I would be only too happy, etc., etc. That car stopped there. But the high command of GF brought every variety of pressure to bear to get those figures—and everything else about the story it didn't like—removed; pressure on Ingersoll, pressure on Luce, pressure on the directors. But the figures stayed in.

• • •

This small anecdote has its larger applications. Despite the desperate wringer it had been in, and still was going through, American Business continued not to welcome journalistic inquiry. It was still accustomed to handing out press releases and having them printed, exactly as mimeographed. The American businessman remained under the genuine delusion that he, unaided, had built America and was entitled to his corresponding rewards. The Depression was something that had *happened*, an Act of God, for which he was not responsible; for which, if anything, he was entitled to sympathy and understanding. This was not the view that *Fortune* took; it took the view that business was indeed entitled to understanding but that the businessman would have to pay a price for it, which was fuller disclosure and franker criticism than he had been accustomed to. And it was this insistence that gained for *Fortune* during the 1930's the reputation of being "anti-business." The disclosure of GF's profits by divisions was a good case in point. Even today, it is a rare annual report indeed that gives even a hint of such information; the company does not want to let "the competition" know precisely how it makes its money. And this is pretty silly, because "the competition" does know. It has its C.I.A.'s. Nevertheless, the pretense goes on, despite all the Counter C.I.A.'s.

• • •

It was highly instructive for me to be working on the GF and Unemployment stories at the same time. Business, which in early 1933 had welcomed F.D.R. as the savior of capitalism, had now turned hard against him and his New Deal; it was "government interference." But essentially what had happened in the Hoover days, as the Depression deepened, was that business had, in effect, dumped millions of men and their families off the payrolls and onto the tax rolls; now it was complaining about the astronomical rise in government spending. The *real* trouble with the New Deal of those days was that it was not spending enough—but this was an unspeakable heresy.

• • •

Well, my two stories went to press on time and I was mightily proud, for they totaled more than 26,000 words. "Nobody's ever done that before, boy," said Ralph McAllister Ingersoll. Harry Luce liked the General Foods story, which had caused him a lot of trouble; the Unemployment story, which had caused him no trouble at all, he did not particularly care for, although he voiced no criticism to me direct. But it kept getting back to me, so eventually I asked him about it. One of the many Luce virtues was that he never dissembled. "I guess I've been doing some talking behind your back, which I shouldn't have done. No—I didn't like it much; I thought it was too descriptive with not enough analysis." And I guess it was.

45 · MR. McCARTER'S VOLTAGE, or, BLACKOUT

IT HAD BEEN PLANNED that after my double-decker I would take things easy for a month, but other circumstances intervened. Schuyler Jackson had been assigned to do a story on the then so-named Public Service Corporation of New Jersey, and the manuscript was a bad flop. What's more, it was a *long* bad flop, for PSNJ was a complicated company that had an all-but monopoly of the supply of electricity for most of its native state, was a manufacturer and distributor of gas, and operated electric and bus transportation for northern New Jersey. There was no one around to rewrite the piece except myself.

I could smell trouble coming. This took no very keen nose, for the president of the company was one Thomas Nesbitt Mc-Carter, a completely unreconstituted Bourbon of a businessman who had not been satisfied with the political management of the United States since the days of William McKinley, and possibly not then. He was the autocrat complete; the second of the three powerful McCarter brothers who all but ran New Jersey as their principality. And Thomas Nesbitt McCarter was not going to like anything said about him or his company unless it was one long, uninterrupted song of praise, which the manuscript was not going to be.

Ralph Ingersoll had opened the story negotiations with Mr. McCarter. "At the start," he had cause to say later, "McCarter gave me an absolutely flat *No* to the whole idea, but by the time I got through with him he was belly up on the floor, meowing to be tickled." (I could well believe this; Ingersoll's powers of persuasion were considerable.) So it was Ingersoll who dispatched the rewritten manuscript to Mr. McCarter, with the usual letter saying we'd be glad to correct any errors of fact and discuss any matters of interpretation.

And it was Ingersoll who an afternoon later stuck his head in my door. "You'll have to be in Newark at eight o'clock tonight, and I've told Al Grover to go with you for protection. McCarter is livid." Then, like all good executives, Ingersoll went home.

• • •

So Al Grover and I were indeed in Newark at PSNJ headquarters at 8 P.M. I think it must have been 11 P.M. before we left. Promptly on our arrival we were ushered into Mr. Mc-Carter's office. He had set a stage for us. There he sat, heavy, florid, jowly, tousle-haired, behind his massive desk. Flanking him in a quarter circle on each side were the company's vice-presidents, treasurer, secretary, to a total, I suppose, of eight. Each face was set and grim, but none was setter or grimmer than Thomas Nesbitt McCarter's. He silently motioned us to two chairs placed directly in front of him and first addressed himself to Grover.

"You write this story?" he demanded.

Grover truthfully answered, "No."

Mr. McCarter pivoted his full bulk until it faced me. "*You* write this story?"

My answer could not be as simple as Grover's. I settled for "I was not the original author but I take full responsibility for anything in the manuscript."

The President of PSNJ took two or three minutes in silently switching glares of contemptuous hate from Grover to me and back again. It was a good unsettling technique. "All right," he said. "Since neither of you *gentlemen* is willing to come straight out and say you wrote this filthy article, I'll tell you what I'm going to do: *I'm going to read it aloud to you, word by word, and you are going to listen.*"

• • •

And he did. Not since Robert Mantell stopped playing King Lear has there been such a performance. Mr. McCarter's build and appearance would not have been favorable to a stage career, but he had everything else—voice, nuance, presence and passion. Particularly passion. The McCarter Theatre at Princeton, his Alma Mater, was not named for him merely because he put up the money. He not only read the story word for word; he did it very well. He went from roaring *fortissimos* to the veriest whispered *pianissimos*, his technique not to comment, but to exaggerate and ridicule. Only once did he give vent to an aside. One never can tell what particular thing will goad a man beyond containment, and when Mr. McCarter came to the innocuous sentence "Although reared a Presbyterian, he now seldom goes to church" it was suddenly too much for him. He dropped his actor's pose. "Goddamnit, what business is that of *yours?*" he roared. Then he reined himself in. He was saving all vituperative comment for the end, and when the end came, I have seldom seen such passion.

The thing that sustained me through all this performance was that *Fortune*'s research notes, carefully gathered from every source we could uncover, had specified that precisely this sort of intensive and sustained browbeating was a well-known and widely used McCarter technique. When at last he had exhausted himself, he turned to his colleagues. "Is there anything additional any of you wish to say?"

Only the treasurer spoke up. "Merely, Mr. McCarter, to express the admiration I think all of us must feel at the restraint with which you have handled this," he said.

Was this man a model ironist? No. This man was the treasurer, and had a green face and had uttered a straight line.

The *Fortune* Research Department notes had listed a specification about Mr. McCarter that I had not used in the story, but it was vividly in my mind. It was that a McCarter tirade always ended with a reference to his dead brother, Uzal, and his long and selfless record of service to his state, whereupon "Mr. McCarter's voice would break, his little pig eyes would brim over, and he would end sobbing at his desk."

And this is exactly what happened. Grover and I took this as our cue for departure, assuring Mr. McCarter's colleagues that we had been much enlightened, which we most certainly had. We had some body bruises, but our eyes were dry as dust. Grover had kept careful notes of all the legitimate points raised, and we later took due note of them. But as I look at that old story today, I can only marvel at how mild it was but what a storm it raised at the time—more violent than anything I have been through since.

• • •

So that ended what was to have been my rest period. By now we were working on the last issue of the year. I was down for two pieces on the Federal Budget, no less; one to appear in December 1934, the second in January 1935. I worked with a will on the first piece, which was a stinker to try to get straight, for although Al Smith had yet to coin his contemptuous phrase "alphabet soup" for the New Deal agencies, they were in full flower by then and were interconnected and cross-funded in wondrous ways. A beautiful chart on their incestuous complexities was prepared and I put the story to press on time. But I never wrote the second story at all. I was in a hospital instead.

• • •

• • •

The *ménage à trois* in which I had involved myself had been getting pretty serious; it involved all three of us, among other things, in a steadily increasing consumption of alcohol. One Friday night I left the office, with things in shipshape condition, and told someone that although I didn't expect to be in on Saturday, I did plan to come in briefly on Sunday. (We paid no attention to the days of the week in 1934.) That Friday night, Val and Jack and I stayed up half the night, drinking and playing our variety of self-invented parlor games. It was four in the morning before we felt any impulse to break up, and by that time we were all drunk and I was much too drunk to go home. But both Val and Jack were eager that I stay the night, so that was no problem.

Naturally, we all had terrible hangovers next day, and for the second time in my life—I *think* it was only the second—I had a drink early in the morning. We all did. And, as on the *Rex* in the harbor of Genoa, the antemeridian alcohol had its miraculous effect; in the beginning a sort of sober euphoria of much finer and more serene quality than any snort of booze taken at the cocktail hour or after. Jack, who was a much hardier soul and tougher guy than I, had to go to the office, and set off for it quite blithely, untroubled by any sense of sin at setting out for work with a morning jag on. Not so with Val or me. We needed another drink quite soon to keep that euphoria going, which masked our sense of wrongdoing. And then another. That led us to wild, abandoned love-making in the very bed where Val had slept with her husband. If he had happened to return— for we did not know how long he proposed to be gone—he or Val or I, or more probably all three of us, might have been prominent in the next morning's *Daily News*. But he did not.

After our adultery, it was only to be expected that Val and I would need more than several drinks to wipe out—which they splendidly did—the extra load of guilt. When Jack finally did come home, it was to find Val and me irreproachably costumed and alcoholically blithe. Not drunk—blithe. It slowly dawned on her and me that Jack was in exactly the same state, so it was only common sense, was it not, that we should have several rounds of drinks to celebrate the affection we all felt for one another. It was. We marched forward again into another thicket of drunkenness of which I can remember only that there was much more alcohol and much less food than the night before. And no games; somehow, we did not have the wit for games. And once again, I stayed the night.

• • •

And once again, next morning, there were several restorative drinks. But nothing wiped out the memory that I had told *some-body*, back long ago on Friday afternoon, that I would be in the office some time on Sunday. And I was eternally resolved, even through the haze of alcohol, that I would be. It was mid-afternoon before I was able to tear myself away from Val and Jack to make good my "promise." I put that word in quotes be-cause I had no appointment, no necessary task, no *real* reason for being in the office at all. I had merely said I would be. (Out of sheer loneliness I often spent a good part of Sunday in the office, reading *The New York Times*.) When I left Val and Jack, they were full-blown drunk again and I was in never-never land, not drunk, but not sober, and quite conscious that I was not sober. There was no euphoria now.

When I got to the office, not a soul was there except for two girls in the typing department who were industriously banging away at typescripts that obviously had to be ready first thing next morning. They looked up casually as I came in and then returned to their platens. But the momentary casual glance had somehow been a terrible thing for me, and when I reached my desk and discovered I was too confused to make anything out of the papers there, a depression hit me with all the force of a collapsing wall. I closed my office door and gazed south at the twilight now dimming the towers of downtown Manhattan. I must have looked out that window for a quarter hour as a resolution formed in my mind. I was disgraced and hopeless, and tonight I was going to end my life. In my befogged mind it was not the alcohol or the adulterous fornication that had been the final straw; it had been just the passing glance of the two typing girls. They *must* have instantly known how I had spent my life since last Friday evening, and this was more than I could bear. I put on my hat and coat and walked briskly to the elevators, waving good night to the typing girls as I passed their glass-enclosed cubicle.

• • •

• • •

In my hotel room I had whiskey. I also had plenty of one-and-a-half-grain Luminal tablets, for in those simple days one did not need a prescription for any of the barbituric-acid derivatives. I poured myself a very cautious drink. It was cautious because I did not want to make myself merely drowsy and then possibly fail to carry out my plan. It was a drink because my plan needed Dutch courage. I thought of what I would be leaving behind, and I was agonized. Life was bitter but it was also sweet, and damn the Creator for making it so. I took another drink, again cautious, and thought "I will be joining Catherine, whether in Chaos or oblivion doesn't much matter." Then I emptied a bottle of Luminal tablets into the sturdy bottom of an Old Fashioned glass and used a teaspoon to crush them to a fine powder. Then I filled the glass to the brim with undiluted bourbon, for at least I was smart enough to know that alcohol and the barbiturates had a strongly synergistic effect.

• • •

I don't know how long I stared at that glass, stirring it occasionally so that the Luminal particles would stay in suspension. I was in such an agony of soul as I had never known before—but was to know again. I was conscious that I was deserting my infant

son, already a half orphan. How could I possibly do such a horrible thing to this little child not yet two? On the other hand *was*
it a horrible thing? Mightn't it possibly be a good thing? Clearing
the docket, so to speak, and removing the ambiguity that would
later confuse him? The ambiguity that was myself.

I don't know how long I thought these thoughts, or how often
I stirred the Old Fashioned glass. Of my parents, or of others
who might love or value me, I confess I thought not one thought.
I wanted permanent oblivion, and my personal world would sur-
vive the experience of my absence. Only my little son and—in-
congruously mixed with him—the unprofessionalism of walking
out on an uncompleted story were the inhibitors.

But the agony was too great. I had lost track of time, but let
us say that it was about 8 P.M. when I double-locked my door,
got into bed in my pajamas, my clothes neatly hung up, all lights
out except a dim one by which I could see the hemlock by my
side, and declared myself ready for the end. It took me three
gulps to down the contents of the glass, for the whiskey was fiery
strong and I had to take time to gasp. But with the final gulp
I lay down, and there was not even time enough for drowsiness.

46 · "THE MARCH OF TIME," OR, THE TREND OF EVENTS

It TURNED OUT LATER that I had done a good job. There was no Hodgins in the office in the morning and no explanation of his absence. His telephone did not answer. Despite all I have admitted to in previous pages, my reputation in the office was of reliability, so that when the lunch hour had come and gone and I still could not be raised, Ingersoll in some alarm dispatched a friend to my East 40's apartment. My first memory was of three people in my room, and this is curious because there were only two: my friend and a hastily summoned doctor. I *think* my state would today be diagnosed as alcoholic hallucinosis. There must obviously have been telltale dregs in the Old Fashioned glass, because my next memory was of the rubber tube of a stomach pump being forced past my gullet again and again. Then I remember nothing more until at some indefinite later time I woke up in a hospital room. And I remember little enough after that. Did I feel the sense of relief that would-be suicides are commonly supposed to feel when they discover their attempt has failed? I don't *think* so, but my memory may well be at fault. Confusion piles upon confusion here; it may well be that the enlightened doctor, knowing the dangers of sudden cessation of barbiturate intoxication, kept me partially sedated with calculatedly decreasing doses of the poison I had taken. I don't even remember how long I was in the hospital, but whenever I think of this now vanished occasion the words "ten days" occur to me. I slept a lot. I remember that Anne visited me, and was concerned, but to this day I remain unaware of who, besides the doctor and the friend who summoned him, knew or knows that my episode of October 1934 was a suicide attempt.

In all this confusion one person stood out. He was Ralph Ingersoll. In the years that lay ahead he and I were to become anything but friends, but in the now the consideration he showed me was perfect. He must have known my true situation, but he never alluded to it, and there was never even the slightest evidence that he communicated it to anyone else, even Harry Luce: otherwise I doubt that Harry would have reposed in me the confidence he later did. Right now, Ingersoll's concern was that the whole situation was *his* fault, which of course it was not, to the slightest degree. "I'm to blame," he said; "I worked you too hard; I put too heavy loads on you, and you just collapsed, that's all." That wasn't all, and I can't believe that Ingersoll really thought it was, but if it was fiction, he inviolably maintained it, even to me.

I was due to leave the hospital on a Friday. What was I planning to do then? Ingersoll wanted to know earlier in the week. "Go home," I said. Ingersoll urgently wanted me to come up to Lakeville with him and his wife. I politely declined. By now my system was purged of its poison, but my mind was back in as bad a turmoil as ever. If I just went back to my routine of overworking, overdrinking and illicit sex it would only be a matter of time before the same thing would happen all over again—pray God successfully, this time . . .

Ingersoll came back a third time. "Look here," he said, "I die very hard on some things. You're coming up to Lakeville with my wife and me for a couple of days of rest and country air and then next Monday we'll go back to the office together. This is an invitation but it's one I'm prepared to back up with force if necessary."

That did it. I accepted, which was what I had wanted to do anyway. But I had to be forced to accept. And one phrase in Ingersoll's speech gave me more relief, *perhaps*, than he knew: "we'll go back to the office together." Although my remorse for what I had done seemed very slight in other respects, I felt disgraced professionally, and Ingersoll's phrase indicated that he was standing sturdily behind me, and that so far as he and Time Inc. were concerned I was just an ordinary battle casualty to be rehabilitated as quickly as possible and be returned to front-line duty.

And that was the way it turned out. The January issue was closed. Arch MacLeish had written the second piece on the Federal Budget that I should have done. I slipped quietly back into the scheme of things.

Had I learned anything from the experience I had put myself through? Apparently not much. I had not, for example, learned that I was in desperate need of psychiatric help. (Nobody else had learned that, either; no one ever made the suggestion to me.) I *somewhat* lessened my consumption of alcohol, but again, at no one's suggestion. Jack and Val and I had a rather solemn meeting in which the three of us agreed we were drinking too much and resolved, voluntarily, that it might be better if we saw less of each other, for we were somewhat vaguely, only vaguely, mind you, aware that our threesome presented us with drinking problems that did not otherwise arise so strongly. Val and I even tried parting; it did not work. So here I was, more or less as I had foreseen, except that somehow, and thanks, I am convinced, to Ralph Ingersoll, my professional reputation was undamaged. Nor had my capacity for work suffered, a fact I continue to marvel at.

• • •

• • •

The official history of Time Inc. records that the first public showing of *The March of Time* movie took place in the since-demolished but then resplendent Capitol Theatre, Broadway and 50th Street, on February 1, 1935. I have plenty of reason to remember that date, quite apart from anything that appeared on the screen.

I suppose some sixty to seventy Time Incers were invited to attend, and for them a special section of loges had been roped off. We were asked to decorate the occasion by wearing formal dress. I took Eleanor Treacy, *Fortune*'s art editor, and this must have been the first official evening occasion when we were together as an office pair.

Before I joined *Fortune* I had often wondered why the name of only one woman stood separately on its masthead, and as its art editor: Eleanor Treacy. I soon found out. She had been the protégée of T. M. Cleland, who had devised *Fortune*'s magnificent original format, although Cleland was a man about fifty in those days and she a girl in her twenties. Cleland, certainly one of the twentieth century's most gifted designers, was not an easy

398

man to get along with and, in a way it was never given me to
understand, the great work Cleland did for Luce left the two men
deeply at odds. But Cleland had been able to insist that Eleanor
Treacy be given the title and post with which to carry out and
continue his basic aims. This was arranged, and this Eleanor carried out, with, in my opinion, a very high competence that commanded my fullest respect. Her knowledge of art and the history
of art commanded even more—my envious admiration. Her sense
of color, in which all women exceed all men, was 100 degrees
more subtle than anything I could cope with. And she had learned
to be a good pictorial journalist. She was distinctly not in Harry
Luce's good graces, but whether she had offended the Calvinist
Luce or the Journalistic Luce I never knew. She was not in Ingersoll's good graces either, but that was easier to understand. Managing editors and art editors on all magazines everywhere have a
long tradition of viewing the same things in very different lights.
I cannot remember what office subject Eleanor and I discussed,
but the conversation ended with her saying, "I think I'm going
to like you," and my responding, "Thank you, I hope you do." No
tragedy ever began more innocuously.

Eleanor was far from a pale aesthete—very far. She was a
lusty girl, who could hold her own in any slanging match, but
also managed to be equally at home in the Museum of Modern
Art, the Metropolitan, a pressroom, Carnegie Hall, or, if business
took her there, a blast furnace. What *did* escape her, I was later
to discover, was the feminine art of ingratiation. When she had
a point to carry, flattery, dissimulation, indirection, subtlety
simply were not in her list of ploys; she had only one technique:
the direct center rush, with the fierceness born of one-yard-to-go.
So she got banged up pretty often—and her opponents, too, knew
they had been in a fight. But for a long time I was a partisan
of Eleanor's and vice versa. And since she was one of the few
unmarried girls in the office, we began to see something of each
other when office hours were over.

• • •

During my first year with Time Inc. I had barely met its second-in-command, Roy Larsen. *The March of Time* on radio had
been a huge success; now Roy had almost totally detached himself
from Time Inc. to collaborate with an authentic Balzacian char-

399

acter, Louis de Rochemont, hugely floating on seas of black coffee, and heaving in labor to make *The March of Time* movie an even greater success. Uncountable months of sweat, coffee and curses went into uncountable prototypes, and then on February 1, 1935—I have three vivid reasons for remembering this date— the first public unveiling took place.

• • •

I suppose all of us thought that the audience would spontaneously rise and cheer this *March of Time* innovation in pictorial reporting. In any event, we were all bidden to a lavish champagne-and-caviar party in Messmore Kendall's huge apartment, which was a sort of private penthouse attached to the theater, with a beautiful window through which the then owner-exhibitor tycoon could watch his theater and what was on its screen, or seek even deeper pleasures. It was quite a penthouse, and in it that night was thrown quite a party. A throng of bartenders and waiters was pressed to the limit of its powers.

Eleanor looked quite enchanting that evening, in the way blondes do when they garb themselves in long white satin gowns. And I lost her for long periods of time to—of all people—Ralph McAllister Ingersoll. Eleanor was a superb dancer. Since I was anything but, this was a pleasure we could not share. But Ingersoll, too, was a splendid dancer, and he, tall and elegant in his white tie and tails, and Eleanor, in her white satin gown, exactly less tall than Ingersoll to be sexually appropriate, made quite a stunning pair. Every once in a while, when they would go into high gear to the beat of somebody's small band honking out the jazz of the mid-thirties, the rest of the dancers on the small floor would stop and become spectators instead, and the managing and art editors of *Fortune*, who had probably spent an hour in the office that morning snarling at each other and would do it again tomorrow, put on an exhibition of ballroom dancing that was really worth watching. Eleanor, becoming flushed, was obviously having the time of her life.

• • •

And so was I. If I had had any aspirations to be a good, not to say, spectacular, dancer, I would obviously have been miserable. Fortunately I had none, and during a comparative lull,

400

I wandered out to the bar. Near there I saw my friend Malcolm Johnson talking to a most attractive lady. His eye caught mine and he beckoned me toward them. "Do you know Mrs. Hobson?"

"I don't think so," said Mrs. Hobson.

My memory tells me she had on some kind of luxurious candy-stripe gown.

"Well, you both work for the same organization," said Malcolm, as if *he* didn't. Then he either disappeared or vanished from my consciousness. It didn't matter. I was confronting a beautiful and striking woman ("beauty" was never a word that Laura would concede to herself, but "striking" was) who was gracious and vivacious; an intense listener and eager conversationalist. Her looks were enhanced, for me, by her prematurely gray hair, a feature, I was later to learn, she herself hated.

Mrs. Hobson and I had perhaps ten minutes of conversation together, and no great themes were struck; we were merely interested in the fact that we had both joined Time Inc. in the same year, she as a promotion writer, and had never met or even heard of each other until now. Somehow we found it very easy to converse, and I remember thinking how rarely I met a beautiful woman who was also gracious; the beauties were cold or condescending, and the horse-faced ones were so full of graciousness that it was hard to escape them. But Mrs. Hobson was both striking and gracious, and I remember feeling disappointed when the general swirl of the party separated us.

I wonder what it means, psychologically, that Laura Hobson has no recollection at all of that first meeting, in fact that she can't for the life of her remember when she first met me at all. But meet me again she surely did, for in one way or another we have been in and out of each other's lives—with some very long lapses, it is true—ever since. She was not Laura Z. Hobson, the novelist, then; her first big success—*Gentleman's Agreement*, book and Academy Award-winning film—was still more than a decade ahead of her. So were a lot of other things.

• • •

• • •

Eleanor and I began seeing a great deal more of each other than we ever had before. And her influence on me was good, in a host of ways. Anne had been powerless to control my drinking, and Val and Jack wildly enhanced it, but Eleanor lived with quiet dignity in a truly lovely backwater, with a garden at her feet, private to those few whose low buildings boxed it in. Here she lived among innumerable books, not *all* on art, and tons of what in those days passed for phonograph records: "shellacs." Maria, a splendid cook and devoted servant, made daily trips down from the Bronx, whenever necessary lugging a carboy of dago red to refill Eleanor's decanters. All this quieted me down a good deal—but not completely. The best way I can think of putting things was that under Eleanor's influence the night-me became somewhat more like the day-me: still suffering, still hypertense, but not cracked apart in the Jekyll-Hyde fashion I had been since Catherine's death. Since we both loved music we spent a great deal of time together in Carnegie Hall, and since Eleanor really knew the world of art and its history, she contributed immensely to such aesthetic growth as I was capable of. In only one such domain was I her superior; despite her close association with Tom Cleland and Edward Wilson, who were designers as much as they were artists, she could do nothing with type and loathed the very problems in typography on which her mentors—and now I—doted.

•   •   •

One Sunday not long after Messmore Kendall's party Eleanor telephoned me with urgency in her voice. "Can I say we're going to get married?"

It took me a moment to get my breath. I was a full-grown adult male now, but I still was not used to the directness of women, particularly when The Sex had such a well-earned reputation for indirection. Less out of resolution than bewilderment I said, "No."

"I don't mean I'm asking you for a pledge," said Eleanor. "I'm only saying that it would get me out of a terrible spot if I could say that to somebody. And I'm trying to play square with you, because of course I could say it anyway, if I wanted to. Now, if anyone is going to be humiliated later it would only be me."

I could not make the two halves of that paragraph quite hang together but the upshot of this strange conversation was that if our understanding was that by saying Yes to her question I was doing her a convenience, then Yes could be the answer, but it must be crystal-clear between us that that was as far as things went.

I did not feel easy in my agreement, and I told Eleanor so. I followed it up with a letter in which I can remember saying "We have gone too fast; much too fast." And we would have to slow down our pace, I went on. The fact that we enjoyed things from art museums and food, from music to being together was a very happy circumstance, but if all this had deeper implications they were yet to emerge.

47 · STRIKEBREAKERS AND KINGS, OR, A PINT OF LAGER *VS.* THE ARISTOCRATIC PRINCIPLE

WHAT *did* EMERGE was that the year 1935 was going to be interesting—journalistically. For one thing Harry had fallen, with a resounding crash, in love with Clare Boothe Brokaw. His new emotional enthusiasms did not lessen his enthusiasms for being editor in chief of *Time* and *Fortune*. On the contrary, I can remember no year when he bubbled with so many new ideas, when his enthusiasm for well-done stories elicited so much praise, and his impatience with the inept was so brisk. "A hell of a lot of *Fortune research* is a great deal better than what we get from it," he said in a scalding note to Ingersoll. "I suggest we publish the research instead of the story. I am serious. HRL." We all knew, of our sad knowledge, that there *seemed* to be a lot of truth in what Harry said. What finished layout looks as beautiful as its first charcoal rough? The research girl, banging out her notes, would often seem to hit an exciting generality, starkly stated, that would then turn into editorial mush after the "literary mind" had played ducks and drakes with it. And indeed some pearls did get lost in the suet this very way. But Ingersoll tried it out, and behold, it was not one of Harry's more inspired ideas. The bold "without exception" in the research girl's preliminary notes would get watered down (and by *her*) first to "almost without significant exception" and maybe later to "oftener than not."

• • •

The year 1935 also provided an episode during which I expected for a while to get shot. The while was brief by the clock but not by me. A skull-cracking strike in some industry—I really

don't remember which—had led Ingersoll to the trail of one Pearl
Bergoff, a professional strikebreaker, whose ploys were as busi-
nesslike as business's itself, and who, because of the still huge
unemployment rate, had no trouble with recruiting. I forget who
wrote the story, but Mr. Bergoff was not at all reticent in the
interviews, and his face bore testimony to many a personal battle
with and for Truth, Justice and the Public Service. The story
went smoothly and closed without incident.

A month later, when the issue bearing the article came out,
Ingersoll's secretary put her head in my door. "There's a Mr.
Bergoff in Reception and he wants to see the man who published
the story about him." This could only mean me; I had edited
the story—and besides, Ingersoll was, as usual, downtown.

I spent several minutes in my office, inhaling and exhaling.
What did professional strikebreakers do to journalists who had
displeased them? Was the sawed-off shotgun already in the violin
case? "Don't say nuttin' to nobody, 'cause we don't want no trouble, see? Move!"

But I *had* to see Mr. Bergoff; an editor who would print a
story and not confront the man involved was a sick chicken indeed. So I made for the reception room and asked the girl in
charge to point out the gentleman who had asked to see me.
It was scarcely necessary.

After I had introduced myself it became evident there was to
be no violence, no threats. The interview was incredible. Mr.
Bergoff was not even angry—he was just terribly, terribly hurt.
The article had made him seem a low creature. As a matter of
fact he and his wife were the parents of five of the finest children,
you wouldn't find such perfect little ladies and gentlemen no
matter where you should look. Furthermore, his business was 100
per cent legitimate; the strikebreaker in times like these was not
only useful but essential . . . . General George Washington
hired mercenaries, didn't he? Was the Father of our Country
a bum? Was that what we were trying to say? He all but broke
down.

So, newly released from tension, I now desired to laugh, but
my guts were killing me for this was, *mutatis mutandis*, the Corporation President complaining that a story did not give a properly accurate sense of the *spirit* of his company. No, Mr. Bergoff
wanted no retraction of anything, that would just make things

worse; he had just wanted to confront the man responsible for the lying slanders and give him a piece of his mind.

• • •

When I got back to my office again it was some time before I could laugh, and when I could, the sound was a little like a sob, too, and although I told the story to all the office mates I could collar, I noticed a fine tremor that did not leave my hands for the rest of the afternoon.

• • •

The American Businessman was Harry's hope and his despair. Harry believed in the aristocratic principle. The British had their Upper Upper Class, who Ran Things, and this suited Harry to a T, for he himself was a Greek scholar, a member of the Landed Gentry, and an Honorable Clerk of the Works. By dint of some backbreaking work the American Businessman might be made to fill an analogous position in *his* society. Poor Harry. In the first place, the parallel was not straight, and neither the social atmosphere nor the human raw material came from the same vat.

• • •

Fortune in those days was a magazine of business—plus. One way to educate a Philistine businessman was to acquaint him with worlds he never knew, or were at the very most only vaguely peripheral to his Daily Report. I forget from whose impulse sprang the story of The Nervous Breakdown, complete with brief directory of sanatoria, but it was a dilly. Dwight Macdonald wrote it, and even this Great Integrator was aghast at the cock-eyed variety of criticisms, perhaps all on the same point, that came back from the eminent practitioners to whom we had sent the piece for review. It was impossible to reconcile them—but then the Lord sent me a memory. In the first edition of Wells's *Outline of History*, Wells and Gilbert Murray, one of the many scholars on whom he relied, had had a Donnybrook over the character of W. E. Gladstone, which Wells traduced; and Wells used up inches of footnotes: statements, rebuttals, surrebuttals, retorts courteous and counterchecks quarrelsome. It made some of the most fascinating reading in the book, although, alas, it all disappeared after the first volume. Why not steal Mr. Wells's idea and print contradictory footnotes to an idea without making the slightest attempt to make them make sense with each other? We did, and it worked fine.

• • •

This same year 1935 saw *Fortune* with a journalistic innovation that still echoes with every election. This was The *Fortune Survey*, which ran for years. The idea was brought to Ingersoll and me by Richardson Wood of the then firm of Cherington, Roper & Wood. It was to flower mightily from the small seeds Wood had planted, for his initial idea was merely that we would apply the comparatively new but firmly lodged mathematical technique of sampling to the quarterly sales of cigarettes by brands and automobiles by makes. But it would have taken greater dolts than we were not to realize that in the technique of scientific sampling we had in our hands a device—a limited and fallible device but incomprehensibly a new one in journalism—to find out what people thought, or thought they thought, about all manner of things. We played it to the limit, and the first survey, with an appropriately weighty preface by Arch MacLeish, appeared in July 1935. It was a hit from the word go.

• • •

George V of England celebrated his silver jubilee that summer and *Fortune* celebrated it for him with a beautiful color frontispiece and a text piece by MacLeish in collaboration with Harold Nicolson. I did something that seemed to me better, purely personally; I went over and watched it. For the first time I saw the "phlegmatic" English public totally out of emotional control. It was a sight for to see.

I had been so lucky as to get to London on the Saturday afternoon that ended the first week of jubilation. I must have checked in at the New Clarges on Half Moon Street, but grubby details like this I don't remember. I made for Piccadilly Circus, where most of the action was. All automobile traffic was shut off, and I was staring at the, to me, utterly new tribal rite of tens of thousands of Englishmen snake dancing down Piccadilly. As I stared, and stared, I got a clap between the shoulder blades that almost sent me through a plate-glass window. My attacker greeted me with a cordial smile. "He's not half bad an old fella, is he?" My attacker was obviously speaking of His Majesty. Although he'd had enough alcohol to accost a total stranger, and a vile American at that, the "not half bad" syndrome had not deserted him—and never would. I *did* think the "old fella" was a more intimate way of speaking of His Royal and Imperial Majesty than I would have used in speaking of my mere fellow citizen, the President of the United States, but things vary, and "I say, what about a drink?" stifled all such thoughts. A pub was twelve feet away, where we each ordered "A pint of lager, please." I tried to put the same intonation into the same words, politeness, slight condescension—and a sense that things would *always* be the same. It was in that last quality that I fell down worst, I think.

I was up against a middle-class Englishman, I decided. "I had a half brother who once migrated to Philadel*phi-a*. I suppose it's a rather ridiculous question, but is that anywhere near . . . your part of the country?" The tentativeness, the pause to find a phrase that would not rouse battling regionalism in me, the concealed hunger for information about this strange land whence I came, speaking my strange version of *his* mother tongue, were all quite touching.

"Ninety miles," I said.

He was aghast. He was knocked all of a 'eap. Damned if I knew what was bothering him but forbore to ask, instead commanding two more pints of lager, please.

As the pints of lager multiplied, our friendship grew and ripened. Of course we never introduced ourselves (there are limits, you know) but we did vow undying friendship. This was just before the increasing jostle inside the pub swept us apart. So long as we could see each other we made futile gestures indicating a bar space over where we could rejoin, but it never worked out. We had been swept apart forever. Nice bloke, too. Wonder about his brother, sometimes.

•   •   •

Left to myself I decided to vary my drinking pattern. There was a bodega across the street that served a sherry so dry it was acid. A pint of bitter at the pub, alternated with the bodega's sherry, did wonderful things. Battling the crowds to cross the street provided essential exercise. When this proved insufficient I joined the snake dance, which, however, produced a malaise. Why not, the thought suddenly occurred to me (where had it been before?), get myself picked up? From the hordes of purse-swinging whores, I chose one. She was frantic, it turned out, for a square meal. Poor girl, she might not have eaten for a week. That was the impression she gave at the porcelain-topped *eatery* (that would have been its American name) where we made our first, long stop. After she had finished her generous meal she looked up brightly at me and said, "Aou abouta bitta fun?"

It was not to be. We got into a taxi and took a long, long ride together. But my need of deviltry had died within me, and all I could think of, damn it, was hygiene, hygiene, hygiene. I stopped the cab short, pressed a ten-pound note into my whore's hand, whereupon we parted. That's half a lifetime ago but it was my last such venture—I'm just not the type, damn it; re-strained not by virtue but by fear.

48 · WHAT LAY BEHIND QUEEN ANNE'S GATE, OR, GUILT

MY STAY IN LONDON with Dick Leonard was supposed to be all vacation, but for me, through choice, it wasn't. Remember now that this was 1935, the occupation of the Rhineland was less than one year in the future, Munich three years. Europe was poised on the thinnest knife-edge in its history.

But if we take Europe to mean England and France, Europe didn't care. America didn't care. Only Germany cared. As Harry and I said goodby, he had said, casually, that if I picked up anything interesting about German rearmament, that would be nice. But his whole attitude was don't go to any *bother;* the British weren't, so why should a tripper Yank have it anywhere but in the back of his mind? Harry had been in England the year before and had been disgusted by the sloth and slackness of this land he loved.

But one result of Harry's trip was that little Time Inc. had signed up Brendan Bracken as its London correspondent. This was very nice, although less resounding than it was to sound later. Mr. Bracken, then of early middle years and flaming red hair, was a modest backbencher M.P. and editor of the *Financial News.* Harry had sent me off on the *Champlain* equipped with a magnum of champagne and a letter of introduction to "B.B.," suggesting he show me some ropes.

Is there any American of prewar vintage—it doesn't matter which one!—who can remember what it used to be like to try to present a letter of introduction to *any* Englishman? First, his secretary cannot catch your name and doesn't want to. Your accent adds to her suspicion. Hers adds to yours, of course. The fact that you have a letter of introduction does *not* mean that you have a letter of introduction; it merely means that you have a partial claim on the lady's attention.

"To what matters does the letter of introduction allude?"

"These are explained in the letter of introduction."

"I see. In that case if you would forward the letter by post I'll see that it is brought to Mr. Bracken's attention as soon as possible. Perhaps you could ring up next Tuesday . . . ." (It is now last Thursday.)

When you ring up next Tuesday Mr. B. (by which I don't mean Mr. Bracken, poor soul, now gone from works to reward— just any Mr. B.), your letter has not met his attention. "He's had a most *trying* morning."

"I'm calling today because you suggested it to me."

"I see. Perhaps it would be better if you could drop Mr. Bracken a note, so that he would have something in front of him."

"He is already supposed to have my letter of introduction in front of him, madam." (The crass American was getting quite vexed, in the way They have, you know.)

"I see. Well, perhaps if . . ."

• • •

So it went, on and on and on. Perhaps it still does. Something brought the *perpetuum stabile* to an end at last, and I was inside the brisk Bracken's office, where a cheery coal grate gave off a mixture of chilblains and what a West Virginia coal miner would call blackdamp. In spite of all this we got down to business fast now that the hazing was over. Mr. Bracken dictated several letters, one of which he gave to me.

"Present this," he said, "without mentioning any names, to the servant who will open the door at 24 Queen Anne's Gate at ten o'clock tomorrow morning. *So* pleasant to have met you."

No. 24 Queen Anne's Gate was a charming little Georgian house in a charming little cobbled street half a block long. On the door was a brass plaque that must have been rubbed for several centuries since the words "PASSPORT CONTROL OFFICE" were scarcely visible.

They also suggested I was at the wrong number of the wrong street. When I saw the interior of No. 24, this impression deepened. In uniform, a few survivors of the Crimean War were polishing things. The civilian visitors did certainly look as if they needed genuine passport control. Queen Victoria had been young when this suite of rooms had been middle-aged. But in this seventeenth-century setting, I was not misplaced. A Crimean survivor caught my eye and made a gesture with his head that said, "Follow me."

•   •   •

When I followed, through an oaken door, the James Bond part (vintage 1935, remember) began. We walked down two flights of most unseemly rough concrete stairs, and then another door opened into the public lobby of a prosaic office building like one on Broadway, with large banks of elevators buzzing up and down. We took one up. Dreary, dingy, seedy sameness characterized every floor, including the tenth, at which we got off. It was a condemned loft building, that's what it was; the hall lights dim, dust thick, paint flaked or blistered; the landlord was just letting it go to hell. Most of the doors were unmarked.

My guide halted in front of one, and we walked into a suite of large, dingy offices. Except, except, that in one casually obscure cubicle, behind a warped and peeling oaken desk, there sat the most perfect picture of a spit-and-polish Regular British Army Major I'd ever seen, Ronald Coleman not excluded.

"Mr. 'Odgkins, Major Morton, sir," said my guide, and vanished.

•   •   •

Major Morton (I am sure the Major *General* Morton of whom I read later, in the war, was the same man) very soon made me deeply ashamed of myself. He was lightning-quick, anticipated your next question before it was half-framed (or framed at all), and flooded you, inundated you, buried you up to your chin with information. This could have been a ploy, of course, and probably was, but what so humiliated me was that it had a counterploy that I had totally neglected while I fumed about, getting past Brendan Bracken's secretariat. This was merely doing one's homework, so that I could later have decoded Major Morton's thousand-words-a-minute discourse into reasonable fact. But I had come expecting a Colonel Blimp or nothing, and it was because I was so mistaken in the former that I came away with the latter. I cannot make out an airtight case against myself—except that even today I occasionally regret that I ever met the charming and handsome Major at all, or ever tried to decipher my scrawling notes at all. I don't know how far up the British Intelligence ladder I was taken, but it was not low, which is why I am haunted—not by the knowledge that I missed a great story, but by not knowing whether I did or not.

One question I did settle to my own satisfaction. Why did the British, after all the camouflage of 24 Queen Anne's Gate, etc., make a high British Intelligence Officer look so exactly like a high British Intelligence Officer? Because, I decided, the Germans would be incapable of believing that the British would do any such utterly damn fool thing.

49 · CAMDEN, OR,
IN THE SOUP, DEEP

In the 1930's, three of the biggest privately owned companies in the U.S. business world were the Ford Motor Company, Singer Sewing Machines and Campbell's Soup. In the face of such companies *Fortune* was helpless; the businesses might be huge but they *were* private, and what they chose not to tell you, there was small way of finding out, and none of verifying. A corporation story on any of the three thus seemed out of the question. Yet *Fortune*'s little Ed Kennedy had, not long before, wormed an interview out of Henry Ford that had revealed more than the Sage of Dearborn knew he was saying . . . which is why the journalistic motto has to be Keep Everlastingly Trying.

For the great Campbell Soup Company, I cherished an ambition: that I could do a full-blown corporation story on it. This ambition rested on a very rickety foundation; it was merely that John T. Dorrance was a member of the M.I.T. Class of 1895, and was by training a chemist, and that Dr. (it was an earned doctorate) Dorrance had then for the next thirty-five years devoted himself, for a number of those years as president of the company, to making the Campbell Soup Company into the largest and most profitable food-canning operation ever to then known.

None of this did me any good; Dr. Dorrance was too old for me to have known; also he took a minimum interest in M.I.T. or its alumni affairs. Worst of all, he was five years dead.

But his death, which had been sudden, pitchforked his much (by twenty years) younger brother, Arthur Dorrance, into the company presidency. And Buck Dorrance, M.I.T. Class of '14, I *did* know. And I proposed to get to know him much better, as fast as good manners would permit.

Here my *Technology Review* background stood me in good

stead, for Buck Dorrance, unlike his elder brother, was a "good" (i.e., dues-paying) alumnus and a careful reader of the *Review*. In an odd way, therefore, he knew me better than I knew him; at least he was acquainted with my journalistic style and seemed to approve it.

When I confided to Harry Luce my ambition to convert my acquaintanceship with Buck Dorrance into a *Fortune* corporation story on Campbell's Soup, he slapped his desk and said, "Go spend the rest of the year in Camden if that's what it takes!"

That was almost what it took. Buck Dorrance was the youngest among all the directors and major officers of the company and a believer (the direct opposite of his brother on this point) in the careful cultivation of the press. So whenever I asked for a Camden appointment, I got it, and a good deal of my time was spent sitting in Buck Dorrance's elegant office. In the 1930's only two Campbell executives had private offices: the president of the company and its treasurer; thousands upon thousands of filing cases made up cubicle walls for all the others. In his office Buck Dorrance, young, quiet, earnest, imperturbable, would talk and talk, with a minimum of emphasis or rubato, his exquisitely kept hands gestureless on the desk before him, about Techniques of Executive Control or The Philosophy of Management. Buck *may* have topped off his M.I.T. years with a frosting from the Harvard Business School; whether or no, he was the type. I went to Camden often; we had many of these meetings and more than one lunch in the executive dining room—as unpretentious as a farmhouse kitchen—and inevitably the question would come up, raised by me: When would the Campbell Soup Company *officially* receive me for the purposes of a corporation story?

Ah, yes, said Buck; he'd wondered how soon I would come to the point *this* time. Well, official conversations were different from unofficial ones, after all, weren't they? But hadn't I learned a good deal about the company through the now not inconsiderable number of unofficial meetings I'd had? Not enough? Well, perhaps we should give the whole matter some additional unofficial consideration . . . .

He teased me like that for months. Was I getting anyplace or was he just having a good time at my expense? I had only one tangible base for optimism. Although he *wouldn't* say Yes, he *hadn't* said No.

• • •

One day, perhaps after a tenth meeting, and just as it was ending, Buck suddenly put an end to the game. "I'll make a deal with you. *Fortune* can do the story if I have *Fortune*'s assurances that *you* and nobody else will write it."

I knew I needed no consultation with Harry or Ingersoll on that one, so we shook hands then and there—and I've been wondering about it ever since. Now let me turn my wonder over to some Professor of Ethics-in-Journalism.

I knew perfectly well what was implicit in Buck Dorrance's "deal," and he knew that I knew it. It was: "In making my condition that you and only you write the story, I am expressing my faith that you will write the story as I would like to see it written, and you are agreeing that you will do that."

And in agreeing that I and only I would write the story, my unspoken reservation was: "I know what's in your mind, Old Buck, and I know that you know that I know it, but I am merely agreeing, literally, that I will write it; not *how* I'll write it. Since I like you, I hope you'll like *it*, but there are not going to be any Special Considerations. You *know* that from reading *The Technology Review*, as well as from knowing me."

• • •

I'm overelaborating a little, I suppose; nevertheless, there was a Favor-for-Favor glint in Buck's eyes that I clearly saw, yet I shook hands in the knowledge that I was going to do nothing about it. The one thing I wanted was to be the first journalist to crack the books of the Campbell Soup Company; all other considerations were secondary. Buck knew that, all right; I had told him we wanted sales and profit figures never before published, and his answer had been far from vague: "Absolutely nothing doing." "Then we'll have to estimate," I said, to which Buck replied, "I frankly don't see how you can."

At that stage, neither did I, but at least there was no ambiguity here. The camel had, however, got his nose into the tent.

• • •

When my researcher, Patricia Divver, and I arrived to go to work in earnest, it was obvious that the order had gone out to

416

kill us with kindness. It was also obvious that one of the five ranking executives we were permitted to see—Production Manager James McGowan, Jr., later to succeed to the presidency of the company when Buck, like his brother, died young—was having difficulty following his orders. He had obviously voted against letting us in and did not relish his defeat. He was doing his best to be the Organization Man and take part in Team Play, but it came hard.

"What is the capacity of this soup kettle, Mr. McGowan?"

"One hundred and fifty gallons."

"And how many of them are there, here in Camden?"

"You can go round and count them, one by one, if you'd like."

"All right. Patty, I think I see fifty in my aisle. How many do you see in yours?"

"I'm not sure whether it's forty-eight or fifty," said Patty, who picked up cues fast.

"Aw, hell, I'll give you a blueprint of every one! Look, I don't mind telling you people you picked a mighty inconvenient time of year to come down here with questions like these."

"Oh? Well, we want to cause just as little inconvenience to—"

"I'm sorry; I don't mean to be short with you. But outside people don't realize that during the month of September we've got to make our tomato pack in this plant for the entire year. Do you realize what that means?"

We said we didn't, so Mr. McGowan told us. It was very, very interesting. We had picked the perfect time for our story, and the significance of the Total Tomato Pack had not dawned on Mr. McGowan. The leverage this gave us had apparently escaped Buck Dorrance's attention, too.

• • •

The purchasing agent volunteered more lore, except that if a figure had a dollar sign in front of it, he would not utter it. "Nobody knows it, but in addition to being the largest *sellers* of canned goods in the world, we're also the largest *buyers*. Now you take lima beans . . ."

We took lima beans. Then we took peas. They were astronomical. We even took okra. These could, so to speak, be roughly triangulated to advantage.

Next door to the plant of every large canner there is always the plant of a large can manufacturer. The two are connected by a noisy overhead conveyor, for this is the only way empty cans can be shipped "without paying freight charges on ten thousand gallons of air," as the canner is always glad to explain to you. As the purchasing agent listened to the clash of the product rolling, sliding, tumbling from the Continental Can plant across the way, nostalgia momentarily overcame him.

"I can remember the time when we had our first million-can day," he said. The reverence in his voice called for a more than adequate reply. "Think of that," I said. "And now you can pack ten times as many."

It was a shot in the dark, but from the splash I reckoned that I had come close.

"More than that," said the purchasing agent. "*More than that.*"

What did this emphasis mean? I decided that it meant I had come close. Maybe 12 million cans per day, or 360 million cans a month—that *could* be a year's pack; if so, it was also what those soup kettles could produce in thirty days of three-shift operation. Now it would be helpful to know how long it took to process each batch, and this was just the sort of nondollar figure the management was not only willing but eager to give out.

There were certain other questions whose answers sounded innocent enough.

Q. I notice you make quite a thing out of the Ten-Ton Club. Just what is it?

A. We pay a special bonus to farmers who can raise more than ten tons of tomatoes per acre of land.

Q. How many members?

A. Oh, about one in seven.

Q. What proportion of Campbell's tomatoes are raised in New Jersey?

A. About two-thirds.

Q. How many farmers does Campbell do business with?

A. I'll be glad to look up that figure.

In short, the Campbell executives were not only willing but eager to supply any figure, if it was not a dollar figure.

• • •

Patty Divver had experienced the same phenomenon; her notebook was quite full of dollarless figures. She and I had also

418

noticed that the last ingredient to go into a 150-gallon vat of tomato soup was a one-pound brick of butter.

What did that cost, wholesale? This was ascertainable, although not in Camden.

So were other things. Fortunately for us, Campbell's Soup's very hugeness made enemies for it, right and left. Buck Dorrance had quoted to me the principle by which brother John ran his totally controlled company. "We have enough surplus," he had said, "to run this company without any profit for fifteen years, and still be very comfortable. *And that's exactly what we will do rather than yield first place in our industry to anyone else."* The whole 1935 world of canning and distributing of foodstuffs knew this too, and it would have been hard to find anyone who liked it. So overwhelming was the consumer demand for Campbell's Soups in those days that it had *all* the bargaining power: wholesale price, quotas of slower-moving items that must be met if the wholesaler was to get as much as he wanted of the fast-turnover items, mostly based, one way or another, on *Lycopersicon esculentum*, or the tomato. Even Campbell's interoffice memos spoke of Soup, not soup, and there was good earthy reason for this Deification. Even in those days of bankruptcies and reorganizations, the Campbell Soup Company was so rich that it had never had to borrow a nickel since 1906 or 1907—the kindly, white-haired, benevolent, shark-jawed treasurer couldn't quite remember which.

• • •

Thus it was that within the grocery trade Campbell was rich in something besides money. That was enemies. Although my agreement with Buck Dorrance specified that I would not seek information from direct (soup) competitors (Heinz was about the only one of consequence), this admittedly unusual concession didn't bar me from characters like Abe Krasne. A. Krasne & Company was the largest wholesale grocer in the country, and although Abe Krasne didn't know the volume of profits of Campbell, he was intimately acquainted with the selling methods of every canner and packager in the country and his hatred for Campbell was venomous. When to Pat Divver's microscopic examination of the ingredients (starting with that butter) and their average commodity-exchange prices, you added an occasional mild indiscretion of a Campbell officer (total daily tomato pack) and then you added Abe Krasne's venom, you came up with something remarkable: a plausible estimate of the annual profits of the Campbell Soup Company.

I shipped off my first draft to Campbell and prepared to face the music. The facedown took place in that bare, spare country kitchen of an executive's dining room where we had met so often before—and the music itself was in a strangely muted and minor key. Every officer from Buck Dorrance down loathed the story, but Buck Dorrance was what Harry Luce had always cherished the hope every American businessman would eventually become—a businessman who was also, in his own way, an aristocrat. Thus Buck had obviously passed down the message that with accuracy might be roughly translated as "Treat this total son of a bitch with absolutely impeccable, unexceptionable courtesy from first to last."

And that was how it went. I had divided my story into three major headings: (1) Campbell the Corporation, (2) The Tomato, Genetics of, and (3) John T. Dorrance, Estate of, and how the Supreme Court of the United States had collaborated in a gross miscarriage of justice concerning it.

• • •

James McGowan addressed a most intelligent question to the second section of the article. "What I can't figure out," he said, while the floor, but not his voice, vibrated with his fury, "is how Pop Hall got his story over to you so perfectly and none of the rest of us did." (Pop Hall was Dr. Harry Hall, the company's chief geneticist.)

The answer was very simple, and I gave it with the same (I hope) exquisite courtesy Mr. McGowan had bestowed upon me. Dr. Hall had never dogged a question; in fact, he had been so bursting with information and the desire to impart it, that although he was twenty years older than I, he had me puffing as he raced from row to row and field to field in his vast and varied tomato gardens. These were not, of course, production fields; what I was seeing for the first time in my life was Mendelianism brought to the service of humanity and the profit motive, both at the same time. So *of course*, Mr. McGowan, Pop Hall had got his story across to me; it turned out, to my naïve surprise, that the world not only needed tomatoes but tomatoes in their infinite variety. Every row of Pop's garden was staked and labeled: whence had come the ancestors; what generation this was (FF[1] stayed in my mind as First Filial Generation); what crossed with what other generations of what genera had done what? Opposed to the cautious, nonresponsive, circumlocutory answers of Management, Dr. Hall, like any true teacher, was bursting to impart.

Pop's surgical instrument was a penknife. "See that?" The penknife scraped the tomato skin. "Pretty thick and waxy. Got to settle for compromises in this business. Waxy skin is okay but only up to a point . . . . Now *here's* something we've got coming along. Taste a hunk of that. Good for juice; good for pulp. Not too much diameter. Plenty deep from stem scar down, and not very subject to catface. A hell of a lot of good tomatoes get spoiled by too much catface . . . ." ("Catface" means defects around the blossom end of the fruit.)

"So, Mr. McGowan, sir, Dr. Hall got his story across to me by deluging me with more authentic information than I could use, although I wanted to use it all. And if you'll pardon me for saying so, that's the direct reverse of the techniques used by some of your colleagues."

When I said "some" I meant "all," and the icy silence that then fell was broken by the truly exquisite manners of Campbell's president.

"I was right in the first place, wasn't I?" said Buck Dorrance. "Never let the press in at all unless you're willing to give a straight answer to every question."

That wasn't, and isn't, altogether true, but it was very convenient to answer Yes, so I answered Yes.

• • •

Once we had shaken hands on our deal, Buck Dorrance did a strange thing indeed. He handed to me the whole dossier on his elder brother's estate litigation—still, as then, the most extraordinary event of its kind. Why Buck did it, I don't know, but I was instantly in possession of a journalistic rough diamond of the heaviest troy weight.

John Thompson Dorrance was a very shy man. He was much more successfully shy than that Johnny-come-lately Howard

Hughes, for example, for in his lifetime he just never did anything, good *or* bad, to attract any journalistic attention. Only by dying did he raise any clamor at all, but then it was a ferocious clamor indeed, for when his trustees filed his will with the Surrogate Court of the County of Burlington in the State of New Jersey the astounding first estimate of the wealth of the all-but-anonymous man was $150 million. If that seems a bit middle class today, remember that the year of this disclosure was 1930, and Herbert Hoover was his country's weary President.

50 · "I, JOHN T. DORRANCE," OR, THE TRUSTEES' AGONY

DR. DORRANCE, whose carefully chosen friends called him Jack, was modest as well as shy. He lived in the township of Cinnaminson, at Pomona Farms, so called, not nine miles from his Camden cannery, and it was in Cinnaminson that he died. There was nothing about Pomona Farms or its 167 acres of fine tomato land to suggest a love of Oriental Display and nothing to suggest that Dr. Dorrance, whose passion was the making of soup, felt the lack of it.

But there was a hitch. Dr. Dorrance had been married to the former Ethel Mallinckrodt for twenty-four years when he died; she, during that time, had borne him four daughters until—thank God!—in 1919 she had presented him with a son and heir. Now things were really shipshape and tidy, for the Campbell Soup Company could now never fall out of the control of the Dorrance family—not, that is, as far as Dr. Dorrance could fix things.

The hitch was that Elinor, Ethel, Charlotte and Peggy, the Dorrance daughters, began growing up. They were pretty—and a poorer launching pad for the social careers of four comely, well-favored young females could scarcely be imagined than Cinnaminson, New Jersey. Something had to be done.

Not too eventually, something was done: the Dorrance family moved across the Delaware River to a big estate in Radnor, one of the Mainest of the fashionable Main Line suburbs of Philadelphia. And, as the four daughters successively came out, at proper intervals, the resources, catering and otherwise, of the Bellevue Stratford, long Philadelphia's headquarters for that sort of thing, ended up barely able to stand the strain.

• • •

But Dr. Dorrance had always been downright fussy about where he lived, legally, and had once even refused a directorship of the Pennsylvania Railroad until thrice assured by expensive legal counsel that this would not in any way compromise his New Jersey residency. Pomona Farms in Cinnaminson was never closed. Dr. Dorrance continued to vote in New Jersey and never gave up his post of Senior Warden of Christ Church in nearby Riverton.

It was all neat as a pin. Dr. Dorrance's was an incredibly detailed will, which, for example, specified that the amount of gasoline remaining in the tanks of his automobiles at the time of his death should pass to his widow.

Decedent's executors and trustees were just preparing to hand over an inheritance tax of $4.4 million to the federal government when the Commonwealth of Pennsylvania suddenly cleared its throat and threw a whole crate of eggs into the electric fan by saying that *its* valuation of Dr. Dorrance's wealth was $200 million, and consequently *it* would like $31 million as its proper share of the Commonwealth's tax.

• • •

From this the thunderstruck executors took immediate and horrified appeal. They went to the Orphan's Court of Delaware County, at Media, Pennsylvania, and there began an interminable legal wrangle to answer the question: Where did Dr. Dorrance live? Upon the bench sat John B. Hannum; among the counsel for the executors was John B. Hannum, Jr. The passionate contention of the counsel for the executors was that Dr. Dorrance lived in New Jersey. They spent several months insisting that he lived in New Jersey, and at the end of that time, Judge Hannum said Yes, he did live in New Jersey, and the Pennsylvania assessment was of no validity. The executors sighed in relief and went home (in Pennsylvania) for a good night's sleep.

But the Commonwealth of Pennsylvania was not satisfied, so it appealed to the Supreme Court of Pennsylvania. By coincidence, among eminent counsel for the executors was Robert von Moschzisker, who had in 1930 resigned as Chief Justice of that very court to become associated with the firm of Ballard, Spahr, Andrews & Ingersoll. But he failed to convince his former colleagues, and in September 1932 they reversed the Orphan's Court and ruled that Dr. Dorrance lived in Pennsylvania after all. It was small relief to the executors that Pennsylvania's more sober appraisal of the estate now resulted in a tax claim of no more than $17 million.

Eventually, the whole business got up to the Supreme Court of the United States on petition of the executors for a writ of certiorari. It now became evident that Judge von Moschzisker had made at least an error of strategy, if not indeed the most expensive legal boo-boo in the history of estate litigation. A peculiar rule (No. 17) of the court of which he had been for nine years the Chief Justice specified that a case on appeal comes before the court on the "appellant's statement of the questions involved" and upon that only, unless the appellee (in this case the estate) undertakes to file a counterstatement. In the Orphan's Court, one argument of the executors had been that a tax levied by Pennsylvania would contravene the "due process of the law" clause of the Constitution of the United States, since New Jersey, as they contended, was entitled to a tax in any event. But in going, as appellee, before his former colleagues in the Pennsylvania Supreme Court, Judge von Moschzisker had not elected to file a counterstatement raising that point again. Thus it was that in December 1932 the Supreme Court of the United States denied certiorari on the highly technical and legalistic grounds that the only federal question involved had not been properly presented under the rules of the Supreme Court of Pennsylvania.

That was that. To eminent counsel the executors now turned to ask, quite understandably, What the hell? Eminent counsel's response was that, although justice was justice, it is possible to irritate a court by inserting in your brief something that is patently a signal flag announcing in advance that if you don't get what you want in *that* court, you propose immediately to go to a higher one.

Under the circumstances, this was not consoling. Pennsylvania assessed the tax, and the executors, after rearguments availed not, had no course but to write out on March 31, 1933, the largest check the Commonwealth of Pennsylvania has ever received. It was a check for $14,394,698.88.

• • •

• • •

Meanwhile, of course, New Jersey had not been inactive. Its State Tax Commissioner had, it so happened, filed demand on the estate for more than $12 million in the very same month that the Pennsylvania Supreme Court had given Judge von Moschzisker his original rebuff. At first, it had unavailingly attempted to get the United States Supreme Court to let it sue to enjoin Pennsylvania from collecting the tax. Denied that, it suddenly became ominously quiet, engrossed in watching the executors sink deeper and deeper into the legalistic mires of its neighbor state. It could afford to wait. "The New Jersey assessment," said New Jersey's Attorney General, *"is a lien upon all the property of the decedent in New Jersey . . . ."* The executors didn't have to think twice to know what that meant. Decedent had no property in Pennsylvania except Woodcrest in Radnor. But decedent had left behind in New Jersey the whole Campbell Soup Company.

So when it thought the time was right, New Jersey looked up blandly and said to the executors, in effect, "We understand your contention has been that Dr. Dorrance lived in New Jersey. We agree with that." Whereupon it began to press in the matter of the $12 million it believed it had coming to it. Thus it was that the executors now found themselves in a dilemma the horns of which were that having argued in Pennsylvania that Dr. Dorrance was a resident of New Jersey, they must now argue in New Jersey that he was a resident of Pennsylvania. It was not an argument into which they could put much vim. The Pennsylvania tax had been paid; every relief from it had been exhausted. But residence, at law, is determined by facts *and* by intent; where the facts are ambiguous, as they were in this case, the intent decides. Dr. Dorrance's intent was clear, as witness his refusal to become a director of the Pennsylvania Railroad until he was assured that that would not jeopardize his New Jersey citizenship. The Prerogative Court of New Jersey sat gravely and listened to the transcripts of the Pennsylvania testimony and found, in February 1934, that Dr. Dorrance was a resident of New Jersey.

One good argument the executors did still have. It lay in Article IV, Section 1 of the U.S. Constitution, which provides that the courts of one state must give "full faith and credit" to the decisions of the courts of other states. But in the executors' faltering hands, even this stout stave snapped short. New Jersey denied the argument on the grounds that *it is applicable only where the courts of the other state have jurisdiction on the subject matter, and the courts of Pennsylvania had no jurisdiction because Dr. Dorrance was a resident of New Jersey!* And it thereupon capped a new sort of climax in estate litigation by refusing even to exempt from its taxation that portion of the estate that had been paid out as a tax to Pennsylvania, even though New Jersey statutes specifically provide for such deduction. Once again, its argument had a breathtaking simplicity: the Pennsylvania tax was an illegal tax and therefore none of New Jersey's business.

• • •

The executors had, of course, one last shot—a sort of jurisprudential silver bullet. They could go from the New Jersey Court of Errors and Appeals back once again to the Supreme Court of the United States. The Supreme Court of the United States now found itself in a painful position. The essence of the whole case, to the layman, is that the executors lost in Pennsylvania on technical grounds and lost in New Jersey on substantial grounds. And so the Supreme Court was constrained to hold: (1) that New Jersey was right; (2) that a serious miscarriage of justice had therefore taken place (in more obscure language, of course); and (3) that in this miscarriage it (the Supreme Court) played a part. To those three points the Supeme Court then had to add a final one: (4) nothing whatever can be done about it.

• • •

I have spent a lot of words in telling this old but still obscure story (also for several pages I have plagiarized from myself, with Time Inc. permission*) because it seems to me that Dr. Dorrance was the very last of his kind—the American Businessman who was interested in *nothing* but his business. Compared to him, his rough contemporary Henry Ford was a man of broad social outlook and reformer's zeal—peace, square dances, soybeans, etc.

---

* Copyright 1935 by TIME-FORTUNE CORPORATION.

By all accounts, Dr. Dorrance was a pleasant man, but God must have meant something by bringing his life to a close in 1930, for Dr. Dorrance was the Frenchman's *vrai type américain*, which can scarcely longer be found. Having made his colossal pile, he did absolutely nothing with it. No benefactions, no Foundations, no imposing granite piles, no nothing. What was perhaps even more amazing—no splurges, no stables, no yachts, no diamonds as big as the Ritz, again, no nothing. Dr. Dorrance just left the whole vast bundle of his wealth to his family, which was of course a very kind thing to do, but not much in fashion today. Moreover, God disposed, even in the 1930's. That portion of Dr. Dorrance's wealth that the warring states of Pennsylvania and New Jersey taxed, stole, gouged, confiscated or otherwise made off with had largely to be used on what was then known as Relief, for the soup-kitchen lines had shortened only slightly two years after the beginning of the New Deal.

• • •

Perhaps Buck Dorrance, when he made me a present of this journalistic pearl of the official record of his brother's estate, expected me to blast the state and federal governments for the obvious and evident miscarriages of justice in which they had gotten themselves so involved. And I did blast them. But the total situation was of an irony so high and dry that to ignore it would have been a prime case of nonjournalism. So I far from ignored it. When one is about to lose almost $30 million wrongfully and through the stupidity of another, there is nothing funny about it, and this of course was the trustees' situation. But I was writing for a wider and more diversified audience, so my viewpoint was not quite the same. Buck Dorrance was deeply disappointed at my treatment of *everything* about Campbell except the genetics of the tomato, but he utterly kept his cool, and when it was all over, on October 1, 1935, he sent me a letter that I still cherish enough to quote from:

> A reading of the proofs which you sent to us late yesterday afternoon has made me appreciate the care with which you have made corrections which we have brought to your attention. Evidently there is no limit to the amount of trouble that you will take to have the article letter-perfect insofar as ascertainable facts

are concerned. Differences of opinion still exist between us, but I have no lack of respect for your conclusions, even though I cannot accept several of them.

•   •   •

That is the real end of the story. But I cannot refrain from three short appendices.

I: As the article was about to come out, the acting advertising manager of Campbell's wrote to *Fortune:* "We would like, for distribution to the members of our organization, 100 copies of the story of our company as it is scheduled to appear in your November issue."

I can't resist including that because it represented a pattern so often repeated during the contentious thirties—furious anger during the writing of a story, coupled with just such a letter when the squawking-and-feathers phase was over.

II: Just to indicate that everything was not sweetness and light, I had not heard my last from Mr. James McGowan. When Buck Dorrance regrettably died, Mr. McGowan succeeded him as president. Some longish time after this change of command I was invited to speak before the M.I.T. Club of Philadelphia. When the evening came and the toastmaster and I were exchanging prespeech pleasantries, he suddenly said, "What in the world did you ever do to Jim McGowan?" Mr. McGowan, as a distinguished alumnus (M.I.T. '08), had been invited to sit on the dais. The chairman showed me his written reply, which was that he would not only not sit on the dais, he would not attend the goddamn dinner, nor be found near the Bellevue Stratford that night, and he had Absolute Zero interest in seeing or hearing the advertised speaker, "whose loyalty to our American way of life I have serious reason to question. Yours very truly."

•   •   •

III: There is, today, a John T. Dorrance Hall of Food Technology at M.I.T. The times do move, and John T. Dorrance, Jr., who was a minor child when his father died, is now Chairman of the Board of the Campbell Soup Company, bigger than ever.

51 · ON BEING A MANAGING EDITOR, OR, ARCH MacLEISH FRONT AND CENTER

ONE DAY IN MID-1935 Ingersoll called Grover and me into his office and began a long, complex, orotund speech. As Harry had been emphasizing for some time, he began, Time Inc. had ceased to be a big little business and had become a little big business. And it was getting harder and harder for Harry and for Treasurer Charlie Stillman to keep themselves in touch with all the aspects of things that needed their high attention. (Ingersoll left Roy Larsen out of the line-up of senior officers because Roy was still so deeply involved with *The March of Time* movie that for an indefinite future he was as good as lost as the company's Second-in-Command.) Hence, said Ingersoll, blowing up to his climax, there must be another high officer: a man whose primary job would be to keep Harry and Charlie properly informed of everything that should concern them. He and Harry had been having many talks about the problem, said Ingersoll, and it was agreed that what Time Inc. needed was a "general manager." But who could fill the post? Harry and Ingersoll had agreed that to go outside the company at this critical stage would be to make a grave mistake. On the other hand, there was no perfect candidate within the company. So, granting that, Harry and Ingersoll had at length come to the conclusion that the *nearest thing* to the perfect candidate was Ingersoll. Therefore, effective next month, he, Ingersoll, would become general manager of Time Inc.

It was a most peculiar speech.

And it was delivered in a most peculiar manner. I think Grover and I were the first to hear it, although obviously Luce, Larsen and Stillman preceded us in the knowledge of what was going to happen. The long, long windup to the climax was peculiar, for Ingersoll, whatever his faults, was no windbag, yet this was a windbag's speech. Its modesty was fake, for Ingersoll, whatever his virtues, was no violet. I later decided that if a date could be set for the regrettable beginning of office politics in Time Inc., this was it. I still later decided that the fake modesty was inserted as an escape hatch in case the job did not work out. It did not, but perhaps *this* wisdom *was* ex post facto.

• • •

In any event, on this particular morning, as I was taking in Ingersoll's speech, I was also thinking, with might and main, "What about Me?" For nowhere was the managing editorship of *Fortune* mentioned in Ingersoll's rough sketch of the new grand design. So after lunch I went to Ingersoll's office to renew my congratulations to him personally and the company on the wisdom of its new strengthening move. (Have I given anyone the impression that I, too, am not a liar and a hypocrite? I hope not, and you can take *that* with a grain of salt, too.)

Eventually I worked the subject around to Me.

"Well, what do you expect?" asked the new general manager.

"I *hope*," I said, "that Harry will designate me as your acting successor, and if he likes what I do he won't take forever to confirm me permanently in the job."

"Well," said Ingersoll abstractedly, "I *imagine* that's more or less what Harry has in mind."

• • •

But Harry never said a word to me. Ingersoll, on moving out of his office, merely said to me, "Well, move in." So I did. And thereafter the memos I got from Harry all made the tacit assumption that I was responsible for *Fortune*'s editorial content. But no memorandum, no conversation, not even a grunt, officially confirmed this. I was to hold several more positions with Time Inc. before I was at last, after twenty-five years, let out to pasture, and each one was duly and formally heralded. But not this one. Not once. Never.

• • •

The staff I inherited from Ingersoll and later, with some additions and subtractions, passed on to Mitch Davenport was insane, unreliable, alcoholic, and, all in all, I think the most brilliant magazine staff ever to exist in America. Please note that I say *staff*. Magazines did not have staffs except for the editor and the wage slaves who mechanically fitted together the contents supplied largely by outside contributors. But *Fortune* (and *Time*) had a resident (subject to its whims) staff, and although it's hopeless, I'd like to describe its major elements.

• • •

There was, first of all, Arch MacLeish. I'll give him the rest of this chapter and then go on to the rest. Arch was older than the group average of the rest of us by five years or more and a sweet, gentle man he was. The rest of the staff looked up to him as was befitting a Pulitzer Prize winner. Ingersoll said one thing in particular about him in giving me his first rapid rundown of the staff. It was "Arch is very easy to handle editorially provided you don't change as much as a comma in his copy without consulting him." When I succeeded Ingersoll I got proof of that in jig time. Arch came tearing into my office one day, the galley proofs of one of his stories fluttering behind him. "Would you mind telling me, if you know, who made this change in my copy?" I knew all right; it was I, who had literally changed a comma to a semicolon by one unthinking dot. I confessed, was mildly upbraided, and then forgiven. But Arch could change his lens aperture on a story from commas to cosmos in a trice. I had suggested to Harry in 1937 a *Fortune* series of articles titled *Background of War*.* Arch wrote most of them. The first, "British Foreign Policy," was a breeze, which rightly stirred up a lot of dust. The second, "The Struggle in Spain," was a hurricane, for Arch's position that the Loyalists *were* the Loyalists was unshakable; Harry's position was not *exactly* pro-Franco, but "Arch is taking on one hell of a responsibility in what he's saying." And there was I, precisely in the middle, because neither principal would talk to the other directly, so strong were their emotions. I studied and studied the story, and came to an honest conclusion, with which I went to the author. "Arch, the first half of this story is so good that I don't truly think the second half lives up to it."

Arch pondered this and next day he said, "I think maybe you're right." Whereupon he thoroughly rewrote the second half.

* Not to be confused with copycat *Time*'s 1939 department, Background for War.

God is not always kind to managing editors but this time He was good to me. Arch had made such enormous improvements in the second half that now, again in all honesty, the first half was markedly its inferior. I asked Arch if he did not agree with me.

There are two kinds of pride of authorship: one is the Standfast type that will brook no changes at all from any outside source. Fortunately for me Arch's was (despite commas) of the genuine type, eager to improve and improve and improve in response to any suggestions with which he agreed. And damned if he didn't agree with me—whereupon he began a furious rewriting of the first half. The result was a story that suited Arch himself better. Harry still didn't like it, but at least it reduced him from the fulminating to the grunting stage and a crisis was thus passed. And in this instance I was so innocent of guile that the way the whole thing had happened never fully dawned on me for a week or more.

• • •

When Arch and Ada MacLeish were not living in Conway, Massachusetts, which Arch never tires of immortalizing, they used as a *pied-à-terre* an apartment at St. Mark's Garth—the same set of buildings that housed Eleanor Treacy. Arch and I with fair frequency rattled down the Third Avenue El to lunch just abaft St. Mark's in the Bowery in what was once a lovely backwater and is now a gathering place for vandals. When great men say startling things, it is all too easy to imagine them said at some literary gathering place, a soiree presided over by some American equivalent of Lady Ottoline Morrell (Clare, for example?), or elsewhere where the intellectual echoes would be resounding. So it's a bit of a comedown to have to report that the most startling thing Arch ever said to me had as it's locale one of the rattan cross-benches of the Third Avenue El's more dilapidated cars.

Arch suddenly burst out "I wish to Christ I didn't want fame so much!" This was a real shocker and a real eye opener; until that time I had assumed that Arch basked quite comfortably in his even then quite considerable fame. It was this sudden confession of discomfort with what is commonly supposed to be one of life's major rewards that endeared Arch to me more than anything else.

• • •

"Don't talk to me about Arch's poetry," Harry barked at me
one evening after he and I had had a business dinner alone at
one of his temporary abodes in Greenwich. I certainly hadn't
been talking very deeply about it, because there is scarcely a
line of it, written by that master of clarity in prose, that I can
understand. I must merely have mentioned it, which had been
enough to set Harry off. What he could read but not understand
put him into a fury. Arch had come into the conversation via
Thomas Mann, whom Arch had recently met. Arch had recounted to us how the author of *The Magic Mountain* had said,
"You are a poet. But in America poets can make no money. How
do you make money?" And Arch had replied with beautiful simplicity, "I am a journalist." (*"Je suis journaliste." "Ich bin
Zeitungsschreiber."*) For some obscure reason this self-portrait
drawn in grease crayon of Arch as journalist sent both Harry
and me up the wall—I, perhaps, because I aspired to be nothing
else; Harry, perhaps, because his higher aspirations were not yet
firmly formed. I apologized to Harry that there was *something*
about Arch that made me feel female-catty. "For God's sake,
don't apologize to *me* for that," said Harry with some heat, going
on to say that his great emotional trouble in dealing with Arch
was that Arch made *him* feel that way, often more than once
a day.

• • •

It is all too true that Arch, in addition to being the most distinguished member of the staff, was also the most efficient. Nor
did he insulate himself from *Fortune*'s daily clashes and clangors.
(More than once he added to them.) He contributed not only
words but thoughts, policies and ponderings. If there was a hint
of condescension in Arch's attitude, it was not toward *Fortune*,
which he dearly loved, but toward journalism and above all
toward business and industry, which he despised. So here was
a strange anomaly indeed. And I happened to be present when
Arch discovered industry, much in the same fashion that Columbus discovered America. It was in Washington, at a small dinner
in early wartime, and if Arch was not yet head of the short-lived
office of Facts and Figures, he was about to be. His deputy, Allen

Grover, also filched from Time Inc., was beside him. Donald Nelson, newly struggling with the impossible job of heading the Office of Production Management, which had not yet beaten him into an unrecognizable pulp, was full of conversation. So was Elmo Roper, happy to be one of Wild Bill Donovan's boys in the Office of Strategic Services. One of my M.I.T. classmates, Albert Browning, was there too. And there was me. This particular alignment of planets sets the date as mid-1942.

It was an informal, not an official, dinner. But as the evening's conversation progressed, I could see it borne in on Arch that *if* we were going to win the war (it was then a huge *if*, for 1942 was the very sump of the war for the newly forged Allies), then one of the forces for victory was the American industrial might, in the hands, then as now, of a bunch of sons of bitches, some with good manners and morals, some with none. Arch had spent a generous part of his life despising their Philistinism, their labor policies, their political outlook (they had only one) and everything else about them. And now, if they did not exist, we would lose the war. This was hard on Arch but he—well, he adapted very easily to the New Industrialists that evening.

52·ED KENNEDY, OR, HOMER DRUNK

ALTHOUGH I HAVE RECORDED my belief that the editorial staff Ingersoll turned over to me, and that I, in turn, later turned over to Davenport, was just about the best resident staff of writers a magazine in America ever had, its principal and persistent trouble was that there was never enough of it.

When Harry Luce made that speech of his at the Time Inc. 20th Anniversary Dinner, over which I presided, he struck a jarring chord that has hummed in my mind ever since: "I sometimes wonder whether the much-advertised opera troupes actually contain as many temperamentalists as are to be found wandering, more or less at their own pleasure, in and out of the Time and Life Building." It was a fine speech Harry made that night, with its lightly put confession that he, the Chief, the Big Boss, the supposed Supreme Commander of the Allied Powers of *Time*, *Life* and *Fortune*, was in only partial control of the thousand and one people and emergencies that cropped up every day and his frank confession that "we'd be a hell of a dead place without all our big and little prima donnas."

• • •

When I first arrived on the editorial scene of 1934, there were six to eight male members of the editorial department, and that was all. Designating the number of "writers" was much harder, because, for one thing, this count included people like Allen Grover and his assistant, who never wrote a line, couldn't, didn't want to, and weren't asked to; their function was to be business-critical and business-sophisticated, hold writers' hands and periodically explain what a debenture was or give elementary lessons in reading balance sheets. But there was a second difficulty;

436

not all the "writers" could produce an acceptable manuscript by deadline time, owing either to alcohol, indolence, incapacity, sexual preoccupation or any combination of these with other things.

● ● ●

I have dealt separately with Arch MacLeish because he was sane and sober, never got sick and had a normal conscience and sense of responsibility. His colleagues called for, and demanded, a different kind of treatment. To proceed at random, which is the only logical way, this was the balance of the writing writers, as of early 1934.

● ● ●

Ed Kennedy: He wrote with beautiful point and grace. Sample opening of a Kennedy story: "The U.S. Rubber Company was born with water in its stock and monopoly in its eye." Ed specialized wholly in corporation stories, simply because no one else could do them half as well. Arch MacLeish couldn't write one worth a nickel because he was then so bored and supercilious about the whole business process. In consequence, his first such story was also his last. But Ed Kennedy brought a high degree of business sophistication to his job, and was more interested in looking *through* than *down on* its practitioners. Unique among *Fortune* writers at the time, he needed business coaching no more than he needed instructions on how to write, which was not at all.

Thus it was that a managing editor would turn an assignment over to Ed with a pleasant thrill of expectation—and also, unfortunately, with an unpleasant thrill of suppressed alarm. For Ed was the drunk of all drunks. It was almost a matter of routine for a *Fortune* writer, after having closed a hard story, to go out and tie one on with such ferocity that it might take forty-eight to seventy-two hours to get the knot undone. No one thought anything much about it. Ed followed this pattern, but he also followed another: he was a continuous drinker—on this level he could function, and function pretty well—but he was also a periodic drinker, given to five-day disappearances. In assigning Ed a story, one could only pray that if there was going to be one

437

of those bellicose, uprooting, smashing, scorched-earth outbursts, whose violence was truly frightening, it would come at the end of the story, not its middle. And they did . . . usually.

But if, under these layers of disadvantage, there lay not Irish charm, there did lie Irish wit. As and when the spirit moved him, Ed would bring out a little four-page sheet called *Timerous*. In content and style it was a beautiful in-joke parody of *Time*. He did not show it to many people; I was honored to be on its complimentary list. That was in the early days, when Ed Kennedy and I were friends. Later I did something—or failed to— that made me, to him, a stench and a hissing. I've often wished I knew what it was.

• • •

In the soft, forgotten days when Harry's journalistic children were only *Time* and *Fortune* he busied himself much more with the editorial staffs than was possible later. He noted, with mounting irritation, the morning hours at which Ed checked in, slowly sagging from half-past ten to noon to post meridian. He issued a summons to the offender.

"Goddamn it, Ed, don't you know that the office rules say that secretaries are due in at nine A.M., researchers at nine thirty and writers at ten?"

Ed swallowed twice before he answered. Then in his meek, thin voice he said, "I always thought I was due at nine." History has drawn a veil over the rest of this interview; I can carry the story no further.

• • •

Charles Wertenbaker: I put him next because he makes such a perfect contrast with Ed. Wert was more than normally fond of the bottle, but he was not a souse, or at any rate not an alcoholic. Wert was a Southern Gentleman first (University of Virginia) and everything else, including writer, second. No double portrait of Wert and Ed Kennedy exists, and that is too bad, for Wert was handsome, excellently built, of a complexion that matched his well-implanted dark hair, and "dashing," whatever that means. He was given to trench coats when I first knew him, and all in all was a casting director's idea of a reporter. I couldn't help thinking that a picture of Richard Harding Davis kept flowering in Wert's mind. If so, much later in Wert's career, it was to bloom appropriately.

But it was during Wert's early days as a *Fortune* writer that he kicked his heels up hardest. Like Ed Kennedy, Wert did not favor office arrival at any officially appointed hour. When he was working really hard on a story he might show up at noon. Since he would then write late into the evening before having a Few Quick Ones, the next day's arrival would be after noon, successively later and later. I began to watch Wert's arrival hour for a reason strictly my own. When it reached 6 P.M. for the start of the workday I felt that my private theory would be borne out; when Wert began arriving at midnight I was dead sure. By slow successive degrees there came the inevitable day when Wert walked into the office at 9 A.M. sharp. He had crossed the International Date Line and lost a day out of his life forever.

Wert wrote a graceful, somewhat romantic prose that did *not* have, as Ed Kennedy's did, the instinct for the business heart of the story. Perhaps he should never have been a journalist at all. I do not think his *The Death of Kings* was much of a book because there was more novelist than journalist in Charles Christian Wertenbaker.

Green Peyton: Green was Wert's younger brother yet it was Wert who pinned the contemptuous nickname "Crash" on this somewhat languorous young man. What was so desperately wrong between the two I never really found out, but they were full brothers and Green Peyton was, in reality, Green Peyton Wertenbaker, but some sort of compact had been sealed between them whereby Peyton was Peyton and Wert was Wertenbaker and that was that. Crash was best in painting large canvases, in which something could be lovingly created and elaborated, and fondled, and extended, and elaborated again, but no sharp point was ever made. Thus he could not cope with the clickety-click of Simon and Schuster, for example; but anyone who wanted to know a whale of a lot about *Diamonds* or *Tea* (two of his most extended length stories) could not possibly do better than sit at Uncle Crash's avuncular knee and hear all about it. His style was extremely leisurely.

• • •

"Goddamn it," said Arch MacLeish to me one day after a session with Luce, "Harry thinks my piece is fine, but he wants me to get so-and-so 'farther up forward.' Everybody around this place, including you, always wants to get *something* farther up forward."

The Pulitzer Prize winner suddenly lost his temper—not at me, not at Harry, not at Ingersoll, but at the whole world of journalism. There was always this clash on *Fortune* between spinning a yarn and coming straight to the point. Few indeed were those who, like little Ed Kennedy, could do both at the same time.

53·ONE OF A KIND, OR,
JIM AGEE AND THE DEEPEST SOUTH

OF ALL THE MYRIADS of people who swarmed in and out of the editorial department of *Fortune* in the 1930's, those who for one reason or another still persist most strongly in the public memory forty years later are James Agee, Russell Davenport, Archibald MacLeish and Dwight Macdonald. When I realize that for at least three years all four of them coexisted on the same office floor, and that for most of this time it was my responsibility to be their "managing" editor, I have retrospective warmth and chills. Of the four, Agee and Davenport, although widely separated in age, died untimely deaths within a year of each other: Davenport in 1954, Agee in 1955. The other two, respectively poet and polemicist, are still going strong as I write this in their (and my) seventies. And of the four, meaning anything but disrespect to MacLeish, whose position in American Letters seems secure for at least a generation, I think the most interesting, as a phenomenon, was Jim Agee.

Both MacLeish and Agee were poets. But there the resemblance ceased. MacLeish was Agee's mentor, not only on *Fortune* but in other ways. But MacLeish, despite his eminence, despite the almost Tennysonian volume of work published and honors won, contradicted all the public's stereotypes of The Poet. He was monogamous. He was gregarious. He was endlessly industrious and completely dependable. Like W. S. Gilbert's Archibald Grosvenor he was a man of proper*tee*, which always helps; also like Grosvenor he had a tendency toward being "Archibald the All-Right." He did not take refuge in alcohol; he liked the grape as a civilized man should. Whatever form his social protests took, he did not cease to wash or shave. On the contrary, he took a pride in his body, which was well founded; it was an athlete's body and MacLeish was a splendid athlete. Nor did this end his list of achievements; after graduation from Yale he had entered Harvard Law School and been the winner of the Fay Diploma, a high distinction, and then he began the practice of law that preceded his writing career.

What I am trying to say is that wherever MacLeish's poetic imagination soared, his dwelling was terra firma. He was oriented in time and space. He was a gem of a man.

By contrast, Jim Agee, a child of twenty-five to Arch's forty-two in 1934, commuted between cloud cuckooland and hell; in these circumstances it was understandable that clocks and calendars and Jim did not live in harmony together. Yet the young Agee I first met in 1934 was no outward eccentric. He was merely a painfully shy young man, liked and admired by every one of his staff coworkers for his obvious talents and unassuming ways. On paper he was so lucid, so vivid, such a master of prose modulation, that it came as a wild surprise that this same fellow was, verbally, so speech-bound that he could scarcely complete a simple declarative sentence. I am speaking of Agee-in-the-office, and Agee sober; I never saw him under other conditions.

• • •

Jim Agee had been on *Fortune* for two years when I appeared, and I remember my feelings of pleasure and surprise at the discovery that the rest of the editorial staff seemed unanimous in feeling that Agee was its most highly gifted member. Naturally, MacLeish did not openly declare him better than MacLeish (he wasn't), but admiration, not jealousy, was the emotional tone that Agee generated among his confreres. And when Ralph Ingersoll, in his unique vulgate, declared him "the best word-bird on the floor," there was none to contradict.

Jim was not, however, perfect, as his post-mortem cult increasingly has it. His failure to distinguish between the fifth and the twenty-fifth of a month, a trifling defect in a Poet Laureate, is more serious in a journalist, which Jim had contracted to be. A similar unconcern with the difference in white space consumed by 5,000 words and by 50,000 words can also lead to practical troubles in the grim world first systematically described by Euclid. So Jim Agee, who also occasionally accepted Assignment A and thought he had fulfilled it by submitting Story A + log e$[A \pm \sqrt{-1}]^n$, was not always a calming influence on the nerves of the managing editor. Ralph Ingersoll had to do quite a bit of wet-nursing on Jim Agee, and Ingersoll, being an intensely practical man, was not slow in switching Jim, as much as he could, from his own glands to mine, once mine were available. I was, after all, his coadjutor.

• • •

Ingersoll was many things, but among them he was certainly a brilliant journalist and a highly creative editor. A great difference existed in those days between *Time* and *Fortune:* the contents of any issue of *Time* was 80 per cent dictated by what *had* happened; the contents of any issue of *Fortune* was 80 per cent dictated by what might or might not happen. The need for *creating* an issue for *Fortune* was correspondingly higher.

In the summer of 1934, a real honey of an article idea popped into Ingersoll's mind, and the schedule slug told all about it: "The Great American Roadside." The idea was not only splendid; it was tailor-made for the talents of Jim Agee.

The idea was splendid because it was so prescient. It then seemed that America had as many automobiles as it could hold, which was unfortunately not true. But it did have close to as many as the then-existing roadways could accommodate, and in a loose sort of way the continent was connected not only from sea to shining sea but from the rock-bound shores of Maine to the Everglades of Florida. The latter connection was probably the more significant, for Florida was slowly recovering from its own private disasters of land-boom collapses and without-warning hurricanes, and North-South tourist travel by car was growing. The Greyhound bus system, having started from nothing in 1915, was still adolescent, and would not even have been that if the nation's railroads had not been in the waxy catatonic trance that had gripped them since 1920. There were few such things in the mid-1930's as "service stations," systematically operated by the big oil companies; a franchised "dealer" had his roadside pumps for this or that brand of gas and somewhat sullenly provided "rest rooms," usually filthy, for those unfortunates who were in urgent need of rest. The Greyhound bus routes had obviously to be arranged with these periodic necessities in mind, and it was this influence, as much as any other, that began to

lift the pump-and-privy out of its squalor and start it on the
way to its present Taj Mahal magnificence. These roadside institutions were in their larval stages, characterized by huge signs,
usually, LADIES and GENTS, or, more flatly, WOMEN and MEN, when
Ralph Ingersoll had his story idea.

But an even more significant development was in its pupal
stage. Painted signs were beginning to appear along the American roadside (chiefly the North-South routes) proclaiming
"CABINS—$1.00." Behind them would be a collection of little cot-
tages, sometimes sleazy, sometimes quite tasteful, which offered
overnight lodging, whether family or illicit, alternative to the
horrors of an eighth-rate hotel in a "city." From this would later
spring the "auto court" and from *this* would eventually spring
the "motel." The word, not coined until the 1940's, had at first
a hard battle with derision until wall-to-wall carpeting, heated
swimming pools, free ice, TV in every room and 28 flavors eventually conquered all. Neither Ralph Ingersoll nor Howard Johnson (nor maybe God) was a good bet to foresee all this in the
1930's, but Ralph Ingersoll was first: having put together gas
pumps, Bar-B-Q sandwiches and "CABINS—$1.00" in his mind,
he stirred Jim Agee into the flux and the result was a memorable
Fortune story. It was Ingersoll's inspiration that got it started.
And it was my sweat that got it stopped. I should explain.

•   •   •

With an assignment precisely to his liking and uniquely fitted
to his talents, Jim Agee took off to explore The Great American
Roadside in some depth that summer. Some sixty days later he
returned and fell to writing in his small and rather difficult
script. Neither Ingersoll nor I ever encouraged a writer to talk
much about his story after he'd returned from the field, and when
I eventually succeeded Ingersoll as M.E. I actively discouraged
it, unless there was an important problem to discuss, on the
grounds that every time the writer described his story yet unwrit-
ten, he leaked some creative steam out of his own boiler. He
also killed any sense of surprise in the editor. Jim was taciturn
because of his office shyness, so a normal and satisfactory Q. and
A. between Ingersoll and Agee could well have been "How did
it go?" "It went all right." And that would have been that. For
all I know, that *was* that.

Jim wrote and wrote and wrote on his assignment. I had a minimum amount to do with the issue in which it was to appear, for I was down for a double assignment the month following, and was mostly in Washington, full of woe. Slowly, closing time for the issue approached and arrived without more than normal crisis. Among the cast proofs I leafed through was "The Great American Roadside." "How come it wasn't late?" I asked.

Ingersoll hesitated a fraction of a second. "I had to go down one evening and take eight thousand words off the top of Jim's desk and send them to the printer," said Ingersoll. "They were *great.*"

"I don't think Jim knows that," I said. "Jim is still in his office writing like hell and I think it's still on 'The Great American Roadside.' I don't think Jim knows the issue is closed."

"Will you be a good fellow and go down and see Jim about the issue being closed? Tell him everything's *fine*. I'm late for an appointment with Orlando Weber right now."

Ingersoll was *always* late for an appointment with Orlando Weber when waves got choppy around the office.

Ingersoll was my superior. He had not issued me an order; he had asked me to "be a good fellow." This I could jolly well refuse to do, but I could not bear the thought of James Rufus Agee sitting sweating in his office continuing to turn out page after page of a story already finished and gone. So I opened Jim's office door, gently. His desk was buried under swoops and sworls of copy paper bearing his script.

"Jim," I said, "Ingersoll's gone to press with the first eight thousand words of 'Roadside,' and it's all finished. He wanted me to tell you it's *great*—and only eight thousand words was the assignment."

Jim said "Oh" with not a shade of inflection; no shock, no surprise, no outrage, no chagrin, no bewilderment. Just "Oh."

• • •

That night, out of the office, I am sure James Agee must have cursed Ingersoll in fifty languages for doing on the sneak what might just as effectively and better have been done in broad daylight. But Ingersoll was not, by nature, a broad-daylight operator.

And I am almost as sure that Agee cursed me equally. After all, I was not only the messenger who brought the bad news;

I was Part of the System. Come to think of it, I *was* Part of the System; also I had made my remark about the assignment being 8,000 words in my capacity as Part of the System. There are times when being Part of the System is not what it's cracked up to be. Perhaps this has remained still true, surviving the semantic change that in the 1960's rendered System into Establishment.

54 · RUSSELL WHEELER DAVENPORT, OR, REAPING WHOSE WHIRLWIND?

IN THE SUMMER of 1934 a glad word began to circulate on the *Fortune* floor: "Mitch Davenport is coming back." Everyone I ever knew called Russell Wheeler Davenport "Mitch," except Harry Luce, who always stuck to "Russ," and Marcia Davenport, then his wife, who seemed to favor "Russell." The reason for "Mitch" was so complicated that it fatigued even Mitch to try to explain it, but the reason for the rejoicing was simple: Mitch could write English prose, always in short supply. (I do not consider myself qualified to assess his poetry.) Even by 1934 Mitch had achieved a reputation as a Time Inc. in-and-outer; he was perpetually "going away again" and perpetually "coming back again." This time he was coming back from I don't know exactly where—except that he and Marcia had been in Germany, Austria and Italy in the portentous years 1932–33.

The moment I met this tall, dark, rawboned, handsome, disheveled, tousled chap of my own age, whose very expensive trousers were always seeming about to fall down, I liked him enormously. And he appeared to like me. Mitch's first new *Fortune* assignment was on the Diesel engine, for the Union Pacific's M10001, America's first so-called streamlined train, powered by G.M.'s Diesels, was on display in Grand Central and the steam locomotive was starting on its long last painful journey to breakers' yards and a few museums, although nobody knew that yet.

Since I was to be the editor of Mitch's story, Harry Luce arranged for himself and Mitch and I to have lunch with G.M.'s boss, Charles Kettering, who had masterminded this motive-power revolution in America. We three obviously wanted to talk to Kettering about the Diesel locomotive, but Kettering, that day, wanted to talk about branch banking—so damned if we didn't talk about branch banking.

At the editing of the Diesel locomotive story Mitch and I had our first Confrontation; it was all that such things should be. "Look, Eric," said Mitch, "some of your changes I like and some I don't. Can we talk?" So of course we talked, finding compromise not at all difficult, and the story went to press with no blood, no tears, and only standard amounts of toil and sweat. There thus began between Mitch and me a friendship and an entanglement that lasted twenty years. It was not a friendship without problems; indeed in its middle years it became for a while so marred and scarred by differences and misunderstandings that I thought it was ended, and so, I am sure, did Mitch. But the happy thing to record now is that we ended as we began: firm and affectionate friends. The last time I ever saw him was in a hospital, but I was the patient and he was the visitor. He had recently been released from a different pavilion of the same institution that was harboring me, but he looked well and his tone was spirited. We spent an hour or more in talk. That was on a late Saturday afternoon. The following Monday, idly turning the pages of the *Times*, I was stunned to see his picture at the top of the column that bore his obituary. He had collapsed and died apparently only a few hours after he had taken leave of me.

• • •

Mitch's gifts were greater than mine, but what initially attracted us to each other, I think, was that we held the same attitude toward our work. We considered journalism an important matter. We did not feel demeaned. We considered *Fortune* an important magazine. We believed in doing our damnedest sweating best, and then redoing it if we thought we could make it better.

One nonprofessional envy I had of Mitch was his relaxed capacity for gregariousness. Thus, after a reasonable while, he could say to me, "We seem to get along. Let's see more of each other." Once *he* had said it, I was unlocked, and we did. But I couldn't have said it first.

Several things made seeing more of each other easy as well as pleasant. We were both night office workers, then, and sometimes didn't leave the Chrysler Building tower until well after midnight. We trusted each other's word sense, so that when we had a paragraph or a caption or a something else about which we felt either (1) smug or (2) hopeless we would try it out, one on the other, aloud. Since we constituted a mutual help and admiration society, in those early days particularly, this was not only good for us, but forged a strong bond.

We also shared a ridiculous pastime. When we would leave the office late at night together our first stop would be an all-night cafeteria. Mitch had a treacherous stomach, so this onetime connoisseur of wines had to subsist on tea, milk, dry toast and maybe custards. He didn't seem to mind. I, for some reason, could digest anything, which was just as well, for that's what I did: the cafeteria's short-order cook could certainly dish out anything.

This interval over, we would proceed to our pastime. Pinball parlors that gave out redeemable coupons had not yet been made illegal, and there was a beauty just a block farther north on Lexington Avenue. Mitch and I would buy a couple of dollars' worth of nickels and set to at adjacent machines. Then the rivalry that was absent when we were in the office, maybe struggling with the Federal Reserve System or the Bureau of the Budget, would burst forth in a fury as we competed for coupons worth tens of thousands of "points" for which we might eventually win a painting on velveteen or a neon-lighted doorstop. We might go through this night after night, with as much intensity as if we were in Colonel Bradley's Casino. We would come out with enough bundles of coupons to choke a horse, millionaires in points, which we did not redeem, for we were shooting for the moon.

This went on for months and months, and then more months, and was a deep and genuine pleasure. We became rival billionaires. And then some goddamn spoilsport, possibly Fiorello H. La Guardia, brought down our whole cosmos: pinball machines were all right per se (it was decreed), but the issuance of redeemable coupons constituted illegal gambling. Our joint closed up, leaving Mitch and me with enough unredeemed coupons to paper Grand Central. A beautiful episode had come to an end.

• • •

Like Luce, MacLeish and Ingersoll, Mitch and I were deeply serious about *Fortune*'s journalistic mission. Although in the winter of 1935 I had only partial responsibility for any actual guid-

ance and Mitch had none, we decided we would constitute ourselves an informal *ad hoc* committee of two for purposes of High
Discussion—a sort of proto-Rand Corporation that had not been
hired or empowered by anybody to do anything, but was full
of eagerness and willingness to do something anyway.

For the first (it turned out to be the only) meeting, a weekend
was the obvious time. As to place, Mitch suggested his "farm"
in Windsor, Vermont, and thither we drove one cold, winter
Friday. In *Too Strong for Fantasy*, Marcia Davenport gives a
vivid description of the farm, which she loathed, commenting
(page 173), "I cannot reconstruct the reasoning by which Russell
thought it made sense to be two hundred and fifty miles from
New York, an eight hours' drive at that time (and no direct rail
service) years before there were any thruways. This was no re-
treat for weekends. It took a whole weekend just to go and
come . . . ."

Well, the conditions Marcia Davenport was describing, circa
1932, were still pretty much the conditions of 1935, except that
Mitch, while still loving the place, had lost his early pioneering
and gentleman-farmer's ardor and seldom went to it. It *was* an
eight-hour drive, not accomplished lightly. But on this occasion
the time went fast, for Mitch and I felt in fine spirits and were
highly conversational, as the temperatures dropped and the snows
deepened and hardened and the northern latitudes increased.
Mitch explained, somewhere north of Brattleboro, that since the
only inhabitants of his 250 acres were Jimmy, the "farmer," and
the livestock, we would have to improvise our living arrangements as we went along and the first thing we'd have to do was
hire a pro tem cook.

At last, in Windsor, the town, we did, and God smiled upon
us, a somewhat lopsided smile it must have been, for He gave
us Amanda, a local red-haired lady who, like ourselves, was in
her middle thirties. I shall never forget the flat, uninflected, utterly emotionless Vermont voice in which she told us, after our
cooking bargain had been struck, that she was a raging and unpredictable alcoholic, "and no power on earth goin' to change
me." She was, she explained, temporarily off the sauce due to
a depressed skull fracture, from which she was now recovering
nicely, sustained when a car she had been driving struck a concrete abutment at high speed. She described the varying fates

450

or conditions of the car's other occupants with an archetypal Vermont economy of speech, and we did not press her since several corpses seemed involved. For weekend purposes, we felt, we already had somewhat more information than we wanted. But whatever vague worries we may have felt, we kept them to ourselves, and Amanda turned out to be a superb (and sober) cook. Country sausage and flapjacks with Vermont maple syrup (not only "real" but local) poured forth from her. So did bacon and a variety of dishes in which eggs, heavy cream and every other high-cholesterol ingredient had been laid on with a lavish hand. In deference to Mitch's stomach, and in view of Amanda's personality problem, we brought not a drop of anything alcoholic into the farmhouse high on its hill, being so cautious as even to cross vanilla extract off the shopping list; nevertheless I am sure my present atherosclerosis got heavy encouragement from that weekend. But today's polyunsaturate dustup was of course unknown in 1935.

Amanda's conduct remained exemplary. If her local reputation, unknown to us, was to heighten another situation that arose before the weekend was over, that was no one's fault but Mitch's.

• • •

We had scarcely settled down before the roaring fireplace in the incredible farmhouse on the hill before Mitch said, "Hey, Eric, I've invited Katie Hepburn up, too; I hope you don't mind."

I did mind. I minded like hell. This blew what had been the whole idea of the trip before it had started. I had come to Windsor looking forward to some *male* conversation, professional conversation about our jobs and problems. Now the sudden introduction of a movie star obliterated the whole purpose of the trip, *as proposed by Mitch*, and, by the way, Humpty Dumpty was never put back together again. Mitch's ability to hold two cross-purpose ideas in his mind simultaneously, in utter assurance that he could integrate them, was a recurring characteristic. Whether it caused him or those who loved him the more trouble, I don't know.

But when a host says to a guest, about a *fait accompli*, "I hope you don't mind," the guest says, "No, of course not," which is what I said. And when Katharine Hepburn next day arrived in the little Ford roadster she had driven from her Hartford home,

451

my lie suddenly became the truth; it was lovely that she had come.

She was not in the least stagy. She was not beautiful. What made her fascinating was a resoluteness of character that shone through everything she said and did. I have not said that the way I want it and if I have made her sound like a character who always knows what's what and that's that, I have done the precise reverse of what I intended. She simply looked at things, pleasant or unpleasant, puzzling or clear, with a steady, level, unblinking gaze. And she was not a monologist. She would ponder, she would state, she would reflect, and *she would listen!* In short, she understood and practiced the art of conversation; she said things worth listening to; she then shut up and paid you the compliment, deserved or not, that *you* were saying things worth listening to. Since Katharine Hepburn and Mitch were old friends (she habitually called him, affectionately, "Davenport") they had much to talk about in which I could not share, but I did not feel at all excluded by the fact that my role, at least that first day, was mainly that of a listener. When two good conversationalists are at work, the subject takes an oddly secondary importance.

• • •

Meanwhile, unknown to us, the little town of Windsor (southeastern part of Vermont; nearest point of national reference either Ascutney Mountain, Woodstock, the fairly upper reaches of the Connecticut River, or Lebanon, New Hampshire, depending on your orientation), several hundred rugged feet below our hilltop, was now aboil—on our account. Katharine Hepburn, despite her best efforts at inconspicuousness, had been spotted by a group of girls as she drove her roadster along the main stem on her route leading to the Davenport turnoff. The rural Vermont grapevine—finest in the world, as aided by the four-party phone line—had flashed the word, and all decoding apparatus was clicking with a speed I.B.M. might, years later, envy. Despite the infrequency of his visits, Davenport was well known in Windsor as a card-carrying City Eccentric. Last night, he and an unknown male companion had been seen in conversation with That Amanda, and no later than noon today, Katharine Hepburn had been positively identified—*and was now alone with the two men in the Davenport farmhouse*. Moreover, she was going to spend the night. Mebbe two nights.

Now it cannot be said that by 1935 Katharine Hepburn was at the height of her fame, for her fame was to rise higher and still higher. But by then she was already a Hollywood Gold Medalist. She was thus fair game, knew it, and tried to take all reasonable precautions. Unfortunately, none of us had taken into account, not knowing, the vividness of That Amanda's local reputation. Where That Amanda was, no good would come. This was not gossip, this was an equation—and *That Amanda was now also at the Davenport farmhouse* . . . . When Mitch, the Movie Queen and I, the Queen striving to look as unqueenly as possible, made what we thought was going to be an unobtrusive trip to Windsor's center, the whole town simply came to a halt and gawked. We got out of there again as quickly as we could. I can't prove anything, but I don't think That Amanda tried at all to quell the leaping flames; self-interest actually lay more in her fanning them. But her cooking stayed on its steady, even, flawless (and sober) course.

•   •   •

That evening an awkward situation arose, as all the laws of Greek Drama said it must. "Unh, Eric," said Mitch, "we've got to go downtown again. Katie has a Problem." It was unnecessary to say anything more, but Mitch said it. "Katie can't possibly go into that drugstore, and even I can't, and Amanda is out of the question, so that leaves only you."

"I'd be delighted," I said, with a heart of lead.

"It would be absolutely lovely of you," said the star of *Little Women*, etc., etc., with a truly sweet smile.

"I figure that if we cross Main Street and head left we can park the car on the far side of the old freight depot," said Mitch. "It's dark as pitch there. That would give you only a two-block uphill walk to the drugstore."

"O.K.," I said.

"Of course it would be downhill coming back," said Mitch, who couldn't stop overexplaining.

So that's the way we did it. Mitch and Katie (I can't quite call her Miss Hepburn here) sat in the front seat of the roadster, isinglass curtains up. That left the rumble seat for me. Oh, it was cold. But things went according to plan. "We'll be waiting," said Mitch as he parked in the lee of the freight depot, and I got out. If it hadn't been so cold I might not have said "You goddamn well better had be," but it was that cold, so I did say it.

I had never before said to a pharmacist "Two boxes of Kotex regular, please," and certainly not to a Vermont pharmacist who bent such a look of hostile suspicion on me that I wondered if he was going to ask for a prescription. But there was no hitch except, of course, that I forgot my change and the pharmacist, being a Vermonter born and bred, pursued me out of his store to give it to me, making some acid remark I choose not to remember. At the end of the two-block downhill trip (things were so icy that the uphill trip had actually been easier) the getaway car was waiting; it took us three criminals up the hill again. In the deep night the wind had grown still a little colder. "That was absolutely darling of you," said Miss Hepburn, and next morning I felt much more a part of the group.

• • •

I kept that anecdote locked in my gentlemanly bosom for twenty years; indeed I had planned to keep it locked there all my life. But, twenty years after, it began to drift back to me that the lady involved was herself telling the story, with that relish and retrospective glee with which things invest themselves after a while, after a long while. So I unlocked my bosom. Bless you, Miss Katharine Hepburn.

55 · TRIALS, or,
TRIBULATIONS

Dwight Macdonald: He was only half on the staff when I arrived, for Harry had detached him to be a member of the Experimental Department. There was always an Experimental Department of one kind or another, but out of this one nothing came. After it expired, Dwight took a long vacation, so long that when he returned I, not Ingersoll, was managing editor.

Al Grover came bursting into my office. "Macdonald's back, and he's grown a pink beard and he looks exactly like those pictures of Jesus Christ!" It was all too true.

There, however, the resemblance stopped. Macdonald and I got along quite well in the beginning and were even cordial toward each other. He was a gifted and methodical writer, whose copy came in on time and needed minimum editorial attention. He wrote at his best when he was indignant about something, which he usually was, although he was not, in these younger days, the professional polemicist and horse's ass that he became as the pink beard slowly grizzled. His prose was impeccable, which made it all the more peculiar that despite a Yale education and an extensive familiarity with all kinds and varieties of literature, he had never been able to shake off a heavy *dese*, *dem* and *doze* Brooklyn accent, delivered in a particularly harsh and grating voice. He and I, however, never fell into bad terms until after he had left *Fortune*. One late afternoon in the fall of 1936 he dropped in to pay a social call. It was a bad day for it; I was struggling to close the October issue. It was the Roosevelt-Landon election year; the one in which F.D.R. first used, with considerable venom, his "Economic Royalists" phrase. Harry had suggested that since we had just given the steel industry unshirted hell it might be fair and reasonable to let one of the hardest-

boiled steelmaker businessmen in the country have his counter-
say. I suggested—and Harry agreed—that we should also let an
avowed New Dealer have a voice in the same issue; thus we
ended up with signed articles by Ernest Tener Weir and Rexford
Guy Tugwell, and, I forget how or why, Republican Senator Van-
denberg. None of the three were masterpieces, and left to my
own devices, I would have junked them all—but, alas, we had
solicited them.

Macdonald, with whom a moment before I was having a
pleasant conversation, saw the page proofs on my desk. "So you've
gone over to the other side," he said.

Harsh words immediately erupted. I was trying to get an issue
closed; Macdonald wanted to begin an economic debate. I said
something about the incompatibility of our two desires.

"I resent your tone," said Dwight.

"All right," I said, "get out of my office and resent it to your
heart's content."

He did. And in May 1937 there appeared in the *Nation* three
articles by Macdonald attacking Luce, *Time* and *Fortune*. I could
never help thinking that my run-in with Macdonald was the
grit around which he built up these pearls, for in the middle
of his second article (on *Fortune* exclusively) Macdonald recounts
his version of this tiff as if the basement rocks of history, politics
and journalism had been set trembling by it. I confess this interested me less than Macdonald's recounting of the *Fortune* editorial process (of which he was a part for five years). Consider
this:

> . . . Adequate time is rarely allowed for research. Lengthy trea-
> tises on the most complex subjects are slapped together in a month
> or six weeks. And a great deal of such time as there is goes
> to waste because of the Hollywoodian inefficiency of Luce and
> his editors, who postpone all decisions until after the last mo-
> ment and chronically fail to make monthly deadlines. The most
> efficient male in the place is a poet. [MacLeish, of course.] Once
> the article is somehow written, it is pulled apart by several edi-
> tors—usually of a lower grade of intelligence than the writer—
> rewritten here and touched up there. Sentences are deleted, para-
> graphs wrenched from their place and stuck bodily in some incon-
> gruous section, where they perch like cows stranded on barn roofs
> by a passing tornado. By the time it is over, the article is a sham-

bles, bleeding internally at a dozen points where vital organs have been excised by the editorial scalpel. The better it was as first written, the more it suffers from being thus dismembered and reassembled . . . .

Macdonald makes a heavy point of Luce's business shrewdness, which has always left me wondering why, therefore, he (Luce) would hire the best *writing* talent available (e.g., Macdonald and *perhaps* MacLeish) and then hire editors—*several* editors "usually of a lower grade of intelligence than the writer"—to ruin the writer's work. It did not, it does not, sound like a solid, money-making system to me, and according to the gifted writer this was Luce's essential publishing aim. Ah, well.

• • •

Wilder Hobson: Wilder was a handsome and well-spoken young Yale man who was a semiperpetual disappointment as a writer. He could *tell* a marvelous yarn about his assignment, but when he came to write it, somehow three-quarters of the zip and bounce and humor—of which he had loads—would have disappeared. "Harry has convinced me," Ingersoll wrote in one of his rare moments of humility, "that I was confused by Wilder's smooth rhetoric," whereupon he turned Wilder's piece over to me. Wilder didn't care. That was the trouble with Wilder: he just didn't care. He could indeed turn out reams of smooth rhetoric, but the great love of his life was jazz, and anything else— except alcohol—was an intrusion. He was, in the thirties, the author of a ringingly authoritative book on the jazz of the period. He was a slide trombone player of close to professional grade— and a thoroughly charming young man. In my opinion he could have been just about anything he cared to be—but he just didn't care to be. Hard work, except at music, which wasn't hard work to Wilder, was distasteful to him. And yet, his manuscripts came in on time. I never saw him looped or plastered or stoned in the office, yet alcohol must have been almost his sole fuel, for by his fifties he had so damaged his liver that his doctor told him one more gulp must be his last. Wilder put up with this prohibition for a short while and then—it was.

In the kindest possible way, Wilder gave me my lumps quite early in my career as managing editor. Lots had obviously been drawn for the job and Wilder had lost. Much to my surprise he invited me to that sinkhole the Yale Club for dinner. (We had never had a meal together before.) The dinner passed in chitchat until the last fork was laid down, when Wilder said, "I've been deputized by the editorial department to convey a complaint. The best way I can think of putting it is that there is too much editorial kibitzing at the expense of editing." Wilder dropped his complaint right there and I was never *absolutely* sure what I was guilty of, but as I walked back with him, my face beet-red in the dark at the gentle rebuke, I decided I must have been fussing too much, making too many little points and not enough big ones—the exact obverse of the Luce method. But I must have done something right thereafter, for I was not criticized again.

Jack Jessup: Whether I really hired Jack Jessup or not, only he knows. He wrote the best letter of job application I have ever seen, explaining why, for example, standing with a hand-clicker on the platform of the Trenton station of the Pennsylvania Railroad (he was working for J. Walter Thompson at the time) to see how many people got off was good preparation for writing *Fortune* articles. Alas, the letter is lost, but it made sublime sense. It came in at the precise time that Ingersoll was turning his seals of office over to me. Nervous as a herring that my first hiring would somehow be a fizzle, despite the fact I was sure this man would not be, I sent Jack and his letter down to Harry, who assumed on no evidence at all that Jack was already on the payroll, wished him a long and happy career, and waved him the hell out of the office. So who *did* hire Jack Jessup? I should like to think it was I, for it was one of the most triumphant hirings ever to take place within Time Inc. Jack and I were to have our later differences, but no one really matched Jack as a *Fortune* corporation story writer—not even Ed Kennedy at his soberest or drunkest best. Moreover, Jack was abstemious with the bottle, so once you had arranged a marriage between him and an appropriate story, your troubles were over and you could have a drink yourself. It was great.

John Chamberlain: In this list I am omitting the baker's dozen of out-and-out disasters who gave every evidence of high competence and then, confronted with a typewriter, denied themselves thrice. I think I was no better and no worse a hirer than Ingersoll, my predecessor, or Davenport, my successor.

John Chamberlain, whom MacLeish and Longwell, and spasmodically Luce, put pressure on me to hire, was in the thirties *The New York Times*'s book reviewer and the author of *A Farewell to Reform*, which was why I had to be pushed into hiring him. But pushed I was by the combination of the heavy forces on the one side and the awful vacuum of enough talent on the other.

John came easy. Either I had overestimated his *Times* salary or he was sick of the job, but I got him from the *Times* with a minimum of ripping and tearing. And he was a great comfort to have around—for a while.

John was not an out-and-out disaster—he was an in-and-out disaster. He was a highly competent writer and a pleasant, gentle man, with a deeply hidden streak of hostility under his sub-sub-surface. As a lesser evil, he had difficulty sticking to the point of the general conversation. "And then John would come in with one of his goddamn inane questions, " Arch MacLeish burst forth one day, after he had come to love John a little less than before— and after John, as he did so many times, had derailed an entire conversation. The real trouble with John burst forth from the events leading up to September 3, 1939. John was not only an isolationist, but was somewhat more pro-German than pro-English. So, alas, was Jack Jessup. The attitude of these two admirable men was remarkably like that of our then national hero Charles Augustus Lindbergh, so far as I could judge, for quite the same reasons: they could not conceive how the drowsing English and the venal French and all the rest of squalid Europe could last a day against Hitler's overpowering might—and they were as obsessed with the idea of *Festung Amerika* as Hitler was later to be with *Festung Europa*. It was plausible, all right, and some very hard feelings were produced at the time among those who didn't seem to feel that any moral issue was involved—or any that involved America. A minority of Time Inc. took the Jessup-Chamberlain view. A majority took the Luce view, which was the William Allen White view of the Committee to Defend America by Aiding the Allies. This was also F.D.R.'s view—but Luce hated F.D.R.'s guts. And then there were the 1940 elections in which brother slew brother along *another* line of cleavage. Why did we not splinter into 10,000 pieces?

56·WHAT BILL FURTH DID, or, CHARLIE MURPHY

Charles J. V. Murphy: One day Laura Hobson called me to say that an old journalistic buddy of hers had just come back to town from an utterly no-adverb unique assignment: ghosting the record of Admiral Richard E. Byrd's adventures at the South Pole under the title of *Alone.*

We met, and I beheld a pleasant fellow indeed: Boston Irish, late thirties, profuse curly black hair becomingly dusted with gray at the temples, which strongly reinforced his impeccable manner and manners. At first I thought this was an act; later events emphatically proved me wrong. I should have been forced to this conclusion a lot sooner than I was.

• • •

Charlie had been assigned to a story on the Associated Press, at the time when that considerable journalist Kent Cooper was at the height of his powers. This coincided neatly indeed with the time when *Fortune* was one of the smallest and newest potatoes in the great weedy patch of the Fourth Estate. Nevertheless, Charlie, in his manuscript draft for this seedling, had managed to say something about the A.P.—I'd give anything to remember what—that vexed Mr. Cooper exceedingly.

I was having lunch with Harry in a Lexington Avenue dive just about then and he was quizzing me about the progress of the month's stories. I came to the A.P. and the hot words Mr. Cooper had flung at Charlie Murphy. To complete the story I had to add Charlie's soothing rejoinder: "But, Mr. Cooper, we don't want to *destroy* the Associated Press."

Now Harry was not a hearty laugher; the chuckle or the grunt, never the guffaw, was his medium. But at the image of a *Fortune* writer reassuring Mr. Cooper that we were positively not going to rip the great A.P. open below the waterline, all of Harry's inward bracing collapsed. He threw back his head and laughed like an Omaha meat packer on his first visit to the *Follies*. Never before or after have I seen him so completely broken up.

Then suddenly his laughter stopped and he turned on me a deeply quizzical face.

"It *could* have been wit," he said. When we came to the conclusion that it was not wit, Harry wiped his eyes but spent the rest of lunch in a sort of dreamlike state, most uncharacteristic.

•   •   •

Now none of this would have taken place had it not been for Albert Lavenson Furth. These being his given names, he was universally known as Bill, and most of his mail was so addressed. His hair was blond and curly, his complexion slightly florid, and everybody loved him because, among other reasons, he loved everybody.

I think the nearest thing to my formal introduction as managing editor was the morning Harry called me down to his office and with no preamble at all shot me the question, *"Do you want Bill Furth?"*

Of course I wanted Bill Furth. I also wanted Mr. Morgan's yacht, but had asked for neither for similar reasons. Why Harry offered him to me and what process of divination told him that Bill was just what *Fortune* (and I) needed are closed volumes. Bill had been press editor on *Time*, and the lamentations there were very loud when the memo from Harry arrived announcing that Bill was being detached from *Time* for the larger opportunity of becoming *Fortune*'s assistant managing editor, and that Bill's former colleagues on *Time* would obviously join Harry in his pleasure at this well-deserved etc., etc. The hell they did. They were sore as pups—not from jealousy toward Bill, but from anger at *Fortune*. Harry never seemed to get around to telling anyone that the whole thing had been *his* idea, and since I was its principal beneficiary, I could not get over the feeling that it would be unwise of me to go into the building's men's room except in friendly company. The two magazines did not like or respect each other very much in those days, just as, thirty-five years later, they still don't.

. . .

There is much to tell of Bill Furth, but I have rather off-handedly chucked him into the narrative here because among the many things for which he was responsible is the longest, most word productive writing career in Time Inc.—the career of Charles J. V. Murphy. I have personal doubts whether this was on balance to the good or the bad—but of this there can be no doubt: it has been unique.

Despite a successful career as reporter and ghost before he came to Time Inc., Charlie Murphy couldn't seem to get the hang of how to write for *Fortune*. And I couldn't seem to get the hang of telling him where, why and how he had gone astray. His first story—on the American Museum of Natural History—was a disaster area from first to last. I can't remember what the next stories were, except that they were no better, and I sadly made up my mind that Charlie Murphy would have to go. I even went to see Laura Hobson to express in person my disappointment that her suggestion had not worked out.

But one evening, after hours, Bill Furth came into my office and conspiratorially closed the door. "Before you fire Charlie Murphy," said Bill, "will you give him to me for three months? I think I can make something out of him."

Now this was most peculiar. Modesty was a vice with Bill; the suggestion that he could pull off a stunt someone else (this time, his direct superior) could not had absolutely no precedent. But I heaved a double sigh of relief: I could stop girding my loins for the firing of Charlie Murphy next day, and there was the possibility—the far possibility—that Bill might succeed, in which case we would be one up instead of one down.

And by God he *did* succeed! He succeeded so well that for a while, in the days before the war burst out in Europe, and as it relentlessly enveloped the world, Charlie Murphy came close to being the most valuable writer on the *Fortune* staff.

462

57 · NEITHER "YES" NOR "NO," OR, COWARDICE

INEVITABLY ELEANOR TREACY and I saw a great deal of each other in the office. We worked well together, with harmony, understanding and respect. And I think I can say that outside the office the same conditions prevailed. But I was scarcely prepared for what was coming.

Late one summer afternoon in 1936 Eleanor asked if we could have drinks together as soon as our workday was over. Of course we could. Midway through the second Manhattan in the spacious basement bar and lounge of the old Murray Hill Hotel, Eleanor came to the point of the meeting with the accuracy of a perfectly trained bombardier: "I love you, and I want you to marry me. I know what your trouble is, and I *know* I can fix it!"

• • •

What did I do in the months that followed? I faltered, and I faltered. This should, I think, have conveyed *some* message to Eleanor, the message I was too pusillanimous to put into direct words; but if it did, she paid it no mind. *She* had been the incarnation of directness; she had received, verbally, neither a Yes nor a No. But it was in her to take that as a Yes; it was not in my nature to make a contradiction—and so, by a dozen or a hundred little or not so little cowardices, I found myself becoming (that is the only way I can think to put it) married to Eleanor Treacy.

We talked about it a good deal, and I found myself a consoling thought: Perhaps Eleanor was right; perhaps she *did* know what my trouble was (I certainly didn't) and perhaps she *could* fix it. At any rate, there was in her mind no shadow of doubt whatever. Eleanor had been reared a Catholic; although she was totally relapsed by the time I met her, skepticism had never taken the place of Faith; in her mind there was simply no houseroom for Doubt—on any subject.

The year 1936 was wearing to an end; soon would come the fourth anniversary of Catherine's death, but the wound would not close—although in a psychically healthy person it long ago should have. And this led me to lay down a law to Eleanor with such considerable force that it stayed on the books for eight years. The law said that since it appeared we were going to get married—no children! One experience with parenthood had been quite enough for me.

I well remember that we had this ancient conversation on the sands of Jones Beach—still sufficiently underutilized for such intimate, private conversation. And I well remember Eleanor's answer. She looked quite pensive and then she said, "Well, I can't say I'm particularly joyful at what you're saying, but I don't *suppose* I'll feel like the Barren Fig Tree . . . ."

• • •

On the morning of October 31, 1936, Margaret Eleanor Treacy and Eric Francis Hodgins were married by the City Clerk in the City, County and State of New York.

AFTERWORD

John Kenneth Galbraith

In 1943, I had reached the end of my road as a wartime price fixer; my military abilities were unappreciated and not very heroically sold, and so I did a stint as an editor of *Fortune* before going back to Washington (and Germany and Japan) for another short tour with the U.S. Strategic Bombing Survey and the State Department. Between the years here described and my appearance, Eric's second marriage had deteriorated and was eventually to lapse. The periods of depression that he describes had become more serious, and so had the alcohol. He had partly mastered the first through a psychiatrist and completely mastered the alcohol through Alcoholics Anonymous. I learned of none of these things from Eric, and I first heard of the AA experience when it became a *Fortune* story. Other people talk of themselves. Eric saved it for his books.

In the mid-forties, as I've said, he chucked the corporate vice-presidency he held—it had something to do with liaison with the business community—and returned to *Fortune* as a writer. We had adjoining offices and shared the same efficient and mildly contemptuous secretary. In the ensuing months I became accustomed to hearing an explosion of laughter from Eric's office. This was invariably followed by an explosion of Eric into my office. He had encountered something that rejoiced his soul and roared in to share it with me. He particularly favored the more pompous insanities of the free-enterprise system, to which Time Inc. itself contributed a fairly solid share. I remember a report composed by the late C. D. Jackson, then head of Time-Life

International, the imperial arm of our enterprise. In the years immediately following the war, T-L International was notably unprofitable. Goods abroad were so scarce that no one needed to advertise; exchange control made it hard to bring home even the subscription revenue. Harry Luce, whom Eric and I both admired wholeheartedly—if, as liberals, a bit unfashionably— as a businessman, editor and friend, did not relish any branch of the company that lost money. Jackson was making the best of a bad situation. His report (by my best recollection) read, "If business conditions in the second half of the year had been as favorable as in the first half, Time-Life International would have been within shooting distance of the break-even point." Eric proposed that we frame it as the year's finest example of triple-conditional financial prose.

In 1948 I went back to Harvard and Eric remained at *Fortune*, but in a state of increasing boredom. Among other things, he had an unfulfilled desire for public service, and he must have told me this. In the late forties William S. Paley called in one day in Cambridge to talk about a commission that President Truman had invited him to head on the prospective supply of raw materials for the American industrial maw. He asked about possible members, and I urged the name of Hodgins. Quite possibly the suggestion came from others as well (one always assumes himself to be the sole source of such inspiration), but in any case, Eric became a member of the Paley Commission and was a highly effective contributor to what was to be an informative, sensible and, thanks to Eric, exceptionally literate report.

It is my impression from some of the fragments left behind by Eric that Bill Paley had a primary role in persuading Eric to write this account of his life.

Oddly, I again had occasion to urge Eric for a job. In the late summer of 1952 I was in Springfield, Illinois, helping Adlai Stevenson with his speeches. We were desperately in need of more talent, and again I brought up the name of Hodgins. The suggestion was immediately accepted. I phoned Eric, and he arrived within a few hours. As a ghost writer he was incredibly unsuccessful. The speech drafts were wonderful—but pure Hodgins. He could not accommodate himself to Adlai's political style and was, I suspect, too honest even to try. There was also the old problem of length. Minimum delivery time for a Hodgins draft would have been around three hours. As it was, Stevenson never quite finished his speeches before the television time ran out. I remember lunching with Eric one day in Springfield. He was deeply, silently in depression over what he considered his failure. I remember my own sadness that day.

Later in the fifties, Eric left Time Inc. to join forces with Elmo Roper—a consequence of a friendship formed when the Roper Poll was a *Fortune* feature. By now he was living a bachelor and rather lonesome life in New York. From time to time he came to Cambridge in connection with some enterprise or other that he had undertaken for MIT. Affection for MIT remained a fixed point in Eric's life. Then one night while alone in his apartment, he had a severe stroke. For anyone else it would have been no more than that. For Eric it was the raw material for another superb book: *Episode.** This tells in the most vivid detail of his collapse, the struggle for help, and then, in devastating detail, of New York hospitals and associated medical care. It also tells of the financial consequences for a man who, for all of his mature life, had been remarkably well paid. Depression again followed the illness, and Eric takes the reader to the Harkness Pavilion and through the hard struggle back to a nearly normal existence. Not the least touching part of the tale is the help he received from a most compassionate Canadian nurse. But she also must have had a wonderfully funny time.

I last saw Eric a couple of years ago at a birthday party at the Plaza. We talked as usual about what I was doing. Eric, who as this book tells was a passionate Democrat and liberal, delivered himself of some inspired invective on Richard Nixon and Spiro Agnew but not a word about this history. I came to know of its existence only after his death.

* Or, more fully, *Report on the Accident Inside My Skull.*